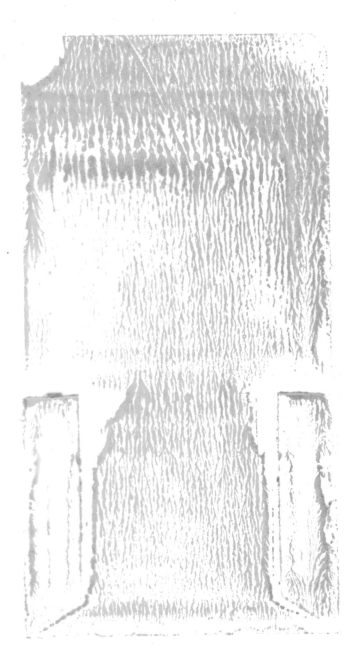

Notes of a Processed Brother

NOTES OF A PROCESSED BROTHER

DONALD REEVES

PANTHEON BOOKS
A Division of Random House   New York

6-20-73

For my mother

But he is Black; so he is a Negro. There is the conflict. He does not understand his own race, and whites do not understand him . . . The personality of the author does not emerge quite so easily as one might wish. An orphan sent to a provincial boarding school, he is compelled to spend his vacations there. His friends and acquaintances scatter all over [the world] on the slightest pretext, . . . the little Negro is forced into the habit of solitude . . . At the extreme, I should say there is a certain accusatory character, a certain resentment, an ill-disciplined aggression, in the long list—too long—of "traveling companions" that the author offers us: at the extreme, I say, but it is exactly to that extreme that we have to go.

Unable to be assimilated, unable to pass unnoticed, he consoles himself by associating with the dead, or at least the absent.

FRANTZ FANON
Black Skin, White Masks

Preface

THIS BOOK is about a learning experience. Primarily, it is the story of a student confrontation with the Board of Education in New York City—a confrontation that failed.

At the end of the 1969–70 school year I had in hand the makings of a small but interesting piece of student history: the records (in the form of notes, letters, speeches, and transcripts) of the New York high school students' struggle for their own Bill of Rights. At that time it was my sole purpose to level a public indictment against the New York City Board of Education, the United Federation of Teachers, and the Council of Supervisory Associations for their role in this fight. Using the materials available, I intended to make a documentary that would show the pathological ways in which professional administrators behave today toward young people.

Each year, students attempt to change some part of the system, but in all too many cases, they are unsuccessful. And graduates leave nothing behind for underclassmen to learn from, nothing to prevent the abortive cycle of indoctrination-as-usual from continuing. Therefore, I felt it was a question of *seizing the time,* of finishing this book before it was too late. The result is a quasi-autobiographical account not only of the New York City struggle, but also of my own development, of the psychology of miseducation, racism, and sex, of the effects of assassinations, strikes, invasions, and the war, and of the emergence of my self-awareness, or, if you will, Black consciousness, etc. If all this infuriates some readers, it will be because I am telling the truth.

Where my personal life is concerned, I am not so pretentious as to believe that I am speaking for anyone but myself. Although my experiences are not unique, I have tried not to generalize my own feelings onto anyone else. This book represents an attempt to expose people to an individual's point of view, to show what's happening within a specific institution, and to involve you in a process (whether or not you identify with it) that involves millions of students every day. In each chapter I have tried to deal with a specific period of growth, a particular segment of our times; in reporting on these things, I harp on hypocrisy and certain well-known prejudices, on common experiences, hatreds, and hangups. Whether or not the book really works depends finally on its power to lead *you* to analyze the situation.

In the course of writing this book I have been encouraged and helped along by many people. I am particularly indebted to Verne Moberg, who took real interest in my writing, helping me put this book together, and whose friendship I deeply value. I also want to express my gratitude to Candace A. Simon, who typed the manuscript, Robert Dawidoff, Carle Peterson, John Dellaverson, and all the members of the 1970–71 Cornell Branch Telluride Association who gave me the benefits of their criticisms. I want to say thanks to my main man, Kenneth D. Hagood, one of the few people I still trust. And of all the people who have helped me, I'd like to thank, especially, my brother, Francis Reeves.

Contents

PART I

OF TWO WORLDS

Br'er Rabbit

Br'er Rabbit gets into conflicts with
almost all the other animals in creation,
and naturally he is always the winner.

Frantz Fanon

WHAT LITTLE I KNOW of my childhood in America I
learned from my mother, Mom Reeves. She was originally a
country girl from Jamaica. My father, Boss Reeves, was born
in Limon, Costa Rica, but early in his life went to live in the
West Indies. Like most Jamaicans who come to America, my
parents moved here to work and get money so they could
buy land or build, back in Jamaica. But Mom and Boss
Reeves stayed on, and I was born in Detroit in 1952, a
second-class citizen of the United States of America—a fact
I learned almost fifteen years later and refused to accept.
Four years after me, in 1956, my younger brother Francis
was born.

Boss was proud of his sons. Our family lived in a two-story
brown wooden house on West Euclid Street, and whenever
we had company there, he'd say, "Why, you know, my son
Francis is the smartest of all the Reeveses. Him was named
after a president—F.D.R." (Francis's middle name was Del-

ano.) Boss's first name was really George, and Mom told me that at first he was going to name me St. George Reeves, but she wouldn't let him. So they compromised and made it my middle name. I've never understood why, but practically all my relatives were named after Biblical figures.

Some of the things I remember best about America in those days are the Black barber, the Ronald Gang, Superman, and the white folks across the street. The Black barber had smooth, processed black hair and a gold tooth. When he gave me a haircut, I ran home and lathered my hair up so that it looked as smooth as his, only my process was white. I tried using black liquid shoe polish, but it didn't work. I also tried to take my teeth out by biting a chicken noodle soup can so that I could get gold teeth like the barber's, but this failed too. I still bear the patch on my forehead from trying to cut my hair off because I wanted it to grow smooth and processed.

The Ronald Gang were those Negroes from up the block. They always beat me up. As soon as Mom and Boss Reeves were gone, they'd threaten to break my ass if I didn't open the doors. The Gang would come into our house and unload everything from the icebox. One day they held me down in the backyard, and Ronald pissed into a soda bottle, gave it to my brother, told him it was orange juice, and forced him to drink it.

Then I got this red bicycle for Christmas. I rode that bicycle every hour of the day and cried on Sundays when Mom Reeves took it away. The Ronald Gang forced me to enter a bicycle race. First prize was the loser's bicycle. We had to race ten times around the block and finish in front of Ronald's house. There were only two people entered in the race, Ronald and I. I tore off like Superman. Ronald was nowhere in sight, but every time I got to the straightaway, there he was behind me. When I turned the corner and looked back, he had disappeared. I rode faster and faster. Around the eighth lap he started appearing in front of me, even though he had never passed me; at least I hadn't seen him doing it. Nobody could ride that fast. I stopped and waited for him, but he never came. I saw him cutting through the backyard, waiting for me so he could sneak out from behind. I went around the corner, told the Gang that Ronald was cheating. They laughed, beat me up, and later that night stole my bike. Boss Reeves said that I was stupid for leaving it outside. Without my bicycle there was little to do but watch television all day and night.

One of the things I watched on TV was Popeye. I loved him because he was an underdog who always took revenge into his own hands. I wanted to beat up Ronald as badly as Popeye beat up Bluto. But my favorite was Superman, "able to leap tall buildings in a single bound."

It was hot that day I decided to try it. I was on the second floor with Boss Reeves's red towel wrapped around my neck. Mr. Betts, our next-door neighbor, was mowing his lawn. "Mr. Betts," I yelled, "look at meeeeee." He nearly died right there when he saw me jump, but before he could get over to our backyard, I was up on the balcony again. "Catch me this time." Mr. Betts ran inside screaming for Mom Reeves. I jumped again. I was taken to the hospital, but nothing was found wrong with me.

Mr. Betts was a big, jolly old white man who played Santa Claus in the winter (I know because one time I almost caught him at it). Mom Reeves used to say he was "walking on the coffin." He had been in the hospital every year that we knew him, and there was something wrong with his lungs, heart, back, and eyes. He used to come over to our house for injections, as Mom Reeves was a nurse. Once when I was watching Mr. Betts clip his hedges, he just fell over right into the bushes. I thought he was playing games, so I left him there. Fortunately, somebody else found him. Old Mr. Betts had suffered a mild stroke.

When I was of age to go to kindergarten, Mom Reeves asked some white folks across the street who had older kids going to the same school to let me walk along with them. They told Mom Reeves it would cost her $10 a week. I learned to walk to school by myself. Tied around my neck I had this chart of a red light and a green light. One said stop, the other said go. Stop and go were the only things on my mind when I went to school. I would look at the lights, then at the chart so I'd know what to do. I almost got killed every day because I didn't know what to do when the yellow light came on. I always got caught in the middle of the street.

■ ■ ■

When I was still very young, Mom Reeves sent me to the West Indies so that I could grow up away from America's racial discrimination. In Jamaica I attended a Catholic school called Mount Alverna and lived in our family's house at 42 Thompson Street, in Montego Bay, with my Aunt Diane, who fled Cuba before Batista seized power. Virtually all of our relatives had Scotch, Portuguese, British, or Irish blood running through their veins. Jamaica still bears marks of the triangular trade—the exploitative trade circuit joining the Caribbean, the United States, and Europe. I don't remember much about that year. Only Willie, the Wilsons, and the sun are unforgettable. Willie lived across the street. All day long he and I would run up and down Thompson Street, bare-assed in the sun, pushing car and bicycle rims. When he got tired, I would sit on the veranda with my Aunt Ettie, who was blind, and stare at the sun. I'd let my eyes tear, then squint, making all kinds of colors. Once I looked at the sun too long, and started bawling my head off. I thought I'd gone blind. Aside from the sun, I watched the John Crow, black vultures who soared on the wind's currents, and from time to time descended from the skies to encircle and devour decaying carcasses on the streets. Of all the animals in creation, I wanted to be a John Crow, to have that feeling of being seemingly as high as the sun itself, the freedom to follow the winds and clear the earth of all that was no longer needed.

The Wilsons lived in Spaldings, Christiana. Every Sunday they would take me to this little run-down wooden church on a muddy hill surrounded by a graveyard. They sang hymn after hymn. The "spirit" would grab some of them, making old ladies fall to the floor screaming "Thank you Jesus, thank

you Jesus." All the women wore white cloths around their
heads. Fat Mrs. Wilson, who played the organ, had the most
powerful voice in the whole congregation—it brought the
bats screeching out from the rafters over our heads. I would
get terrified and often hide under the benches until the service
was over. We left for church before the moon went down and
got back around noon.

Mrs. Wilson died a few years later and was buried on the
hill by the church. Up until that time I still refused to believe
that human beings could die: I just couldn't conceive of anyone I knew dying. I used to go up to the hill and stare at her
grave, hoping she'd bust out.

I returned to America—I don't know what year—and remained until 1958 when I made my second trip to Jamaica to
attend Knox College in Spaldings, Jamaica, B.W.I.

Knox was founded in 1947 by the Presbyterian Church of
Jamaica as a center for Christian Education. Over two thousand students attended the school, and half of them were day
students from Christiana, Mandeville, and Spaldings. The
boarders came from Haiti, Antigua, Dominica, Martinique,
Guadeloupe, Grenada, Trinidad, Cayman, Nassau, and
many parts of Central and North America as well as from
Scotland and elsewhere in Europe. The headmaster, the Reverend Mr. Davidson, was a missionary of the Church of Scotland. The ethos of Knox was discipline. It was said that there
was enough discipline to prepare us for the kind of society we
would live in. Everyone was required to wear the Knox uniform so that the rich would be no different from the poor.
Students were usually admitted at seven years of age and
went through elementary, preparatory, and secondary
school, graduating at about twenty with a Cambridge diploma, which is equivalent to a high school diploma in the
U.S.

The founders of Knox felt that it was more important to
acquire habits of studying and learning rather than merely to
absorb a certain amount of knowledge by a certain time. The
school's aim was to nurture rather than exhaust a person's

strengths and to enable the full person to overcome the difficulties which he would meet in a wider sphere of life, in the
real world. Knox emphasized athletic activities and the competitive spirit between groups rather than between individuals. Each student belonged to one of four competitive groups
called Grants, Murray, Forbes Dennis, and Webster. All ri-
valry was consumed in athletic competition. The fundamental principle behind the Knox system of education was that
children were individuals who needed to be taught individually to develop their own potentialities as responsible
members of a community. As you got older you received a
specific amount of pocket money determined by your age. In
a sense you could say that Knox was an international community in which all members existed for the collective good.

We were expected to act sensibly and to cooperate in creating a system which allowed a proper degree of freedom to
develop self-control. Anyone who did not cooperate was expelled. This was made unequivocally clear before admission. Expulsion was a harsh punishment: it meant that you
could not attend another secondary school on the island.
There were a few unwritten rules. Cursing warranted suspension. If you were late for a meal, you missed the entire meal.
There was a moment of silent prayer and hymn singing
("Onward, Christian Soldiers") before breakfast and inspection before every meal. If your bed was untidy or shoes
unclean, you were whipped or made to clean the entire dormitory—or both, as it usually happened. Although the people
who ran Knox claimed not to believe in corporal punishment,
they felt that "punishments were always made to fit the
crime." Students were suspended for cursing and smoking
and expelled for arguing with teachers and using knives
against other students. The ultimate punishment was expulsion from the school community for consistently refusing to
cooperate.

These rules didn't apply to me yet. As I was an "overseas"
student and too young to take care of myself, I, along with
four other boys, stayed at Girls' Hostel. Benito, who was

from Venezuela, couldn't speak a word of English. Toby, the youngest, was an American. He was crazy—he loved to lock himself up in closets. Toby was a true American, the blond-haired, blue-eyed type. Dudley and Gunther were Jamaicans. We knew nowhere but Knox: it was our world and our universe.

We were not allowed to read comic books because they "distracted from study." We had to stand while speaking to teachers and always say "yes, sa." and "no, sa." Our classes were held outside, and they told us stories of Dickens and poetry by Poe.

The four of us tried to teach Benito as much English as we knew. Up to then I was unable to spell my name or read. Miss Bent, our housemother, read to me letters that my mother sent, and I would draw pictures of Miss Bent and myself and have them mailed to my mother. I drew pictures all the time, of the sun which I looked at for hours, of the landscape, flowers, animals, and people.

After supper the five of us were expected to go to our hostel, read, and play quiet games until bedtime. The older students went down to the school buildings to do "prep" (homework). Girls' Hostel had a quadrangle. The side opposite our side, where we slept, was the senior girls' dormitory. The windows were always left open and the curtains pulled back. The five of us would pretend to sleep until we heard the girls coming. Then we would climb close to the window where we saw an international group of naked girls. No Miss Universe contest was more thrilling. It drove me crazy to see those girls and not be able to touch them. This happened every night until Miss Bent decided that we were "of age" and sent us to live in the Junior Boys' Hostel. Toby, the American, was not as dumb as we thought. Those closets he hid in were close to the girls' bathroom, and he had drilled holes in them so that he had a clear view of the girls bathing. One day I got caught in there. The older girls did a job to my behind and mind, scratched me up real good, and left me crumpled in the closet. Rachel, who was the only one who had mercy on me, put ointment on my cuts. I couldn't believe, I refused to believe that her hands were actually touching my body. I had seen her naked many times.

That afternoon I missed supper and went over to the girls' side of the hostel and pissed all over their beds. I was just beginning to realize that revenge had to be taken into my own hands. For a long time I had believed in letting people beat me up until they either got tired of doing it, or until they arbitrarily stopped, suddenly shocked at the brutality they had inflicted on me. Life doesn't work that way. If it hadn't been for Miss Bent, I probably would have been killed that night when the girls got back.

The five of us were split up and sent to the Junior Boys' Hostel. It was a difficult period for us. We cared greatly for each other and not at all for anybody or anything else. We knew only vaguely who we were and where we came from. Our security had been in unity. Now we were forced to start growing up. Benito had learned to speak full sentences in English, and the rest of us, except Gunther, had stopped wetting our beds.

GENERAL REPORT ON: REEVES D. CLASS 4 1961

. . . is lively and artistic. He is also rather too disturbing an element in his group too often. He has very definite powers of leadership, which he has not always used to the best advantage of the school. However we have discussed this problem with him regularly of late and he is becoming aware of his responsibilities in this respect and is trying to improve . . . Whenever possible he will avoid reading in preferences for drawing and writing. It would help him a great deal if he would read purely for enjoyment . . . In arithmetic, he works unevenly. I am not sure of the reason. It may be he memorizes more often than he really understands. Perhaps he is merely careless at times.

Older boys in the Junior Hostel always tried to beat me up because I didn't do what I was told. In turn, I bullied boys my age and younger. Our hostel was governed by strength. Each of us was aware of the strengths and weaknesses of those we

lived with. Only strength was respected. We shared our deepest secrets and revealed our innermost fears. Every hour of
every day we followed a structured program from hymn singing and inspection in the morning through breakfast, classes,
lunch, dinner, and lights out. Only on Saturdays after inspection and Sundays after church was there free time. On Saturdays when we received our two shillings and sixpence pocket
money, I forced boys my age to contribute a shilling to buy
food, which was distributed to members of my tribe. I was a
little feudal lord. On Sundays everyone was required to go to
church, a little more than a three-mile walk. Afterward we
went to the bush. We were all warriors of various tribes, and I
was head of the largest tribe, consisting of about twenty boys.
We chopped down trees, destroyed each other's forts, and
threw stones and sticks at each other. Our heads and knees
bled, but we kept fighting. We got sick from germs that plants
carried and became weak from drinking rain and river water.
We hunted and killed goats and wild pigs for feasts. We swam
naked in the river and dove from the falls down into the river
between sharp rocks to prove our courage. We ate mango,
guava, naseberry, and starapple. We killed green humming-
birds and brown lizards with slings and all kinds of things
that weren't human. We became exhausted from the heat and
fell where we stood until the sun went down.

The land itself seemed to make us lords of all we surveyed. We stood on the hills watching the heavy dark clouds
floating toward us with rain. We would run down to the
road's edge and actually watch the rain falling on the other
side while we remained dry only a few feet away. We ran
from the rain but always lost the race: nature always caught
up with us. The rain and thunder left as quickly as they came,
like life did from the animals we killed. We were natives of the
rain and land and sun—and felt like masters of the world.

We feared only the Rastas, black men who lived in the
bush and smoked weeds that made them crazy. They wore
their hair long and dirty and never cut it and greeted all
strangers by saying "Peace and love, Brother Mahn." Their

weeds were ganja—marijuana. We heard stories of these giants—of how at times they were friendly but then suddenly would turn crazy. They would eat our heads if they caught us killing their animals. They would make soup with our penises. Therefore, we never explored their land or stoned or killed their animals.

I spent as much time in the bush as my health permitted. Whenever I had asthma attacks I was left alone and not given medication for long periods of time, days and even weeks. I was left alone gasping and vomiting on myself. Only on nights when my attacks were so fierce that my wheezing awakened everyone, was I given any attention. Sometimes I'd get fanatic, savage, and hostile, trying to tear the sinews from my chest. Sometimes I was given injections that lasted for only a few hours. Other times my head was placed under a heavy blanket while I inhaled steam from a hot pot of herbs.

Mom Reeves had sent me a glass instrument containing liquid which, when sprayed into my mouth, gave me instant relief. I remember having an attack one night. I went through a psychological battle, trying to convince myself that nothing was wrong with me, that I could breathe, that I was free. But the asthma came, it hit and ran and hit. The attack was on and I went stumbling around in the darkness searching for the instrument. I reached out for the instrument, heard it fall and break. In the darkness I fell to the floor and tried to suck up the liquid. It was useless. I only caught splinters in my tongue and lips. I pulled up a huge wooden chair, placed it at the entrance of the dormitory, and sat there wheezing and gasping, gazing at the full moon and clouds as they assumed different formations.

Hate ran through my body and mind because I was left there. I tried walking down to the sanitarium. It took me a great deal of time to cover the twenty-five-yard walk. I stood with my hands on my sides, my head raised to the sky, calling out for the nurse. She finally appeared in the light on the veranda. The night insects instantly swarmed around the light. They could be seen from the road. The nurse stood there; her face could not be seen clearly, but her cold harsh voice could be heard clearly. "You asthma dog, shut your trap." She slammed the door. Bitch! Where was this God and Jesus, I thought to myself. I was afraid to even question their existence, afraid of them finding out and punishing me. But I had nothing to lose. I struggled down the path along the bushes to the center of the field. I was waiting for God. "There's no one here but me." I waited for him, but he didn't show. I was afraid to say it but thought that he probably didn't exist.

I was sick most of my years at Knox. I remember nights after prep, when everybody had gone up to the hostel, I was still struggling up the road wheezing, coughing, and spitting. It was at these moments when I hated people who were healthy. I used to sit in front of the window and watch people playing in the rain and mud. Any time my asthma let up, I'd do everything I saw healthy people doing.

HEADMASTER'S COMMENT

I am concerned about Donald's asthma and even more about his reckless disobedience of doctors' and nurses' instructions. He cannot afford to be careless and must develop a more sensible attitude.

George Scott

When I wasn't suffering from asthma, I was suffering from being an American—a second-class citizen who knew absolutely nothing of the "Black experience," which was inherently American. My relatives, my experience, my entire foundation up to this point was West Indian, yet I was damned as a Yankee.

Jamaicans are a people of pride and arrogance. They, like any other group of people, love themselves. This ethnocentric feeling permeated the school, not only Jamaicans against Americans but Bajans against Latins against Cubans against Haitians against Trinidadians, etc. We never argued over race. A person's skin color meant nothing. Nationalism transcended all. Jamaica's internal differences were over class status. It was always possible for various nationalities to unify and direct their venom toward America. America had perpetrated various indignities on the Caribbean, and I was held responsible. America had troops all over the world occupying lands belonging to other people. American tourists and agricultural advisors and the philanthropic bilateral foreign aid program had left a sour taste of hatred for America. Jamaicans I knew told me that America respected no one, no nation, that she wanted respect and yet looked down on the world. I told them that my mother and ancestry were West Indian and that I too wanted to belong to the Caribbean. But they forced me to speak, to defend a country that I was born in but never knew. I stood up for Uncle Sam. I told them, those West Indians, that they drank American soda, ate American candy bars, smoked American cigarettes, and loved American cowboy and war movies. I told them that "Uncle Sam" was the most powerful nation on the earth. They responded to that by telling me about something called the Bay of Pigs, an anti-Castro invasion that failed. They told me that America represented a lie, that the dark-skinned man wasn't free, or an equal to the white man in the eyes of white Americans. I knew very little of America and could say virtually nothing to defend her. I didn't want to.

Only a few years later, when Cassius Clay was letting the whole world know that he was the greatest, it was possible for me to brag about America. While the Caribbean had no great affection for this country, the grandiosity that was (Cassius Clay) Muhammad Ali was powerful, poetic, prophetic. And, ironically, the American Champion unified our spirits. We had been told stories of some fantastic animal named Br'er Rabbit who got into confrontations with every animal in creation, who occasionally whipped the entire animal kingdom. Br'er Rabbit won even when he lost. We grew to see Ali as Br'er Rabbit. Everything he was, we wanted to be part of. I should say the reason we loved him most was because he was an American so intolerable to America. Every time he won it was a victory for us, against America.

Despite all of our differences, when it came to our school

we were one unified body. We had school spirit. We were the
first country school in Jamaica to have a swimming pool. We,
the students, built it with our own hands. We uprooted and
burned the bush, cleared away the stones, and raised money
to buy cement and employ contractors. We were all proud of
the pool when it was finished. It belonged to us, collectively.

I soon outgrew the bush and disbanded my tribe. When the
school administration found out about our killing the animals
in the bush and chopping down the trees, we had to pay for
the trees and got whipped for killing the animals. I became
interested in girls and fish. I had many jars filled with multi-
colored fish and frogs that I had caught from the tanks which
supplied our drinking water.

I went with Barbara, who was Chinese. She brought me
food whenever I was late and had to miss meals. She helped
me in math. At night after prep I would meet Lorna in the
bush. She was Jamaican and so black that she was called
Bull. On Sundays after church I would swim with Heather,
who was Jamaican but white. Heather was very frail and
turned red in the sun instead of tan. I spent most of my time,
however, with Gay, who was Trinidadian. Her skin was a
smooth golden brown. Her hair was long and soft. Her older
brother and other older boys warned me to stay away from
her because she was too good for me. But Gay was mine. One
night Calvert, a senior boy, slapped me over and over again
until my whole head felt numb and my body limp. He just
kept saying, "Stay away from her. Stay away from her . . ."

I told Devon, who was like an older brother to me, and he
stabbed Calvert in the arm, and warned him not to bother me
again. Devon was later expelled, and I no longer tried to be
with Gay.

Of all the girls that I knew at Knox, Puss Giddy was by far
the wildest. Her real name was Norma something-or-other—
I never knew her last name. During break, our ten-minute
free time before lunch, our class would sit on the walls outside talking about whose hood was big enough and long
enough to get into Puss Giddy.

Giddy was something else; she always wanted you to feel

her up. One day in projects class the teacher assigned us some work and left the room. All of us started going crazy. Gloster closed and bolted the door, and all the boys backed Puss Giddy up against the wall, snatching off her tunic, feeling whatever they could get their hands on. There was a hell of a lot of noise in that room, girls laughing, guys pushing each other down to get a better feel. I watched it all because I was sick. But even if I had been well that day, I would not have joined in, because at that time I was seeing a senior girl named Joan.

I thought I had fired in my pants the time I met her at a dance. The school's rules forbade close dancing, but Joan and I were way in the back under the dim lights, grinding the soul out of each other. My penis was being ripped to shreds on my zipper. In between dances I ran over to Philip, and he and I went into the bathroom. I pulled down my pants and showed him my penis. "Have I fired yet?" I asked. "No," he said. "You'll know when you fire; you'll feel it like a tingling in the head of your hood. Something will come out of it that you've never seen before."

I never did fire on Joan and couldn't understand why.

I was in the sanitarium when I met Frances, a tall raven-haired American. I was recovering from an asthmatic attack, and she a sore throat. The sanitarium had only one bathroom between the partition which separated boys from girls, and one afternoon I entered the bathroom and saw Frances standing before me naked. She didn't flinch, but stood there smiling at me. Later that night we fucked, both of us for the first time.

Girls were too temperamental, so I stayed with my fish. I was deeply immersed in painting and running and living. I wrote to my mother, but it had been such a long time since I had seen her that I forgot what she looked like.

My life came to be a series of unending punishments. One night Gregor, Wayne, and I decided to steal some food from Mr. Porteous, who was our housemaster. On that night he was on prep duty. We left prep early, raced up to the hostel, and entered his room. We saw tuna, crackers, sardines, fruits, American peanut butter, and candy bars. Much of this stuff I had not tasted since I came to Knox. We were hesitant to take anything that would be noticed, so we settled for two cookies each.

The following morning the three of us were told to miss breakfast and to report to Mr. Scott's office. Scott was hated by everyone who came into contact with him. I hated him more than anybody because he had married the senior girl who had taken care of me when I lived at Girls' Hostel. When we got to his office, he told us that we would have no meals for that day, that we would have one meal a day for two weeks, that we would not eat with other students, that we would be whipped, that we were suspended from classes, that we would clean the shit from the pig pens. We were forced to write letters to our parents, stating that we had stolen "goods" from the housemaster's room.

We were beaten forty times and given five more lashes each time we fell to our knees. While other students were in the cafeteria eating, we had to stand in the quadrangle opposite them with our arms outstretched, holding piles of books on each arm.

We spent the entire day lifting buckets of dung. We were plagued by insects and couldn't stand the smell of our own bodies.

The three of us set a trap for Porteous. We lined the entrance to our dormitory with thin fishing wire and tied a bucket filled with rocks over the entrance. After lights out we started making loud noises and banging on Porteous's door. Porteous rushed out, running after me. I headed for the trap and stepped out of the way. Porteous rushed into the wire, cutting his face, hands, and neck. He lay there struggling on the ground trying to free himself. Monty had lost his courage and failed to pull the rope so that the rocks would fall on the victim. I pulled it.

BEATTIE HOSTEL
HOUSEMASTER'S REPORT   1964

. . . It is a pity he is not ready to accept authority. He can at times be dishonest and violent. I am hoping for an improvement next term. His asthma has not troubled him during the second half of the term so much. He does not always follow the instructions and arrangements laid down for him by the nurse.

M. D. Porteous

The two-week punishment was hardly over before I got into a fight with a senior boy, Edgar Munn. I was caught fighting with a steel peg in my fist and was sentenced to three more weeks on the pig farm besides being beaten in the evenings. I was beaten by "Sarge," headmaster of Jones Hostel, until my body felt like it was covered with ants.

In the late evening I was reporting for my meal. As I entered the door, someone was pulling my collar. The next thing I felt was my head bouncing off the cement. When I looked up, I saw an older girl standing over me. She said that I should have manners and always let older people, especially girls, through doors first. When she turned her back I grabbed her and pulled her out into the road. We fought from late evening until night. She had reopened old wounds on my knees and had mercilessly beaten and slapped my face. I bled from the nose and lips but would not be beaten by a girl, no matter how old. It was a disgrace for a man to be beaten by a woman. Each time she thought that I was finally finished, I came back for more punishment. Crowds gathered around us. Older boys kept picking me up as I fell and throwing me back to her. Girls became almost fanatic, screaming for someone to stop my bleeding. I grabbed a stone and let fly dead center of her forehead. As she fell, I descended on her, strangling her. I held her neck firmly, wanting to squeeze the life out of her. She began to kick, exposing her legs. She stopped moving and began to cry. I was pulled off her, victorious. I did not wipe the blood from my face and felt proud of the blood on my torn shirt. I felt good to see that nappy-headed bitch crying.

I was given another six weeks of whipping and shit lugging. By this time I had become well-known because of my punishment. Everyone who had received punishment was respected within the student family.

Of all those beatings I received from headmasters that I thought were unfair, Ross's was by far the most unjust. It was on a night when all of us were restless. The lights were out, but we were still talking and running around in the dark hitting each other with pillows. I had been standing with my back to the window when Ross pulled me through the window, kicked me down the concrete steps, and struck me more than several times with a club. I rolled and tried to dodge his blows but my back felt paralyzed. I lay motionless with my hands covering my head. As he stopped beating me, the pain in my back lessened. I rose to my feet, headed for the road, and picked up two rocks. I went back for Ross.

"Lick me now you damn heathen Jew, you," I said. And people from both senior and junior hostels were crying out, "Clout him with the stone, Reeves." I was crying, nervous, and liable to do just about anything. Ross was scared and backing away. I was just about ready to let go one of those stones dead center of his head, when from behind, two prefects grabbed me around the neck and hands. I struggled, but they beat me to the ground and held me there face down.

When I calmed down, I was given the cross punishment for the rest of the night. That is, I stood in the middle of the quadrangle with my arms outstretched holding two huge dictionaries in each hand. After an hour those dictionaries feel like tons; your arms, veins, and bones feel like they're going to give out. You feel like a nail or some cold metallic spike is being driven through your chest. And if those books dropped, the weight would be increased. As soon as I had learned to write letters by myself, I had told Mom Reeves of those punishments. Those people had no right to beat us the way they often did. These letters never reached their destination. There was one red mail box for the school. Before the mail went out to Spaldings, the headmasters of each hostel would check the mail—who had written to whom could easily be told by the address and return address. Porteous often steamed open our letters. We found this out much later, when he was caught doing it.

By the last day of my six-week punishment I was icily determined never to be whipped again, never to disobey. I became deeply immersed in athletics. In physical education we were required to run a four-mile course. Patterson was the champion in our age group. When I was sick, from the sanitarium window I used to watch him finishing races. No one was ever close to him when he finished. I had always wondered what it must feel like to lead two hundred people over a four-mile course. I was determined to run with Patterson.

At the sound of the whistle two hundred of us set off to cover the distance. I ran with Patterson, and as we passed through the gates of Knox, there was no sight of other runners. For two miles I followed Patterson. I remained only a few feet away from him. Not once did he turn to look at me because he didn't expect anyone to be there. I ran through the bush and gullies along paths of beaten red dirt. I began to tire, could not possibly keep up the pace. My mind said run, run. The stones were cutting my bare feet and caused blisters which got swollen on the hot tar roads. My lungs felt like they were going to explode, but I was more afraid of losing. I began to give up when Patterson looked back at me and told me not to stop, not to give up. The pain was so unbearable, I began to cry, but kept running. As we approached the Knox hill, the last mile, he felt the challenge, began to run faster and faster. I would not come so far to be robbed of victory. But on the last fifty yards he pulled away from me as if I were standing still. The defeat overwhelmed me.

He repeated the same finish four times afterward. And each time I became more determined than ever to take his championship. Although I had failed to beat him, I became obsessed with my new ability. I began to punish myself religiously. Every Sunday and Saturday I ran the course twice, once in the morning before breakfast and once after lights out. Late at night I stuffed my pillow under my blankets and stole out of the dormitory. I was always afraid of running at night because there was total darkness in the bush. Only when the moon was full could I actually see the ends of the road. In those days I half felt that the full moon had something to do with my asthma. Superstition seemed to be fact: a full moon meant an asthma attack.

When Patterson and I raced again, I defeated him. And when I had equaled his victories over me, we came to respect each other and afterward always ran the course together and finished together, never again trying to outdo each other.

As the cross-country season came to an end, I became interested in track and field. I won the Class IV division title. One of our most memorable meets was against Priory, an all-white school in Kingston. As an athlete, I began to feel the status that the school accorded us. We represented the school in all its glory, nothing brought us closer together with each other than sports. On the day of the Priory meet, suffering from asthma, I had to defend my title. I went to the sanitarium and stole some drugs. I stuffed myself with pills and three bottles of cough syrup, then fell asleep until the meet began. I lost one of my four events.

When the track season ended, I joined the swimming team. During the football season I kept goal for Grants Junior Boys' Team. In the first season our team won, but in the second season I failed miserably as goalkeeper. The last game all hell let loose against us. We were tied four all. The rain was coming down hard, and the mud had people slipping and sliding all over the place. I was standing there guarding the goal when up field the other team broke free with the ball. The rush was coming down. I was scared.

"Where's our guys?"

The crowd was going wild. The guy who had the ball panicked and kicked it before he was in good position to score. It fell dead only a few feet away from me. I was so anxious to pounce on the ball that I slipped. I got up, slipped again. By this time the opposing team was down on me. I was lying on my belly in the mud, looking at the ball, stretching out my hand. All I saw was a foot coming at my face. It connected with my head, and I felt a cold numbness, then nothing at all. I was knocked out. People never stopped teasing me about how dumb it looked. We lost four to five.

I spent more time playing sports and in the sanitarium than I did in classes. I was out keeping goal at the time when I was supposed to be at music lessons.

SUBJECT: PIANO

TEACHER'S COMMENT   CHRISTMAS 1964

Since half-term I have scarcely seen him—mainly due to attacks of asthma. During the lessons that he had he showed very little aptitude either physically at the keyboard or mentally in grasping the elements of musical notation. I think he genuinely wants to play, but I do not believe he has the slightest conception of what is entailed in the learning of a musical instrument.

In general my teachers said that I was a "good student and most capable in academic work." Yet, I received grades of F in English Composition, Literature, Reading, Math, Spanish, Projects, and Religion. Everybody had a different story or explanation for my failure. I got B's in art and woodwork. I did, however, get an A in general science. Mr. Jones was the teacher.

Once a student had caught a rat in our cafeteria and named him Roger. We always saw rats in the cafeteria. Up by the roof where the rafters connected with the wall, the rats would come out and hurdle the wooden beams. During dinner when they came out, everybody would cheer for them as they cleared a beam.

One day Mr. Jones and I were alone in the lab. He said that he was going to dissect Roger. He put Roger in a large bottle with cotton soaked in chloroform and screwed on the top. I stood there watching Roger struggle frantically to get free. He got weaker and weaker and finally stopped moving. His tail stiffened, then fell limp; one eye closed; the other, already closed, had been pulverized and left hanging from Roger's head in the act of capturing him.

"Is he dead?" I asked.

"Yes, he's dead," Mr. Jones replied.

I was fascinated. I'll bet Roger didn't know what hit him. There seemed to be no end to the many ways that subhuman things could be killed. Life seemed not to have any real meaning since it could be taken away so easily. Watching Roger die caused me to think about Desmond Morrow, the new American. There was something mentally wrong with him. A lot of people had tried running away from Knox, but few ever succeeded. Morrow believed that he could run from Jamaica to America. Everybody knew about this, even the headmaster who assigned me the task of running around the bush with Morrow until he got tired and frustrated. He tried to run away a lot of times, and while running would say all kinds of things about escaping. He was never certain what he wanted to escape from, but you could sense in him some terrible knot that he wasn't able to loosen.

Whenever we had short vacations, I stayed with relatives on the island. I soon realized how isolated Knox was. Knox was not Jamaica; Jamaica was not Knox. Knox had given impetus to my life. I had covered miles running through the countryside. I saw Jamaica washing clothes in rivers, her people living in huts made of tin and cardboard, eating barely enough food to give them enough strength to work more, believing in God, the Son, and the Holy Ghost, cutting cane, selling fruits and fowls and living to die. As I traveled through the island, I saw beauty everywhere. Its lush green mountains were embroidered with flowers of many colors. I took the train from Kendal, through Mandeville and May Pen, Spanish Town and Kingston. As we traveled through the morning dew in the high mountains, we seemed to be riding on clouds. My relatives took me to Dunn's River Falls, Fern Gully, the harbor at Port Antonio, and Montego Bay. When we traveled to the sea, I rambled up the white coastline and watched the huge white yachts slide into the cove. In places, the island remained primeval, untouched. The brilliant sun pierced the clear water. Many times I followed its rays beneath the water and followed the chains that held the buoys above. I swam even farther—through the labyrinth of coral formations down to the bottom among the rocks, draped in golds, purples, blues, and greens. I saw tiny fish swimming in perfect order, and even when I motioned to frighten them, they stayed together. The water of the Caribbean was so clear that larger fish in the deeper seas could be seen from far away.

When I stayed with my relatives, I became aware of the Jamaican way of life. The first thing they taught me was two methods of killing chickens.

I must say that for a time I enjoyed killing chickens more than anything else in the world. I'd snap their necks with my bare hands or cut their necks off with the machete. I laughed when I saw the headless chickens flying, jumping through the air, bouncing, and banging into objects around them. Often I took aim with my sling and struck them in midair as they flew. On occasion I'd kill every chicken I could get my hands on, one right after the other. I don't know why I loved it so much, maybe because of the way they walked, or the way their eyes seemed to be tacked into their heads in a fixed position, following your every move, or maybe it was because they shit that green-yellowish, pastelike mucus all over the place. Whop! Off came their heads, whatever the reason.

I watched the way the people dressed and lived. They loved to gossip about dead people and discuss other people's business. They would express shock at the tale of the death of a person who had died thirty and forty years ago. Sometimes I don't think they even knew these people. They were obsessed with land, possessing it either to build on or be buried in. Uncle John would say, "You're not a man until your two feet are standing" (and here he would plant first one foot on the ground, and then the other) "on land that you can call your own." They claimed superiority to American Blacks because they were "self-governed and American Blacks were merely governed."

Despite their arrogance, they were a beautiful people. I would soon realize that Afro-Americans harbored just as much arrogance and abhorrence for the West Indians. In fact,

I would see that all races of people had inherent assumptions of superiority to those outside their immediate circles.

Knox had been my whole world. I cursed the earth that it was built on more times than I can remember: I was torn between the bitter and the sweet and valued the sweetness as I valued the lives of those who meant most to me. I was a native child who saw things with his eyes but did not analyze or interpret them in his mind. It was more like being born blind than being born with sight and losing it. It was good to live and grow with people of different nationalities, races, and socio-economic backgrounds. People were identified by nationality and not race, never discriminated against because of race. That all of us—Black, Red, White, Yellow, and Brown—had a common oppressor, who put out the lights and punished us and forbade us even to hold hands with members of the opposite sex, yet taught us to survive together, made us one and gave us the ability to distinguish between allies and enemies.

In retrospect I try to describe the feelings I had when I was in the bush and was seeing things with my unaware eyes, things that only now have meaning to me because I now understand what I saw. At the time, it was enough just to see, to experience; I never felt it was necessary to understand anything.

I never understood life and death. We were born, yet as soon as we had sense, we knew that death was inevitable, that one day we would all up and die. Why was there life if death existed? When we did not identify with what we killed or what had died, it meant absolutely nothing. But when something close to us died, we were reduced to tears, reduced to murmurs and outcries of—why? *We* felt inside that our worthless lives should be taken instead of a person whom we felt close to, whom we consciously or unconsciously depended on for love and guidance.

The environment in which we lived at Knox was virtually a utopian vacuum, pure in the sense that people defined themselves only in terms of one another. To Knox I owe my foundation and character, both the good and the bad in me. The drastic difference between the life people had there and the existence which masquerades as life here in America, left me with an objective vision through which I could remain a detached observer and yet an involved participant.

Ignorance was not the problem. It is pretentious to believe that knowledge was the answer because I had been conditioned to accept the truth as it seemed then. I had been conditioned to worship strength, and sought to strengthen my body. The sexes were isolated; therefore, every opportunity we got to be alone we used to the fullest extent. Despite everything that had been done to us at Knox and everything that we felt for our brothers and sisters (whom I left in 1965), we remained individuals and not members of groups.

I would soon realize that Knox was no more hypocritical than any other institution. The difference was that here at Knox physical wounds we suffered always healed, but the devastating process of indoctrination which tried to break our spirits as individuals and our self-determination was harder to cure.

Later, when I returned to Knox for my second stay, I had already lost my childlike innocence. By then I had begun to realize how alienated I was from *the world* and had become aware of the color differences in people, all because I had lived in America.

The Brownsville Papers

> The town belonging to the colonized people, . . . the Negro Village, . . . is a place of ill fame, peopled by men of evil repute. They are born there, it matters little where or how; they die there, it matters not where, nor how. It is a world without spaciousness; men live there on top of each other.
>
> *Frantz Fanon*

EARLY IN 1963, I left Knox, supposedly to be cured of asthma. During the period that followed I witnessed events that had absolutely no meaning to me, probably because of my youth. The period when Martin Luther King led the "March On Washington," John Kennedy was assassinated in Dallas, and Lyndon B. Johnson stepped into the White House was a time in my life when there were many questions and no answers. I felt disoriented: sometimes I thought we were back in Detroit, but actually we were in New York City. I saw Mom Reeves and someone I only vaguely remembered—my younger brother Francis. We no longer lived in a two-story brown wooden house but in a dingy, cold, one-room, back apartment at 222 St. James Place in Brooklyn. The three of us slept in a huge bed. Where was Boss Reeves?

Mom Reeves kept talking to herself, said that she was determined to stay off something called welfare, and that after all her years in nursing, she wouldn't let her life end in ruin because of any man. She worked day and night, and I was left in charge of Francis. Sometimes we saw her every other day, and even then she just came in to get a clean uniform and check on us. Our room had a stove, a window by the fire escape, and a bed. At night I'd throw the garbage out on the fire escape but soon had to buy candles to keep lit by the window to frighten the rats away. I had broken the chain for the window, so it could not be fully closed. Mom Reeves instructed me not to leave Francis alone, but I often did.

New York was something else. I'd never been in a place where everything was made of cement and iron. The trees were planted in little patches of dirt on the sidewalks, and there were broken glass and men in the streets. America was a filthy place.

Guys killed each other for rum. Once I saw two men fighting: one had a piece of glass that he kept jabbing in the other man's face. People just walked by as if nothing was going on. What knowledge I had of America prior to this was fragmentary recollections and stories from Mom Reeves and pictures in *Look* and *Life* magazines. Now, instead of the whistling of night insects, I heard only cars and sirens and men fighting.

I was temporarily enrolled in Public School 11. The teachers dressed me up like Abraham Lincoln and gave me a script to memorize. I did a good job at acting—after I freed the slaves, they put me in a talent class. I didn't stay at P.S. 11 too long. Mom Reeves had got up enough capital to buy a two-family house on Alabama Avenue in Brooklyn. It was located behind a synagogue in an area that was mainly Jewish. We were the first Black people in this neighborhood, and almost immediately everyone on our block began to move out. Even the people who lived next door, whose children's children had grown up in this community, were planning to leave.* I never got along with those Jewish boys.

---

* In 1940, most of the 170,000 residents were white. By 1950, the total population had dropped to 142,000, and whites were moving out. In 1960, there were 118,600 people. In 1971, the population was estimated at 100,000 with 85 percent Black or Puerto Rican. In May of that year, the riots broke out in Brownsville. We even made *The New York Times*—right up there with Harlem and Watts.

They teased me because of my accent, and when I beat them
up, they came after me as a gang. I carried cooking knives
with me at all times.

A few weeks after our arrival in Brownsville, Boss Reeves
showed up. I was happy to see him; it had been some time.

When the school year began, Mom Reeves enrolled me in
P.S. 190.*

The students laughed at me because of the way I spoke and
dressed. I wore tight pants that were at least a foot above my
ankles and cheap shoes. They said that I had just stepped off
the banana boat. I had been trained to stand while speaking
to a teacher and never to call him by his name. So even the
teacher laughed at me when I stood and said "yes sa," and
"no sa." They called me "monkey chaser." (Monkey Chaser?)
The mere fact that I existed made me a problem.

Mr. Gittelman, my teacher, sent notes home to Mom
Reeves stating that I was a disruptive element in class because I asked "too many questions." When I stopped asking
questions, he said that I "refused to cooperate." Mom Reeves
beat me—she didn't believe my side of the story.

When your parents got one of these notes from school, you
had to get it signed to verify that they received it and take it
back to the teacher. One day I got home before Mom Reeves,
and there was that familiar envelope from school. I got some
old bills with Mom Reeves's signature on them and copied it
over and over again until I got it down pat. If Mom Reeves

---

* "The public school is the greatest and most effective of all Americanized agencies. This is the one place where all children in a community or
district, regardless of nationality, religion, politics, or social status, meet
and work together in a cooperative and harmonious spirit . . . The children work and play together, they catch the school spirit, they live the
democratic life, American heroes become their own, American history
wins their loyalty, the Stars and Stripes, always before their eyes in the
school room, receives their daily salute. Not only are these immigrant children Americanized through the public school, but they, in turn, Ameri-
canize their parents carrying into the home many lessons of democracy
learned at school." "Report of the Superintendent of Schools," Annual Report of Education of the New Haven City School District, 1919, in C. F.
Cnudde and D. E. Neubaner, eds., *Empirical Democratic Theory* (Chicago:
Markham Publishing Co., n.d.).

hadn't called Gittelman to check up on my behavior, I would have gotten away with it, too. I didn't understand why Gittelman hated me so much. When I got into school after he'd found out that I forged the signature, he looked at me and said, "I've got you—you little bastard." The following week he tried to transfer me out of his class but failed.

Gittelman exploited my abilities in art. I drew all the scenery for the class play, and yet everybody was given a part except me. He wouldn't even let me be a tree.

As I became more Americanized, I started to chew gum in class and remained seated while speaking to the teacher. I began to wear long pants and asked questions only when I was told to. Gittelman began to make me stand in the corner every morning because I was still asking too many questions, even though I only asked questions when I was told to.

I knew how to take vengeance and told other boys in my class about hunting in the bush and how important it was to be strong. We became a gang and in the late evening after school would wait for teachers who bothered us and beat them up. It was always dark, so they were unable to identify us. My basement became headquarters. We stole axles and baby carriage wheels and used them to practice weight lifting. We removed cartridges from pens and concealed knives, took cans of hair spray and made crude flamethrowers, took mops and broomsticks and taped nails and long screws to their heads to make spears. We killed stray cats, and other non-human things. Our gang had four Americans, five Puerto Ricans, and an Israeli. We fought other gangs and soon established ourselves as rulers of the lunchyard—it was our territory.

Raymond, one of the Puerto Ricans in our gang, challenged me; he wanted to be "boss." I was boss. He said: "There are more Puerto Ricans in the gang than Negroes."

"Don't call me a Negro."

I thought that the word "Negro" classified me as an American, and that's the last thing I wanted to be.

Raymond and I started fighting. Just about the whole school was down in the lunchyard watching us. He probably would have beaten me if the police hadn't shown up. What a sight it was to see hundreds of fifth- and sixth-graders running all over the place amidst police, police cars, and ambulances. Raymond and I climbed over the fence and went to my house. We settled our dispute and had dinner. I made him my bodyguard. Gittelman sent a note home about the fight. Again I had gotten home before Mom Reeves but had been locked out and forgotten my keys. I was real nervous—she'd kill me this time! I saw her coming up the block and could have stuffed the postcard in my pockets or just thrown it away, but, no, I stuffed it in my mouth. When she found out what was going on, the gang was no longer allowed to meet at my house.

I started going to the after-school center regularly. I played dodge ball and got to be quite good at it. Once six people were left on the court, and it was five on one. I was alone and getting arm-weary, so I threw the ball blindly. It struck a guy in the face. He got mad, came running and swinging at me. I stepped back and slammed him in the eye. Gittelman told me to "get my ass in the office."

They told me I wasn't allowed back in the center anymore, so I got my coat and left. As soon as I got outside, guys started coming from behind cars and everywhere. They encircled me, and the boy I hit in the center stepped forward and punched me in the mouth. All of them started to beat on me. They pulled my coat over my head, kicked and punched me, and hit me over the head with a baseball bat. I broke free and ran into a toy store. I was bleeding from the nose and mouth. The owner called Mom Reeves. She came for me, and we went down to Brookdale Hospital where they took X-rays of my head and put my right hand in a cast. The following morning Mom Reeves and I were in the principal's office. He sat right there grinning at us, looking over at me.

"Well, Mrs. Reeves, he's been giving us trouble ever since he got here. You know the saying, 'Those who live by the sword will die by the sword.' " Mom Reeves got real mad.

"Now you listen here, Mister. This is my son, you understand? If you know who beat him up—"

"Please, Mrs. Reeves. These gangs have been beating up teachers and students. When they fight amongst themselves, it only rids us of a problem."

Mom Reeves gave me a long talk and on Sunday took me down to the Church of St. Marks on Kingston Avenue and Union Street. I had lost my courage after my defeat and became an altar boy and worshiper. My job was to snuff out the candles on the altar. The congregation couldn't leave until I put out the lights. On days when we had Communion, I'd steal a sip of the wine. A great number of times I prayed to God, asking him to return my courage so that I could seek revenge on my enemies. Gradually I realized this was no big deal they were letting me in on. One Sunday somebody was bothering me, and I told him to go to hell. The Reverend heard me and told me to go home. I never mentioned it to Mom Reeves. On Sundays, instead of going to church, Francis and I would go to Prospect Park Zoo.

For the entire year I had been taking allergy tests at Brookdale Hospital. When they got through, I was given a list of things I couldn't eat or be near. The way I figured it, I'd have to be in a coffin six feet under the ground in order to follow their instructions.

Shortly after President Kennedy's assassination in 1963, I went to Knox. Mom Reeves said that she was sending me back so that I would "learn to be a man" and not feel inferior to anyone. Francis went with me this time, and we attended Knox until 1965. This time when we left I knew there would be no returning. And upon coming to the United States, I made a vow to myself that I would not "see race, discriminate, judge people on the basis of skin color, or read books that would make my mind impure with alien and racist ideas."

When I got back to Brownsville, I was shocked. In a few years, a once clean and beautiful community had been transformed into a malignant cancer. People stopped using the word "community" and called it a "ghetto" instead. I looked up "ghetto," and it was defined as a place where

Jews were restricted to live. But there were no Jews here. I had not been aware of the forming of the Black community. The Jews were gone, all of them except those who owned the stores. In time, even they left and were replaced by numerous Puerto Ricans with their bodegas. Each summer Brownsville became darker and darker. The streets were filled with shit and garbage and broken men.

Brownsville was intoxicated with violence. The Puerto Ricans and Cubans across the streets constantly stole soda from the Coke factory up by Linden Boulevard. During the days they'd watch people leave for work. Virtually all the homes on the block had been robbed. They took a fan and two radios from our house, and the garbage can too. We got off lucky. By now the culprits were even stealing bathtubs and pipes.

As the sun got hotter, so did the tempers of the people. Everybody lived in constant fear. I can't remember how many times I saw shooting in the streets—Blacks gunning down other Blacks. By the fishmarket on Alabama Avenue a whole crowd of people stood idly by, trying to get a better look as a Black man was raping a Black woman in broad daylight. You could never find the police when you needed them.

The Puerto Ricans turned the water pump on at nights. They wet me up once. I went inside and got my slingshot and started firing marbles at them. One of them came up on my porch, and we started to fight. He tried to drag me into the street so that his friends could hit me with bricks. Mom Reeves came out after me, and she got hit on the leg.

The only friends I had in Brownsville were the McPhersons and Derrick. Pedro and Medrano McPherson were brothers from Jamaica. Derrick was also West Indian, but you could hardly tell—he'd been Americanized. The five of us (my brother included) used to stick together.

One day we saw three murders. In the morning we were on Pedro's stoop talking. All of a sudden some Puerto Ricans came running down the street. One stopped right in front of

us and drew a pistol, took aim at the other one, and shot him
dead. The five of us ran upstairs. We stayed at Pedro's until
late afternoon when we went to my house to fix our bicycles.
Some people across the street began arguing and fighting. A
man was fighting with a half-naked Black woman. He said he
wanted his kid, and the next thing we knew, another man on
the roof fired a shot into his leg. He lay there for a good while
bleeding before the police showed up. Late at night there was
a knifing, and whoever did it saw us. The five of us cut out,
as if we'd seen a ghost. Despite everything, I can't remember
one moment when we were actually afraid of the violence that
surrounded us.

Around midsummer, fires became the number one specta-
tor sport.

People were always talking about Harlem. As bad off as
Harlem was, it produced Malcolm X, Claude McKay, Claude
Brown, Adam Clayton Powell, and other giants of the Black
community. Brownsville produced nothing but rows upon
rows of gutted buildings, enough to house thousands of
people. The thought just kept running through my mind.
Where were the people who lived in those houses? Everything
was being torn down, and nothing was being built up.

I got a job with two Jewish veterinarians. They gave me
a white jacket which I was really proud of. I felt like a scien-
tist or a technician. My job was to clean the shit from the
cages, but I drew pictures of the dogs and cats and sold them
to get some extra money. I put in some long hours with the
doctor, watching him spay cats and remove all kinds of things
from the intestines of dogs. I lived in a neighborhood where
everybody had to have a dog. If you didn't have a German
shepherd, you were nothing. I worked all summer and made
$125. Joel, the younger veterinarian, told me that he knew a
man named Sol who had good puppies for sale. He drove me
out to the Jewish community where Sol lived. Sol didn't let
me select the puppy I wanted—he already had one picked
out for me. I didn't have any sense: I gave him all the money
I had. He and Joel split up the money right in front of me. I

named the dog Napoleon, took him home, and put him down on the kitchen floor. Mom Reeves came out and looked at him. For some reason Napoleon couldn't stand up for more than five minutes before his back legs would collapse. Mom Reeves said that I was crazy, that they had sold me a dog with a calcium deficiency. I took the dog back to Joel and told him politely that I didn't see how he could have let Sol sell me this sick dog. The doctor put down in front of me $75 worth of medicine for the dog.

"I haven't got that kind of money."

"Well, you'll work for nothing for the rest of the year."

I agreed and went home. In a few weeks Napoleon got stronger, and his coat appeared much healthier. Then one afternoon I came home, and Mom Reeves was waiting for me. She'd left Napoleon in the backyard, and some Negroes had jumped over the fence and stolen him. Stolen a dog? There seemed to be no winning in Brownsville. Everybody— the Jews, the Negroes, the Puerto Ricans, *everybody*—was trying to take your eyes out of your head. I spent an entire week walking all over Brownsville trying to find my dog, thinking that those Negroes had probably eaten him. I quit working for the veterinarians because I was tired of lifting shit and taking it.

Life was difficult. Not even the dogs wanted any part of it. At one point I had four dogs: Roger, Tab, Dog, and Fanny. The first time Roger saw the kitchen door open, he bolted for his freedom. We never saw him again. Dog bit a kid and was taken away, and Tab got locked up because she was considered too vicious. Boss was glad when Tab got put away: he hated dogs.

(When Francis and I had first caught Tab, we locked her up in the basement. Boss came in late one night and went downstairs to check the boiler, and Tab almost killed him down there in the back room. Ever since that day, Boss swore Mom, Francis, and I put the dog down there to "assassinate" him. Even today he'll tell you the same story.)

I was left with Fanny, the little mutt. When I had the other dogs, I didn't pay much attention to her. I wouldn't even be seen with her. She knew nothing about streets and traffic, and the first time she went for a walk with me, two cars struck her at once. She spun around in the air and fell dead in the street. I couldn't believe that she'd died and found myself unable to cry although I desperately wanted to. All these other stray dogs were roaming about wildly, unleashed—why weren't *they* killed?

At the end of the summer Boss Reeves took me over to George Gershwin Junior High School on Van Siclen Avenue in Brooklyn to get me enrolled. They didn't know what grade to put me in because the grading system in Jamaica was much different from here. I had to repeat the eighth grade and was placed in an after-school oral reading development class because of my West Indian accent.

I found it difficult to believe that Gershwin, one building, had almost twice as many students as Knox. The situation there was like it was in so many places in New York— Blacks, Italians, Jews, and the cops fought after school. It took me a while to settle down. I had gotten into a fight in wood shop. Mom Reeves had bought me a velvet jacket and Wayne, a Jewish boy, accused me of stealing it. Russell had got me by surprise and slammed me over the head with a bench, but I hit Wayne in the eye before he knew what was happening.

There were certain dress requirements you had to follow to be accepted socially. You had to have a black leather coat and white Converse sneakers ("Cons"). If you didn't, you were a chump. On the very first day that I was tipping* to school with my new leather coat and Converse sneakers, I got mugged. This Negro called me across the street—said he was lost. Soon as I turned my head to point in the direction he should go, he had a blade up against my throat.

"Take off your shoes and that leather coat," he growled.

---

* All the guys "tipped" when they walked. You flicked both your feet, the right foot more than the left. You also bounced but not too high. You could swing your hands but they had to be held in a fist so that everybody knew you were tough.

Take off my shoes? He was going to take my Cons? I started running backwards. I moved away from him so fast that I left him standing there with the blade still in the air. I knew he was startled because it took him some time before he began to chase after me. There was no way in hell for him to catch me, especially with my mind on that blade in his pocket. I ran straight into Mr. Garfunkel's office. Mr. Garfunkel was the school's strong man. He used to take care of all the bad guys. His desk was filled with blackjacks, knives, pens that concealed knives, pipes, and other confiscated weapons. Mr. Garfunkel called the police station, and I rode around the school with the detective, trying to point out the mugger, "my assailant."

I started playing around with a lot of girls, all of whom were Cuban. There was something different about American Black girls, and at that point I just couldn't put my finger on it. I didn't know whether I was becoming feminine or they too masculine. I ran into some difficulty when I asked Pattie, an Italian girl, to go steady with me. News of it spread quickly throughout the school. I couldn't see what the big deal was. My friends never stopped laughing at me and teased me about it all the time. Pattie also got upset. One day she showed up after school with a Black girl. When she introduced me to her, she seemed to be trying to sell the Black girl to me. In fact, she walked off and left the girl with me. I couldn't figure it out. Only much later did I understand what was going on.

I began to run again and became captain of the track team. That same year I joined the soccer team and the Printing Squad, which had won the Ben Franklin Medal of Honor. I became very friendly with all my teachers, especially the principal, Mr. Flinker. Also, I started spending a lot of time painting and had a one-man exhibition of animal portraits in oil hung throughout the school and in Mr. Flinker's office, and any time I got money, I'd buy paints and canvas. The school gave me a scholarship to take art lessons at Pratt Institute on Saturdays. I enrolled in a design class but didn't like the idea of designing Alka-Seltzer and soap boxes. Boss

Reeves didn't like it either and said I should get a trade, something I could make a living out of—like fixing shoes.

I got a job in school working for service credits, not money. You could get credits by working on the audio-visual, lunchroom, and lab squads. I got my credits in the lab, working with Mr. Prager and Mr. Kipp. Mr. Prager's hands were deformed. He had a normal build for a man his height, but he had arms of a ten-year-old. I thought he was crazy because he'd always be sitting behind the desk talking to himself. He'd say, "Good morning, Mr. Prager, can I get you something? Maybe some soup? Yes, won-ton." He loved won-ton soup with banana splits. My job in the lab was to prepare the frogs for dissection and dry cell batteries for the doorbell-ringing experiment, a globe to show that the sun shines on one side of the earth at a time, and the magnets for the attracting-repelling experiment.

At Gershwin they had what was called a G Major Day when all students who had rendered some service to the school would receive special awards. The assembly program was just like a graduation ceremony. When that day came around, I had to make a speech. They had selected me as a model student in the oral reading development class. It was a big day. All the parents as well as the students showed up wearing new shoes and clothes. I read the speech without making a mistake. Afterward, I had to hand out these envelopes containing the awards.

There was absolutely nothing in the envelopes, not even a thank-you note. They had us parading around like fools. The principal gave one boy a "scholarship," but it was nothing but a rolled-up piece of oak tag paper. Blank pieces of paper. Some students started crying.

I was kind of angry myself, but Mom Reeves just smiled and said, "Well, it's nice to know that at least somebody cares. You kids need the incentive." She just said that to cheer me up—she knew that they had made fools out of us, both students and parents. Parents love to see their kids on stage, getting pieces of paper.

In 1966 both worlds I lived in, Gershwin and Brownsville, were torn with racism. As I watched the metamorphosis and the Black man's inheritance of the ghetto from the Jew, I decided to study this transition. I had nothing else to do with my time, and it was a fascinating change. (Up to this point I still wasn't reading books.) I wrote down everything I saw but read nothing to give me greater insight. I went around taking photographs of gutted buildings, of the filth in the streets, wishing I could capture the stench on film or paper. When people asked me what I was going, I told them that I was working for the Washington Commission on Poverty. When I told them that, they practically forced me inside their homes to make me look at the niches and rat holes they lived in. So I wandered through the ghetto, writing down what had already become a cliché.

I observed that when a Black man owned a liquor store in the ghetto, that functioned as a crowning blow to its people because what little money the men and women there earned, they lost through drinking and gambling. In the cold of winter and the heat of summer, you could see these men, what was left of them as men, sitting in corners bathed in their own urine and lying in the street with dog filth. At night I saw these men of the streets turn upon and beat and sometimes even kill each other for reasons that I never could see, never understand. At times it seemed almost merciful that they took each other's lives—to be free.

Rape was also a very big problem. On those nights when Mom Reeves worked late, Francis and I would wait for her at the bus stop. In the Jewish community, separated from ours by Linden Boulevard, a five- and a seven-year-old girl and a six-year-old boy had been raped. And there was some excitement on my block when the detectives came to arrest the boy, almost twenty years old, who had committed the crimes.

I also wrote about my work in the Head Start Program, which I started after I left the job with the veterinarians, how the program was a failure because the children were all of the same race and from the same background and from the same ghetto coffin and were never exposed to other children of different backgrounds or races. Even the job structure of the program seemed strange to me. The coordinator or supervisor was Jewish, and all the parents who worked as teachers' aides were Black and had to ask for the approval of the coordinator for funds or activities. I thought it interesting because here you had Black children, striving for a "head start" which hopefully would lead them to individuality and independence, yet their elders were still asking for guidance from a stranger —a person who didn't even look like them and wasn't even a member of the community in which they lived. But I said nothing. I observed.

On Fridays sometimes I got paid. I would walk down to the Manpower Center on Sutter Avenue and wait on a line. Often the Black people who were in charge of dispensing the checks would tell us that they had been misplaced when actually they were stealing our checks all along. Black adults had robbed Black youth, and we were helpless to do anything about it. The very same people who were robbing us had both the checks and the receipts in their possession so that there was never any evidence of injustice or crime until the culprits were caught—at the end of the summer.

I was still observing. I saw that as the Jews made their exodus, the Puerto Ricans opened up numerous Spanish-American food stores, toy shops, and candy stores. I also saw similar attempts—successes and failures made by Black people—who opened up soul food stores. Business boomed for them during the summer, but the craving for soul food died out during the winter when it was too cold to go anywhere, even for fried chicken.

Most important were the school and welfare because those were things which I always heard people talking about, not only in my house, but in the barber shop, in the supermarket, and on the streets. Here are some of the things that I wrote about what I heard and observed in those days. I started in 1965, when I was twelve years old.*

---

* In December of 1968 my ignorance would be equaled by that of the National Commission on Urban Problems, who discovered that "slums exist, in large part, because slum dwellers are too poor to afford anything better."

When I look back at the ghetto I have to admit that the Jews were right. The Blacks did destroy their own community and turned it into one of the worst ghettos in New York City.* The Black people are not united . . .

For the few Blacks who want to get ahead "there is always" (?) a helping hand. In George Gershwin Junior High there is no competition for anyone who is interested. The result in being interested is that you will receive Art Scholarships, your works exhibited in the Principal's office, high grades and good standing with all the teachers. You could be stupid and not know it because everyone else was a little bit more stupid than you are and not interested. Therefore, when you are confronted by true competition, self-image is destroyed because you find out that you really don't know anything. You realize that you weren't taught enough and that you suffered at the expense of those who were not interested. Time lost can never be regained. So in the ghetto they beat up teachers after school, curse teachers in the classrooms, and sniff glue in the bathroom . . .

Ghetto youth find opportunities in school but what happens when they enter the real world, looking for a job? A job calls for a good academic education, so he is a failure because of the school or his lack of interest. In this situation it is difficult to say, but for those who had to suffer at the expense of those who were not interested, the schools were a failure. Ghetto youth are deluded. They drop out of junior high or high school thinking that the opportunities are there just for the taking. They do not realize that the schools are artificial environments, separated from the community, separated from reality. They teach you and tell you that what you get out of it is the only thing that really counts, and you should do your best. Sometimes, many times your best is not enough, and if you are Black and in the ghetto, it's just tough.

The middle-class Negro hates the Welfare Negro, and many high-class Negroes are just as mean if not worse than some whites. In general Black people are not interested in the contribution to the whole; Blacks hate to see other Blacks getting ahead.

The Jewish people, in general, are an enterprising and ambitious people. They have expanded their presence in this society,

* On April 21, 1971, Mayor Lindsay took mayors from eleven other cities on a bus tour through Brownsville. The devastation prompted Kevin White, of Boston, to remark that the area "may be the first tangible sign of the collapse of our civilization."

through building and educating their own race within the environment. The Jewish people had owned all the stores in the ghetto, even after they abandoned it when the Negroes started to move in. They still own all the major recreational facilities in the Brownsville unit . . .

Jewish children are exposed to people of their own race* and religion who are teachers, doctors, lawyers and other professionals of high esteem, all of whom have a great influence on their aspirations. Whereas a ghetto youth is constantly exposed to the dreaded four-letter words and filth which are the constant dialogue in his home. And he is denied participation in family affairs if there are any affairs to participate in. The ghetto youth has no association with anyone who has a "big shot profession," and this has a kind of psychological effect on him . . .

Welfare is a good idea with bad people. Some Puerto Ricans and Blacks on Alabama Avenue do not deserve to be on welfare, and the middle-class Blacks resent this. I can't see anyone coming into this country with the sole purpose of getting welfare rights. Their children, who should be in school, are out on the streets sniffing glue, mugging people, chopping down telephone poles, breaking into Coke factories, and roaming the streets. So the middle-class ghetto dwellers resent this, their hard-earned money has to be shared with people who should and could get out and work for themselves. They do not give a hell about their apartments because they do not belong to them. If you look at these apartments today, they have been burned, gutted and leveled to the sidewalk as if they had never existed. Here you have people with too much time on their hands, just waiting to get checks. Hence the rackets. You have a Puerto Rican mother with three children and no husband. She moves into an apartment and soon the common-law husband joins the family. Early in the morning they leave the apartment and the children are left with their grandmother. Then the mother and the father proceed to their jobs, and in this way they are able to get welfare money plus their weekly wages. So what happened to all the big investigations? People who have to work hard for their money HATE the idea of welfare. Those who take advantage of the situation will make things bad for all involved. Now I see these things, and I see my mother working sixteen hours a day to keep our home, so naturally I too resent this idea of welfare. I am blind to the good it does because

---

* See my note on pages 280–81 regarding Jewishness and race.

I ONLY SEE THE BAD; and since you learn by what you see in the ghetto, this becomes fact.

The middle-class ghetto dweller is chained to the ghetto if he is a home-owner. No one in his right mind would want to buy a house in the middle of Brownsville.

■ ■ ■

At that time I was visually oriented, I lived by what I saw. I compiled my notes (which I called "The Brownsville Papers") and handed them in as an extra-credit report to Mrs. Forman, my teacher, who was Jewish. Two or three days later she asked me to meet her in the library during my lunch period. We sat opposite each other. She said:

"Have you ever heard of Stokely Carmichael?"

"No, I haven't."

"Do you know who Martin Luther King is?"

"He led a march to Washington."

"Do you know what it was for?"

Why was she asking me all these questions? I thought she was giving me a quiz.

"I don't know why he went to Washington."

"Do you have a lot of trouble with Blacks?"

I told her that I didn't understand the meaning of her question. She sat there silently shuffling through my papers.

"Have you read any books by Black authors?"

"No."

"Do you realize what you've said about your people?"

"My people?"

"Your people would call you an Uncle Tom if they read this."

"Who is Uncle Tom?"

"An Uncle Tom is a Black man who sees through the eyes of a white man. An Uncle Tom is a Black man in white skin."

Black man in white skin? Even though I didn't understand any of this, I felt uneasy inside. How was that possible—for a Black man to have white skin and to see through eyes that didn't belong to him?

I believe at that age I knew only good and evil. I'm not quite sure how it got into my head that one thing was *bad* and another thing was *good,* but I did distinguish between the two. So (like many children of that age) I couldn't see beyond the surface of things or the gears that made machines work or the experiences that made people what they were or act the way they did. I saw only the result, never the cause. I was a victim blaming other victims.

Mrs. Forman told me at the end of our conversation that I should start reading more books. I didn't have time to read. Reading messed people's minds up, I thought. Besides I didn't like to waste time sitting down. I began running again.

I was the only distance runner in our school, and I never lost any of my races. Boss Reeves would brag about me to all his friends. He'd say, "Not even a horse can beat my son. Him can run like a kangaroo."

There was a big meet coming up at Randalls Island. No one in my family had ever seen me run. They only saw the medals. However, this time the Reeves family and company were coming to see me. Boss Reeves kept bragging, making bets that I'd win. It was the first time in my life that he had ever put his confidence in me. I felt sick, under mental pressure. I was afraid of losing and got nervous anticipating defeat. Every morning for a month I worked out at Gershwin's track.

Saturday morning we went up to Randalls Island. I'd taken some Scott's Emulsion to clear myself out so I wouldn't weigh as much. Mom Reeves had a Kodak camera. I told Francis to take my picture coming across the finish line. Boss Reeves had bought me a new pair of shorts and spikes. It was a half-mile race, two laps. At the sound of the gun I quickly moved out and away from the pack. I was on the second lap, victory was inevitable, then suddenly—bang! I felt like I'd been hit in the stomach with a lightpost. I did a flip in midair, and fell to the ground. Fucking charley horse—a cramp in my stomach. Mom Reeves had some smelling salts. When I opened my eyes, Francis was standing over me taking pictures. Boss

Reeves said nothing to me. I had let him down in front of his friends and felt like shit.

It was during the winter when Mr. Flinker called me into his office and asked me where I was going to high school. I told him Thomas Jefferson High School where the majority of our class was going after graduation. He told me that there were two high schools that specialized in art but that an admissions test was required. He made a phone call and later told me to select my best works for a portfolio. I asked him what a portfolio was. Amazed, he looked at me and smiled. But he never told me what a portfolio was. I got my works together and wrapped them up in wax paper.

The two specialized art schools were the high schools of Art and Design and Music and Art. The admissions tests were given on different dates. I went to Art and Design first.

It was a very modern school with escalators and semi-professional layouts of sculpture, photography, and design mounted on clean displays that lined the walls. There were many student artists applying for admission. We were escorted to a room and seated around a model. She was really a fine-looking girl. When she smiled at me, I thought, man, I've just got to get in. After the linear drawing of the model we were to pick two out of three choices of scenes to draw: a hot beach, pots and pans, or a dream—to be done from memory. I drew a hot beach and pots and pans. Afterward we were instructed to show our works to an art teacher. My portfolio consisted mainly of still-life oils and dog portraits. I was interviewed and smiled at.

The following week I took the admissions test for the High School of Music and Art, which had a reputation for being one of the best schools in New York City. It was a cold, snowy morning, very dark—a blue haze. Music and Art was a castle on a hill, located at 135th Street and Convent Avenue right next to City College and around the corner from Columbia University. Music and Art, a mass of gargoyled masonry, rested on a hill called St. Nicholas Terrace, overlooking Harlem and surrounded by Morningside Park. There were many

steps leading up the hill—I counted them as I climbed.
When I reached the top, I turned around and looked at Harlem. The only thought that ran through my mind was that
Brownsville was more of a ghetto. I was actually proud of my
ghetto, actually hurt because it had not received as much
publicity as Harlem. As I entered the doors of Music and Art,
two white girls greeted me, asked me who I was, where I
came from, and wished me luck. This school seemed more
jovial than Art and Design. I was late for the test. It was very
similar to Art and Design's, but the interview was much
longer, and they seemed to take a greater interest in my artwork, which was understandable since A & D was more concerned with design than painting.

After the test, I sat in the auditorium for a while. I listened
to students playing jazz and Latin. I was amazed to see students my age playing all kinds of musical instruments with
such ease and professionalism. Everybody seemed to be together here. Then I saw something that made me sick: it was
one of those hippies, with long hair and wearing faggot colors
—pinks, purples. Then a whole mess of them came in. I left
immediately. I hated men who weren't men. I hated men who
tried to look like women. In Brownsville faggots were beat
up; at Knox weaklings weren't tolerated.

As my last year at Gershwin slowly drew to a close, I became depressed. I had some good times there and graduation
meant an end to many friendships. We were all looking forward to high school, and after that, we would get jobs. I knew
very few people who had serious intentions of going on to
college.

I graduated with so-called honors in English, history, and
Spanish. Also, I got a $150 art scholarship and an honorable
mention in science.

I think they gave me the award in science because they felt
sorry for me. Twice I had tried to win a Westinghouse scholarship. We had a special day set aside for science projects
where judges would come around and examine your exhibit
and question you about it. Well, the night before I'd taken
Mom Reeves's wooden wig form (the head women use to put

wigs on) and had gotten some clay and molded the head of a Neanderthal man. I stole my mother's wig and my brother's tape recorder and put them all in a box, then left early in the morning for school. Once inside, I went into the bathroom and made some Neanderthal sounds.

I took my place behind my desk in the gym. (Everybody who had an exhibit had a desk there.) I sat until the three judges came around to mine. One of them asked me to explain my experiment, and I anxiously turned on the tape recorder, which was hidden under the desk. My man started to talk, "Um-ba-ba, Um-ba-ba, Um-ba-ba, Nin-gum-gu-wah." I thought it was ingenious, that they'd be impressed.

The judges had me thrown out and told me not to come back, but I didn't give up. The following year I made a comeback with a laser beam made of magnifying glasses and a Kodak movie light flashbulb. I had four large magnifying glasses mounted behind each other on a cardboard stand with the flashbulb, and I had everything covered with newspapers.

The same three judges showed up. "Mr. Reeves," they said, "didn't we tell you last year that we didn't want to see you in here again?"

"Yes, but I've really done some hard work this time." They looked at my exhibit.

"What's under those newspapers?" they asked.

I had the newspapers over the magnifying glasses so that the beam of light wouldn't be "disrupted by the molecules in the air"—that's exactly what I told them. I then plugged in the flashbulb light. Within seconds the newspapers caught on fire, burned my whole exhibit up, and it took a while before anybody could get to the plug and put out the flame.

When it was all over, I was kind of depressed, but Mrs. Forman told me not to worry, that somebody named Einstein wasn't an instant success either.

■ ■ ■

Anyway, I valued Bruno, my woodland turtle, more than the scholarship and awards. Mr. Dubin, my science teacher, gave him away because someone had poured acid on his shell. Bruno was my friend. I would sit and watch him crawl and eat. I fed him hot dogs. There was something about this turtle that caused me to think whenever he ate. I kept him in the basement, and sometimes he'd get lost and I wouldn't see him for months. Just when I had given up hope, he would show up. When I ran to put food before him, I always expected him to gobble it up, but always he approached it with caution, placing his foot on it to make sure it was dead. He'd bite it first, pull back, strike again, and finally start eating. He was slow and cautious with everything he did. He seemed to be determined to live, to be struggling silently. I often wondered what thoughts ran through his head when he was in the darkness of his shell surrounded by the darkness of the night. I wondered if he just lived for the sake of living until his power failed and death came. He served no purpose to me or anyone else. Why was he living? How did I know that he was a he? Where was he born? In fact why was he born? I decided that I was spending too much time with Bruno and went to find work.

It seemed that throughout all my life I had been lifting shit. In Jamaica it was pigs, with the veterinarians it was dogs and cats. At my new job in the Head Start Program in my old school, P.S. 190, I saw Gittelman and the other teachers. My job didn't keep me too busy, and the kids were really great.

It was becoming evident that Brownsville was witnessing another onslaught of immigrants. West Indians and Puerto Ricans were coming in full force. My relatives came in from all over the Caribbean, some from Latin America. My Aunt Diane told me things about Cuba's revolution, about the murder and confiscation of property. At that time her comments had little meaning to me. I was more concerned with making friends with all the West Indian families that had moved into our neighborhood. I kept running into them on the streets and knew they were West Indian from the way they looked, walked, and dressed. All they had to do was open their mouths, and I'd go running over to let them know that I was West Indian also. But at each encounter I was turned down, put on the defensive.

I wouldn't lie. I was born in America, but I was West Indian. Many Black Americans hate West Indians. I felt that they had come way the hell from the Caribbean to put down America and denounce me as an American. They seemed to be two-faced hypocrites who came here only to talk about times "back home." What were they here for? Education and work? They came from Jamaica and stayed in our house, ate our food, used the telephone and ran up all these bills, and didn't even lift a finger to help my mother pay for them or help her clean the house. Francis would openly tell these people "to get the fuck out and find work."

Francis was ten, four years younger than I was and yet almost as tall. He was about as lanky as I was at his age, but unlike me, he was always reading. Whenever we had company, people would always say he was smarter—but I wasn't interested in being smart. That didn't mean anything except that you knew a lot of things that everybody else didn't know, and if everybody else didn't know these things, then I supposed that nobody cared. Even some of my own relatives thought that way. Most of them found work taking care of elderly, rich white people or cleaning rich white folks' homes. They always worked in white people's homes and would never even consider the idea of cleaning another Black person's home. They said that the education here was poor in comparison to Jamaica's. Hell, I had been in parts of the island where the people still looked at cars with strange and frightened fascination, where people had not seen electric lights—now they looked at me as if I didn't know these things. I told them to hell with Jamaica. I was forced to say it—"I'm an American."

As soon as I'd said that, I knew that I had nowhere, no so-called motherland. It was and is important to have some earth upon which you can plant your feet, somewhere that can host generations, not uprooted people in ghettos.

I was ostracized, not from any one specific thing but from any and every thing that had any meaning in my life. I looked forward to high school and getting a job so that I could travel to Central America to see where Boss Reeves was born. I had been accepted at both schools and was casually advised to go to the High School of Music and Art. (The guidance counselor and I were crossing the street, and I asked him where I should go to school: it was just chance.) Everyone on my block—that is those West Indians and American Blacks—knew that I had made a specialized and prestigious high school, one of the best in the city. I made damn sure that they knew it.

Only three students from Gershwin were going to Music and Art—Louie Rodriguez, David Barrios, and me. Louie and I became close friends before school opened. Sometimes I'd go over to his house to have dinner. He had two brothers and two sisters. He was the second oldest son and Papo the youngest. The oldest boy had been drafted. Louie's oldest sister was planning to go back to Puerto Rico to live with her grandmother.

I really liked Louie's family. They were down-to-earth people, the grass roots. All this business of politics and international affairs had nothing to do with them, so I thought. Mr. Rodriguez was a handyman—he worked with his hands and made a comfortable living for his family. Though he wasn't educated, he had what many educated people lack—common sense.

Papo worked after school and often bought new clothes. I admired him because of the way he carried himself. Even though he was younger than I was, he always worked, seemed independent and appeared to be a man.

Dinner at Louie's was never quiet. They were always playing music, mostly Latin stuff. Not only was Louie a sharp dresser, he was cool at dancing too. We always ate greasy Spanish food. Louie told me to stop wearing jeans because I looked like a tramp. Before school opened, Louie and I took a trip up to Music and Art just to see how long it would take. The trip was well over an hour's ride, without subway delays.

We had received postcards congratulating us again and informing us of the date school would open.

PART II

LOST

Sophomore

LOUIE AND I went to school together on the first day. When
we got up to Music and Art, we saw hippies all over the
place. It was obvious that Music and Art was predominantly
Jewish (that is, white) and that Louie and I would be outnumbered if there was a fight after school. At Music and Art,
nonwhite students totaled 34.2 percent of the two thousand
members of the student body. When we got inside the building, we were instructed to report to our official classrooms, or
homerooms. Louie and I agreed to meet after school, and
split. When I got to my homeroom, about six other students
were sitting there, none of them talking to each other, all
reading paperbacks. I said "hi!" They looked at me, said nothing, and started reading again. I sat in my seat and started
drawing on the desk. Eventually everyone arrived, including
our official teacher, Mr. Sines. I caught sight of another Black
guy and went over to him. Just to start a conversation, I said:
"Hey man, there's a lot of Jews here."

"Yeah," he said, "there's a lot of whites here." It was at

this point that I stopped calling white people Jews and called white people, white people. Much later I saw how inaccurate my assumption had been.

Up front Mr. Sines started shouting: "Everyone be seated, no talking, shut up. I've got to read this to you." He read the rules of the school. I didn't get a copy and had unknowingly picked up the wrong bulletin.

I was just getting bits and pieces of what was being said—cutting and lateness, wear appropriate dress, no loitering, no leaving the room, no using telephones, no destroying furniture, no talking, no walking in the halls without a pass, no this, no that. The rules even told us how not to be late—get to school before the bell rings. Damn, I was in a daze. I was in high school. When I looked around the room, most of the other people had just about fallen asleep; a few were laughing and pointing out to each other how ridiculous the rules were.

I was there reading my bulletin—"For Teachers Only"—which said that if a student left the classroom without permission from the teacher, it was to be regarded as an act in open defiance of school authority and subject to whatever penalty the school deemed fit.* It was just like being at Knox —where supposedly punishments were always made to fit the crime.

After the rules, Mr. Golub, our grade guide, came in. The grade guide is the person responsible for making your college recommendations and checking on your averages while you're in high school. This baldheaded, starchy-faced man started rattling off an obviously memorized speech of sympathy and concern for guiding us in the right direction. He used the analogy of a ship without a rudder—we, the students, had to provide the rudder before he, the captain, could guide us to the right course. He left abruptly, and immediately the students started talking about his wrinkled and dirty white shirt, comparable to his attitude toward us.

---

*The complete lists of rules and regulations for both teachers and students appear in Appendixes A and B. I really think you should take a look at them—now.

We were dismissed. As I came out the front door, I saw what I had never seen or thought was possible in America: a Black guy was kissing a white girl in the middle of the hall, and no one said anything, no one looked at them. And for a moment I was looking at them, but my eyes didn't see them. I saw Knox. I saw my friends there and the absence of race. I saw the dichotomy that had torn my life ever since I had set foot on American soil—Jews and Black folks, now whites and Black folks. I realized that although I consciously struggled within my mind, absolutely determined not to see race, I saw race and saw *through* race. The sight of a Black kissing a white would have meant nothing to me before elementary school and Gershwin. Now I found myself referring to human beings as Blacks and whites, colors.

I went to go find Louie, and we went home together. I couldn't understand why I was conscious of the white people, and yet I knew that I was aware of it because of Gershwin and because of the furor that erupted when I asked the Italian girl to go steady with me. In my mind she was a person, but in other minds she was white. I had been conditioned to refer to people's nationalities and religions rather than skin color. This is not to say that I consciously discriminated on the basis of national origin or religion; it is to say that I didn't consciously discriminate at all.

The second day of school we went to class, and almost immediately I knew that I was in for trouble. In Spanish class I couldn't understand one word of the conversation, and yet I had received an honors award in junior high school. And, of course, math was a problem. I had failed math in junior high school and would proceed to fail it twice more.

As for English, one of the most characteristic days I remember was the time we were going over some European poetry and each of us had to pick two poets, read some of their work in front of the class, criticize it, then conduct a discussion about the poets. I chose Francis Thompson and some other fellow. Thompson's stuff dealt mainly with death and suffering.

I read some of his poetry, which had real meaning for me because of my own problems with asthma, but at that moment I wasn't in the right mood to appraise his work adequately. I stood there in front of the class thinking about what I should do—make up something to take up time, or admit the truth. I elected to do the latter.

I turned to the teacher and said, "I really can't say anything about this, 'cause this man is obviously going through a lot of changes, and none of us in this class is in the right frame of mind to understand his feelings."

The teacher looked at me. "I think you'd better give it a try."

"I'm not trying to cop out," I said. "I'd be butchering his work. I mean, I'd just be saying something to get a mark. I wouldn't be giving you my honest opinion."

The two-way discussion made the rest of the class impatient. Even though they knew that what I was saying was true, they had long since given up on this learning-for-learning's-sake bit and had conformed to what was required to please the teacher—to shuffle by. No one in the room believed that I was serious about my feelings. Everybody thought it was just a put-on. Anytime people said things like that to me, I always took it to mean that they were putting themselves in my situation and telling me how I would have to react, based on their feelings and behavior patterns. In other words, I often found that people had preconceived notions about other people's behavior patterns.

I was still standing up front. She said to me, "We're waiting. Give us your opinion of the poet. Is he great, mediocre?"

"I think he's great."

She replied, "I think you're afraid to admit that his work is no good."

"What? I think he's great and that we're not prepared, in this setting, at this particular time, to discuss what he has written. Everybody just can't wait until the bell rings to get out of here." I read one more poem about suffering, said that if you couldn't feel what he had written at least to a small degree, then you couldn't say anything about the man.

So for the rest of the period she had me up front butchering this man's work. I said, "He's great, line five *proves* he's great, and listen to this, and look here, look at those words he uses —can't you *feel* the pain?" I clenched my fist, tried to show pain in my face—was I doing O.K.? This went on for the rest of the period. Finally, the bell rang, saving the day.

There are very few teachers who have the ability to question a student, probe for some response without twisting and pulling at the student to say what they want to hear. Very few teachers have the ability to probe in such a way that the actual *discovery* is still left up to the student. Most of these teachers have been at it for so long that they aren't even aware of what little patience they have or how uncomfortable and untactful their methods of questioning really are.

I thought it truly amazing, truly wonderful to be in a school where everyone was either an artist or a musician. The art students used huge canvases covered with rich and vibrant colors. Each student had a particular style, seemingly striving for greater perfection. The work there could rival that of some of the best professionals or at least could be displayed in museums. Music and Art was a school where supposedly the "cream of the crop," the best student artists and musicians in the city, came. Why then would we later abstain from art and music, even loathe it?

I was looking forward to biology because I thought I'd finally have a chance to work with animals. I was soon disillusioned, entirely let down, when I received a hardcover book and reading assignments.

My crafts class could easily have been mistaken for a nursery school cut-out-and-paste session. I found myself making paper boxes and painting a toilet plunger. Music and Art seemed to try to impose new art forms and exhaust an individual's particular interests and artistic abilities in handling subject matter that he feels familiar with. In some cases, it was beneficial; the majority of times it wasn't. Some artists graduated and never touched a brush again.

The only class I really liked was gym. Gym teachers and the class were always cool. Still, you got the same routine every time. They lined you up in either size places or alphabetical order. All you wanted to do was play ball, but the gym teacher had to tell you: "This is a gym, and we don't want any street shoes in here. Now you see those things hanging from the ceiling, those are ropes. You're going to learn how to climb them. In order to climb the ropes, you got to start from the bottom. When you get to the top, don't let go and don't, *don't* slide down the rope—you'll get rope burns on your hands."

In junior high school there had been a primary emphasis on social life. It was difficult to approach education any other way, given the conditions that existed in Brownsville. Although Gershwin was well integrated, Blacks and whites came from separate communities. The color line was Linden Boulevard which separated the Black and Puerto Rican communities from the Jewish community. Brownsville should have been declared a disaster area. The ethnic composition and socio-economic backgrounds of the students seemingly justified the sacrifice of rigid academics for social activities. In essence, by the time many people graduated from Gershwin (Blacks and Puerto Ricans, especially), they were no longer able to adapt to academics. So effective was the socialization that it was difficult to accept any other way of life. We needed social activities. Brownsville was a world in itself, and so was Gershwin, and both worlds were physical and violent. I was nonverbal, unable to communicate with words, yet I graduated from junior high school with all these so-called honors. The truth of the matter was that I had not been prepared for academic work. I was an average student placed in competition with people who had little interest or ability in studying. At Music and Art, faced with real competition, I was unprepared to handle academic life. In fact, I was so helpless that the English teacher told Eva, a girl in the class, to sit with me and explain certain things as we went along. I sat all the way in the back of the class and had a tutor in all my subjects except art, crafts, and music appreciation.

During the first week, in our quizzes and spelling tests, I fell flat on my academic face. I bought a dictionary for English and caught various words that were being used among the whites in class. For two weeks I was caught in a fit—what the hell was going on? I was failing everything and didn't know whether I was going or coming. The English teacher spoke to me after class and said that I seemed to be in a daze. She smiled and told me not to be so "petulant." I had thought that petulant meant dumb and took it as an insult.

Louie was in the same bind that I was in. He was planning to quit Music and Art and go to Thomas Jefferson High School. He said: "Man, this isn't the place for us." And Louie was right. We weren't used to this sustained, rigid, academic pressure. As bad off as Gershwin was, we'd always had friends there, always went to parties and basketball games, always had fun when we were together.

Louie dropped out after about three weeks. He later became a Jehovah's Witness preacher. I told Mom Reeves that I also wanted to transfer to Jefferson. I told her that I didn't want to go to high school at all. I told her that I couldn't do the work and that there was no way for me to catch up. She got angry and told me that she had sent me to Knox to become a man, "never to accept defeat," always to have confidence in myself. If I was a coward, I should quit, she said, run scared. Against my better judgment I decided to stay.

I was lost without Louie. He was the only friend that I had in Music and Art. I couldn't stand the hippies, and the other Black students seemed very far away from anything that I was all about. It was difficult to make friends if you didn't use drugs or smoke dope, added to the fact that I was "clean looking." Everybody belonged to a closed clique. Eventually I made friends with Barrios, the other student from Gershwin. He was in a clique and introduced me to others. Barrios, who once dressed in penny loafers, collegiate sweaters, and pants, was slowly becoming one of those hippies. Anyway, every morning our clique would meet in the auditorium, and Barrios and I would get our kicks by teasing and making fun of other people. We called this "ripping off." Barrios didn't live too far from me, and I'd ride over to his part of the neighborhood where all the whites lived. When he rode over to my house, he was afraid. One day he said that he wasn't coming to where I lived again, that I'd have to go to him.

We started going to school together on the subway. Barrios had a loud mouth. He was obviously impressed by all the big words and new things that he had learned at Music and Art and would always insist on discussing Black people, why we live the way we live. The subway was always packed with Black folks, and Barrios would be screaming at the top of his voice, "Then why don't Blacks get jobs or stay in school, or work like everybody else." Once we went down to Forty-second Street, and a Black guy tried to sell us a watch. All the way back home he was talking about how Black people were hustlers and did shoddy things to make a living. That was the last time that Barrios and I rode the trains together. I got so hot and angry that I was almost ready to beat the shit out of him. We stopped talking. In school I was ostracized from our clique, so I said to hell with them.

I began to feel totally isolated, totally inferior. I stopped talking to people, spoke only when I was asked a question, hardly ever got asked anything. I started to read a book on How to Make Friends, but that was dumb, and I never got past page ten. I became a clown, a comedian. To make friends, I made jokes about myself, about all the races I'd lost. But people were laughing *at* me, not with me.

Early one morning I went to the gym and asked an old sandy-teethed, white-haired man named Mr. Kunitz if there was a track team at M & A. He said yes and gave me a medical form. The following week I was working out with the team. Most of the guys on it were seniors and juniors. I got to be really friendly with them, especially Terry, Tony, Lamont, and Herndon, all of whom were Black. I was the newest member of the team and had to get a time trial to see what event I would be best in.

During the winter we worked out in the 168th Street Armory across the street from the Columbia Presbyterian Hospital. Our coach, Mr. Holzer, was white, had two bad feet, and was never really an athlete. In school he was a librarian. Our team was pretty lousy, but we worked out hard. After a few weeks on the team, I realized that the seniors were more concerned with their times than with the team as a whole. I guessed that they were trying out for college scholarships, but I wouldn't let any of them beat me in my event. I remember one afternoon when I had a time trial, I was so determined and anxious to hit "a fantastic time" that I didn't warm up first. I went right to the starting line, tore down the straightaway, went into the turn, and felt my leg muscles tighten into a cramp. I fell hard on my elbows. My muscles kept tightening and tightening.

Mr. Holzer came over and tried to massage my legs. I screamed out, "Get your fucking hands off me, off me, off me." The cramp got tighter and tighter and finally wore off. When it did, guys on the team said jokingly, "Are you ready to start working out again?" I stood up, laughing. Then it came again and I fell. It was worse this time. The pain was unbearable. I closed my eyes, lay motionless, bit my tongue so that I wouldn't cry. The cramp wore off again.

Mr. Holzer and other members of the team picked me up and took me upstairs where I got dressed. Mr. Holzer said that he'd wait for me outside, and everyone left me except Mark, whose legs were always in bad shape. In fact, the doctor said that he shouldn't run. When he ran, both of his legs had to be bandaged. I got dressed and he helped me downstairs to Mr. Holzer's car. We went over to the Medical Center. The doctor gave me some Darvon, a pain killer, and Holzer drove me home. I had to stay off my feet for a week. When I finally got better, I came to practice and watched.

Eventually I started working out again, not trying to outdo anyone. I felt better now and wanted so desperately to run again, to stride, to run as fast as my power would permit. I knew that it was only a question of time before I'd be O.K. again. What really frightened me was thinking about what would have happened if my injury had been so bad that I would have doubts about my recovery. I envisioned myself as a cripple attempting to walk.

As I was unable to work out for long hours, I devoted a lot of time to painting and drawing. I did two large pen-and-ink drawings of birds and a cathedral under construction. Both were entered in an art exhibition. I also did a number of African animal portraits. My friend, Medrano McPherson, was a junior at the High School of Art and Design. His work was much neater than ours at Music and Art. He used many more professional art instruments than we did. Some of his worst design things would have been the best in our class. I learned a number of things from him and began to do a lot of extra-credit art work. I didn't consider it extra-credit because I wanted to be a professional artist. My teacher told me that "all this isn't necessary—you shouldn't spend so much money on art supplies." The students in my class said that all I was doing was trying to get an A. I didn't like this drawing for a mark bit. There can be no grade on art, only appreciation or the lack of it.

Everyone was in constant competition to establish themselves as "The Best Artist." Few people really loved art for its own sake; few were given the chance to do so. Many of us had come from junior high schools where there were only one or two really good artists; now we were just small fish in a sea of millions. Then, too, many people took Music and Art as a second choice if they didn't get into Bronx High School of Science or some other specialized school.

When my legs finally got better, I became anchor man on the two-mile relay team. Anchor man is an honorable position because he delivers the payload. When that baton is placed in your hands, the entire team's efforts depend on your ability. You have the ultimate responsibility not only to yourself but to your teammates. I hated this position, not really the position, but what happened to me. The senior guys were so bad that for the entire season every time the baton was placed in my hand, the other teams were already finished. It was humiliating. At the Randalls Island Borough Championship, I was replaced as anchor man, which made me mad. The relay team now consisted only of seniors, and they knew that though we were poor in meets against Catholic schools and schools in other boroughs, we were the best in Manhattan. Now at the last moment, after all the humiliation, they deprived me of the chance to win my first medal—to break Novice. They won the borough two-mile championship. I had never practiced the triple jump, and yet Mr. Holzer entered me in that event. Inexperienced, I fouled my first two jumps, ran through the pit on my third.

The following week came the Novice meet, which gave all those who had not won medals at the Borough Championship a second chance. There were so many of us that we had to be broken up into more than the usual number of sections. I was placed in the fifth. The five fastest times won medals. Therefore, it meant that even if you won in your section, another person who placed second or even third in another section could have a faster time than yours and win the medal.

We all stood nervously at the starting line, then the gun. I moved out quickly but soon remembered what had happened to me a few weeks ago. Slowing down a bit, I thought of time, of tension, of time going and not stopping, of my legs tightening. Everything was lost as we entered the second and gun lap. I felt that familiar dryness in my throat, that numbness in my jaws, that pain in my brain, that tightening in my legs until they felt heavy, feelings now moving higher and higher, going slower, but in my mind moving with the speed of the wind. And then ever so suddenly the sensation and rhythm were interrupted by a challenger. Over my shoulder I could glimpse his blond hair and Brooklyn Tech insignia. Although much smaller in size and stride, he rode me. We were much farther ahead; no one behind us would be counted. Now it was a two-man race. Entering the last turn, I closed my eyes, afraid to face defeat, pleaded for radiating power, the extra burst, not coming. Opening my eyes, I saw he was still there. Give up, I thought, there's no choice: push, push, he's as tired as you are. Is your will stronger? About twenty yards to go, listen to the crowds cheering, listen, push and push harder, lean forward and reach the tape before him, the medal is yours.

It was good to win, to have old coach Kunitz congratulate me by slapping me in the face, and then grin with his sandy yellow teeth. Even a few students from my official class congratulated me. It seemed now that finally I was being accepted and permitted to live, admitted into the world. The season brought more challenges and victories. I became known, began to have the chance to speak confidently to people because I had something, something I was good at.

Sometime on April 4th, 1968, when I was running, I heard the news of the assassination of Dr. Martin Luther King. I went home and watched the six o'clock news. They showed pictures of people and dignitaries from all parts of the world lamenting his death, extolling him as a great Black leader.

The funeral of Dr. King appeared strange. All the white dignitaries were inside the church while the Black people who were regular members of the church were kept outside and stood in the streets, surrounding the donkey wagon. I would see much later what the death of Dr. King and his philosophy actually meant to people who followed him.

I had heard about Dr. King when I learned about non-violence and civil rights. I had admired him because everyone else admired his courage to do what everyone knew was impossible. He was always trying to get Congressional bills passed for Black people. I had seen him only once before on television when he was getting hit with stones by whites in the South. I actually thought that he would have been better off in the North.

The following morning I was going about my usual school routine. All the newspapers carried headlines of Dr. King's assassination. Though I never read the news, I noticed that Dr. King was getting as many headlines as President Kennedy did when he was assassinated. When I got up to school, the students were milling around in the streets, some standing in front of the doors dissuading anyone from entering the building. They said that no one should go to school today because of Dr. King's assassination, that we should be in mourning. I went inside, but the teachers were standing in the lobby, annoyed because they wanted to teach. I heard one say, "The learning process cannot be disrupted. We have a responsibility to teach."

I went to my room but no one was there, not even the teacher. I went back outside. Everyone was together, looking happy.

The Black boy who I had seen kissing the white girl on my first day of school got up on a box and told everyone to be quiet. He said that we were going to Central Park "To Remember Dr. King." I had not noticed it before, but the boy had an artificial leg. I was really fascinated because I was happy to see that he didn't let his disability hinder him.

We all left school and went down to Central Park. The musicians from our school began to sing and play their instruments. Everyone felt really good, really happy being together. I thought that if I were dead, I wouldn't want any of them at my funeral. How could you be happy when you're supposed to be mourning? Nobody was mourning: everyone was having a good time. Then people from other high schools started to pour in. Some, all of them Black, ran up onto the stage and disrupted the music. They said that it was "time to get whitey," time for the end of nonviolence, time for revolution . . . "Right, Ralphie?" "Rap on, brother." The students from Music and Art couldn't deal with the situation because they were from another culture, allegedly one of passivity and love and peace. The threat of physical force, which had always been present in my life, frightened them. I was afraid of their world, they afraid of mine. I thought that the entire façade was a cheap way to escape school, and I went home.

Dr. King was forgotten and business as usual set in. An

abundance of symbolic funeral coverage, television commentaries, and rhetoric had inundated my mind. The more I heard about King, the more I wanted to know.

Immediately following Martin Luther King's assassination, President Johnson got on TV and pleaded for "calm" as scattered violence erupted throughout the Black communities of the nation. At the same time that Johnson was calling for a joint session of Congress, Army troops were sent into Washington, D.C., and the National Guard was sent into Chicago, Detroit, and Boston. More soldiers were sent into Washington and Chicago, Baltimore, and Pittsburgh. On April 9th, King was buried. On April 10th, the House of Representatives passed a Civil Rights Bill "designed to topple racial barriers in 80 percent of the nation's housing." The vote was 250 to 171.

I now had five heroes: Washington, Lincoln, Muhammad Ali, President Kennedy, and Dr. King. Ali was the only one who was not dead. As time passed, my list would change.

As the school year was coming to an end, I started seeing a girl named Linda. We cut school one day and went to Central Park. She was the first American Black girl I really liked. I didn't consider her a girl—she was a woman, and I was proud of her because she was fine and didn't take shit from nobody.

The General Organization (student government) elections were also coming around, but I didn't have any particular interest in anything outside of track and Linda. My official class went to the G.O. assembly to hear speeches made by the candidates. We sat up in the balcony and had a good view in this church-type auditorium. Sam was the only Black candidate running. All of them made speeches, but I didn't pay any attention to what they said.

Before the assembly started, the orchestra began to play. I had been so accustomed to the squeaking sound of the junior high school band that I appreciated fine music. I couldn't believe that students could produce such perfection and felt proud to be there. The music students could rival any professional band. I remember seeing Blacks and whites making music together—producing this exquisite sound—and wanting more than anything to have some of my friends from Gershwin here so that they could see Blacks and whites working together. I thought that nothing could bring people together the way that music did. All prejudices and problems disappeared in rhythms of jazz and Latin soul. I had never had a taste for classical music but was overwhelmed when I heard students playing it. During the summer I wrote to Linda, but she never wrote back, so I understood that our relationship was over.

A few days before school ended, there was a concert in the auditorium. The music was so good that I turned to a friend and asked, seriously, "Are they really playing or is the sound coming from backstage?" After the concert, I just *had* to get a saxophone. I told Mom Reeves that I wanted to play, and she bought me a tenor sax and enrolled me in the Institute of Music in Manhattan.

(The money wasn't available for her to just go out and buy me a sax. Mom was the kind of a parent who'd bend over backward to give her children those things that really meant something to them, not toys or things we wanted on the spur of the moment, but things that could significantly benefit our lives in one way or another.)

My sax playing was kind of hard on the notes. Boss Reeves would leave the house when I took it out to practice. Francis would slam the door. My career as a musician came to an end after only three weeks. What happened was that I got an instructor who was a homosexual.

During the last few days of school we had to give back our track uniforms and textbooks. Mr. Holzer said that he wouldn't be coming back next year. He told us to report to the library where he gave those of us who had won medals a letter or insignia to be worn on a sweater or jacket. I just couldn't believe that this was the way things ended, not in a library. We were Music and Art's track team. We represented the school and spent hours of each day practicing and running for the school. We ran in the rain, throughout winter, and in the sun. And at the end, we just came into a library to pick up some stupid piece of cloth. I thought that we should have an assembly so that we could be recognized. They had assemblies planned to recognize the smart kids—those who had ninety averages.

Elitism and egocentrism are characteristics that many non-athletically oriented people see in athletes who are proud of their accomplishments, who want the same recognition that is accorded to writers and philosophers. Artists, musicians, doctors, lawyers—all try to be the best in their fields. So then why is it that after an athlete goes through months of agonizing pain, developing stamina and strength, and is victorious and proud that he has been able to compete and win, non-athletes say he is egotistical?

The athlete is always lonely, even in a team sport. In track and field often an athlete passes his prime before he wants to quit. He sets a new record that he knows tomorrow someone else might break. Track is a question of time, of seconds, of tenths of seconds. It is a question of mind and body, of discipline and strength, and uncertainty. Many people cannot relate to this world, in fact, condemn it.

An athlete's body can last for so long before he's finished and must move on to some other way of life. At thirty, an athlete can *look back* at his career. And in the meantime, the athlete is often abused, used, and in the end, forgotten.

People in athletics are not always involved solely for competing against others. Those men and women who are not physically built to be athletes and yet train and punish themselves religiously, usually are competing with themselves. It often happens that when an athlete sustains an injury and a doctor tells him "You're finished," the athlete refuses to accept this decision and declares I can come back, I'm not finished; it is really a question of proving something to one's self, a disciplined and solitary struggle which involves ego, self-confidence, and self-respect. The crowd respects the runner who comes in last and finishes what he has set out to do. How much respect do we have for the athlete who gives up in the middle of the race just because he cannot be number one? Or how much respect do we have for the champion who, faced with the prospect of defeat for the first time, quits at the outset rather than struggle to the end?

Students at Music and Art looked down on sports. I knew they did. No one from our school ever came to see us run or to cheer us on. Students at other schools would show up in full force, rooting for their teams, giving them some inspiration. We always showed up in tattered grey uniforms, wearing demoralizing expressions of certain defeat. The only people who took any real interest in the track team was the track team. The rest of the school was so dead, stagnant, and immersed in academics that the people seemed not only unfriendly, but cold and cynical about anything outside their immediate clique.

When I received my letter, I took it and threw it away. I went to my official class and got my report card. I had a low average and had failed math again. I had to enroll in summer school at Thomas Jefferson High School. The more I thought about Music and Art, the more depressed and angry I became. All the drugs and damned hippies all over the place. After the Dr. King demonstration, the hippies started demonstrating against the war. What possible significance could demonstrating in front of Music and Art have upon the war in Southeast Asia? If I was Johnson, I would draft the whole lot of them and dump them over there, to either fight or die. As for Music and Art, it was nothing but a tomb. Everybody was concerned with getting the highest average. The students had no love for the school. It was just a building with chairs and desks that they occupied during the day.

What's Happening?

I DON'T REMEMBER where I was or what I was doing, but I know people were rushing to get home to watch the six o'clock news. Somebody important had been assassinated—it was Robert Kennedy. I followed the events on the sixth- and eleventh-hour news. Once again the reporters donned artificial expressions of sadness and spoke in deep tones. They interviewed the peace candidate, McCarthy, and Humphrey, and Nixon; all were in agreement that they were genuinely saddened by the death of R.F.K.

Already the political strategists were reassessing the primaries and the campaign. Once again, *Time, Look,* and *Life* magazines carried color photos of the national tragedy.

Two months had passed. Dr. King's murderer, James Earl Ray, was still on the loose. R.F.K.'s assailant, Sirhan Sirhan, was caught on the spot. Two days after R.F.K.'s death, James Earl Ray was caught in London.

People around Brownsville said that the CIA had something to do with King's assassination. When I was in the barber shop, I heard one fellow say that if Kennedy hadn't died, they never would have caught Ray. "They got Ray because they knew Black people would start asking questions about how come when the white man gets assassinated, it takes only a few days to track down the killer, and when the Black man gets assassinated, you can't find the motherfucker who done it?" I got my hair cut and left. I learned most of what I knew in that barber shop. I listened to the men talk of numbers, O.D.'s (overdoses of drugs), women, and other things. The white man was often discussed. Talking about the white man often brought powerful Black men to tears right there in the shop. They all hated the white man; no one trusted him. I remember Black men who clenched their fists or held their hands up in midair, screaming, "Somebody got to flick the revolution. I just got to crush one of those motherfuckers, split his brain open with an ax."

I learned from those men who had been in prison that the white man wanted to know everything the Negro knew, and all the shit he didn't want, he made sure the Negro got it. The white man, I was told, put drugs in Brownsville so that the Negroes wouldn't know whether they were going or coming. I knew this to be true because the barber shop was a front for drugs. I saw Black people selling poison to themselves. One of the things I remember hearing in the shop was about this white man who had tried to rape the sister of some of the meanest brothers in Brownsville. They caught that man in the act, took him up to the top floor of a project building, and "pushed the motherfucker off to see if he could fly." He couldn't.

With the close of school, I had to find work. I got a job in the Neighborhood Youth Corps. Everybody who worked for the Corps got $32.82 a week. In the mornings I had to go to summer school because I had failed math. I met a Puerto Rican girl, Zoraida, in school, and we started seeing each other regularly. Zoraida's problem was that she was trying to be white; in fact, she told me she was white and could pass for a white person. Sometimes we'd be walking down the street, and we'd run into some of her white friends, and she'd tell me to slow down while she walked away from me, like she didn't know who I was.

She used to tell me all kinds of things about her family life, how her brothers were in Vietnam and her mother beat her constantly. She showed me the marks. I really felt sorry for her. Whenever I got paid, I'd spend practically all my money on her. I felt that I had an obligation to take her to places outside of Brownsville. For her, I was an escape. On the last payday, she told me that she no longer wanted to see me, that she didn't want to hurt me, but that the summer was over, and she'd have to go back to her school and friends who were white. I wasn't really broken up over the whole thing. I just found it difficult to accept. I should have learned my lesson right there, but I was going to do it again at a time when I wouldn't be able to shrug it off as easily as I did then. I had nothing but time on my hands.

In Brownsville sundown became an understood curfew. People seemed to be walking around looking for money or for people who looked like they had money. Some of the girls I knew who had graduated from Gershwin were now becoming first-class prostitutes. The streets were like scenes from days of the Old West—cops chasing Blacks, people shooting each other in broad daylight. Fires were commonplace. Pedro, Derrick, Francis, and I played stickball most of the time. At night we'd go down to the Brownsville Recreational Center and swim, then afterward, we'd sit around and talk about Jamaica or the gang fights in Jefferson High School or Gershwin.

Mom Reeves, Francis, and I moved to Queens Village. Mom Reeves got a job at the Men's House of Detention. We quickly settled into our new house. We were now in the middle class—what that meant to us was living in a house with no roaches.

On the six o'clock news they said that school might not open on time because of some dispute between the teachers and the Board of Education.

The United Federation of Teachers claimed that due process had been violated when the Ocean Hill-Brownsville Governing Board, a Ford Foundation-financed experiment in decentralization, transferred eighty-three teachers from the district. Decentralization and community control had become axioms of Black self-determination. The Governing Board was led to believe that it had the power to control the community's schools, to determine what was best for the community. The UFT, with its large Jewish membership, confronted the Black people of Brownsville and told them that they could not control their own communities. In Brownsville people learn from what they see, and all they can see is Jewish prosperity and Negro deprivation.

John H. Niemeyer, acting consultant to the central board, informed the Ocean Hill-Brownsville Governing Board of its power to dismiss teachers who they thought were unacceptable to their district. He assured them that there would be no challenge from the UFT. The board was also told not to publicize the issue. But certain board members saw to it that the issue was widely exposed through the mass media. The roots of the strike went back to the previous May when the Ocean Hill board ousted nineteen teachers and supervisors. The teachers were charged with sabotaging the decentralization plan in addition to unsatisfactory work. Following these charges, the teachers were cleared by a trial examiner, but the Ocean Hill board refused to reinstate the teachers. For the Governing Board this was a test of its power to hire and dismiss teachers in its district. To the UFT the decentralization plan was an open challenge to its concept of job security.

On the first scheduled day of school I went up to Music and Art. I saw those same teachers who had so righteously spoken about their duty, their responsibility to teach, out marching on a picket line. The doors to the school were chained shut. On the terrace several hundred students stood quietly. Other students were gathered in scattered circles, but soon they broke from their circles and formed an opposing picket line and began chanting, demanding that the school be open.

I went back home. Why should I be so anxious to get inside? That night old Coach Kunitz called and said there'd be practice during the strike. I started running and practiced every day of the strike.

Students and a few teachers throughout the city began organizing liberation schools. Our school was in a church somewhere in the Bronx. I stopped going to track practice because I liked the liberation school, felt like I was learning something. I wasn't sitting in a stuffy room with some machine up front calling the shots all the time. There was no bureaucracy, no late pass, no cards (called "Delany cards").* You could choose your own program, suggest curriculum, take whatever courses you wanted. If anything went wrong, you'd stop a teacher who actually listened, a parent who listened. The liberation school became a community where every student who came wanted to learn, and every teacher wanted to teach. There were no grades or tests; what you learned was for your own benefit. You weren't competing against anybody. The conventional grading system doesn't help the students; it's only a convenience for teachers, a comparison of students to each other, of a number to other numbers. There was no cramming or cheating in the lib schools because tests weren't given.

For the first time students felt the beauty of learning what school could be like. The school was ours. We were learning from each other. Many so-called educators think it is impossible to have fun while learning. "You don't go to school to have fun. You go to school to learn!" Everybody's heard that. We weren't learning anything here that we wouldn't have learned inside the school. The difference lay in the spirit in which we were taught.

Mayor Lindsay took the liberty of personally ending the

---

* I had an art teacher who was just about crazy. Besides marking down the days you were absent on the Delany cards, she used to give you a big "N" for naughty, "O" for outstandingly naughty, "T" for trouble, and "TT" for double trouble. I'm serious: she'd say, "I heard you talking—yes I did," and she'd rush over to her Delany book and say, "Hahhh, I'm giving you a big red N." The whole class thought she was insane. She had us drawing boats and trees for the entire year.

first strike when the original nineteen teachers voluntarily transferred out of Ocean Hill. The Mayor did not inform the UFT of any resolution, and the strike was resumed. Another strike settlement was reached, but this time the action of the community had not been counted on. Through adverse conditions focused around the dispute at P.S. 271, another teachers' strike was called. Although the Ocean Hill board was suspended, the community would not capitulate to the UFT or Board of Education. The UFT reduced its original goal—the destruction of the experiment—to the demands for the removal of the district teachers who had harassed UFT members and for the reinstatement of the UFT members. But Mayor Lindsay and the Board of Education would not act until formal charges were filed and upheld. All this time racial tension was building. Negro anti-Semitic and hate literature was circulated to all the homes during the nights.

There were only a handful of teachers who defied the powerful machine of Albert Shanker, president of the UFT. These teachers were teaching on their own time throughout the strike. Our particular teacher was Miss Carol Fineberg, who taught history. She was really a great person, always trying to get you to think, to say what was on your mind. And if your answer was wrong, she'd make you see your mistake. She and I became good friends.

I met another teacher in the liberation school, Miss Francine Mirro. She was really a fine-looking woman—she was kind of short, had a very pretty face, and was young. I felt uncomfortable around her most of the time because she knew so much, and I, so little. Sometimes I listened to her speaking to other teachers and students; as soon as she looked my way, I was gone, afraid she'd ask me something. She always wanted me to read. I showed her my Brownsville survey, and she began talking to me about Black consciousness, about my identity as a Black man. She made me feel that I didn't understand what it was to be a Black man and insisted that I read because I was going to get myself into trouble if I didn't. Sometimes it really burned me up inside to have Miss Mirro tell me those things. At the same time I became very dependent on her.

I developed a tactic that I used for a long while which saved me the trouble of reading. Sometimes when I'd want to find out something, I'd immediately go find Miss Mirro, and instead of asking her a question, I'd get her annoyed by making some stupid statement and pretend to defend it. She'd blow up, tell me why I was wrong, and then go through a long rebuttal with factual information supporting her argument. Whenever she'd quote an author, I'd remember the author, the quote, and information; then whenever I got into an argument with someone else, I'd start using the same names and quotes she had given me, so that I also would appear intelligent.

The strike dragged on. Twice the strike had been over. Even though I dug what was going on in the lib schools, when the Mexico Olympics came on television, I split. I stayed home and watched the whole thing, John Carlos and Tommy Smith receiving their medals and then raising clenched fists during the National Anthem. At this point I saw no meaning behind this, only a regrettable feeling that race was entering into something I valued which served as my escape.

The team began working out at Van Cortland Park in the Bronx. The cross-country season was difficult because of our new Black coach, Mr. Bob King. He had taught Phys.-Ed at Brandeis High School and coached us in the afternoon. He, unlike Mr. Holzer, was really an athlete; in fact, he had been a state champion in cross-country and captain of Morgan State College track team. He had titles in the hurdles, quarter-mile, and 220. With an experienced athlete as coach, the track team steadily gained momentum. Membership grew, and our spirits were raised.

During the third strike parents and teachers used force to open up Music and Art and get education underway. I started paying more attention to what was going on; that is, I listened to the six o'clock news. The school strike was gradually becoming an issue of race—of Blacks against whites. Albert Shanker kept making statements that infuriated Black people. The implication was that the (Jewish) UFT was an enemy of the Black and Puerto Rican communities. At times it looked like he was calling for a siege to see who could hold out the longest. I remember hearing somewhere that once the Romans had surrounded the Jews at Masada and that they were waiting for the Jews to surrender. Rather than surrender and be slaves for the Romans, the Jews killed each other—it was like "Give me liberty or give me death."

Right now the UFT had the Black community surrounded and was slowly moving in for the kill. Tensions heightened and erupted into a racial holocaust. Blacks began attacking whites and vice versa—Black anti-Semitism versus Jewish racism. Police en masse stood in front of schools keeping parents, students, and even defiant teachers from entering. In other parts of the city the people used force to open their schools. It became evident that once the schools were open again, violence would make its entry into the high school system. Despite all their lectures on obeying the law, the teachers defied the Taylor Law, which forbids strikes by public employees. In the eyes of the community they were outlaws.

On Friday of that week the appellate division decided to uphold the decision of a lower court ruling that the principals were illegally appointed according to regular Civil Service procedure. The Board of Education was responsible for their appointment. And through negotiations the principals, including the only Puerto Rican principal in New York, Luis Fuentes, were assigned to different posts. The Governing Board of Ocean Hill was suspended, and Rhody McCoy was forced to comply with the courts ruling or be relieved of his duties.

Ten weeks had passed before the strike was finally over. Massive student agitation continued, and students began organizing unions along ethnic and political lines. The teachers' strike, deemed racist, had set the tone for widespread student violence that would be justified by the fact that "even our teachers," who espoused the law, broke it. They had barred 1,120,000 students from attending school three times for a total of ten weeks. Fifty-seven thousand teachers had failed to report to classes.

At that time I accepted what was happening, remained ignorant, and said that the strike meant nothing more to me than a union fighting for job security. I had also thought that if it had not been the strike, something else would have brought about the confrontation because it was inevitable.

The far-ranging repercussions of the strike stemmed from the liberation schools. The liberation schools made us see what our problems were, made us see the difference between education and indoctrination. We began to recognize that we had voluntarily relinquished our freedom to the bureaucracy of rules and regulations. We saw that learning did not end with a test or quiz. We understood that learning was an end in itself.

The teachers' strike marked the abandonment of non-violence as King's assassination had marked the end of the liberal renaissance. The teachers' strike had given birth to the high school student movement. It opened up the eyes of a whole lot of people. I was not one of them.

PART III

MISFIRE

Students Unite

OCEAN HILL HAD lost the confrontation, and the strike was finally over. Numerous schools throughout the city hosted spontaneous student rebellions, fires, police repression, and arrests. Old Glory, her stars and stripes no longer waving, was either burning or had been replaced by the red, green, and black—the colors of Black nationalism and liberation. The Afro-American Students' Association came to the fore with seventeen non-negotiable demands, saying there would be no peace until the demands were met. Representing the administration's response were the police (now called "pigs"). A contingent of New York's Finest pigs surrounded many high schools, supposedly to prevent violence. The increasing estrangement between teachers and students erupted in an outpouring of racial hate. It was the students who suffered and lost most from the strike, and it was the students who got penalized after the confrontation. Protests began when the Board of Education announced that there would be an extra forty-five minutes added to the school day, to make up for lost time. At the same time, the teachers received pay for the days they were out on the streets striking.

The newspapers carried extensive headlines about violence reaching the high schools by way of the colleges. Walter Degnan,* principal at Dewitt Clinton High School and president of the Council of Supervisory Associations, said that he felt sure that Communists and college students were involved. But the truth of the matter was that students, on their own, were exposing the injustices and disrupting the system that was responsible for the end product of high school education —void.

Of the 65,203 students who were originally admitted to the class of June 1968, 12,238 did not complete their junior year; 25,712 did not complete their senior year. And of those 65,203 initially admitted students, only 19,509 were granted academic diplomas. The other 15,603 students were given general diplomas, worthless pieces of paper. The largest majority of dropouts (pushouts) were Black and Puerto Rican students. Most of the general diplomas also went to them.† Any time such large numbers are involved, the entire onus cannot be placed solely on the student.

The composition of the rebelling crowd mirrored the current catalytic element in the society—the Black Panthers. At this time the concept of Black consciousness and nationalism began to take hold of the nation. There was now a concerted effort being made by some in the splintered Black community to become a collectivity. Reorientation of thinking and eradication of the devastating effects of white institutions on Black minds was the first priority—Black Power, Black is Beautiful, Black History, Black Pride, Black Teachers. The paranoid, anachronistic high school bureaucracy, unable to accept change, unwilling to look for the social reasons behind disruptions, relied on police to repel any and all forms of new

---

* A name to remember.

† All figures cited are taken from *A Report on New York City High Schools,* conducted by a special task force of the Citizens' Committee for Children of New York, Inc., issued on January 5, 1970.

ideals and efforts to implement demands for change from the irrelevance and dehumanization it is built on.

While the city was embroiled in revolution, Music and Art was bathing in passivity and traditional isolation. At the same time, right across the street, Black and Puerto Rican students at City College were having a running confrontation with President Buell Gallagher. Ultimately they seized South Campus, changed its name to Harlem University (for the people), and said that they were protesting the administration's refusal to negotiate in good faith. Gallagher resigned, stating that "outside politically motivated groups make conciliation impossible." He was denounced by the Black and Puerto Rican community as a liar, a provocateur of violence, and a perpetrator of racism. They went further to denounce the Faculty Senate as a group of spineless, gutless men with power, men who represented nothing but castration. They proclaimed that their goals were with the people and the elimination of racist education.

Yet Music and Art remained so silent that the *New York Post* printed an article about it called "A Peaceful Neighbor." It said that our school was "sandwiched between a sea of tumult and revolution," that while our older peers were dabbling in the art of revolution, we were "dabbling in paints and oils and figuring out an intricate Bach Fugue."

Nationwide, the coming year would witness $200 million worth of damaged school property and over 13,000 fires—the amount of damage totaling $52 million.

Yet I had no idea what was going on during this time. All that I saw and knew was limited to the confines of the building. It seemed that I had picked up where I left off during my sophomore year—in the dark. I had a few more friends now and started seeing this really beautiful girl called Marleen. The best thing about it was that Miss Mirro wanted us to stay together. I also had Miss Mirro for history. Gladstone Cooper, from Panama, was my best friend. He was a sophomore and fellow teammate. At that time we had much in common, our main interest being social activities.

More and more guys started coming out for track. Mr. King was a great coach and didn't mess around when it came to practice. We functioned as a team. All of us would sit around after practice and talk about the workouts and upcoming meets. Mr. King wanted to take us to the Penn Relays. Music and Art had never entered because our school never had a team that could win. Mr. King said that he wanted to get us out of the bags, our uniforms. The team needed money.

Gladstone and I started talking about school spirit and getting cheerleaders for the team—we never had any—and getting the whole school together by organizing dances and boat rides, etc.; whenever we spoke, I thought about Knox and how together we were there, how friendly. Despite the fact that Music and Art didn't have many of the problems that most of the city's high schools had, it was impersonal and unresponsive to the needs of nonacademic students. Music and Art's interests focused primarily on the honors students, the grade grubbers, and bookworms. Social activities were looked down upon as a deterrent from academic excellence and the quest for prestige. To deal with the unresponsiveness of the school, Black students had formed a fraternity to sponsor social functions; the school still remained apathetic and dull.

I went to find Miss Mirro during my lunch period. We met in a vacant office. I was frustrated and angry and told her that I couldn't stand the boredom. She suggested that I get some friends together and try to do something.

At the same time we were getting a new principal, Mr. Richard Klein. He was young, for a principal, and always wore a smile. Unlike the other principal, whom I never saw, Mr. Klein was always talking to students, always walking around checking on classes, commenting on your artwork— his door was "always open."

Gladstone and I went to see him, told him that we wanted to get some school spirit, some new uniforms for the track team, some cheerleaders and dances, and a prom. Up to then we had never had a prom. He was really receptive and sympathetic to our desires, but he kept sending us to the General

Organization (G.O.). "That's the organization that should be handling these things. You should make them represent you." We persisted, told him that all we wanted was his O.K. to get some money for the track team so that we could buy some uniforms. He said that we should speak to the G.O. officers.

I had never been in the G.O. office before and knew nothing about any student government. The G.O. is a student association whose primary functions are to hold social activities, raise money for school activities, gifts, and charities. You get to be a member of the G.O. by paying dues. (Paying dues was a prerequisite for participation in extracurricular activities.) All clubs and other extracurricular activities are formed through the G.O. with final authorization resting with the principal, who assigns faculty advisors to the groups. Just about everyone in the school thought that the G.O. was a joke. Those who didn't think that it was funny saw it as an extension of school authority and a mechanism to get college credit, in terms of extracurricular activities. All of this had nothing to do with what Gladstone and I wanted.

During homeroom we went down to the G.O. office. The organization had one president, who didn't want to be president, two vice-presidents, two treasurers, and a secretary. The G.O. also had a faculty advisor, Mrs. Helen Shapiro. She didn't look as old as she was, but she did look like she had gone through a great deal of tension and frustration. Her face was like a statue come to life.

I politely told Mrs. Shapiro that Gladstone and I wanted to speak to her about getting some money for the track team. She fired back, "Wait in the corner until we're finished with our official business." Gladstone and I waited. The president, Steven Mencher, was really articulate and had a commanding way about conducting the small meeting. Gladstone and I got tired of waiting and split. We grabbed two copies of the G.O. constitution on the way out. For two weeks after that we kept coming back and got the same response—"Wait in the corner."

The G.O. constitution said that if a class representative was irresponsible, a two-thirds vote of the class could have him removed. The only way that the G.O. or Mr. Klein would take you seriously was if you represented someone besides yourself. I needed some official capacity. Our official class representative, Henry, was totally irresponsible, never told us anything that went on (not that it really mattered, but it was his duty). I told Betsy and William that I wanted to have Henry dismissed and run for the position myself. I was kind of nervous about how people would react to this. It would have a bad reflection on me because Henry was a nice guy.

The morning came. I fumbled over my little speech, people laughed, and I got elected class president. I went down to the G.O., and they still paid no attention to me.

I told Miss Mirro what happened, and during lunch we went to talk on a back staircase. I told her that I wanted to start another organization to replace the G.O., but she urged that I organize a political party, with posters and policy statements and everything, to take over the G.O. At first I thought she was joking, especially with the kind of people in Music and Art.

In class she started a discussion on political parties. We smiled at each other during the discussion, and I listened to what other students had to say, especially Karen. She was really intelligent, got all A's on her papers, and kept reading all the time. Personally I didn't like her, but I made friends with her anyway because I knew that she was smart and could help me organize.

Karen, William, Betsy, Gladstone, and I formed what we called the United Student Party (USP). Word quickly got around school that a "conspiracy" was being formed. All sorts of crazy rumors circulated. There was so much boredom that people just made up stuff to create excitement, and they believed just about anything they heard, even their own rumors.

I met Hassan Adeeb in one of my art classes. He joined the party, and it was our luck to have him because his uncle was a printer. Hassan got two other people to join, Holly and Janet.

Our party was well integrated—five Blacks and two whites. We had a few meetings after school but clowned around most of the time. However, we did talk about strategy.

I went down to the G.O. office and told Mrs. Shapiro that I wanted to impeach the Student Government, and she angrily told me to leave the room. Karen said that our best chance now would be a referendum to oust the president of G.O. so that our party could run in the new election.

The G.O. said that they would send out a bulletin to see whether or not the students wanted new elections. Rather than give us the opportunity to write our side of the story, they presented both arguments with their position obviously much stronger than ours. That night I stayed up typing carbon copies of our position, and in the morning put them up all over the school. Before official period all the bulletins had been removed, on Mrs. Shapiro's orders. I went down to the G.O. office.

"Where's my stuff?"

"No one is allowed to put things on the walls or doors without getting official permission."

"Well I'll speak to Mr. Klein. Can I have my stuff?"

"It's in the garbage."

I was beginning to dislike this lady.

We had elected a ticket in our party, but we needed a secretary. Karen was running for treasurer, out of necessity, "Spiro who?" Goldwitz was running for vice-president, and I was up for president. We decided that the ticket should be integrated. It now stood with me as the only Black. Karen took over the job of writing bulletins as she was much better at it than I. When I did them myself, the bulletins were often made up of quotes from *Newsweek* concerning the Nixon-Humphrey presidential race that I cut out and used for our campaign. Honestly there wasn't any difference.

Hassan began printing the posters and stickers. We still needed a secretary; Hassan declined, and so did Janet and Holly. William avoided being asked, and Betsy was apolitical, a flower child. Betsy was worried about me. She said that I was going to get corrupt and power-hungry and egotistical. I didn't know much about the political process and told her that I couldn't understand why she said these things would happen to me. She'd just say, "If only people knew how naive you really are." That night I looked up the word "naive" in the dictionary. People just kept using these words that they obviously thought I knew.

Gladstone became my campaign manager. People began taking interest in what we were doing. Many (including me) assumed that I was the first Black student to run for president. Actually the first Black student had run when I was only four years old.

The elections were scheduled for February 21st. It was early in January that signs of opposition appeared. There were now two other candidates for president: Liz Abzug and James Bednarz. In mid-February we were required to show Mrs. Shapiro the speeches we would read to the student body. I told her that I wasn't going to write the speech. She took it as open defiance of her authority. The truth was that I didn't know how to write a speech. Miss Mirro spent every lunch period with me right up to the time of the election going over my speech. One day, for some reason unclear to me, Mrs. Shapiro and Mr. Klein asked if I didn't mind having the elections on February 21st. I said no and couldn't understand why they'd asked me that question.

Mrs. Shapiro looked at me and frowned: "Looks like you have a lot of support: all these girls working for you every day, people making posters, the principal backing you, and you don't even know what's going on."

"Looks like I should be president, doesn't it?"

"Listen here, young man, you're rude and impudent and I won't stand for it."

The speech assembly came. I was nervous. All the days that Miss Mirro had sat in the empty auditorium listening to me make the same speech over and over had come to an end. Most people have a nervous fear of standing in front of large crowds of people—I know, I was scared shitless. There was just one thing in the back of my mind, "Don't look at the people look at the clock." The clock was on the wall in back of the auditorium.

Abzug spoke first; you could hardly hear a word she said. She spoke about draft counseling and the war in Vietnam and the need for us to do something. She went on about buying books for the library on women's rights.

Bednarz had the audience laughing all the way through his speech. He said that the art here was a farce, that he had been drawing boats and trees ever since he got into Music and Art, that in art survey he had covered the sculpture of Greece, the whole Roman civilization, and the Renaissance in one class period, that there was a film strip of ancient civilizations of the Tigris and Euphrates Rivers showing the people as white as the best honky around. He labeled both me and the G.O. as a farce and said that, if elected, he would resign.

The last speaker, Eric Bibb, son of Leon Bibb, was a candidate for secretary. I remember being in a stupor as I listened to him. He had no written speech but had a definite mastery of oratory. Even more fascinating was the fact that he was Black, looked like a common hustler on the street, and possessed so much intelligence. The entire auditorium was still as he spoke. Without raising his voice, he challenged the administration, the values of the liberal white institution, and its gross insensitivity and unresponsiveness to the Black community. He pointed out that there were three Black candidates running for office, all of whom would need Black votes, and yet the administration scheduled the elections on the same day when the majority of Black students would be out of school attending the Malcolm X Memorial. Malcolm X had been assassinated on February 21, 1965. Eric said that the white establishment had not only institutionalized racism, but also used the mass media to create so-called leaders of the Black community to totally negate and neglect and dilute the contributions of the revolutionaries who fought for the people.

The assembly remained silent as he went back to his seat.

There seemed to be a sense of guilt in the air. Minds were questioning, asking where he got the courage to say all that he did. My mind was asking—who was Malcolm X?

Suddenly Mr. Klein jumped up on stage, grabbed the Black girl who was running for vice-president by the hand, practically dragging her across the stage over to the microphone.

"I want you," he said, "to tell everyone whether or not you were asked by the administration if you wanted the date of the elections changed."

I got angrier and angrier. In fact, everyone watching got angry seeing Mr. Klein drag the girl over to the microphone and pressure her into making this humiliating submission, to exonerate himself in front of everyone. It was a public indignation. The girl timidly admitted that she had been approached by Mrs. Shapiro. He now called on me to defend his position. I hadn't known that this was the reason why they'd asked me if I wanted the date of the election changed. I went behind the rostrum, waited until everybody was quiet:

"I'm sorry, I just won't be used by the administration."

The applause was thunderous. Klein departed through the side aisle. Had I, as Mrs. Shapiro would tell me, knifed him in the back? People came rushing toward me smiling and shaking my hand. Miss Mirro kissed me on the cheek, another girl hugged me and said what Klein had done was "blatant tokenism." Had I knifed Klein in the back?

Water Carrier

APPARENTLY MR. KLEIN wasn't too pissed off because he sent me a letter congratulating me on having won the election. Karen, Eric, and Goldwitz had also won.

I told Mr. King that our team would finally have new uniforms. Miss Mirro and I laughed about it.

During classes, students and teachers congratulated me. Our new history teacher, Mr. Coony, devoted the entire period to discussing the elections. In the beginning I thought he was a racist. He started to put me on the defensive. He said, "You're Black, and now you're in the white man's system . . ." I told him that it was no longer the white man's system; it was mine because I was Black and president.

There was an uneasiness in the class, not only because of the closed discussion between Mr. Coony and me, but also because there were only two Black students in the class. Mr. Coony even asked me if I didn't think that Kipling was right about the white man's burden—going into the jungle and getting the savages out of the trees and making them act civilized and pray to God the Christian way.

I didn't want any part of this discussion; I hated to talk about Black people and white people. Why should the fact that I was G.O. president have to set me up as a special target, or make people treat me different?

I told him that there was nothing "civilized," that there were only groups of people believing in values *they* thought were civilized, that everything external to their immediate values was uncivilized. I told him that I saw a movie where two Black warriors in the jungle were fighting because one of the warriors had killed that other warrior's daughter. During the fight, the one who sought revenge was knocked unconscious, the other escaped to the white man's land—civilization. He cast off his animal skins to wear a white shirt and tie. He laid down his spear to pick up a shovel—to do "civilized work." The law of the jungle demanded that it must be a "life for a life," that it was the duty of the warrior, the father, to avenge his daughter's death. In his pursuit, he went to the white man's land, found the other warrior, but failed at his first attempt to kill him. He was placed behind bars and appeared in the white man's court where the judge told him, "It is not your duty to kill another human being; that will be decided by the courts." I cut my story short and asked Mr. Coony, "In this case, did the white man's law have more validity than the law of the jungle? Was this warrior not acting on the values he knew to be true?"

Mr. Coony replied slowly by saying that I knew what was civilized and was fooling myself by believing that the law of the jungle could possibly be valid.

The period ended. This business of being G.O. president wasn't good if I had to go through more stuff like this. I started to perform much better, to make a conscientious effort to improve myself, to line up with other people's expectations of me.

In the afternoon I had to miss two classes to attend the Parent/Student/Faculty Advisory Committee meeting that Mr. Klein had invited me to as the new Student Government president. It was explained to me that the committee advised Mr. Klein on decisions he had to make about the school.

This was the first time that I had been in a meeting run by parliamentary procedure, and to me it was really frustrating. Nobody listened when I tried to say something: they just told me I was "off the motion and out of order." I sat and listened. First they spoke about teacher evaluation by students, then "mandatory electives" and curriculum. One of the department chairmen on the committee said that because of the changes occurring in our country and society, the students should be allowed to take academic electives if they wished, and that this would not "subvert the foundation of the school." The science teacher said he feared physics might be abolished because students couldn't fit it into their programs.

They spoke for I don't know how many hours, and in the closing minutes of the meeting, the chairman turned to me and said, "Mr. Reeves, you've been painfully silent during this discussion—isn't there anything you wish to say?"

"Yes. How come there isn't any paper in the art rooms for students to wipe their hands on?"

I wish you could have seen the looks on their faces. I guess in relation to what they were talking about, my problem was inconsequential. But at that time nothing was more important to me. There was a moment of silence in which I could see in the eyes and expressions of those around me that I had said something out of place, even though they really couldn't have expected more of me; and Mr. Klein did answer my question. He said that "the Board of Education doesn't allocate enough money for all the supplies needed in every class."

I didn't want to argue that point, but there were only two art high schools in New York City. How could it be that there weren't enough brown paper towels?

Afterward, Miss Mirro and I took the subway together. On the way, she told me that many teachers were saying that I was unable to handle the job, wasn't interested in anything but sports, and couldn't chair meetings because I didn't know parliamentary procedure. I let Eric chair the meeting, because he was more articulate than I. On the train she wrote out a list of recommended readings. She said, "Even if you don't read books, here's a list of magazines you should read."

That night I thought about what was being said, thought that the only reason they doubted my abilities was because I was Black. I'd show them that I could surpass Mencher, my predecessor.

The following morning Mr. Sines, my official teacher, told me that I had to be in the G.O. office during official periods from now on. The fact that I was "president of a school" still had not sunk in. I arrived at the office about five minutes after the period began, and Mrs. Shapiro started to bitch about how irresponsible I was. We began planning an "agenda." I told her that I had to use the bathroom, but went to the library, to the dictionary, to find out what this word agenda meant. When I returned, we planned the meeting.

Once in "power," the first thing I did was to get uniforms for the track team. The second thing that happened was that the council passed a motion stating that if students were not given "complete censorship rights" of the school newspaper, there would be "no more student money to pay for a useless and untimely newspaper." It was carried by a unanimous vote. The other important motion passed directed the G.O. President to write up a format of student policy "when and if" the principal gave the students a chance to control their own paper. So the Student/Parent/Faculty Committee met and agreed to the following guidelines:

1. Articles for the newspaper can be submitted by any student in the school.

2. A G.O. appointed committee will sit as part of the editorial board of *Overtone*.

3. The policy on *Overtone* shall be as follows:
   a. No profanity.
   b. The subject matter of the articles should deal with information that has significant relationship to students.
   c. There should be a fair balance of opinion on articles dealing with controversial issues such as: Race, Religion, The War, Teachers, and Administrative Policies.
   d. In the event of a deadlock or uncertainty by the editorial board, articles in question will be brought before the G.O. for decision.

e. The principal and only the principal will read the paper in
its entirety before it is printed and distributed to the student
body to assure compliance with these guidelines.

Open discussion was something that had been denied before. But I used it because I detested parliamentary procedure.

I was always concerned with accomplishing more than the
president before me, not only because Mrs. Shapiro and other
teachers thought that I was unqualified for the job, but because I wanted to do everything Gladstone and I had set out
to do. Gladstone was no limelight individual. He always remained silent and acted on common sense.

By this time, veteran members of the United Student Party
were now working for the G.O. on their free and lunch periods. We had a lot of interesting people around. There was
David Sheppard, a Black artist and musician. Although he
had a heart condition, he was loud and hyperactive, one of
the most talented cats in the school. He was like a cancer
because he would start out like a small, unnoticeable growth
and would quietly expand until finally he dominated the entire body. There was Eric Bibb, also Black and a musician
and the intellectual among us. Janet, a musician who had
been like a dormant volcano, was now erupting and shooting
out scores of ideas. Karen, a musician, pushy woman, sneaky
—not to be trusted—was always contemplating the *coup
d'état*. William and Betsy, my friends. Barbara Anderson,
Black and a musician, looked much younger than her age.
Leon, always trying to be like me. Hassan Adeeb, pushing for
me to do what I said I would do and Goldwitz, now called
Spiro T.

The idea that I was president began to reach me. I was
president of the High School of Music and Art, an intellectual
school, renowned, with a proud tradition. Yes sir, I was president, and my friends were "The Thinking Machine," accomplishing more than we set out to do.

While we were deeply immersed in our "official business,"
and I was busy with my new-found toy machine, at City Col-

lege masses of students were preparing to embark on a trip to Albany to protest the proposed budget cut in the city university's funds. The cuts would terminate admission of new students to SEEK and College Discovery—programs that offered disadvantaged Black and Puerto Rican students the chance to gain so-called higher education.

It seemed logical for Music and Art, a sister school to CCNY, to lend a hand, so Goldwitz chartered some busses and "The Thinking Machine" organized a trip for people who wanted to go to Albany. No one from the administration provided any obstacles; in fact, Mrs. Shapiro had calmed down quite a bit and was even happy to hear that we were "going away."

The morning of the trip thousands of students from CCNY and bands of our students were swarming all over St. Nicholas Terrace and Amsterdam Avenue. There were rows of busses and scores of marshals getting groups on the right busses. Goldwitz had us walking around in circles for about two hours. I was making the trip with Marleen.

I had always considered her to be the most beautiful girl in the school. She was everything I wanted in a woman, except that she didn't take any interest in track and really didn't care for the G.O. either. But she was always good to be with.

On the bus there were some people hiding on the blanket racks and under the seats—there were just too many people. They remained well hidden from the driver, and so did the wine and grass. We began our journey. Everybody started talking to me about the G.O., making friendly jokes about me, the president. When they offered me some grass, I said jokingly, "I'm not into smoking grass. I'm the *president,* remember?"

It took me a while before I realized that I was the only Black person on the bus. I went over to Goldwitz and asked him why there weren't any other Black people with us. He said, "All the Black people went on Black busses."

I couldn't understand what Black students had to fear or hate about these whites. I mean, I had hated them too, despised them because I thought they were rich kids who wore jeans and old shirts like me as a costume—only to identify symbolically with the poor while retaining their material wealth. They were harmless, only loving each other, smoking in peace, for peace. I watched them passing it around to each other, like sharing food, or happiness. I had never smoked. First of all, I was an athlete and wanted to keep my body pure. Also, I had seen what other kinds of drugs had done to my friends in Brownsville: killed them. These whites weren't like those I had seen on the six o'clock news, stoning Martin Luther King or applauding Wallace. They were from a different culture and rejected everything their parents believed in. I couldn't help but pity them—caught between their elders who rejected and repressed them and brainwashed them with racism, and Black people, whom they desperately tried to reach as allies but who coldly turned them down. They were left isolated in their own culture which no one, not even themselves, understood. These whites received the hatred their parents created for them.

When we arrived in Albany, there were already over ten thousand students ahead of us. Albany seemed to be a dirty little mud puddle of a capital for a state like New York. The action centered around a huge grey building called the State House. Located on its front steps were speakers' platforms.

The students on our bus looked to me for leadership. As I stepped off the bus they asked me what to do, where to go, when to get back. My memory jogged, put me back in the bush at Knox with my tribe.

Almost immediately the demonstration began to fail. "Militants" took over the microphones with their "fascist-honky-motherfucker-revolutionary" talk on the grounds of the State House. People who came to listen got turned off and began to leave. The "enemy," the people locked up inside the State House, peered down at us through the windows, waving and smiling. In a matter of minutes, it seemed like a lot of cops started showing up. People started back for the busses—"just keep on trucking, brother."

Goldwitz and I finally got our group together and cut out. It was now night, and everyone was high from either wine or grass. People seemed to be screwing everywhere, even in the racks. I was preoccupied with Marleen. We arrived in New York City at Columbus Circle late at night.

The following morning we had scheduled a forum to give the student body an opportunity to question the newly elected G.O.

By this time there was a new member to the G.O. family, Miss Fineberg, whom I had met in the liberation school during the teachers' strike. Miss Fineberg was going to replace Mrs. Shapiro, who had served here way before I was born and had even taught Miss Fineberg when *she* was a student at Music and Art.

That morning I told both of them that I wanted to change the purpose of the forum to discuss the incident at Albany. I told Shapiro exactly what happened, and to my surprise, she seemed understanding. She, like Miss Fineberg and Mr. Klein, were afraid of the repercussions should the discussion become "too heated and get out of hand." I told them that although I didn't know parliamentary procedure, if the discussion got too hot, I'd adjourn the forum immediately. Mr. Klein smiled in harmony with Mrs. Shapiro and Miss Fineberg.

At the forum I explained what the purpose of the rally had been and that it had failed because some individuals had used it as an opportunity to voice their own opinions. This ultimately alienated the masses of white and Black students and turned what should have been a united effort into a racial confrontation. I also told them that there seemed to be an undercurrent of racial friction growing at our school and that we should try to find a solution before it was too late.

The forum did become heated. I really wasn't aware that there was so much hate and racial tension there. I'd never known how people really felt until I heard them speaking from the heart in public. People had asked me what I thought about it all, but rather than answer, I told them that I was too concerned with keeping order to have an opinion or feelings. Inside I knew that Music and Art was nurturing a cancerous, racist seed that would inevitably germinate. It hurt me because I had grown to love the school and all it was, all it could still be.

The following day Klein sent the Student Government a letter, congratulating us. Unaware that I was a tool of the administration, I was actually proud—even this early in my term—of accomplishing more than those who had been elected before me.

It was Janet and Holly who came up with the idea of having a Martin Luther King Day. Our entire staff labored round the clock to make it work. The program consisted of Dave Harris's band, "Big" John Martin's voice, a chorus, and my reading of Martin Luther King's "I Have a Dream" speech.

The next day, Klein sent a letter to the Executive Board of the G.O. and complimented us on the program. He offered his highest compliments to each of us for our great contribution to the cause of fellowship and understanding among all peoples. He said that we were a credit to the school, "a most unusual and outstanding and dedicated group of student leaders." And he even wished us continued success in "whatever ventures" lay ahead.

Some of the students even wrote us letters telling us how much they liked the Martin Luther King Day. One student said:

I'm a Freshman, and I want to thank you for what you did. I felt at one with everybody. I felt good holding hands with people I didn't know and singing and really feeling good. Thanks.

Although I was slipping badly in track, everything was really beautiful. I seemed not to have an enemy in the world, only friends. It was obvious by the number of people who hung around the G.O. office that finally we were reaching people and getting them involved.

White girls that I once stared at in the halls and in my classes were now approaching me. Having so many women at one time was a novelty for me—it was one big continuous movie of walking in parks, of spending late nights on subways, of looking at fountains. Because I was now a prominent bachelor, fresh game, and one of the Big Men Inside The Four Walls, all of the groupies were after me. For The Big Man there is no prophylactic strong enough to ward them off. Groupies are those little promiscuous power-seeking status-crazed girls who shimmy and clamor around after *the Leader,* the symbol of masculinity, the recognized number one top dog. Vickie Ginsberg had been a groupie. Before me, she, along with the other groupies, was after Overlay, one of the top guitar players in the school. Bad thing about groupies is, they never seem to know where they're going.

While I loved these girls, none of them seemed interested in what I was doing. Because Vickie was the only one who was interested in my work, which at that time was the most important thing to me, I asked her to be my girl. Everybody told me I was making a mistake, but I said fuck 'em.

A note placed among my books said that Vickie reminded them of the little old lady who sat in the back of a crowded bus. The only reason she moved to a seat which was vacated in the front of the bus, they said, was so that she could be closer to the driver. It was not until a full year later that I would find out that my friend William had left me this note around the time I started going with Vickie. By then I would clearly understand its meaning. She was borrowing status.

Hassan Adeeb, my friend from campaign days, told me that I had done the wrong thing and that if I valued his friendship, I'd get rid of Vickie. Many girls who had been familiar around the office typing and working were gone. Hassan now looked into my face and said, "You were a good Black cat, and candidate for all the sisters, and here you picked up with this. You're a slap in the face."

And so Hassan was gone. Miss Mirro was worried and tried to reason with me, telling me to stay with Marleen. And Karen, who had written my speeches, would no longer lift a finger to help me and looked upon me as a traitor. We were no longer a team—my rashness supported by her sound logic and intelligence. Gladstone seemed silent as usual, merely observing, but I could sense that he too thought I had fucked things up for myself. Even Mrs. Shapiro momentarily unwrapped her authoritarian cloak to let me know that she didn't particularly care what I did, but that Vickie was the wrong person for me. Up until then she had never impressed me as being anything more than a child with a cute face, big breasts, and interest in my activities.

My affair with Vickie began on the fifth floor behind the steel plate leading up to the sixth floor. I had chemistry on the fifth floor and she, music on the sixth floor. The bell had already rung, yet we remained there behind the metal plate, talking. We were talking about some stupid thing—I don't remember what. All I knew and felt was this urge to hold and kiss her. She looked so fine. Her blue shirt was open far more than it had to be to look stylish, and she was so lively and warm that day. I pulled her close to me in the middle of something she was saying and kissed her forcefully, felt her arms fly around my neck and back, fingers digging into my shoulders, pulling me into her even more tightly. Methodically I unbuttoned her shirt, palmed her tits, slid my tongue over both of them soft and warm, sucking each as she held my head, gently, and slowly pressed me harder against her. My dick began to stiffen and lay pressed on my stomach rubbing against her cunt. I was ripping my poor penis to shreds against the zipper of my pants even through my B.V.D.'s. The pain was too much; as soon as I stopped rubbing she started. Jesus Christ! she was going to *castrate* me right there. I backed off and slid my hand up between her legs. At the touch, she moved one foot to open more. Like a stiletto my index finger shot out and began fishing. She remained silent except for those deep sensuous breaths of warm air that ran down my neck giving me gooseflesh. She laid her head on my shoulder and pressed herself against me. The euphoria turned my cock to stone sweat, and even tempted me to chance opening my fly . . . We had just finished when the bell rang—as it did the next day and the next and the next. I would fail chemistry, but it was just one of those things.

Vickie was always around. As I had never envisioned the day when I'd take an interest in her, I told her everything about the girls I saw, asked her advice on how I could love them all without hurting them and losing them. Yet I did hurt and lose all of them.

When I had asked her to go with me, others felt, when she reported the news to them, that she acted as if she had won a contest. My thinking was guided by the belief that my friends would remain with me and accept Vickie, but I was wrong. Ignoring this problem was self-defeating. The "majority support" was still there, but having "support" was a far different thing from having friends, as I soon realized. I began getting cold looks from other Black students. On the team, the guys kidded around, calling me "Uncle Don." I couldn't understand this because everyone knew that I had been seeing other white girls. There was no furor before, why now? The fact didn't dawn on me that I no longer had a closed personal life.

Vickie, I could tell, was more in love with *what* I was (G.O. president and athlete) than *who* I was. To her I was nothing but a status symbol, an attention getter. At times I just laughed at how obvious she made things. The first thing she told me was that Leigh, president of the senior class, used to be her guy and that some big name in SDS had also gone out with her. The biggest joke came when she brought in this magazine to show me a fellow on the front cover who also used to be her boyfriend. I never asked her if I should feel honored to join the list. But in all honesty, I was also using her, as a sexual outlet. None of the other girls I had seen could put up with the relationship I offered—a whenever-I'm-not-busy-I'll-see-you type of thing. As I saw it, there were only two kinds of girls who would accept that kind of relationship—one who really loved you for what you were or one who loved to possess you because of what you meant to other people. Vickie was the latter.

At that time her personality was blurred by the overwhelming external pressures. All I knew was that I was losing my friends and that people I didn't even know were trying to tell me what to do. I'd had enough of that shit at Knox and had to have the freedom to do as I saw fit, to act independently. I bothered no one; no one should bother me, especially over a trivial two-faced relationship.

At that time, I saw Black students erecting a clique within a clique, constructing their own networks of organizations and a social world of their own. They began to reinforce each other's insecurities by doing virtually everything together, leaving them wholly inadequate to stand up and do anything alone. They were getting to be like white people. The once loose and splintered Black student populace was slowly becoming a collectivity. I viewed this negatively because I didn't understand what I saw.

My inability to relate to this enforced cohesiveness came from many factors inherent in my childhood. I was unable to relate to this political Black consciousness because I was too familiar with the Black people who lived in Brownsville.

In Brownsville, it was an eye for an eye, a life for a life. Each man saw out of his two eyes his view of the world, all he wanted from it, all who got in the way of his having it, and all that was necessary for him to eliminate those who stood in his way. Only the strong survived; the weak withered away and died. I had been conditioned to live by the laws of our realm, so naturally I was a loner, unwilling and unable to see why *strangers,* even though they might be the same color as I, wanted to tell me what to do with my life. It wasn't (of course) my decision to be born, but now that I was here, it was my life to live as I, and I alone, saw fit.

The Fire This Time

MY RELATIONSHIP WITH other Black students, especially Black girls, grew steadily worse. The Black community cut me loose because I had broken the taboos of the group by getting sexually involved with the "enemy." While I continued as G.O. president, few Black students spoke to me. My closer brothers told me that the only reason I was being hounded as an Uncle Tom was because of Vickie.

I had been seeing a sister in my sophomore year. She and not I had ended the relationship, but that made no difference to anyone but me. I was not seeing a white girl because of a bad experience with a Black girl. If the only reason people were calling me a Tom was my relationship with Vickie, well, fuck them. Vickie helped me in my work. My increased political popularity had illuminated our relationship. But now I lost all credibility as a spokesman for the Black students. I had no desire to fit into any handshaking–fist-raising–daishiki-wearing so-called revolution. This was no revolution; it was total conformity. An overripe sense of guilt and insecurity that made them flock together. I never feared any white man or thought less of myself because I was Black. Black men have been enslaved by white men as well as other Black men, by gods and taboos. I noticed that in the West Indies, Black women were equals to their men. But here in America, it seemed to me that Black women not only dominated their men, but even restricted their freedom. No one would limit *my* freedom. The master enjoyed the privilege of expressing his individuality; the slave was forced to assume a group stereotype. The Black denominator of enforced cohesiveness had created blindness among these students. They conspired against me and created wretched lies and rumors about me. I assured myself that I would never need them. I could do what I had to do alone. They were trying to put me down, and I wouldn't let them.

Vickie and I were in an ironic situation. Earlier there had been no real sincerity or warmth between us. But now everyone and every force that tried to tear us apart only strengthened our determination to remain together. The harder they tried to break me away from her, the closer I became. Black girls had even thrown stones at us one morning when we were walking up the hill. And that incident, more than anything else, made me callous and determined to stay with Vickie. My attitude antagonized Black students. I was regarded as an insult. Then too, I must admit I enjoyed playing the outlaw, consciously knowing that my presence with Vickie aroused all kinds of hatreds and prejudices in other people.

Black people want Black Power. I had power which they felt was not being used for Black students. Contrastingly, a Black girl began organizing a union for Black students. It was rumored that she had received the directive from SNCC to form a Black Security Council. During the organizing of this union, someone by the name of Darryl Chisholm, a senior, emerged as spokesman for the BSC. As I was concerned solely with my social activities program, I paid absolutely no attention to the progress of the union within our school. In April, Black students' unions throughout the city were calling for strikes to support seventeen non-negotiable demands. One morning, word got around in our school that there would be a false alarm after second period and that there would be a demonstration. We students would strike for demands that we had never seen.

Mr. Klein said that he would not recognize any demonstration, that it was a regular school day as far as he was concerned. He said that demonstrators would be marked as cutting. Nevertheless, the false alarm went off, and police cars could be heard outside. Students were leaving the building and congregating in front of the school. The overwhelming majority of white students remained inside. Even a few Black students refused to participate in the demonstration. They contended that no one could define their blackness on the basis of missing classes.

Shapiro urged me not to go outside and told me that my duty was to set an example as a responsible student leader. Shapiro must have regarded authoritarianism and paternalism as virtues. I told her that I would not go outside and then left the building. I left because I wanted to get information and, if possible, try to stop the disruption.

There were about two hundred students outside. Darryl stood on a rock overlooking his followers and ordered them to move onto the hills in the park. Darryl understood his audience. He knew exactly what they wanted to hear and when to say it. Darryl began to address the crowd. "We're going to close Music and Art down. The school will not function until the demands are met." He then started to read the demands, but fell off into a rap about some American eagle becoming the prey for a powerful Black Panther. Some of the people were staring at me and asking why I wasn't inside with Klein.

When Darryl saw me in the crowd, he started to criticize the G.O. and the "puppets" of the administration who worked with me. He was denouncing my organization, and that hurt my pride. I wanted to respond verbally but didn't because I was in an unsympathetic crowd.

I started back to the building by myself. Vickie came running after me and asked me to hold her books because she was going to join the line.

"What do you mean you're going to join the line? Do you know what most of those students think of us?"

She responded by telling me she had a mind of her own, smiled, and walked away. I admired her spirit.

When I got back to school, police cars were lined up in front. The school's doors were closed, but I was able to get in through an emergency exit. I was surprised by the comparative normalcy inside. Again I left the building.

Everybody was lined up like an army battalion ready for arms presentation. They stood there silently facing the school. I went over to Darryl and some guys who looked like college students. They were having a caucus and instructed me to wait until they were finished.

Finally they were through and Darryl walked away chanting:

Power to the people, we want Black Power for Black people . . . Who will survive, America? Very few people and no more Toms.

It was a poetic, powerful, and almost comical sight. It reminded me of the Biblical story of Joshua blowing down the walls of Jericho with his trumpet. But the event was all too symbolic for me. Music and Art wasn't going to fall that way.

Again I went inside, this time to find Mr. Klein and urge him to meet with the leaders of the demonstration. In a stern voice, he said:

"I'm the principal. The demands have not been presented to me officially . . . The students outside are cutting classes." I stood there in silence. This man was actually more concerned with what was "official" and what "should be" than what was and what the lives of those demonstrating were like.

Police cars were now stationed at the far end of the street. The crowd started to move over to City College. Policemen jumped out of their cars and blocked the street. Photographers were all over the place. Many of them didn't look like they had press credentials. They appeared to be hunting for specific people. One photographer followed Darryl's every move.

I sat there on the fence watching. It was fascinating to see the drama of people in conflict. This crowd, this demonstration, was only serving a particular purpose at a certain location in a particular period in history. Tomorrow no one would have any idea of what had occurred on this street. And then as quickly as the crowd had vanished, they returned from City College with more numbers. In the distance, the sound of more police coming—people demonstrating—me watching. What did demonstrating mean? What did it accomplish?

There were hundreds of people, some from City College, others from our school, and many community people. I was shocked to see Vickie in the front line marching with Darryl and four other people. The crowd discovered the emergency exit and stormed inside the building. Although I didn't have any intentions of joining them, I hoped that they would destroy the entire school, not only because of Mr. Klein's attitude, but because the school was trying to ignore a problem. I wasn't inside, and I wasn't marching. I thought both sides were wrong. Only a handful of the demonstrators knew exactly why they were demonstrating. At the same time, those who remained in the building were guilty of apathy. Personally, I just felt it meant disruption in my social activities program.

Large crowds had always fascinated me, and for some reason I felt that something, not necessarily a person, was always watching me, watching something else. It was not a fear, only a consciousness that I was perceiving something. This question of life and death, which remained unanswered, related to a third factor, time. Inanimate things—chairs, desks, hallways, etc.—were used by all kinds of students and teachers, as time passed. The inanimate things remained; the people went on.

Some of my friends came outside to sit on the fence with me. I listened, ambivalently, as they told me how Klein had tried to stop the demonstrators and that someone called him a pig and that he had been pushed aside. The exhibits on the wall had been torn down. Black students who attended classes were harassed. Finally people started leaving the building.

As I walked through the halls and rooms, I smiled because Klein had paid the price for not listening. But why must the building suffer and not the people? I felt like an archeologist who had just discovered some ancient tomb that had been pillaged by thieves. Chairs, desks, and bookshelves had been overturned. Cabinets had been smashed, their contents torn and littered. Paintings were on the floor. The locker room was littered with coats, and the place smelled like dog shit. In the auditorium, glass was shattered over the stage. This old institution had entered a new era. No longer would it dwell in academic, intellectual passivity. What would the administration do now?

Teachers were standing around talking and preparing for an emergency faculty conference to "discuss the problem." One teacher approached me and asked if I had been part of "that mob demonstration." I said, "No, were you?"

Miss Fineberg came running toward me and invited me to attend the conference. Mr. Klein was addressing the faculty, and when he finished, there was no doubt in anyone's mind that he had done "all that was humanly possible" to stop the demonstration. Then he called on teachers from the floor to comment on the problem. One teacher was angry that Darryl had not been "suspended, expelled, and arrested." (At the same time?) Miss Fineberg agreed with the teacher. The conference was adjourned.

The building was ready for closing. I was wandering around. Mr. Klein was still in his office, so I went in.

"Are you going to do anything to Darryl?"

"No, if I suspend Darryl—that's just what he wants."

"I don't understand."

"If I suspend Darryl, he'll have all of Harlem up here."

Mr. Klein was afraid of Darryl. Darryl had security through his advocacy of violence. I was to learn later that violence and fear, which I could not endorse, were the best security for a militant leader or minority. Violence and fear forced the majority to negotiate and to ratify demands made upon it.

Mr. Klein and I left school together. Vickie was waiting for me outside, and on the way home we talked it over.

That weekend I, along with Tony, Terry, Lamont, and Mr. King, went to Pennsylvania for the Penn Relays. Because of the violence, I had not been to practice in over a week. This was the first time that our school had sent a relay team to Pennsylvania. Athletes who represented the United States in the Olympics would be there. We had placed last in our meet prior to this one, and now we were expected to compete against some of the best high school teams in the country.

I was lead-off man and was able to hold a close second. The track was made out of a fiber that was unfamiliar to us; it seemed to make you move. I handed off to Lamont. He started to fall behind but held his ground in third place. We had a chance. Terry took the baton and put us back into second place. Then Tony, our anchor man, tried desperately to hold first, then second, and finished third. We won—at least we won something. We were all happy, and our coach was thrilled. All of us had cut down on our times. Mr. King had brought all of his college friends to see his team win. This time we didn't let him down.

On Sunday I called Vickie to tell her the news of the track team's victory. I also told her that I needed help in a speech concerning the demands. She suggested that I come over to her house. I was still unable to write my own speeches, so I went. I felt awkward going to the middle of a Jewish community to write a speech directed to Black students. I went anyway. When I got to her house, her parents weren't there. I was really getting nervous. Vickie called out for me. She was down the block with two other girls. I walked over to them, and she introduced me to her sister, Ellen, and her friend, Susan, who seemed to be timid, obviously a virgin, I thought.

Vickie and I then went to her house. Just as we entered the backyard, her parents arrived. I wasn't invited inside. Instead, everybody sat in the backyard. Vickie's mother went inside, got a small Sony TV for her husband. I just watched them, thinking back to Brownsville of the people sitting on the streets with nothing to do except kill each other. I watched these people here in this backyard all dressed up in the whitest, brightest tennis attire. Her father was sipping some iced tea; her mother just sat there staring at me, never once moving her eyes in any other direction. When I looked at her she opened her mouth, released a plastic smile, and asked me if I wanted to see the wallpaper in the kitchen. She opened the door so that I could see the kitchen from where I sat in the backyard.

I hated these people. Who were they? Vickie had told me that her mother had been exposed to prejudice as a child and had even changed her last name so that it wouldn't sound Jewish. Her family was nothing but a bunch of Uncle Tom Jews. In Jamaica people would call them "Hurry Come Ups." Hurry Come Up people are those who work only to reach a position where they can look down on other people. Hurry Come Up people seem to think they are superior even though they privately fear they are nobodies.

I didn't see how it was possible for Vickie to come out of this environment and love me. In fact, she didn't love me. I was an escape, a momentary outlet from this bogus way of life. It was a thrill, a fantasy come true for her to be with me, always hustling. One of the things we started doing together was shoplifting, which I had learned growing up. But for her it was a novelty. I knew it was because all her life, just about everything she owned was bought on a Bloomingdale's credit card. But I have to admit, even though she was often scared, she was good at shoplifting.

That day at her house I told her my feelings and she wrote the speech for me.

By Monday morning, there was no way in the world for anyone to know that there had been a demonstration at school only two days ago. There was not even discussion concerning the violence. How in the world could these people proceed with business as usual after what had happened Friday? I showed my speech to Mr. Klein. He said bluntly that he wouldn't approve the speech. When I told other students Klein's reaction to my speech, they encouraged me to read it without his approval. I had never taken such an extreme action by myself before.

There were rumors circulating throughout the school that the administration was making phone calls to parents to inform them that their children had disrupted classes and endangered the lives of other students. We soon found people whose parents had been called by the administration. Mr. Klein also issued a statement praising those students who remained in the building and condemning the demonstrators for using "fascist tactics."

I went to the cafeteria and onto the microphone stand. Up to this point, I had been observing when I should have been leading. Now I knew that my actions could be no worse than either Klein's or Darryl's.

". . . Although the students were wrong in not presenting their demands 'officially' to the administration," I said, "the administration was equally wrong in not attempting to meet with the leaders of the walkout . . . Since when is walking through an open door considered a fascist tactic?" I went on to inform the students of my plan to hold an open forum and how the faculty rejected my plan. I then requested a vote of confidence to support my position on the open forum. Attendence for that day was recorded at 1,795, and only five students voted against the plan (or maybe I should say had the courage to vote against the majority). The forum was the only way to head off another BSC demonstration. The majority of students still had not seen the demands. The administration's solution was to ignore the confrontation and to continue with business as usual.

I had never seen any reason for Black students at Music and Art to attack whites either physically or verbally. The whites here were merely scared liberals. I felt that Blacks should attack only those people who attacked them or had the courage to fight back. It used to make me sick when I watched the BSC alienate their own white support. If anyone should have been attacked, it was the administration for creating hostility within the student body so as to divert any hostility from itself.

Mr. Klein and Mrs. Shapiro were outraged when they heard that I had given the speech despite their warnings. I was called into Klein's office where he blasted me. Sensing that I was only making matters worse every time I denied Klein's charges, Shapiro told him that she would talk to me, and we left the office. On the way to the G.O. office I said to Shapiro, "You know, for a while I felt like he was my father."

His anger was not a simple matter of authoritarianism although he tried to make me feel that it was. It was more the kind of self-pitying anger a person expresses when he is let down or when a friend becomes an adversary. Mr. Klein had urged me to run for office and given me more control over the G.O. than any other student had before had. I'd been in his office more times than any teacher or department chairman. Up until now we had made a good team.

But I was beginning to think for myself. I mean I started to think about reality and to let my thinking govern my actions rather than remain mentally locked up and stagnant. My activism was what Mr. Klein could not tolerate. I sent him a letter stating that my primary obligation was to the students who elected me.

The following morning Klein took us from our classes for one of two fifteen-minute assemblies. After the first assembly people told me that Klein was answering the accusations that I had made in my speech on Monday.

As Klein began to speak everyone shut up.

"Since the beginning of the school year a group of students has been meeting with me to institute reform . . . Our

school is one of the most liberal institutions in the country
. . . No reasonable request has ever been turned down,
and my door is always open for discussion . . . There is no
need for any mass forum. The Student/Parent/Faculty Committee will take care of this issue."

I was burning with anger. The SPFC took care of *Mr.
Klein,* and that's about all. He failed to acknowledge that the
G.O. was the group that had been working with him or that
we had instituted anything of permanent significance. I felt
my nerves tightening. I had never addressed an assembly
without a written speech. He was just about to dismiss the
group when I gathered the courage to wave my hand to be
recognized. If it had not been for the shouts of encourage-
ment, I would never have gone up on stage. I went behind the
rostrum and lowered the microphone.

"Mr. Klein, I'm thoroughly disgusted with your actions today . . . How do you justify pulling us out of our classes to
defend yourself?"

Darryl was in the balcony trying to read the seventeen demands over my voice but was quickly shouted down. I continued and told them that the SPFC should be abolished and
that I was still in favor of having an open forum. I then
pointed out that Mr. Klein had just told them that his door
was always open and yet, right before their eyes, he tried to
avoid recognizing me. The assembly was then dismissed.

Old Coach Kunitz came over to me smiling and told me
that he didn't know where I got the courage to tell the
principal that I was so disgusted. As usual, the coach gave
me a friendly, rough slap in the face and walked away.

At first there were only a few students searching for information, but soon the entire crowd of nearly three hundred
people had surrounded me, staring and waiting for me to say
something. I started fumbling over my words and could hardly
hear myself as they gathered closer. I got behind the rostrum
and told them that we would hold our own forum right now.

Word got around about the impromptu forum, and the auditorium filled to its maximum capacity. I sent for Darryl,

and he showed up with the entire membership of the BSC, who lined up across the stage behind me. It looked ridiculous. What were they trying to prove? I then called for Klein who, upon sitting in a chair that I provided for him, discovered that someone had placed chewing gum on it. (He had more suits anyway.) It was a gigantic drama. The white man seated between two Black leaders. Malcolm X versus Martin Luther King. The dream of racial harmony within these four walls was witnessing its final erosion. The polarization was complete.

Darryl pulled up a chair and stood on it, overlooking everybody and down at me. He read the demands:

WE THE BLACK STUDENTS OF THE HIGH SCHOOL OF MUSIC AND ART, (IN THE INTEREST OF THE SCHOOL AND THE COMMUNITY) UPON RECOGNIZING THE HYPOCRISY OF THE EDUCATIONAL SYSTEM, DO FORMULATE THESE DEMANDS:

1. That the school employ more Third World instructors.
2. That the amount of incoming Third World students (especially from the community) be increased considerably as of September 1969.
3. That there be a revision of the entire curriculum to relate to the needs of all Third World students.
4. That Black History (not Negro History) be taught by teachers who can directly relate to the experiences of the Black population.
5. That there be established in the school, a student committee for the purpose of evaluating teacher activities and attitudes.
6. That there be more community activity inside of the school.
7. That there be taught a language of the Third World. (Preferably Arabic or Yoruba)
8. That the students be given the use of any school facility for their mutual needs. (A bulletin board must be supplied for the Black Student Organization—The Black Security Council)
9. That there be formed an advisory council for the purpose of

college and scholarship guidance in the interest of all Third World students.

10. Guaranteed college admission for all Third World students.
11. That there be an end to all involuntary transfers and automatic suspensions.
12. That there be formed a Third World cultural workshop in relation to the semi-annuals.
13. That there be an end to the censoring of guest speakers and all communications media in the school, e.g., bulletin boards, etc.
14. That there be established a political science class orientated towards the Third World movement.
15. That the Black Student Organization become an established, functioning body within the school.
16. That all freshmen and sophomores, upon applying to the school, be informed of the Black Student Organization.
17. The establishment of a Third World committee to investigate future student demands and to help in the revision of the curriculum and all other outdated school restrictions, e.g., advisory code.

> Note: Third World students includes all Black, Latin, and Asian students.
> Note: All classes demanded must be fully accredited.

Power ——————————————————— then peace.

His whole presence on stage was one of I AM MILITANT. His style was polished, his oratory powerful, emotional, and effective. At the end he said, "Freedom is non-negotiable, and that's why our demands are non-negotiable. We will use any means necessary to win our freedom."

The auditorium, packed with nearly two thousand people, fell silent. Darryl and the BSC filed offstage. I said, "Would one of you care to remain and answer some questions concerning these demands?" When no one responded, a few people in the audience spoke out, denouncing the BSC as a bunch of bullshitters and phony revolutionaries. Darryl got mad. "The next motherfucker who opens his mouth I'll off." He was shouted down. Klein rose to give his side of the story but was interrupted by an ASPIRA member who presented, officially, the seventeen demands.

Someone from the BSC told me that I was wanted backstage. As soon as I got behind the curtains, I was pushed into a small back room which apparently was filled with the BSC membership. What the fuck was going on? I felt like I was in Brownsville again.

I was on trial as a traitor to the Black community, an Uncle Tom, and a jive-assed errand boy for the administration. The trial got very heated, and occasionally people challenged me to fight. I wasn't afraid to fight, but I thought that it was best not to this time. The only sympathy I had came from the Black athletes who knew me before I had got involved in the politics of M & A. People were shouting and cursing at me. I felt emotionless, unattentive. My ears started to ring. My head felt numb. Eventually they started to argue among themselves. I felt at ease listening to other people decide my fate. I didn't speak, just watched mouths moving. The trial ended without verdict. Because of this session I was determined more than ever to do whatever I could to destroy the BSC.

I left the room. Klein was onstage speaking. Karen, Leslie, and Frances were crying. They thought that I had been beaten up. But Vickie appeared to have no emotions about the incident. She simply smiled at me and said, "I didn't think you'd want to have me crying, like them." I thought that it was a strange thing to say. Why should her emotions for me be based on what other people were doing?

The forum lasted until late afternoon. The following morning a number of letters were placed on bulletin boards. One of them said:

The BSC made bigger fools of themselves—seeing them struggle for power with every opponent showed these phony revolutionaries for what they are . . . It made me feel unified with my school . . . Nothing was accomplished by the forum except social tension was brought to the surface . . . The majority of students here are against violence.

And there was a letter addressed to me and "those who worked with me for the betterment of the school," telling us that we shouldn't capitulate to violence. The writer assured us that the majority of the students supported the G.O.

Any letters opposing the BSC came from the anonymous category. Whites were afraid to speak out openly against the BSC.

The Student Union had its own views concerning the demands. They wrote a leaflet addressed to the white students of Music and Art urging them to support the demands of the Black students. They said that "whites have to realize that Blacks must lead their own people in the struggle for liberation" and pointed out that "change that benefits an oppressed minority will . . . benefit the entire population." The leaflet also urged students to recognize the common enemy and not allow themselves to be divided on the basis of ethnic differences. "In order to move forward we must rid ourselves of all the racist tendencies society has implanted within us . . . WE MUST UNDERSTAND THAT NO ONE IS FREE UNTIL EVERYONE IS FREE."

They included an explanation of how each of the demands related to the white students. For example:

* It is not only important for Black students to see non-white people in a teaching position, but it gives white students a true image of the Black man as a productive unit of society. This helps to destroy the favorite myth, perpetuated since slavery, that Black men are stupid and shiftless.

* The primary goal of education should be to teach us to relate to one another as individuals with respect to background and culture. Therefore, the ethnic composition of M & A should reflect that of the New York City school system. To deny us this is to guarantee the inability to relate to people different from us.

* The revision of the curriculum would benefit the entire student population. Since most of us agree that our education is inferior, one way to improve it is by providing us with a true and full picture of *American* history. The course of the relations between Black and white *is* American history. It must be taught unmutilated. To do this, the entire curriculum must be revised.

* This would assure that no student would be subjected to the arbitrary regulations or punishment of any teacher.
* M & A is now existing in a vacuum. Whatever we, as talented students, have to offer should rightfully be extended to the community. If we are not relevant to the community, then we should remove ourselves to make room for an institution that is.
* This would keep students in touch with themselves and the faculty, and allow issues to be discussed before losing relevancy.
* As it exists now, college is another repressive institution. College is a class privilege, offering a draft deferment and a high-paying job when you get your degree. Certain segments of the population (Third World and poor whites) are systematically excluded. To compensate for this, the colleges must be opened to all the people.

The issue of demands soon became dormant. Klein retaliated to charges from the Union, and the Union responded to his notice.

In Mr. Klein's notice yesterday he said:
Most students are so caught up in their own problems and so tied down by their schedule of classes plus outside commitments that they have no idea of events taking place all around them.
Apparently, Mr. Klein has his share of problems too. Enough, it seems, to also make *him* unaware of the events all around him because—

THERE WERE POLICE STATIONED IN OUR BASEMENT YESTERDAY (ON DUTY FOR CITY COLLEGE) AND YOUR PRINCIPAL DIDN'T EVEN KNOW ABOUT IT

The Union made more charges. Klein retaliated. Everybody got tired of reading the leaflets morning after morning.
Since I didn't have anything else to do, I started to attend classes. I became really troubled when I discovered that I could no longer draw or paint as well as I could before. My work was no longer outstanding, and I seemed to be losing incentive. I started going to track practice again. Although I

won all my events and worked out hard, Mr. King said that I was capable of doing better and that he knew my renewed interest would only last for a week or two. Guys on the team didn't like the idea of my not coming to practice, then showing up at the meets and winning. Mr. King said that I was destroying the team's morale. But I loved running. I loved to listen to my spikes pounding on the gravel as I ran. I loved the pain in my legs and chest after a hard workout. Track gave me the freedom to experience the limits of my body, freedom to fathom my mind.

On May 1st, I was in history when the fourth false alarm of that day was sounded. Although we could smell smoke this time, teachers instructed us to remain seated. We were told that the only valid signal would be preceded by a warning bell. The halls were now clouded with smoke. We remained seated, listening to students running through the halls. Mr. Coony was under strict orders from the administration not to pay any attention to the false alarms. It was obvious that Coony wanted to let us out. Finally his better judgment won over. He said, "Everybody get out," and we took off in different directions.

Ever since we'd been going to school we'd been practicing for an "emergency." The procedure that we were taught became routine. The teacher would tell you that during a certain period there would be a secret, emergency fire drill, and therefore we had to get a lot of work done. When it did go off, we were told to line up. (In size places or just any way. In some schools it was boys on the right, girls on the left, or vice versa.) You were then instructed that during such emergencies you were not to panic. You were supposed to quietly follow your official teacher through your designated exit and into the streets. But now, "The Fire Next Time" was here, and it was every man for himself. When the real fire came, the regulations and procedures just disappeared. In fact, they had as much value as human life does in war, which is to say no value at all.

As I stood in the street watching the reactions of the students and teachers, I wondered if the people would stop business as usual or would tomorrow be a regular school day. Many students were glad to see the fire. Some never thought that it could happen here. Ever since the forum on racism, I knew that it was not only possible, but I had been waiting for it.

After the fire I was invited to attend a faculty conference. During the meeting, I saw that the faculty behaved no differently from the way we behaved at our meetings. They had all the petty attitudes and arguments that we had. I couldn't help but laugh at the way they were acting and understood why they took such precautions when it came to inviting students to their meetings. Anyway, I spoke, assuring them that the majority of students did not condone the burning, that the G.O. would help out in whatever way possible, that I stood by the "silent majority and nonviolence." The faculty loved me.

The following morning I made a speech. "That fire was *started* by someone—it was no accident . . . If you don't believe that Blacks and whites can work together, if you believe that burning will solve your problems, then maybe you should get the hell out of this school . . . Let us build, not burn."

Unlike any other speech that I had given, this talk made the students react with ambivalence. I couldn't figure it out. Were the majority of students in support of burning? Or were the majority constricted by their own fear, in their own vacuum of silence?

I was called up to the principal's office and seated between two detectives, one white, the other Black. They said that, while investigating the fires, they had come across information which led them to believe that my life was in danger. They offered me police protection. I declined their offer. I told them that my friends would help me out. I was in the G.O. office joking about my assassination when students came into the office and told me that the BSC was after my ass. I started carrying my knife to school regularly.

My mother had continually warned me that I and no one else would be the one to suffer. She said that I was being used by students who were afraid to speak up for themselves and that when the reason for their fear was removed, I'd be left with my face in the mud. Sometimes the things she said caused me to be uncertain. When I expressed my uncertainty to Mrs. Mirro, she said:

"Donald, if you start thinking like that, then you might as well give up . . . The difference between you and a great man is that you question your sacrifice, and a great man isn't aware that he is making a sacrifice."

No one had ever paid any attention to the G.O. before my election. I had grasped as many of the principal's responsibilities as I could. When he wanted something said that was unpopular, I'd say it and take the criticism. This gave the G.O. significance. Whenever I made speeches, I based my being right or wrong on the amount of applause I received. I never thought that people were following me because of me. I had very few friends, and visible support only in times of violence. My lack of calculation led many to suspect that I was incessantly calculating ways to obtain power. I felt that I must take initiative at all times. But this was an impulsive feeling, not a calculated one. This was the only way to strengthen the G.O., and so far it had worked.

False alarms soon became a part of the regular school day. Cherry bomb explosions were an added attraction. There were sometimes three and four fires around the school in a single day. These fires were only minor ones.

On May 8th, there was an alleged frame-up. A fellow named Walter Crump, a member of the BSC, was automatically suspended from school. He explained the incident: "I was late for a class. I had to walk through the gym. Mrs. Weiss was holding a class and physically prevented me from going through. She asked, 'What's your name, boy?' I said, 'Puddin' tain, ask me again and I'll tell you the same.' I walked away, calling her a 'freckled-faced bastard' . . ."

Klein called me and the other G.O. people into his office,

said that he personally couldn't get involved in defending himself against the charges being made against him by the BSC. He wanted the G.O. to defend him. We fell for it. On the spot, Klein arbitrarily suspended Crump.

Klein later called a hearing to announce his charges against Walter—who was not invited. Klein read some of the incidents on Walter's personal record. He said that Walter wasn't being suspended simply because he called a teacher a "freckled-faced bastard"—"That just topped everything off." The meeting was adjourned, and Walter was still suspended.

Walter put out a bulletin:

On May 8, I was automatically suspended from school, because the administration stated that I threatened Mrs. Weiss's life, also "insubordination," harassment of teachers and students "detrimental to the social welfare of the population of Music and Art" and in all, a dangerous student. I was never given a preliminary school hearing, was suspended from participation in the semiannual [recital], and received a special delivery . . . letter . . . [stating] that a suspension hearing will be held . . .

SUPPORT WALTER! COME TO HIS HEARING! THERE ARE BOARD OF EDUCATION DIRECTIVES PREVENTING THIS KIND OF ACTION. WE CAN NOT ALLOW THE ADMINISTRATION TO EXERCISE ARBITRARY, UNJUST, AND ILLEGAL PUNISHMENT TO REMOVE STUDENTS THEY DISLIKE FROM THE SCHOOL.

Under the Board of Education's suspension guidelines, a principal has the power to suspend any student from school automatically, with or without reason, for up to five days, at which time the student has a hearing scheduled. The purpose of the hearing is to "officially" suspend the student. The student in question has no rights. He is not allowed to cross-examine witnesses who testify against him. He is not allowed to have an attorney. He cannot present evidence. How can the verdict be legal when the process is illegal?

In history I had been reading about "China, A Victim of Imperialism." I remembered that as a result of the Opium War in 1839–42, England compelled China to permit extraterri-

toriality. This is the right of a foreigner in China to be tried
for any offense in a court of his own country, rather than in
China. The similarity of injustices between the Board of Education's directive and extraterritoriality was striking. Both
were just as criminal in method and result.

Crump's case became complicated when a girl was hit on
the leg with a cherry bomb that was thrown from the fourth
floor. It was rumored that Mrs. Weiss's son had been walking
with the girl who had been hit. Immediately following that
incident, some revolutionary blew up a toilet bowl. Darryl
explained to us the toilet bowl was blown up to make people
wake up and that the fires had been set for the same reason.
Personally, I thought that neither Darryl nor the BSC had
anything to do with the fires although they certainly must
have known who was responsible. I thought that Darryl was
taking advantage of the situation, but I kept my thoughts to
myself.

The media did not print a single story about the fires.
Everything was hidden from the public. Therefore, people
continued to think of Music and Art as a prestigious institution. I wanted to destroy the false images that were being upheld. This school, along with its people, politics, and attitude
toward art, was destructive.

I felt down, so I went to classes. The only exciting part in
my day became Spanish class. From my seat I could see a
building that was under construction. Every ten minutes or so
there would be a whistle followed by an explosion.

One morning Klein informed the G.O. that the city was
threatening to cut the education budget by ten percent. He
was very receptive to my idea of a mass demonstration at
City Hall. When teachers heard of this demonstration, they
too were pleased. Psyches that had been seriously wounded
since the Shanker Strike rebounded at the thought of a
"march" with students.

The budget cuts were a blessing in disguise. The seventeen
demands could not be passed without the restoration of
funds. Those who attended classes would eventually find

themselves in overcrowded rooms, receiving the bare essentials of an already inadequate education. Fifteen popular teachers would have to be dismissed. Finally, I had an issue to bring everyone together.

I called a meeting in the G.O. office to organize a demonstration. Fineberg started interrupting and eventually took over the meeting. I, in turn, walked out. I went down to the P.A. system in the cafeteria and called for an 11 A.M. walkout for the following Monday. Klein felt that I had purposely crossed him, and blasted me. When teachers approached me to work out a compromise agreement calling for an early dismissal on Monday, I replied, "We have to do it our own way. We don't need Klein."

Darryl pledged support for the budget cut demonstration. The sudden alliance between Malcolm X and Martin Luther King was a shock to everyone. What could be called white radicals said, "Fighting for more money for the same garbage, most of what we are taught in school, is shit." It was personally repugnant to some students to join hands with teachers. Darryl reneged his pledge of support.

Monday morning the walkout went off as planned. About five hundred turned up at City Hall for what I considered a fairly successful demonstration. The students were happy to see themselves in *The New York Times* and on the six o'clock news. When I was being interviewed, I tried to publicize the fires at the school. The reporter cut me off abruptly.

After the demonstration I went back to school along with about 150 other students. When we got back, Fineberg called a meeting with a few students and started working out arrangements for an "administration-approved" demonstration. I objected to the way in which this was done. Again I walked out. The students who had just marched with me were now supporting Fineberg.

I called for a 10 A.M. impromptu meeting in the auditorium. I would call for another 11 A.M. walkout. Mr. Klein and Mr. Irving Orfuss, the assistant principal, came into the lobby and prevented many students from entering. Two hundred managed to get in. While the students with me in the auditorium wanted to strike, I knew and told them that we didn't have enough people for a successful demonstration. They suggested that we march through the school and attract support. I told them no. Those who wanted no part of what we were doing should not be forced to join us. I went outside to about fifty students who were waiting for me. I explained our situation, and we walked back into the grey gargoyled building.

The common enemy was gone. Klein thought that I had crossed him. The conflict was among Darryl, Fineberg, and myself. I regarded Klein's intervention as an intrusion in a personal battle between Fineberg and myself. Everything that I'd tried to do to bring this fucking institution together only caused frustration to me and other people. If the cuts were so drastic, then why weren't the teachers out demonstrating? Why must we always have our actions "approved" by the administration? Why must Fineberg fuck everything up?

Cliff Notes

As I ENTERED THE LOBBY, Klein came rushing toward me and ordered me into his office. I stood by the door as he said, "Donald, I find it necessary to suspend you. You are to leave the building within thirty minutes or I'll have you arrested."

I stood there half senseless. My nerves tightened. I said nothing and left his office, amazed that he'd do this.

Many students were congregating in the lobby outside of Klein's office. They still wanted to walk out. I told them that Klein had suspended me and that I didn't think that the school was worth saving. To my surprise, many of these students were angry with me because I didn't call for a confrontation. I left them arguing among themselves. I went to clear out my locker. When I got downstairs, the lobby and hall were filled with teachers and students. I told my friend Francesca Michledes to tell Darryl about my suspension. I knew that Darryl would use my issue for his own purposes, but I was sure that in the process, Klein would feel the repercussions.

Students were shouting at me:

"You're a fool for letting him do this to you . . ." The crowd was becoming very hostile. I opened my umbrella and began forging my way out because the next thing Klein would do would be to have me arrested for inciting to riot. Vickie was waiting for me outside.

She and I went walking down Morningside Park and sat on a bench at the foot of the hill. We sat there looking at Harlem.

"Vickie, I'm really suspended. This is going to be on my record forever. They're going to send it to my colleges. What's Mom Reeves going to say?"

We were sitting on the bench talking when we heard a lot of noise and screaming coming from the school. It sounded like a riot. A few students came walking down the hill.

"Don, there's a rumor going around that you turned on the gas in school . . ."

Vickie and I split for Central Park and stayed there for the rest of the day. I momentarily forgot about things and we kissed and played around in the grass and fell asleep. When I woke up, questions just kept running through my mind. I couldn't believe that one man actually had the power to just pick up a book and arbitrarily lay down the law. I couldn't see what gave Klein the right to call police to arrest me. I couldn't yet see the connection between schools and the police. I had rights. I was a human being. How could that book with rules, the principal, and the police be related?

Vickie and I left the park. I got home only to find a certified special delivery letter informing my mother that her "child" had been suspended and that she was expected to be in Klein's office Friday, June 6th, at 10 A.M. I told Mom I was innocent, and she sent Klein a letter telling him she'd meet him when she didn't have to work.

Later that afternoon I got a call from Pamela Howard of the *New York Post*. She told me that my dismissal had precipitated a three-hour sit-in in the school's cafeteria and that my suspension was being used by the BSC to air their gripes over

the expulsion of Walter Crump and the administration's refusal to act on the seventeen demands. I gave her all the information she needed for the story. I told her, "It's beautiful:
here you have a Black boy who believes in working within
the system, and the white administration has stabbed him in
the back."

The following day the *Daily News, The New York Times,*
the *New York Post,* and the *Village Voice* all carried stories
of my suspension and the three-hour sit-in. In the articles,
Klein said that I had played into the hands of militant students who wanted to see the school destroyed. But this wasn't
true because it was he who gave the militant students a legitimate issue to protest about. In *The New York Times,* Klein
said I was a "good boy." In the *Village Voice,* a teacher who
had assumed an unofficial role as advisor to the BSC called
me "Gunga Din, the school's water carrier." None of these
things seemed to bother me. I refused to believe they were
happening.

At my house that night, Wednesday, June 4th, I received a
call from Klein.

He talked about the disruption that my suspension had
caused and told me how Darryl was using my issue to gain
support for the demands and for Walter Crump.

This time I could see how Klein was using me. He was lost.
He had called for a walkout tomorrow, and there was no one
to lead it. He was afraid that Darryl would have full support
in the school that day. I wasn't scheduled to return until Friday. If I went back now, I'd be arrested. I questioned this, but
he gave no concrete answer, only urged me to come in tomorrow to discuss it further.

■   ■   ■

The following day I was in Klein's office when two hundred students from the Student Union and Black Security
Council entered the cafeteria and barricaded the room. The
school was in a state of chaos on the first floor; the other four
were proceeding with business as usual. Klein was a fool for

suspending me; he only revived the dormant issue of the demands and gave the militants an issue to attract support. At eleven o'clock I was in the principal's office when Dr. Nathan Brown, Deputy Superintendent of Schools, told Klein that the matter would soon be out of his hands and that vans of police were on the way. Klein turned pale. Actually, the police were already converging on the cafeteria from both exits. The school's exits were blocked off. Klein and I went down to speak to the students.

The Board of Education had called the cops. The students wouldn't listen to Klein as he pleaded with them to leave, as he told them that the situation would be out of his hands. He feared bloodshed, losing his job, and staining this liberal institution with the blood of white kids (what of Black kids?). Eric, the Black intellectual bear who was now out of hibernation and a leader among the militants, urged the confrontation, wanted white kids and society to know what happens to Black people who step out of line. Klein was now surrounded by police in their riot helmets with black night sticks raised, ready to beat us in our school, our cafeteria.

I had nothing to do with any of this: Klein had made the initial mistake. These kids were now asking to have their heads whipped in. As they began arguing among themselves, I said to Klein, "I can clear this building and prevent any trouble, but you'll have to drop my suspension—no hearing, no guidance counseling, no letters to college or to my mother."

He looked at me and then at the police, ready to move in on the students, and agreed to my terms. I asked him to give me fifteen minutes. We went into his office where I met the captain of the police squad and borrowed his bull horn. I told my friends to go around to classrooms, open the doors, and tell people that the demonstration was on. I went through the halls, telling everybody to get outside. I told them that the police were here for a bust. And in the midst of it all, some teachers got angry and screamed at me for disrupting their classes. While police were ready to brutalize students down-

stairs, they began to circle Delany cards to mark students as
cutting their classes. The floors were finally cleared. When I
got outside, another busload of police was just arriving. I ordered everyone back into the building to the auditorium.

I went into Klein's office and told him and the police captain that we weren't leaving for City Hall until the police
were gone. The captain ordered his men to leave the cafeteria, but they still surrounded the school. I went back into the
auditorium and told everyone to converge at the side of the
building, facing the cafeteria, to show support for the Occupying Forces, the group who took over the cafeteria, and
urge them to join our demonstration. This was the first time I
had acted with total independence. I knew that Miss Mirro
was inside the cafeteria, supporting the Occupying Forces
and not me. I now elected to follow my judgment.

Darryl came outside and jumped up on the City College
wall. There were a thousand or more students standing in the
streets, all surrounding the police vans. Darryl urged them
not to go to City Hall, that the demonstration was an attempt
to subvert their cause by diverting student energies against
City Hall and away from their real enemies, the teachers and
Board of Education. We seemed lost and deaf to what was
being said. No matter what was said, I was determined to
confront City Hall to restore the budget.

As Darryl left and went back inside, a teacher got up on
the wall and called for a cadre of fifty students to remain behind "to show support for the students downstairs against any
police action." At this point I demanded that a "cadre" of
teachers remain behind, not students. Students always had to
"remain behind," and there was nothing to prevent the Board
of Education from bringing in more vans of police to deal
with any number of students. I told everyone that we were
ready to go, but not until the police were gone. We began
chanting: GO GO GO GO GO GO GO GO GO—louder and louder.
The teacher later emerged to announce that Klein had promised that there would be no more police and that negotiations
were underway. The police started moving out. A member of

the Occupying Forces requested time to read the demands
before we left:

DEMANDS

1. Remove police now. They cannot reenter the building whether called by Klein or anyone else. This means, in addition to no uniformed police, no narcos, no plainclothesmen.

2. An end of all automatic suspensions.
   Proposal: institute Student Court.

3. Walter Crump must be reinstated. Klein must write a letter stating, in effect, that he wants Walter back. Don Reeves's suspension must be taken off the books—he must not have a hearing.

4. The seventeen demands must be met. Discussion must be reopened; we must see positive steps toward meeting them. We will not accept Board of Education regulations as an excuse.

5. Total Amnesty.

6. Restore the education budget. No budget cuts.

7. Abolition of Student/Parent/Faculty Advisory Committee.

8. No failures at all (mandatory, suggested, etc.) because of lateness or absences. Unlimited cuts.

9. Open faculty meetings.

10. No music student will fail or be transferred if he is poor in theory.

11. Abolition of uniform examinations and finals.

About seventy-five students from City College's Black and Puerto Rican student community marched from a rally on the South Campus to Music and Art. About fifteen of them entered the cafeteria to support the Occupying Forces. There were cheers, and we moved down the hill to the subways and City Hall.

At City Hall we were joined by our sister school, Performing Arts. Together we circled the building and began chanting, "Don't cut the budget—No—No!"

A representative from the Mayor's Office came out and said that the "Mayor's Office" would meet with a group of us.

We saw "The Mayor's Office" but not the Mayor.

We demonstrated for three hours. Inside we were double-talked by all kinds of statistics and buck-passing tactics, and eventually we cut the discussion short.

None of us had any way of knowing that this budget cut was only a hoax, a trick designed to make someone in the City Government appear to be a hero when the $30 million was "found" to restore the budget. Richard Streiter, an aide to the Mayor, told us that the City simply didn't have sufficient revenues to provide adequate services. The recent legislation enacted in Albany supposedly resulted in a cut of $30 million in State aid for the New York City school system for the 1969–70 school year. Streiter told us that, with specific reference to Music and Art, the school has one of the most intensive and highly financed programs in the city.*

"Given that all the high schools in the City will be affected by the budget cuts," Streiter pointed out, "Music and Art would still have the most favorable average number of classes per day and the best teacher-student ratio in the City."

I went outside and told the students exactly what happened. I became hot and angry because City Hall had passed the buck again. The budget cut affected all schools, not just Music and Art. I told the students that we should take the demonstration down to Lindsay's home, Gracie Mansion.

---

* According to the *New York City School Fact Book* put out in 1969 by the Institute for Community Studies of Queens College of the City University of New York, the average student in a New York City high school then took an average of 5.1 classes per day, exclusive of health education and required music appreciation. The figure for Brooklyn Tech was 6.6, Stuyvesant 6.25, Bronx Science 5.94, and Music and Art 7.1. Even more significant was the fact that the average teacher-student ratio in the New York City high schools was 1:19.5 while at Music and Art it was 1:15.9. Music and Art also had one of the highest ratios of graduating to entering students (1:1.3) and shared top honors of all Manhattan schools with Stuyvesant High School in having awarded 621 academic diplomas for the 1967–68 school year.

Again we moved on the subways, rushing the gates, crowding the cars.

It was a long walk from where we got off. Our numbers seemed to have grown considerably due to the addition of students from other schools. At Gracie Mansion the police began arriving en masse and blocked off the street. I rushed for the captain and was almost attacked by a cop who thought I was going to attack the man. I told both of them that we didn't want any trouble, that we wanted only to make our situation known to the Mayor. They blocked off another part of the street so that we could demonstrate.

Lindsay was throwing a party for a number of politicians and civil rights people here in the city.

Some students ran over to me and told me that I'd better get back up to Music and Art because the police were coming back to bust the Occupying Forces. Shep, Reb, Tom, and a desirable redhead and I took a cab back up to Music and Art. Goldwitz was left in charge.

I didn't even know the redhead's name. I'd just seen her on the train. All she had on then was a hat and what looked like an old stretched-out undershirt. At the moment I sat down across from her, she opened her legs. Why had she even bothered to wear anything, I wondered. I'm sure everyone else on the train had been thinking the same thing. She opened her legs, and I began examining her beaver. I knew she was watching me, yet she smiled and opened up even more. So now there we were in the taxi playing. She was wild, digging, scratching, panting. The cabbie almost ran a red light. Shep and Reb were in the back seat, quietly taking in all the action. I knew they'd tell Vickie. Reb did, but it was worth the hassle.

Once up at Music and Art, Miss Mirro and Gladstone came running out to me.

"Get out of here. Your presence will only cause more trouble."

"Why?"

"Word got around that you were bringing the school back up here. They're sending for the police."

"I'm not bringing—"

"It doesn't matter. The Occupying Forces are planning to stay in overnight. You better get out of here. Go."

We left. None of them said anything to me on the way back down to City Hall. I was deep in thought. Miss Mirro had always been on my side, always helped me, and now she was part of the opposition. Or was she on the right side?

We arrived at City Hall and saw only five students. Lisa said that Goldwitz had destroyed everything. She told us what happened, and we then went to her apartment to watch the news to see how "effective" our demonstration had been. Of course, we only wanted to see our faces on the TV. We heard that negotiations at Music and Art had broken off after Klein agreed to total amnesty for the day's actions. They were to have been arrested at any moment, by orders from the Board of Education.

The following day, Friday, June 6th, at 11:20 A.M., negotiations between Klein and the Occupying Forces broke down because of the insistence upon the part of the students that "total amnesty be granted for any future actions as a condition for any further talks." In response to Klein's refusal for total amnesty, the Occupying Forces moved into the cafeteria for another takeover. They also distributed a bulletin about the negotiations, and I was shocked to find out that Klein had told them he didn't suspend me—that I "just left the building" on my own. But I didn't say anything; everybody was using everybody. Klein was lying, and the Occupying Forces were just using my name to gain support for their cause. I had more or less bribed Klein so that all decisions concerning disciplinary action against me were dropped prior to the occupation of the cafeteria.

Around 4 P.M. their numbers had dwindled to about seventy, but they seemed determined to remain all night. In their desperation for support, they asked me—who they hounded as a Tom—to sit in with them and support their cause. I refused. The Board of Education sent word that no all-night sit-in would be tolerated. At about 5 P.M. they filed out silently.

As the militancy began to die out, a conservative backlash became apparent. First leaflets were distributed throughout the school. It was a "Call for Unity," supporting both Klein and myself, urging the more moderate students to speak up and have their opinions heard over that of the radical minority, urging the student body to realize that reform takes time and takes a coming together of minds to form a rational, sane way of accomplishing things. They ended by saying that just because all demands of one group are not realized immediately, it should not be a cue to take over.

Despite the conservative backlash, the administration continued to negotiate with the Occupying Forces.

The president of ASPIRA sent Klein a letter stating that their club was not invited to participate in negotiations and that no one could speak for them. I also sent the faculty a letter telling them that in responding to a small minority who imposed reforms on the entire student body by means of force, they were capitulating to violence. I pointed out that we who had been trying to achieve reforms through nonviolence had not received the recognition they had given to the small minority who advocated violence. I also told the faculty that the BSC didn't represent even a fourth of the Black population in the school, and they could take no action without the opinions and participation of the "passive majority," while the Student Government represented.

With no hope of negotiations with the administration and me supporting Klein, the Black Security Council now turned its venom against me. During third period the entire membership of the Council, headed by Darryl, took over the cafeteria. It was not a sit-in but an open challenge for the "House Nigger" to answer charges of Tom and Tokenism.

Darryl got up on a table, kicked over the trays and dishes, and began to speak: "Reeves, you're nothing but a House Nigger, an Uncle Tom, and a puppet—a tool of the administration. You failed to see that we have a common exploiter, discriminator. The entire G.O. is filled with puppets. You follow the backdoor tokenism of Martin Luther King. You bite when Klein tells you to bite. Even after he suspended you, you lead his demonstration, the white man's demonstration . . ."

At this point a Black girl interrupted, "Reeves, are you a man? You're not. You're a homosexual; you represent castration, you're not a Black man, you're dirt—a Tom . . ." Seemingly all at once various people began denouncing me —all of them Black. The majority of students seated in the cafeteria were witness to this. They were white and remained silent and watched how Black people deal with those who defy the taboos of the group.

I jumped up behind the microphone stand and began to speak. Gladstone tried to stop me; he said I was playing into their hands. I told them that they had never given me a chance, that both King and Malcolm had had different programs for the problem but both met with death, and now only a coalition of whites and Blacks could win.

If they had had guns, I would have been shot up beyond recognition. Next I turned to the white students and told them that they were cowards for not defending what they believed in.

G.O. elections were coming up again. Three people were nominated for the office of president—one had a 67 percent average making him ineligible under the rules set down in the G.O. constitution, and the other candidate had failed three subjects.

The constitution was unjust: *all* students should be allowed to run for office. As for their intellect and capabilities—those should be the concerns of people who are voting. If they elect an idiot, then an idiot is elected, and in this way people might learn to pay more attention to whom they are putting in a position to represent and speak for them.

The constitution stated that I really didn't have to run again to be reelected, but I followed Miss Mirro's advice and asked for a vote of confidence to equal the number of votes I had originally received. The elections committee also sent out a bulletin stating that if the students wanted new elections for the office of president next year when we came back, that would be arranged. Many teachers wanted me to take back that statement because they feared that "the militant students" would have an opportunity to "get into power."

We had the elections—David Sheppard won the vice-presidency, Karen was reelected secretary, Vickie (moving up closer to the driver) was elected treasurer, and I received the vote of confidence, 1,705 to 80.

By the time the school year came to a close, $1.2 million worth of public school glass had been broken in New York City alone. Despite the demands, demonstrations, fires, and teachers' strike, Music and Art had a graduating class of 513 students, of which only twenty would not be attending college. The graduating students received $36,000 worth of scholarship money.

On the last day of school, Mrs. Shapiro and I had a long talk. She wasn't coming back the next year. Miss Fineberg would be taking her place. For some reason, I now felt kind of close to Mrs. Shapiro, like a relative or a friend.

When Klein had suspended me, Mrs. Shapiro realized that it was unfair, and so she and I became very close. We began to talk to each other as two human beings and stopped playing our separate adversary roles. She told me that I should call her up from time to time to let her know how things were going. I kissed her on the cheek and left.

I saw Mr. Coony taking his lunch break. He and I walked over to Columbia University and discussed virtually everything that had happened. He wanted to know whether or not I still believed in nonviolence, and I told him I didn't know. It was impossible for me to deny what was evident,* that as a result of the sit-ins the school was now going to hire more Third World instructors in the math, music, and language departments. The principal was getting in contact with commu-

---

* A Congressional questionnaire reported that 18 percent of the nation's high schools experienced "some form of student protest" in the 1968–69 school year . . . 40 percent of schools where there were protests altered school rules as a result of the demonstrations." *The New York Times Encyclopedia Almanac* 1971, p. 536.

nity leaders in the arts, setting up programs to encourage more Third World students to prepare for the entrance requirements. Klein also asked the Board of Education for money to hire professional artists and musicians to augment M & A's regular program and revisions in the curriculum, like the inclusion of Black literature. The BSC had won what they considered to be an important victory.

The same reforms one student body fought for or requested in one year almost invariably will be taken away the next year and brought up again in coming years. In this way there are no lasting effects. Students seeking reform keep running over the same beaten path year after year.

Icarus

(So I Thought I Was Going To The Sun)

VICKIE HAD GONE to France with her parents and, like many other students, I entered my final summer in high school only to find myself in the streets again, looking for a job. As I was walking around, the only thing on my mind was those white kids—those so-called white radicals who wore jeans and green jackets, lived in the best apartments on West End Avenue, Central Park West, and the Village, and who denounced me as a "bourgeois capitalist" and then left on their European tours. I was by no means from a poor family —a lot of people would be ranked under my family's economic status. The only problem was that I never looked at people who were worse off than I was to define my status or position; I always looked at those above me. Still, there was no way in the world anybody was going to convince me that because I wore clean shirts to school, I was a bourgeois capitalist.

During the second week of vacation, Karen and I began revising the school's constitution and soon realized that it was a waste of time. As long as the Board of Education bestowed veto power upon principals, the Student Government would remain under administrative control—an instrument of the administration. The only way to get power, we thought, was through revising the Board of Education by-laws, in favor of the students. But even then we saw, in the case of arbitrary arrests, suspensions, and expulsions, that the principal would not have to adhere to any laws. Within his domain, the principal is unaccountable for his irresponsible actions. Karen and I were left with the problem of student self-determination, and we didn't have enough time to find a solution. It was summer, we had been through a hard year, people were now relaxing (in fact, falling asleep) and having fun, and so we decided to put away school business and wished each other a happy vacation.

I finally got a job packing pipes at Burger Industries, a steel factory. My feelings about the factory were ambivalent. Every day I grew more and more bitter at how easily I had been thrust into the lower depths of society and made to feel invisible. At the same time, it was rewarding and psychologically strengthening to be part of the proletariat, alienated even from myself. "Why am I here?" I always asked. I stood in one spot, moved my arms to another spot, lifted sixteen pieces of cold steel, and placed them in an iron cart. I could feel my mind dying, losing contact with the world outside the factory. Those around me—forty and fifty years old—existed by doing this kind of work. I would have the chance to escape, but what of the other people? A man over sixty worked beside me. I thought that if he didn't die from smoking, he surely would die from lifting the pipes. And yet when I offered to do his work, he laughed at me, told me he could do it by himself.

These men in the factory didn't talk about class struggle or see capitalism as an instrument of oppression. They complained about poor working conditions and low wages and people tearing up the country. Their sympathies were not with students who told them to revolt—and who were unable to show them how their lives would be improved "after the revolution." Any time you have a man who doesn't even have a high school education, earning $4 and $5 an hour, owning his own home, car, and making a comfortable living for his family, you had better have something substantial to show that man before you go telling him to destroy the source of his income. Men in his position aren't concerned about any power elite: they don't even know what that *is*. The sad part about it all is that the students I was soon to meet would assume a superior attitude whenever they tried to "educate" the worker, because of who they were, where they came from, and the very manner in which they moved.

Miss Fineberg wrote me a letter inquiring about our progress on the constitution. I went to see her to discuss the previous school year and to get things straightened out between us before September. We spoke for a good while but really didn't resolve anything. She gave me two books: *Soul on Ice* and *Black Protest*. On the subway I began reading *Soul on Ice,* and for the first time I found myself reading something I understood and enjoyed. Cleaver's prose was cutting and powerful. I was very conscious of the fact that here was a writer who was a convict, an ex-rapist, and a revolutionary. Every time he would say something that struck a nerve in me—you know, things that you usually underline—I stopped and thought it out.

Soul on Ice was the first book that I actually read with dedication, from cover to cover. It started me thinking about times at Knox when boys would masturbate in front of each other to prove that they were men. And I also began to see how oppressed the Black woman was in American society. As Cleaver saw it, the Black woman had been deposited in the kitchen and made into Aunt Jemima—her beauty, her dignity, everything about her, totally neglected. And I could see in Brownsville, where hundreds of Black women had been abandoned by Black men, left with seven and nine children, maybe one still in the womb, that the Black woman had been dealt a merciless blow.

Through the decades she'd been left at the very bottom of

society—neglected, exploited by white men as well as Black men (sometimes by Black men who left her at the hands of white men).

I later saw how the Black family structure had been scarred during slavery and destroyed. Slavemasters denied Black people the sacrament of marriage. The legacy of slavery, its lasting effects in relation to the Black family structure, have been oversimplified and stereotyped. The Moynihan Report attributes the "crumbling of the Negro family" to the legacy of slavery and asserts that "unless this damage is repaired, *all* the effort to end discrimination and poverty and injustice will come to little." I don't believe that. I'm inclined to believe that Dr. William Ryan's analysis and critique of the situation is correct. He says:

Moynihan was able to take a subject . . . bring it into a central position of popular American thought, creating a whole new set of group stereotypes which support the notion that Negro culture produces a weak and disorganized form of family life, which in turn is a major factor in maintaining Negro inequality.*

Ryan concedes that there are problems with the Negro family but also points out:

Three out of four Negro families are intact and headed by a man, . . . seven out of ten Negro children are living with both parents, and, . . . according to records, the overwhelming majority of Negro babies are born to a man and wife who are legally married. Almost four million *white* families are headed by a woman, compared with slightly more than one million Black female families. About 100,000 *white* girls are reported to produce illegitimate babies each year. There are close to five million *white* children under eighteen—along with perhaps two million Black —who are not living in households with both parents . . . Controlling for income reduces the apparently huge Negro–white differences to relatively small differences on most measures, and on some, eliminates differences altogether.†

---

* William Ryan, *Blaming the Victim* (New York: Pantheon Books, 1971), p. 62.
† Ryan, pp. 65–66.

The differences are due . . . not to culture, or values or a racial habit of promiscuity cultivated on the old plantation; the differences are due to the effect of social and economic forces, and to the discriminatory withholding of information, resources and services *today*.*

Ryan concludes that "it is not that Negro inequality cannot be eliminated until the Negro family is strengthened, but rather that the achievement of *equality* will strengthen the family." †

What Cleaver had to say about Black men and white women was very real to me and started me thinking about Vickie, what our relationship was and what it wasn't. I was especially impressed by Cleaver's explanation that the Black man's libidinous attitude toward the White woman was a desire for "forbidden fruit." However, I do not believe in his Black and white prototypes; such a structured division as he conceives it seems foolish to me. I didn't see any "Ultrafeminine" women or consider myself a "supermasculine menial."

And just how the hell was somebody going to tell me that

---

* Ryan, p. 73.

† Ryan, p. 85. *Time* magazine (April 6, 1970) printed the following "Situation Report":

The economic gap between white and black is still tremendous, but it is narrowing. Negro median family income rose from 54% as much as white income in 1965 to 60% in 1968. The difference is less dramatic if the South, where half the blacks still live, is excluded. In the North Central and Western states, black family income runs 75% to 80% as high as white income.

The number of Negro families existing below the poverty level ($3,553 for a nonfarm family of four) dropped from 48% in 1959 to 29% in 1968. Poverty depends partly on whether there is a man around the house. During the 1959–68 period, the number of nonwhite "poverty" families headed by men declined from 1,452,000 to 697,000, but those headed by women rose from 683,000 to 734,000. The number of black families with incomes of $8,000 or more tripled in the 1950s and nearly tripled again in the 1960s.

But blacks' wages tend to run much lower than whites'. The Negro who completes four years of high school earns less than the white who finishes only eight years of elementary school. The black with four years of college has a median income of $7,754—or less than the $8,154 earned by the white who has only four years of high school. "Underemployment"—work in seasonal or part-time jobs—is more common than for white. Result: a black family often has to have two or more workers to earn as much as a white family with one member at work.

the reason I was going out with Vickie was because when my forefathers were slaves, their white slavemasters didn't let them fuck his wife? That's bullshit. America is obsessed with stifled sex. There is a mystique affixed to the interracial affair because it is forbidden. Like homosexuality, marijuana, or scag, it is placed in the same context as sodomy or baby rape. The sickness of those overcome by this mystique can be seen when the same white men who lynched Black men who made even the slightest advances to their women, were also fucking Black women, and men. So the Black man wants revenge? Or does he want to be like the white man, a dual fucker?

A mystique *has* been developed about the white woman, that she is taboo, a goddess, a so-called Ultrafeminine to many. It is a fraudulent mystique accepted only by those who do not have sense enough to know better, and those whose minds have been warped by a dichotomous Western society. When people are guided by prejudice and ignorance, they'll accept just about anything that's put before them. How the hell can I believe the white woman is a goddess when I look around me and see all the ugly women there are in this country? America, historically—all throughout Black and white literature—has cultivated a guilt mystique over the interracial affair.

When two people engage in an interracial relationship, because of the pressures and risks involved, it is more serious than relationships within the same race. It takes two people of extraordinary courage and defiance of society, with a deep love for each other, to deal with an interracial affair, for all the odds are against its working—a racist society, racist parents and friends and relatives. It is a chance you take that can generate a love that is impregnable and indescribably beautiful; in this love two halves form a utopia, and the warmth inside that world compensates for the overexposure to hate, prejudice, jealousy, and resentment. The love in an affair like this will be inward and strong, coming from the two people involved and from no one else. When there is a schism in this kind of relationship, both people are placed in a difficult position, psychologically and socially, because if they have had to reject their parents, friends, relatives, and the morals of the society in order to engage in their affair, there is absolutely no sympathy, no love, and no one to help pick up the pieces. The fall is very, very hard. And if there is a divorce between the parents of two different races . . . who will take the children? How does society look upon a Black man with no wife and white children? Or a white woman with Black children?

It seemed to me that a society that created such a situation, wherein two people could not freely love each other, needed radical solutions. For that matter, I used to believe that intermarriage carried to the extreme would mean destruction of race (for any race, not just Black and white). Nothing would have pleased me more than a nation of colorless people.

What I could not see at that time was the idealism of my thinking, or the reality that in *this* society, intermarriage means destruction for only one race, the Black race. Integration through intermarriage would leave Black people in an ethnically divided situation. No ethnic group really favors intermarriage simply for reasons of ethnic weakening. No ethnic minority is in control of the means of production, etc. And in a sense all ethnic minorities are victimized by the racist society and the roles they have succumbed to in that society, by force or circumstance. It is primarily the white supremacist, power elite, and institutions that maintain the roles of ethnic oppression.

The growth of the Black population is running the white population out of the cities and into the suburbs. But it is only a question of time before whites will have to deal with the legacy of slavery. Until such time, white people will continue to control the cities, depriving Black people of self-determination. Most major cities in America have their Jewish, Irish, Italian, and Polish sections, all a direct result of ancestral origins. So why is it that so many ethnic groups denounce the Black man's struggle for self-determination as separatist or racist? Do Jews ask Germans to establish a wider community or do Italians ask Spaniards to help them determine their goals? Yet when Black people decide they would rather control their own communities, they are labeled as racist or separatist. Even the government has served as an influence and force to keep Black people down. The cities will be in ruins by the time Black people are in control of them. America will be in shambles by the time there is a Black president—if ever there will be a Black president.

I read through *Soul on Ice* as quickly as I could. I wanted desperately to read *The Autobiography of Malcolm X;* Cleaver seemed to be a disciple of Malcolm X, and I wanted to know why.

After Cleaver, I read Malcolm X, and my whole outlook changed. For the first time in my life my eyes were really opened, and I saw and began to understand the manipulation and deceit going on in society. I became angry at the ignorance that had always guided me. I became angry at those who used me. I became angry at myself for being such a fool, believing that I could save my soul without reading. I'd been dead for sixteen years and hadn't even known it. I had incarcerated myself in my own limited universe. I had seen things with my eyes but hadn't analyzed or interpreted them in my mind. I had seen only the stereotype of Malcolm X—the pure personification of loathing, a hate preacher, a demagogue— and this is all I had ever known him to be.

Malcolm X was a man. He was unreservedly committed to the cause of Black liberation, and Black nationalism, and the building of Black dignity. He spoke a language of clear historical facts. He was here to remind us Black people that we had a problem because we often failed to see that we had one. Malcolm's words showed me the unity he had with Black people, and how estranged I was from the Black community. He told Black people the truth, that we fought in all the white man's wars and bled for white folks, but when it came time to defending our own children and interests, we didn't have any blood. He said that America never worries about legality when her interests are at stake and that if violence was right for America, then it was right for Black people to do whatever is necessary to defend themselves right here in this country.

I went down to the Queens Public Library and looked up the microfilmed *New York Times* articles on Malcolm X. What held me to Malcolm was not his hatred of the white man's brutality and exploitation of the dark man, it was what Malcolm X, the man, represented—a positive reaction to a racist society.

In his book, *The Evolution of a Revolutionary,** George Breitman wrote:

On January 18, 1965, he [Malcolm X] gave an interview to representatives of the *Young Socialist,* and this is how he answered their question. "How do you define Black nationalism, with which you have been identified?":

I used to define black nationalism as the idea that the black man should control the economy of his community, the politics of his community, and so forth.

But when I was in Africa in May, in Ghana, I was speaking with the Algerian ambassador who is extremely militant and is a revolutionary in the true sense of the word (and has his credentials as such for having carried on a successful revolution against oppression in his country). When I told him that my political, social and economic philosophy was black nationalism, he asked me very frankly, well, where did that leave him? Because he was white. He was an African, but he was Algerian, and to all appearances he was a white man. And he said if I define my objective as the victory of black nationalism, where does that leave him? Where does that leave revolutionaries in Morocco, Egypt, Iraq, Mauritania? So he showed me where I was alienating people who were true revolutionaries, dedicated to overthrowing the system of exploitation that exists on this earth by any means necessary.

So, I had to do a lot of thinking and reappraising of my definition of black nationalism. Can we sum up the solution to the problems confronting our people as black nationalism? And if you

---

* George Breitman, *The Evolution of a Revolutionary* (New York: Merit Publishers, 1967), pp. 64, 65.

noticed, I haven't been using the expression for several months. But I still would be hard pressed to give a specific definition of the over-all philosophy which I think is necessary for the liberation of the black people in this country.

I bought Malcolm's *Message to the Grass Roots* and heard him describe the House Nigger and the Field Nigger. The House Nigger loved the master more than the master loved himself, would give his life for the master quicker than the master himself would. If the master's house caught on fire, the House Nigger would fight harder to put out the blaze than the master would. Whereas the Field Nigger, beaten from morning till night, was wiser and hated his master. When master's house was on fire, he didn't try to put it out—he prayed for a breeze.

I sat in awe as Malcolm X told me that I was a House Nigger. Reading those words, I was more ashamed of myself as a person than angry at the individual who used them against me. This happened because I respected Malcolm X.

Herein I saw Klein as master, myself as the House Nigger of Music and Art—fighting harder than master to put the blaze out. I couldn't believe I had been so ignorant that I'd fallen for it. The Student Government was a game, a joke, a circus in every respect. It was a mechanism that gave flunkies a chance to play government. It was a device of tokenism, and I was a sucker in the game. I had boasted of a list of so-called accomplishments, found it gratifying to receive those jive letters of congratulations from the principal, and proceeded to do more "good deeds." I had fallen into a trap that had me sitting around a table supposedly negotiating peaceful reforms with the administration. In fact, I wasn't negotiating anything.

Anything that means anything to the administration couldn't just be abolished by simple "discussion," on the spur of the moment. I should have realized that when you "negotiate," you must have strength to back up your position. I was a fool to think that I was negotiating with the administration when Klein had all the means to abolish the Student Government and kick me out of school whenever he felt like it. I began to understand why many students never had any tolerance for the Student Government. At the same time I thought it was wrong to prejudge the results and generalize the actions of all those involved in the Student Government Game.

I saw that I had been completely at a loss. I realized this was because I had always based my being right or wrong on the amount of applause I received. I now saw applause as being nothing but an indicator that you were saying what people wanted to hear—which may not always be the right thing to say, because you could be appealing to their biases, prejudices, and insecurities. The more cutting and sharp the truth that comes out, the more people are apt to lower their heads or become angry. Sometimes people will get so angry at the truth or opposition to their beliefs that they never listen; instead they just wait for the chance to pounce, to refute, to cough up only what they had to say.

I became angry not only at my ignorance but also because I had been used. This whole process of Student Government had been co-opting me, preparing me to be a worker and recipient of tokens for the rest of my life. It was a process that used me without my even knowing it—until now.

I began to understand, through reading, why Klein could not directly confront the Black Security Council and Black community: in a white institution, in the middle of Harlem, it would be suicidal. I could now understand why the community people got infuriated over Klein's assertions that, if Black parents would trust and believe that he had a common purpose with them and their children, M & A would remain "one of the top schools in the nation." It was self-deception to believe that the system's administrators and the people they oppress and manipulate have a common purpose. Black parents and students are working to change society's institutions while the administrators are working to preserve them as they are. Klein was intelligent. He was a manipulator and deceiver who understood that it was wise to use my black skin to fight other Black students. And so many times I had been stupid enough to let Fineberg adjust my speeches to a tune of tokenism.

Martin Luther King (the compromiser) received a hearing from society because of the threat that was Malcolm X (the rigid, uncompromising one). Whites used "the compromise" and compromised only when the threat was present.

As I reconstructed the events of last year, I saw how Darryl used Malcolm's works effectively, and I used Martin Luther King's, so that we represented the epitome of the countervailing forces of the Black struggle in America. The whites chose me, King, instead of Malcolm. I got the publicity—and Darryl got nothing. They chose the compromise—crumbs instead of the whole loaf. What happened last year had to happen because the time was ripe for it.

I had had no sense of Black consciousness—that was an American phenomenon. I had been taken from one environment and placed into another, but I retained the values of the first culture. What I had failed to understand was that the emergence of a Black collectivity was a direct result of the racism that has pervaded practically all institutions in society. And the institution most efficiently designed to withhold truth and preserve racism was the educational system. I read how so-called educated men tried to formulate theories and studies to prove that Black people were inferior to white people.* In history, scholars failed to include the contributions of Black people. The educational system disseminated lies and half-truths, depicted an image of the dark man as a savage, a wild beast, a second-class citizen, and then created a righteous image for the heroes of the white race. George Washington, "Stepfather of Our Nation," was noted for his loose sexual behavior with Black women. He was also on record for trading a Black man for a keg of molasses. He was a

---

* One of these intellectuals is Arthur Jensen, who wrote "How Much Can We Boost IQ and Scholastic Achievement?" in the *Harvard Educational Review,* Reprint Series No. 2 ("Environment, Heredity, and Intelligence"), June, 1969, pp. 1–125.

slave trader. Wilson, the so-called great humanitarian, signed an executive order segregating Black federal employees and dumped twenty-nine Blacks out of high positions as soon as he was elected. Lincoln, the so-called great emancipator, said that Black and white people could never live together as equals.* Book after book showed me that it was in the American tradition to assign superiority to the white race and inferiority to the Black race. It was nothing but historical indoctrination, subjection to only a half truth—a lie. With only one set of values, there could be no decision as to what was right or wrong, only an unquestioning acceptance of whatever was being presented. The educational system would do whatever was necessary to maintain stability† and repress any alien political ideologies that might intrude.

The American Creed is nurtured through a very powerful social process carried on in institutions not of education but of indoctrination. Because of the very unanimity with which the creed is presented, rejection of it is almost impossible. To reject the creed is to take yourself out of society. And when you look at all the institutions within the society which comprise its identity and which create divisions among people you can see that education is always the basis or foundation of a culture, that the people are dependent on the "truth" and

---

* Lincoln's own words, in a speech in Charleston, South Carolina, on September 18, 1858, were:

"I will say, then, that I am not, nor ever have been, in favor of bringing about in any way the social and political equality of the White and Black races [applause]: That I am not, nor ever have been, in favor of making voters or jurors of Negroes, nor of qualifying them to hold office, nor to intermarry with White people . . . And inasmuch as they cannot so live, while they do remain together there must be the position of superior and inferior, and I as much as any other man am in favor of having the superior position assigned to the White race."

† On February 8, 1969 at South Carolina State College in Orangeburg, three Black students were killed, twenty-seven others wounded. The only injured policeman had been hit by a piece of broken banister, and all but two or three students had been hit in the back or in the soles of their feet while they were lying on the ground. The misunderstanding began with an attempt to integrate a bowling alley. At Jackson State in the spring of 1970, a 28-second fusillade killed two students and wounded twelve others in what *Newsweek* called a "completely unwarranted and unjustified case of literal overkill."

views exposed in those institutions. If those views perpetrated half-truths, broke the spirits of individuals, if as "liberal institutions" they failed to liberate people, it was (and is) the duty of those who realized it to abolish it. The historical and cultural continuity of Black people had been disrupted by enslavement to the Spanish, Portuguese, and Anglo-Saxons. The demand for Black history was a logical cause and effect reaction. Any time mainstream historians negate and neglect the contributions of Black people to the building of this country, the truth must be presented through other channels.

Although provincial and unrevolutionary in concept and structure, community control represented Black dignity to Ocean Hill. It was not the Board of Education or the UFT that the community was fighting against; it was the white power structure. It was a rebellion against white control of Black communities, a rebellion against two-faced liberals who called themselves friends while aiding and abetting the enemy. It was a stand by the Black race against the white race, a confrontation in which, as Lerone Bennett pointed out, "the constitutional rights of live human beings are at stake and are neither ballotable nor negotiable." It was the survival of the Black person as a thinking individual that was on the line. The people of Ocean Hill were protecting their schools as the only hope for achieving Black dignity and the coming of a Black generation. The spurious argument that Black control would give the schools a primarily political function had no weight. During the mid-nineteenth century great masses of immigrant children from diverse backgrounds were Americanized, completely assimilated and acculturated . . . Stars and stripes waving before their eyes, they adopted American heroes as their own. Were not Jews also immigrants? They were also victims of this Americanizing, but to some degree, beyond changing their last names, survived to remain as one people with an identity. Yet they declared themselves enemies of the Black and Puerto Rican communities.

I studied Black history, not only of the Caribbean where the first successful slave rebellion took place in San Domingo

(Haiti) in 1789, but also Afro-American history. I read how individuals and small groups of white people like John Brown divorced themselves from the white racists, supremacists, and segregationists to fight for Black liberation. I read about W.E.B. DuBois, the intellectual organizer of the Pan-African Congress and the NAACP, and about Marcus Garvey and the Universal Negro Improvement Association.

I saw the emasculating effects of the Southern caste system and the failure by Booker T. Washington, who monopolized the Black leadership for almost a third of a century, to understand it. In fact, Washington aided the white forces who advocated total disfranchisement of Black people and erection of a legal system of segregation. Washington represented compromise and concession. DuBois saw Washington's policy as it was, Uncle Tomism. In response to this, DuBois demanded that Black people "strive for the rights which the world accords to men." Subsequently the "Niagara Movement" was formed. The movement's second annual meeting, in 1906, was held at Harper's Ferry at the scene of John Brown's martyrdom. And at that time, DuBois stated the goals of the Niagara Movement. I read all of those goals, and I could see that sixty-three years later many of those goals had not been accomplished. I saw how all through history America has treated the Black man as an animal. In modern times, what Malcolm said is true: the Black man is dumb enough to fight in America's wars supposedly to liberate other peoples when he himself is not treated like a man in America. Even when Black men fought valiantly in defense of America, when they returned from overseas, were they treated any differently?

James Baldwin, in his book *The Fire Next Time*, wrote:

The brutality with which Negroes are treated in this country, simply cannot be overstated, however unwilling white men may be to hear it. In the beginning—and neither can this be overstated

---

* James Baldwin, *The Fire Next Time* (New York: Dell Publishing Company, 1962), pp. 94, 95.

—a Negro just cannot *believe* that white people are treating him as they do; he does not know what he has done to merit it. And when he realizes that the treatment accorded him has nothing to do with anything he has done, that the attempt of white people to destroy him—for that is what it is—is utterly gratuitous, it is not hard for him to think of white people as devils.

I saw that despite the intellectual giants that sprang forth for the oppressed, Black people had tried probably more different ways to integrate into the society and were exposed to more secretive and blatant injustices and repression than any other minority in this country except the Indians. Each time leaders rose from the Black populace, the government sought to make examples out of them to intimidate the Black masses.

The simple analogy of the House and Field Nigger was pertinent not only to me—the situation applied universally. Administrators represent authority and control. Where the administration lacks support from the parents or students to exercise constraints, it will inevitably revert to coercive measures or attempt—through letters, speeches, or meetings—to win the consent of the students or community. If the disruption centers around issues involving only students, two means of winning consent are used by the administration: one is to "cut off the radical leadership from its followers," the other is to co-opt those student leaders who in some way reflect the sentiment or possess the confidence of the student body. As a result of either method, the legitimate student vanguard is neutralized, and the new elements on the administration's side will lend respectability or legitimacy to the administration's authority and control; the end result is the stability of the authority and the elimination of dissent.

We saw the same thing in "crisis patriotism" during the March on Washington. The Black masses initially had prepared for revolution, and the administration in Washington, D.C., called in the "leaders of the Black community" and made available to them everything necessary to stop the insurrection. The March on Washington was a sell-out. As Malcolm rightly pointed out, they had Black people marching between the feet of two dead men—Lincoln and Washington. The leaders of the March were temporarily given power in order to win solidarity in a time of seemingly inevitable disruption. Yet when the crisis was all over, they were told to "get out of town by sundown."

I saw how school administrators used power. I also began to understand why white students had started saying: ALL STUDENTS ARE NIGGERS. When white students started demonstrating against the war, they were exposed to the same kind of brutality that had been dealt out to Black people throughout the era of boycotts, sit-ins, and civil rights demonstrations. In the eyes of school officials, the student has no rights as a human being; he is regarded as property and has only one function and capacity: that is to learn. The student may deviate and question what he is learning, but there can't be too much deviance from "the lesson plan," which is designed and geared for Regents' examinations.

Principals used co-optation to isolate the radical leaders from their followers. Sometimes it was done skillfully; other times it was an open bust. Whenever students took sides with the administration, they were given carte blanche to deal with the "militants." Administrators have always said that they want to see "students dealing with the troublemakers," and in doing so they pit student against student. The high schools are nothing but oppressed colonies ruled by benevolent—sometimes malevolent—dictatorships. They had us, the niggers—the natives—fighting against ourselves. As Fanon says, "Oppressed people kill each other all the time." We took on the labels of liberal, conservative, revolutionary, and radical.

We often failed to discriminate between words and the reality of their meanings. We often failed to recognize in our heads the reality of our situation. A student body is a transient element; the administration is permanent. Each year administrators become more and more skilled in repression. They accumulate a storehouse of information about students and keep files that follow a student wherever he goes. When the student makes one wrong move, everything is there to intimidate him. Look at the case of Walter Crump. Despite our incessant and valid complaints about the conditions under which we are miseducated, we still take the tests, shuffle, and get by with information we know is already obsolete.

Up to this point the essential failure of the student movement was lack of communication. Administrators try to prevent communication among students because information starts people's minds working and makes them question things. The administration benefits by keeping us in the dark. Our actions remained uncoordinated, spontaneous, and always reactive. When you react to something, you're being controlled. The demonstrations thus far were by-products of the teachers' strike, the draft, and the war in Indochina. When the student strikes came, they were often devastating but not crippling because they were isolated, uncoordinated, and spontaneous.

Even in times when we sat down to plan a course of action, we got bogged down in rhetoric about the ruling class, firebombs, and guns. We needed to make specific distinctions between symbolism and grass-roots action. Engaging in symbolism or deceptive pseudo-revolutionary rhetoric was repeating the same error that America finds itself committing—believing its own propaganda. We let the media build and glamorize an image for us and subscribe to the illusion and symbolism that has been created. We must stop stereotyping ourselves to death.

The student who goes to classes during a demonstration is labeled "apathetic." The student who disrupts classes is called "militant." All Black students with Afros are considered advocates of Black nationalism. White students with long hair are thought to be hippies or radicals.

The television generation is one that follows fads. The mass media and other accessories of the system have exploited the high schools. We have fallen victim to stereotypes of ourselves, always being categorized and lied to by the media. The media set the trap and we fell for it. Many high school students declared themselves "revolutionaries." The most important thing that a person can do is to arrive at his own beliefs, then acknowledge and practice them. Although it is too simplistic to say that revolution is the violent overthrow of an elite and the creation of a new ideology, we know that revolutions involve murder, and picking up weapons and having the courage to use them, to kill other human beings, guilty or not. Revolutionaries realize that once they pick up the gun, it cannot be put down until the reason for picking up the gun no longer exists. A revolutionary's duty is to live "to make the revolution," and then make his ideology work. The revolutionary leadership is composed of highly skilled and educated tacticians who plan the course of action and who educate the masses, who often forget that they have a problem that doesn't end with the coming of winter. When I read about Mao, Che, Castro, Lenin, Marx, Malcolm X, and Ho Chi Minh, I began to understand what a revolutionary is, and is not.

Not everybody believes in revolution, but most people have the ability to see a problem and confront that problem with different methods and solutions. When people can't put you into a social category, they get confused and unstable. If you wear a suit, you're a bourgeois capitalist—yet you talk about revolution. You've got an Afro and wear a daishiki—yet you talk about crawling back on the plantation. You carry a gun, yet you say you stand for peace. You wear jeans and long hair, yet you want war not peace, slavery not freedom. When you don't verbalize what category you place yourself in, conservative, radical, revolutionary, people arbitrarily put you into a category they think you belong in. To see a problem, to use any means necessary to solve or eliminate that problem is the only thing that is important.

People often rely on symbols, posters, buttons, or clothes to identify with what they want to be but realize they will never be, either because they are unwilling to accept the consequences, or lack the courage. A revolution, as Malcolm pointed out, is bloody, hostile, and overturns and destroys everything that gets its way. Revolution knows no compromise, no negotiation. "By any means necessary," the dictum of revolution, must be taken very seriously. A lot of people will put up an argument, but I agree with Peter L. Berger's comment: "It is all important to be aware of it. Violence is the ultimate foundation of any political order. No state can exist without a police force or its equivalent in armed might. This ultimate violence may not be used frequently. There may be innumerable steps before its application, in the way of warnings and reprimands," * but it will be used.

I read about the school desegregation cases: *Brown* v. *Board of Education* in Topeka, Kansas, *Briggs* v. *Elliott,* and *Davis County* v. *School Board.* In each case, the plaintiffs were Black children and their cases had been taken before a court of law. I wanted to bring the Board of Education before the courts because they were in violation of the Constitutional rights of high school students, and also directly responsible for institutionalizing racism and dividing students along class lines. As far back as they go, almost all our schools are structured to separate people. I hadn't always seen it, as it was done skillfully. The white and middle-class kids were put in Intellectually Gifted Children (IGC) classes and Special Progress (SP) classes. Although the school was physically integrated, academically it was segregated. When it came to high school, the white and upper-class students went to academic high schools while most Blacks, Puerto Ricans, Latins, and lower-class whites were dumped in vocational high schools, taking general and commercial courses and receiving a "general diploma" that was nothing but "a ticket to the army." (Those students graduating from the vocational schools could not even keep their jobs, the training was so inadequate.)

Every student should be entitled to a college education. Any nation that can maintain armies and navies around the world, pour billions into space explorations and foreign aid, and then throw away "surplus" food has enough money to

---

* Peter L. Berger, *Invitation to Sociology* (New York: Anchor Books, 1963), p. 69.

build facilities to give every one of us a college education.

I studied the disruptions in various high schools in 1968–69 and saw that in each incident, the high school bureaucracy ultimately relied on the police force; in the colleges it was the National Guard. I saw that uniforms gave men the right to brutalize and kill in the name of justice, and that if civilians did the same, they would be jailed for murder or put to death. And I also began to see that, for all of the publicity and big talk and underground newspapers, there were actually few people who would really fight the repressive forces in our schools.

I made an outline of the high school system in terms of its handling of demonstrations. Things were set up in such a way that the Board of Education invested its power in the principal, through the superintendent. The power that was shared here was not in the hands of the public (the people) or of democratically elected representatives, but with key men directing bureaucracies. These men were not accountable for their actions, and as a consequence, they got away with virtually anything. I would soon see that even the courts of law enforced the arbitrary decisions made by the high school system. Whenever the principals felt that their power was being threatened, police were called. And these administrators weren't restrained in any moral sense because they had no morals. Some schools have liberal principals, others conservative, others archaic ones, and an entire high school will assume the personality of the principal. But the primary concern of any administration is to follow and administer the laws that have been set down for it, not to improve the conditions in the institution or to make it relevant and responsive to the needs of its constituency. Collectively these high school principals, irresponsible demagogues, formed a dictatorship —an elite group who took the offensive at any sign of encroachment on their power, who used issues of race and violence as fear tactics in order to gain the public's support and retain power.

Principals are always on the defensive. Most principals are paranoid. They are afraid of encroachments on their "authority" and defend the system at the expense of justice to students. Freedom of speech, the right to assemble, freedom of the press—all the rights this country says a person has—are viewed by principals as infringements of their power. They rule within their domain as autonomous figures whose ally in times of community intervention (i.e., the teachers' strike in 1968) is the United Federation of Teachers. The teachers' union had secured rights and protected its members from arbitrary decisions, harassment, and also from established machinery for grievances. Only when the Council of Supervisory Personnel and United Federation of Teachers are faced with a common enemy, the community, do they unite as one block. The high school bureaucracy doesn't want the community involved in school affairs.

The problems at Music and Art were minute and healthy in comparison to those at other high schools. Throughout the disruptions, except for one injury, the confrontation was waged by use of heated rhetoric. I thought that the essential failure of high school students was confining themselves to the problems of one school with one man. To fight against the immediate problems may be a necessity, but it meant opting for instant gratification, which is inconsequential if it doesn't have repercussions somewhere else. By this I'm saying that taking over a building or room to solve an immediate problem may be a necessity and may be noble, but if it doesn't reach people in other places in some way, then the action is of minute importance.

I saw Music and Art as being in the best position to consolidate the colonies by virtue of the fact that we had music. Music brought people together, made them color-blind. Racism had to be overcome before we could get on to solving our problems. I thought that by establishing a cultural exchange program, we could set up a citywide network. First, Music and Art would send music groups to various high schools, specifically: Ben Franklin, Thomas Jefferson, Charles Evans Hughes, Brandeis, Julia Richmond, Seward Park, Washington Irving, Christopher Columbus, Dewitt Clinton, Evander Childs, James Monroe, Morris High, Roosevelt, Walton,

Taft, Boys High, Wingate, Erasmus Hall, Eastern District, Tilden, Woodrow Wilson, Francis Lewis, Jamaica High, John Adams, Long Island City, Richmond Hill, Newton, William J. Bryant, Grover Cleveland, Andrew Jackson, and Springfield Gardens—all schools which have large percentages of minority groups. Once we played and established a friendship between our school and theirs, the political students from each of the schools could establish communications on a permanent basis in order to settle our problems with the principals.

Of course, the principals would be informed only of the superficial function of the Cultural Exchange Program (which by itself was valid to stimulate racial harmony by showing various racially torn student bodies that Blacks and whites can work together to produce something beautiful). As for the other function, the principals would never allow any permanent political communications among students of various schools because that represents a danger to the administration. Apathy is functional both in school and in society because it permits the government to do just about whatever it pleases with a minimum of pressure from the public.

I kept reading and thinking. I went to museums and exhibits and just about any place where I could increase my knowledge. The one thing that reading showed me was how little I knew and how much more I'd have to learn. However, I didn't become indecisive because the world was more complex than I thought; I was only shocked that most of what I was just learning many people already knew, and yet they didn't apply their energies to tackling the problems or injustices they complained about.

I came across "The Brownsville Papers," the report that I'd started compiling when I was twelve years old. It showed me how easily a person could be deceived by the complexity of the system and even turn on the victims of that system rather than on the people who are actually responsible for the crime.

Brownsville was an exploited colony mined with economic

traps. Along with everything else, easy credit loans bearing high interest rates were keeping everybody down. Things were so bad that by 1971, four out of five families in Brownsville were on welfare, and the unemployment there was about twice the citywide rate. But welfare in itself was not the problem; it was the system that tailored people to fit into welfare and then categorized the victims as social liabilities that was at fault.

But it wasn't just such economic traps; there were educational traps too. In fact, *any* channel that Black people tried —economic, political, social, or academic—they found themselves trapped. And all the reading I'd done since my report on Brownsville just added more evidence.*

■ ■ ■

With only three weeks left in the summer I quit my job at the factory and bought a ticket for Freeport, in the Bahamas. I went to spend some time with Willie's family. On the first night Willie and I talked about old times. Neither of us could

---

* According to another "Situation Report" in *Time* Magazine (April 6, 1970):

Grade School. Only 58% of black school children complete the eighth grade, as against 73% of their white classmates.
High School. About 40% of black teen-agers finish high school, compared with 62% of whites.
College. Black enrollment has almost doubled since 1964, but the relative black total has barely changed: only 6.4% of U.S. undergraduates are black, compared with 5% in 1964. They number 434,000; almost half attend black colleges, mainly in the South. At major integrated universities, perhaps 3 out of 100 students are black.
Graduate School. Blacks account for an estimated 1% of doctoral candidates (most of them in education), less than 3% of medical students.
Teaching. Though 10% of public schoolteachers are black, few become administrators. In New York City, where 32% of students are black, the school system has 24 black principals—out of 893. In 1968, blacks constituted less than 1% of the faculties at 80 public universities. One major predominantly white university (Michigan State) has a black president.
Integration. Almost 40% of the South's black children now attend partly integrated schools, compared with only about 1% in 1964. Even so, three-quarters of Southern black pupils still attend schools that are at least 95% black. Outside the South, the proportion is nearly 1 out of 2.
Payoff. Black educational achievement does not lead to equal income. In 1968, white males who completed grade school earned more ($6,452) than blacks who completed high school ($5,801). White high school graduates earned more than blacks with four or more years of college.

get over how much we had grown since those days on Thompson Street in Montego Bay when we used to run bare-assed up and down the street.

When we were at his house he told me that somebody had sent me a thick letter. How could anybody know I was there? I picked up the envelope: familiar writing on it, it was from Vickie. I had not written to her since I began reading *The Autobiography of Malcolm X*. In fact, I was determined to have as little as possible to do with white people from then on. I opened the letter and was shocked to find out that she had written to my house to get my address and sent me a thirty-eight-page letter, telling me about France, pleading with me to write, and saying how much she cared, wanted to have my children, etc., etc. At this moment I didn't know what to do. I had planned to go back to school and make friends with former enemies and attend Black Security Council meetings and apologize to the brothers and sisters for my past actions. But I just couldn't pick up and leave Vickie. At the same time I knew that they would never accept me talking black and fucking white. I tried to rationalize this in every conceivable way, and I came to the conclusion that our relationship was a *personal* matter. I loved her. Yes, I'd read and reread *Soul on Ice* by Eldridge Cleaver, all of Frantz Fanon's *Black Skin, White Masks*, and I supposed there was much truth in what each man had to say about black/white relationships. But I *knew* my personal feelings, and for all of what they had to say, they didn't touch me. Fanon, in writing *Black Skin, White Masks*, hopes that:

Those who recognize themselves in it, I think, will have made a step forward. I seriously hope to persuade my brother, whether black or white, to tear off with all his strength the shameful livery put together by centuries of incomprehension.*

I am willing to admit that I do not always understand just why it is I do certain things, or what in my subconscious

---

* Frantz Fanon, *Black Skin, White Masks* (New York: Grove Press, 1967), p. 12.

causes me to act the way I do. But Ralph Ellison states my complaint when he writes in the *Invisible Man*:

All my life I had been looking for something, and everywhere I turned someone tried to tell me what it was. I accepted their answers too, though they were often in contradiction and even self-contradictory. I was naïve. I was looking for myself and asking everyone except myself questions which I, and only I, could answer. It took me a long time and much painful boomeranging of my expectations to achieve a realization everyone else appears to have been born with: That I am nobody but myself.*

Every time I found myself defending my relationship with Vickie, it was in *response* to a criticism, generalization, or stereotype. It's not my business to *advocate intermarriage,* nor am I blind to the *necessity* of brothers and sisters loving one another and sticking together. After all, I, and I alone, hated my father because he abandoned my mother and left her alone with me and my brother, who were to see her wasting away every day for want of the love my father would not provide. And this is what was tearing me apart, this self-contradiction and the realization of how many Black women have been used and dumped by Black men. If I was following in their footsteps, it wasn't because I didn't know better. At that time I just didn't know that "losing" me to a white girl would cause sisters any real pain, and even if I had known, I don't think it would have made much difference. That was the conflict.

I loved Vickie. I loved my people, and I realized that society condemned my relationship with a white girl. Yet I didn't give a damn about what society thought (although it would have been helpful if society had left me alone to do as I pleased with my life), and there had to be some way I could help my brothers and sisters while loving Vickie.

No, I didn't accept everything my mentor, Malcolm X, taught me. I couldn't. For most of his life he said:

* Ralph Ellison, *Invisible Man* (New York: Random House, 1947), p. 13.

Let's again face reality. In a world as color-hostile as this, man and woman, black or white, what do they want with a mate of the other race? . . . What is bound to face "integrated" marriages, except being unwelcomed, unwanted, "misfits" in whichever world they try to live in? *

Now, I just couldn't go along with that. America wasn't the only place to live. I wasn't color-hostile and didn't care two cents about what society deemed fit and unfit.

For most of his life, Malcolm X was against integration in any sense of the word. Often he'd say the only thing he liked integrated was a cup of coffee. Yet on January 19, 1965, almost a month before his death, Malcolm X appeared on a television show in Canada and said in response to a question about integration and intermarriage:

I believe in recognizing every human being as a human being—neither white, black, brown or red; and when you are dealing with humanity as a family there's no question of integration or inter-marriage. It's just one human being marrying another human be-ing or one human being living around and with another human be-ing. I may say though, that I don't think it should ever be put upon a black man, I don't think the burden to defend any position should ever be put upon the black man, because it is the white man collectively who has shown that he is hostile toward integra-tion and toward intermarriage and toward these other strides toward oneness. So as a black man and especially as a black American, any stand that I formerly took, I don't think that I would have to defend it because it's still a *reaction* to the society; and it's a reaction that was produced by the society; and I think that it is the society that produced this that should be attacked, not the *reaction* that develops among people who are the victims of that negative society. [Emphasis added.] †

I wrote Vickie a letter, telling her that I also wanted to marry her. But that same evening I started seeing Donna, a girl from Nassau. She worked during the day but at night we

---

* Malcolm X, *Autobiography of Malcolm X* (New York: Grove Press, 1964), p. 276.
† *Autobiography of Malcolm X,* p. 424.

went to the beach; sometimes we swam, and other times we didn't.

In the letter I wrote Vickie I told her how I started reading and wanted to tell her about things I was learning and my plans to make Music and Art the center of political activity. I told her about Malcolm and sent her a passage from his autobiography so she wouldn't get upset.

You may be shocked by these words coming from me, but I have always been a man who tries to face facts and to accept the reality of life as new experiences and knowledge unfold it. The experiences of this pilgrimage have taught me much and each hour in this Holy Land opens my eyes even more . . . I have eaten from the same plate with people whose eyes are the bluest of blue, whose hair was the blondest of blond and whose skin was the whitest of white . . . and I felt the sincerity in words and deeds of these "white" Muslims that I felt among the African Muslims of Nigeria, Sudan and Ghana.*

After that I wrote Vickie many letters about Malcolm X, asking how she felt about him and the influence he had on me, but she never answered my questions; instead she told me that she loved me and that my letters were very beautiful— my writing had improved, she said. This angered me because I was not writing letters to show her how well I could write. I gave her my emotions when I wrote to her, not romantic prose.

Freeport was beautiful and free of cancerous racism. Each day I made up for the living that I had lost in America. The island was clean, and I went to the beach every day and night. Once I stayed near the bottom looking eye to eye with a little fish. Suspended there in clear water, staring at that little fish, nothing else in the world seemed to matter. At night I stood on the coastline watching the water and thinking about what was at the other end of those waves.

My relatives were facing difficulties: they would soon have to leave the island because the government was making it

---

* *Autobiography of Malcolm X,* p. 340.

hard for the indigents to get work. They were deporting the "undesirables." It soon became clear to me what was going on. Freeport was just being developed, transformed into a playground for tourists. They didn't want "common folk" wandering all over the place, scaring the tourists away.

The "common folk" came from all parts of the Caribbean. They spoke Creole (which was a patois of French), broken English, and Spanish. All of them were Black. In Freeport, I saw the Europeans and Americans erecting fabulous white hotels and playing rugby and golf and basking in the sun together while the "common folk" served them lemonade and fruits, and it made me feel like a native in a colony. I thought about things I had read about Europeans. In 1800, they knew only the coastal areas of Africa; by 1900, Africa had been divided among the European exploiters; thirteen years later, European nations controlled 93 percent of African territory.

In the sixteenth century, Central Africa was a territory of peace and happy civilization. Traders travelled thousands of miles from one side of the continent to another without molestation. The tribal wars from which the European pirates claimed to deliver the people were mere sham fights; it was a great battle when half-a-dozen men were killed. It was on a peasantry in many respects superior to the serfs in large areas of Europe, that the slave trade fell. Tribal life was broken up and millions of detribalized Africans were let loose upon each other. The unceasing destruction of crops led to cannibalism; the captive women became concubines and degraded the status of the wife. Tribes had to supply slaves or be sold as slaves themselves. Violence and ferocity became the necessities for survival. The stockades of grinning skulls, the human sacrifices, the selling of their own children as slaves, these horrors were the product of an intolerable pressure on the African peoples, which became fiercer through the centuries as the demands of industry increased and the methods of coercion were perfected . . . *

On the day I left, my friends and relatives came to see me off. I wanted to return as soon as possible. It was an ambiva-

---

* C. L. R. James, *The Black Jacobins: Toussaint L'Ouverture and the San Domingo Revolution* (New York: Vintage Books, 1963), p. 7.

lence similar to what I had felt when I left Knox. There was the beauty of my friends and relatives and the natural beauty of the island; at the same time I saw the natural beauty of the island and people being destroyed by the growth of capitalism. Leaving the islands that day, I thought it deeply ironic that Jamaica, which I loved so much, had actually banned *The Autobiography of Malcolm X*. Even there, my relatives felt, the repression stemmed from clandestine American involvement.

I arrived at Kennedy airport late that night. The busses and subways were running slow. I got home, banged on the door, heard the sound of a dog barking. A new member of the family? Mom Reeves came downstairs and put the dog away before I could see him.

"How was your vacation?"

"It was O.K. What's the dog's name?"

"Caesar."

We sat around the table, but I could sense an uneasiness in her actions and words. I could see that something was wrong. Where was Francis? Dead?

"Where's Francis?"

"Sleeping."

"Then what's wrong?"

She hesitated to answer.

"Your turtle Bruno's dead."

"He's *dead?* How could he *die?*"

"The dog bit his head off."

"Why?"

PART IV

COASTING

September Notes

THE 1969–70 SCHOOL YEAR started off on a low note. Different cliques gathered, questioning each other superficially, "How was your summer?" Already my former enemies were giving me the "evil eye"; members of the Student Union were making mocking jestures at me, bowing and laughing. I could understand their resentment toward me, yet at the same time I thought it unfortunate that they wouldn't permit me to discuss my mistakes so we could work together. As Klein had violated my trust, I had violated their trust.

I went over to City College to get some coffee. I was pouring cream in it, thinking about Malcolm's analogy of how when you had black coffee that was too strong, you made it weak by integrating it with cream; when I looked up, I saw this guy over by a corner staring at the wall. He just sat there facing the wall. I smiled, laughed. Out of curiosity I went over to him.

I had never seen Darryl in such a state of depression. He seemed to have lost something: he didn't look anything like the power he once was. He seemed to have an abandoned look about him and no longer wore an Afro. His hair was even shorter than mine.

"Hi," I said, pulling up a chair. "I've read Malcolm's autobiography. I've come to see that everything you said about me was true, and now I understand what you were trying to do."

Darryl leaned forward and in a very low tone replied, "I've done a lot of reading and thinking. The papers called me a 'charismatic schoolboy—a Cleaver-schooled revolutionary.' I've stopped talking because I've been thinking that you can't be a 95 percent revolutionary. I hope you don't forget that . . . You can't function as a spokesman for your people if you've got a white woman. Black or white, the people won't let you."

I understood what he was saying about the white woman, but not the rest; still, I listened.

"I'm on the outside now, no crowds, no demonstrations, just got too much time to think. It's funny, you can lay your life down for people, be at the vanguard sticking your neck out for them, and suddenly they'll desert you, even turn on you, try to kill you. I stuck my neck out. For what? Life goes on."

I saw in Darryl something that I hoped never to experience for myself, this agony of once having been something, then being nothing, abandoned, displaced. For five years he had existed only for one school. Beyond the school's walls there was a void, nonrecognition of who he was. In two months, overnight, the whole world had changed, reducing him to another face in the crowd. He still had his own distinct Black identity, that had been built up by other people's recognition of him, but his ego was hurting now that he was out of the closed environment which confirmed his old identity; it was impossible to maintain it even within his own consciousness. His reading and thinking had stimulated a transformation that led him to reinterpret his past. Actions he was once proud of, he now denounced as nonsense and unrevolutionary.

Our conversation ended abruptly, Darryl saying, "Keep the fire burning." I went back over to Music and Art with no deep emotional understanding of what Darryl was going through. As he had spoken, I had tried to understand. But only much later was I able to discover the real meaning of what happened that morning.

When I got back, Vickie and I had a long discussion about our relationship. She had always tried to make me feel that she was making a great sacrifice to be with me. I told her that the difficulties worked both ways, that I was finished ass-licking and hiding from her parents, that I didn't have to prove myself worthy of her, that I was tired of running and riding seven fucking miles over to her house at one and two o'clock at night to see her in some park for a few minutes. I was tired of playing around on back staircases and sneaking phone calls when her parents were out.

"Your mother knows what Uncle Tomming is, and degradation. Your parents got a lot of goddamn gall to put me down because I'm Black . . . No more of this using your friends as a front to get out of the house to see me. Lay it straight to your parents."

"Do you know what they'll do to me? They won't pay for anything. They'll take me out of school. They won't pay for college . . ."

"Aw shit, your parents love you. They raised you from birth, and surely they aren't going to throw you out because of me. Trouble with you is you're too dependent on their money. It's your decision to choose between me or your parents' money."

"You're asking me to reject my parents?"

"I haven't asked you to reject your parents. I asked you to reject their money."

My conversation with Darryl had triggered something in me. All morning I was arguing with students and teachers. No one understood what had gotten into me, why I had become so serious. I spoke to teachers about the failure of the school system as I now perceived it. Some agreed with what I had to say; others claimed that *I* was creating the cause and effect, advocating destruction.

Even Mr. King seemed to be laying down a hard line for me. I told him that I wouldn't miss any practices this year. He said, "You're wasting your abilities on this political stuff. These people don't care about you; think about yourself. You got to go to college. You could have won the Cross-Country Championship last year, but you didn't come to practice. And you won the gold medal in the quarter mile only because Terry fell. Winning medals doesn't count in your case. You have the potential to make records. This business of your showing up at the meets and winning medals without practice destroys the team's morale. It isn't fair to the other guys who've been working out. If you miss three practices, you're no longer co-captain; if you miss four, you're kicked off the team."

I understood what Mr. King was saying and respected him. I felt cornered because I loved track, and yet I had another commitment.

Later that day Miss Fineberg, David, Karen, Vickie, and I had a meeting with Klein. The topic of discussion was projects and programs for the coming year. Klein's primary concern was to implement last year's demands. I sat there in silence for a good while, and near the end of the meeting I told him that I wasn't interested in last year's demands, that they had nothing to do with me. I told him that there should be a Humanities Day for Malcolm X and a Cultural Exchange Program sponsored by this school for students all over the city. We had an abundance of talent that was being stifled, I said. It should be used to inspire other students. I suggested that we go into racially torn schools and play jazz, blues, rock, all forms of music. "It's important that those schools see Black and white students working harmoniously to produce something beautiful and creative instead of destructive. This program must be organized along racial lines."

They all looked at me in disbelief even though what I had said was not militant or extreme. Never before, in their presence, had I categorized people in terms of Black or white. Never had I initiated any discussion pertaining to race.

After a long, silent moment we discussed the possibilities of organizing the program, and Klein said that he'd talk it over with the music teachers. In the meantime we set to work organizing three committees that had been demanded the year before by the Occupying Forces: judiciary, censorship, and curriculum review.

Almost immediately the Black and white Student Unions began forming alliances to attack the Student Government, me in particular, because I had no right to implement the committees. They said that I had done nothing to bring these committees about. Admittedly, they were right, but I couldn't see why as students we were so eager to attack one another since none of us had any power. And it was the administration's decision what should and should not be implemented. Why attack me?

To avoid any confrontation with other students, I told the Unions that the matter was out of my hands, that they could meet with Klein and do whatever they wanted. This angered them more than anything else. It was obvious to me that they were looking for a common ground to attack on.

Two weeks later I went to see Klein to find out if the plans for the Cultural Exchange Program had made any progress. He acted as if he didn't know what I was talking about. I was burning inside, but calmly I asked him to call my old principal at George Gershwin Junior High School to see if he was interested in the program. Klein told me to leave the room while he made the call. When I came back, he said the lines were busy. I then asked him to call the principal at Thomas Jefferson High School in Brooklyn. Again he ordered me to leave the room before he made the call. When I entered his office this time, he said that the principal at Jefferson thought it best not to bring "outside groups" into his school because things were "shaky," and he didn't want to "upset anything."

"What do you mean *his* school? The school doesn't belong to him. Didn't you tell him the purpose of the program?"

"I discussed it with everyone, and we're in agreement that it's too risky and not feasible."

"Who is 'everyone'?"

"At this point your program doesn't have priority."

"Why should your plans always have priority? We were elected by the students, and our programs should have priority. And who is 'everybody'?"

Realizing what was coming down from the administration, I went to the students. A suggestion box was set up outside the G.O. office with a sign on it:

WHAT DO YOU, THE STUDENTS, REALLY WANT?

After two weeks we received one letter. We all huddled around the table as Ben opened it:

WE WANT MORE CHICKEN AND NOODLES IN THE CHICKEN AND NOODLE SOUP.

In the same day more letters:

NO MORE ROACHES!

WE WANT TO EAT LUNCH OUTSIDE WHILE THERE IS STILL SUNSHINE.

It was difficult for me to laugh at these letters. It was hard for me to accept what was happening here. It came as a shock because I had expected to hear about more important problems. I couldn't see how any group of people could regress just over a summer. I got angry and began walking out in the middle of meetings and forums with Klein, teachers, and the Student Council. I wasn't going to sit down at a table to discuss "systematic extermination of the roaches." As for Klein, he refused to believe that the roaches existed. He wanted proof and got it. Then a new issue came to the fore—"WHY CAN'T WE HAVE BICYCLE RACKS?"

It had been almost three weeks since the administration abolished the Student/Parent/Faculty Committee and replaced it with the Consultative Council. The Council, as the administration conceived it, had the same representative constituency as the SPFC. However, the administration agreed to abide by all decisions passed by a majority vote of the Council. The administration actually thought it generous to abide by agreements arrived at through "the democratic process." Even the parents and students on the Council were fooled by this deception. Justice had been denied to us for so long that fragments of it appeared to be monumental concessions.

Matthew, a friend, pointed out that "the roaches are coming over here from CCNY because they are cold." The administration hired exterminators, and the roaches were killed.

Even though the Council voted unanimously to permit bicycle racks, the administration vetoed the decision, stating that Board of Education by-laws do not permit such things.

The students were now demanding that they be let outside while there was still sunshine. They were complaining that they were going blind from the darkness in the halls and the cafeteria. The administrative assistant pointed out that students could not be let outside because "they might escape and never come back." The administration suggested that if the G.O. provided padlocks for the outside exits, letting the students outside might be arranged.

Two major decisions were arrived at: that one day should be set aside for the students to be "let loose to paint their own thing on the walls of these hallowed halls"; and that the auditorium would be available to music students for an all-day jam session. These were solutions "as a sort of boost for student and teacher morale and a general overhauling of the lack of atmosphere."

The whole school was going insane. On the back staircases you couldn't even get space to make out any more, and grass and other kinds of drugs were circulating as freely as bubblegum. Walking upstairs on days when there was a strong breeze, you could get a contact high. We used to joke about the back staircases being like motels. One day I ran into the bathroom to take a quick leak before gym. I was late. I pushed open the door to the john, and there was this girl sitting there. I said, "I'm sorry." I ran outside to look at the door—the sign did say: MEN. I went in again, this time to another stall; I couldn't believe it—there was another girl, smoking a joint.

"What's going on? I got to get to gym. I got to take a leak," I said smiling.

They answered, "This bathroom has been liberated."

"From whom?"

I went to gym. I couldn't accept all this nonsense. We went from forums to fires, demonstrations to negotiations, chicken and noodles to roaches. At one point we had been alive socially and politically. The entire school was now stagnant. My plans for a Cultural Exchange Program and Humanities Day for Malcolm X fell dead. By erecting a bureaucratic maze, the administration was now stifling activity within the Student Government and, as expected, with no external pressure, it found no need to make any concessions to us. The student body had become factionalized just as the administration wanted. All attempts at forming a coalition with internal groups had failed. We students should have been allies, but instead we were criticizing each other. I began attending meetings of the Black Security Council. But they still rejected me, made me feel more uncomfortable and unwanted than a white liberal. Nobody listened to anything I said. I felt invisible. They cursed me behind my back, but it always reached my ears by way of so-called friends who took pleasure in telling me these negative things. The BSC branded me permanently as an Uncle Tom, an Oreo. They continued to let my relationship with Vickie get in the way of political progress. They had assumed a righteous attitude of "Blacker than thou." Eventually I told them, "To hell with you, to hell with all of you. None of your asses is Blacker than mine."

I tried to reach the rest of the student body with two major objectives:

Briefly, the by-laws are the rules that govern the school. Within the closed structure of the high school, the by-laws transcend the U.S. Bill of Rights and the Constitution. The by-laws vest the school administration with dictatorial powers and leave us as subjects on pitiful advisory committees, using parliamentary rhetoric, and reaping token and temporary reforms. These by-laws must be revised along democratic lines.

The second objective is a Cultural Exchange Program. . . . Black and white people in the same classroom doesn't mean integration. It is a deception to believe this.

The Exchange Program will give us a chance to meet students of different educational and cultural backgrounds. By concurrently working and holding social functions we can go deeper than M & A's shallow classroom acquaintance relationships. We've got to start thinking universally.

I continued to tell them about the desegregation cases and how, likewise, we could bring the Board of Education before the courts for denying students their rights.

It was painfully obvious that my message did not meet receptive ears, that I was a voice in a vacuum.

Moratorium

THE *New York Post* of October 8, 1969, carried a story by Warren Hoge about the "avalanche of protest" against the war as we prepared for the October Moratorium. He wrote:

Mrs. Martin Luther King, Jr., will lead thousands of war protesters in a candlelight procession from the Washington Monument to the White House. Students will install a large historic bell in the administration building and take turns ringing it every four seconds—once for each of the more than 38,000 Americans killed in combat . . . it's all part of the October 15th Vietnam Moratorium. The target is President Nixon, the only man who has the power to order the troops home, the goal of the movement . . . President Nixon told a White House news conference, "Under no circumstances whatever will I be affected by it."

Around the same time, I got the following letter:

As the person chosen by your high school to be its representative to the City Council, your school and the City Council expect you to attend all General and Special meetings when and if called. The City General Organization Council is the representative body for the city's 275,000 public high school students . . .

My sole intent would be to disrupt the City Council meeting and propose an alternate policy.

Another delegate was needed to attend the City Council meetings with me, so during third period we held a Student Council meeting, and Sarah was elected. She was a very beautiful person, not only in body but also in mind. We were to develop a relationship in which she made it her duty to check up on me constantly—to make sure that I spoke the truth, that my speeches contained accurate facts.

After the Student Council meeting I decided that I might need additional help in disrupting the City Council meeting. Gladstone, Vickie, Terrie, and David accepted the invitation enthusiastically. They were genuinely interested in the Moratorium.

We took the subway down to the High School of Art and Design and found the lunchroom packed with so-called representatives from New York City's ninety-one public high schools. The meeting was called to order, and we were introduced to three so-called advisors of the City Council: George W. Castka, who could easily pass for Santa Claus or Happy, a dwarf out of *Snow White,* was the Assistant Administrative Director; C. J. Sullivan; and Pauline DeMaio. This trio manipulated and controlled the City Council from start to finish. Only when I adopted Klein's mastery of deception would I be in a position to confront them all together. Both Sullivan and Castka were old-timers, obviously failures in climbing upward in the Board of Education's hierarchy. I treated them the same way they treated us, as stupid, inhuman functionaries who were supposed to accept unquestioningly whatever was being shoved down our throats. Even though I knew that these advisors received their subversive and repressive directives from upstairs, they were also part of the problem and had to be confronted on that level.

One of the first student speakers at the orientation meeting was Arthur Swartz, a representative from Bronx High School of Science and one of three candidates for president of the City Council. He told us that he and ten other students from the City Council were part of a Board of Education committee that had formulated certain rights for high school students. They submitted them to Superintendent Lester who in turn told them not to call him; he'd call them. The longer Swartz spoke, the sadder and soppier his tale was. I started laughing out loud trying to disrupt the meeting, repeatedly asking, "Who is this guy?" I started questioning him on every point. He got so confused that he almost broke into tears. Castka relieved him; no sooner did he begin to speak than I started right in again. Soon other students fell in line and started shouting. As the shouting subsided, Castka handed out a short history on the G.O. City Council.

During Castka's verbose speech in which he pointed out that the Board of Education had adopted a new policy of "listening" to students, I stood up and questioned him, interrupted him, and laughed. Many of the students wanted answers to my questions, too. He tried to ignore me. I kept shooting off my mouth. As other students joined in with me, he saw the hopelessness of his situation. Finally he broke down and shouted angrily, "Since you think you know so much, young man, why don't you come up here and run the meeting?"

I stormed up to the front and hurriedly tried to adjust the microphone. It slipped, pinching my little finger. There was a wild burst of laughter. It was probably good that everyone was laughing at me. The fact that I was human got dramatized at just the right time.

As the laughter subsided, I began to speak:

I don't care if these advisors say I'm disrupting your meeting. You're nothing but a bunch of G.O. flunkies. You don't represent anybody but yourselves, and don't let this man convince you otherwise. You don't represent the students who are on drugs.

You don't represent suspended students or those who are being busted and oppressed . . . We are being used by the Board of Education. This Council is an impotent offshoot of the establishment; it's a sandbox government, the kind of harmless student council you hustling kids use to show college admissions offices. It shows that you've learned how *not* to make trouble . . .

The Council is a joke. Look at the rules here:

"No meeting shall be called without the consent of the advisors.

"The legal right of the principal of each high school to veto student recommendations is unquestioned . . .

"The purpose of the city council is to teach democratic procedures within the restrictions placed on the organization by its constitution. And who ratified this constitution? *The associate superintendent in charge of the council . . .*

"All amendments shall go into affect when approved by the associate superintendent . . ."

You don't represent 275,000 high school students. You don't even represent yourselves. This Council is another mechanism used to co-opt us. It is a circus—you are the puppets, these advisors, the puppeteers—and this sham is the same old game of making us think that we have power when in reality we have none . . .

Both Castka and Sullivan tried to take the microphone away, but they were shouted down. I continued:

It was set up by the Board as a scapegoat. Whenever there is a crisis involving so-called outside groups, the Board refuses to give them a hearing, contending that this Council, this farce, is the legal representative group for students. It was set up by the Board of Education not to function in the interest of all students, but for an elite few. Do you realize that the majority of high school students aren't even aware of the existence of this organization? In fact, the majority of high school students aren't even G.O. members. We are even more powerless than a paper tiger. We exhaust our energies by devoting too much time organizing and administering conferences. What has this Council ever done for your school? At no time has it offered universal appeal and relevancy for the 91 schools that it supposedly represents. This business of sitting down with the Board of Education is nothing but a process of co-optation. They use you and me. They tell us to use democracy, yet the Board of Education and high schools are undemocratically governed.

What is important now is not City Council. October 15th is only a week away. On that date the anti-war movement has scheduled a Moratorium, which means that business must stop. If this is the representative body for students, it must function in their interests. Right here we have the ability to go back to our schools and organize for that day. We offer Music and Art as the center for high school coordination for the Moratorium. We will get the permits for the mall and sound equipment. We will also get speakers and music. It is imperative that we stop what we're doing. The high schools must become an effective force against the war in Vietnam . . . We should break down into divisions and organize within our boroughs. Central communications can be maintained through Music and Art. Most important, this communication cannot break down after October 15. This unity is needed to amend certain Board of Education by-laws in our favor.

After I spoke, Castka tried to regain control of the meeting. But it was too late. People were all over the tables, breaking down into separate caucases, beginning to plan.

Castka stood there, red as a cherry, screaming over the microphone that the Board didn't permit such action, that we must follow his orders, that he was in charge, and that things had to be done according to parliamentary procedure. He even sent for the custodian to lock up the cafeteria, but nobody moved. Realizing the hopelessness of their situation, Castka, Sullivan, and DeMaio began to make friends with me. Grinning into my face, they first tried the ego approach, commending me "as a leader." Then came the appeal to rationality—"Things must be done within a system." And finally, Act III, I could have any materials that I needed to organize the rally if I would follow their "sound advice."

While they were speaking, my mind was wandering, going back to my junior year when Klein had used me. But now I could see it clearly, the manipulation and deceit, and I told them to kiss my ass.

When the meeting was over, a few students from Walton and George Washington High Schools came to the front and charged me with trying to put Music and Art in the limelight. They said that Music and Art people thought that they had superior intelligence because they went to a specialized school. These accusations were kind of ironic because the only things special about daily life at Music and Art were the absence of gang fights and overcrowded classes.

The following week was marked with around-the-clock work. Music and Art students were the last to know that their school had become the high school communications center for the Moratorium. Klein and Fineberg had all but put a gag around my mouth. The students on the so-called radical fringe within the school tried to confront me. They wanted Music and Art students to attend workshops rather than organize the citywide rally. They got angry at me because I wouldn't drop what I was doing to do what they wanted.

I overlooked all these internal roadblocks. I didn't pay any attention to the obstacles imposed by Klein. When he barred me from using the school P.A. system to make public announcements, I went outside and got bull horns. When he told me it was illegal to use bull horns in his school, I went outside again, got leaflets from SDS and Panther centers. I had no time to pay any attention to the hassles of Music and Art. At the same time, I was commiting myself to SDS and the Panthers because I was using their stuff. I was the democratically elected president of a white liberal institution, yet I was forced outside to exercise freedom of speech and press.

As the Moratorium gained more public support, the Board of Education made its political move. Expediently, they ruled that public school students would be permitted to use classroom facilities to observe the Moratorium, and predictably, the decision was applauded in the *New York Post*. Only much later would these political moves in the mass media have any significance for me. Not until then would I see how the Board of Education brainwashed the public and turned them against the students. Even I would *use* the media and pay the consequences, in terms of publicity.

Citywide organizing was going on as planned. David had gotten the music together, Terrie the sound permits, and Swartz and I went down to the Moratorium headquarters to explain to the people what we wanted and to ask them to provide speakers. We expected Jim Bouton, Adam Walinsky, and—the only one of the three who showed up—Jimmy Breslin. In the midst of all this, Vickie and Lisa were arguing over who should be on stage introducing the various speakers and music groups. It was obviously a fight over who'd get to be in the limelight. I was busy calling up other schools to find out how they were doing. Despite the Board of Education's public statement, many students were being suspended throughout the city for trying to publicize the peace rally and demonstration. The administration at Music and Art wasn't sticking to the script either, so we did our communicating underground—used the phones when the office people were on lunch breaks, stole paper after school, came in early in the morning and used printing machines.

October 15th ended two weeks of strenuous work. We had all just come from morning workshops at the Ethical Culture Society, where Algernon Black, the director, and others spoke about the war and human commitment.

It was a brisk and beautiful morning; for a change you felt good to be alive. Everyone was happy. We walked and ran through Central Park across the Sheep Meadow. At the band shell we set up the sound equipment.

Our sister school, the High School of Performing Arts, showed up with a theater group as an added attraction. The musicians were tuning their guitars, and marshals were busy cordoning off the area around the concrete shell. The foliage was brilliant and clear in the sunlight, and the coldness of the air made it seem pure enough to inhale. The vacant benches on the ground around the shell became densely packed, hundreds of people became thousands, well over fifteen thousand. There were Black people, Puerto Rican people, white people, all together, all united. As I stood there onstage behind the rostrum, I was fascinated. I found it difficult to believe that this idea had grown out of the minds of five people, that all that was needed to organize it was dedication and sacrifice, not cumbersome committees and large numbers of people. As I stood behind the rostrum lowering the microphones, I looked over the crowd of thousands, with more still pouring in, and thought back to the days when I was afraid to speak in front of a classroom of thirty people.

When I finished my speech, two Black sisters began to sing "Tell Me Why You're Crying, My Son," and I stood there motionless, watching peace signs waving at me. I returned the peace sign and walked off.

After my speech there was anti-war music, singing, and speeches that all seemed to blend into one another; the truth and facts were played in many different keys but always came out sounding the same. As the program went on, the press showed up asking for me, but I got lost in the crowd. They started calling for me over the microphones, but I didn't respond. The media always singled out individuals (usually men) in movements. They built them up so high that they appeared to be more important than the movements and often became divided from them. Instead of covering the Moratorium, which was a failure, they would rather have reported how old I was, where I lived, went to school, if I was on drugs, what I thought about all the wonderful people out there or some other shit like that.

I watched Swartz and Vickie onstage, jumping around in front of the cameras and reporters, screaming over the microphones, telling the people to shut up, move back, line up. It was such an obvious ego trip. Sisters in the crowd where I stood were getting angry. One yelled out, "Get those fucking honkies offstage!" I went to tell Vickie to cool it, but she told me to get off the stage and keep the people back. She was all wrapped up in another world. I'd never seen her like this before. I split from the Moratorium scene.

I found Lynn, a girl I had met in Spanish and played around with in my junior year. We went walking through the park and I told her what I thought of the Moratorium.

Even before we had started organizing, I realized what the end result would be, a kind of fascinating beauty. In fact, it was so beautiful that it was hard to grasp hold of the mind and hurl it into the horrors of the battlefields of Vietnam. Standing there listening to the same speech over and over again took your mind away from the realities of war, the burned babies, scorched earth, and scattered fragments of human limbs. Although I was against America's aggression in Southeast Asia, the Moratorium itself meant very little to me. I had used its organizational strategy to serve my own purposes, which I considered practical, but which everyone else thought trivial.

The Moratorium strategy is the easiest and least effective method of protest. There have been mass demonstrations before. In 1968, there had been one in Chicago during the Democratic Convention. There had been a Civil Rights March on Washington, D.C. Our extensive protesting pressured Johnson into stepping down, but who replaced him? The fallacy of the Moratorium strategy is that too many people have misconceptions that the war is run by one man alone. They fail to see that the war is a complex of government, the military, and big business. Masses of people singing songs, ringing bells, wearing armbands, buttons, and holding candles means nothing; it only cleanses guilty consciences, provides colorful photographs for magazines. Once guilty consciences are cleansed, then what? And how many people in those demonstrations actually feel that the blood of thousands of dead American and Vietnamese lives is on their hands? No matter how many people the Moratorium could put on the streets, there are always more people inside the four walls of their homes, watching it on TV. The Moratorium would not achieve an end to the war; it would only make martyrs out of hoarse voices, weary feet, and sore behinds, and vent frustration that ultimately would present no threat to the Establishment.

This Moratorium was already arousing the anger of the factory workers and people who didn't understand that we had no right to be in Indochina. A conflict between supporters and opposers of the Moratorium was inevitable; it was only a question of time.

There were Moratoriums scheduled for November and December and every month after that until there was "total withdrawal of American troops." How long would people keep coming out on the streets? How long would they carry pig heads on poles—symbols of Nixon and Agnew—before they realized that this was hopeless? The system that caused Vietnam had to be uprooted. If not, nothing would be gained.

Unless the Moratorium produced more than headlines for *The New York Times,* it would use up the energy in the student movement. The whole thing was like a light bulb just before it's ready to burn itself out. It burns very brightly but only for a short time.

My latent role in this symbolic protest was to see just how effectively an organizational plan could be carried out by using the City Council as a base to organize the high schools. It took two weeks of organizing on short notice to bring fifteen thousand people out into the streets. We had more sound equipment and leaflets than we needed for the job, and there was no doubt left in my mind that Music and Art had the capacity to organize the students of the other ninety public high schools throughout the city for an all-out confrontation with the Board of Education.

Lynn and I looked up at a plane spouting red smoke. Two anti-Moratorium parachuters dressed in red, white, and blue landed amid a crowd of onlookers in the Sheep Meadow. The pigs took them away. Afterward we played around in the park for a while.

After a while we came upon a stream embedded between flat, slanting rocks and went to the highest one. There we sat talking about each other, about why things weren't working out between the two of us, and eventually, I pulled her close to me and kissed her. We left the rocks and continued to play in the Sheep Meadow. We lay on the grass for some time, holding each other tightly, feeling as much as we could of each other's bodies. Still holding each other, we rolled and rolled and rolled over the grass. We talked for a while after, and as the sky got darker, we got ready to leave the park—through separate exits.

In the cold of the night, I got a call from Vickie. She put it straight—told me that my ego was crushed because I had to take orders from her, that she was involved now, and wouldn't have that much time for me. I yelled back. She ended the relationship. I said, "Well, fuck it," and slammed the phone down. Mom Reeves came downstairs. "Listen here, I don't want any cursing in my house."

Friendship Circle

PEOPLE WHO WERE supposedly my friends took pleasure in telling me all the negative things that were being said behind my back. I saw it coming, like a fist in the face: I was fighting a losing battle. Within Music and Art small waves of jealousy began to build up against me, and Fineberg began to throw more fuel on the fire by using class time to denounce me as being irresponsible for leaving the Moratorium rally. Even people who had worked with me organizing the rally interpreted my leaving the demonstration as "selfish and harmful" because if I had stayed to be interviewed, we could have gotten more "publicity." When I explained why I didn't want any publicity, that the rally was important and not I, they interpreted that as a holier-than-thou attitude and an ego trip. At the same time, if I had stayed to have my picture taken, I'm sure I would have been accused of the same thing, ego-tripping.

There seemed to be no getting around the criticism. The most cutting came from Vickie. She had bought all the magazines that had covered the rally. In each article, I had been given the credit for having the idea while she and Swartz were described as "kids having a good time." She stood there ranting, "Look at this shit. You weren't the only one who spoke, and yet they only mentioned *your* speech, your name. Look at all the other people who worked on organizing—only *you* got the credit. The only reason they put you in the limelight is that you're Black—a Super Black. If a white person had made the same speech, it wouldn't have meant anything."

I wanted to punch her in the face.

But there was truth in what she said. White people *were* beginning to pay attention to what Black people had to say. What was happening, though, was that whites who could not psychologically accept Black people as their intellectual equals or even superiors began to say that Blacks were getting a hearing not because of what they were saying but merely because they were Black. The implication being that if a Black intellectual was cloaked in white skin, he would no longer be considered an intellectual. Apart from this her whole attitude was characteristic of domineering, ego-ridden whites, who hate to see Black people making strides that surpass them in any way.

Within my friendship circle I was being buried alive. By making my name and actions a constant theme for debate, both teachers and students were building me up to be bigger than I was, to be something that I wasn't. As Klein and Fineberg began to stifle political activity within the school by canceling all but one of the scheduled student forums and prohibiting informational bulletins, I was completely cut off from the student body as a whole. I acted without consultation from anyone. I began to identify myself with Roger, who was dropped in a bottle of chloroform with the lid slowly being tightened. I spoke to Miss Mirro, whom I now called Fran, and to my surprise she recommended that I resign even though I had over three months left till the end of my term.

"Everything is working against you. Darryl tried, and you saw what happened to him."

"I'm not Darryl." I used to hate it when she compared me to other people.

"You're on the same course. The repression is going to come down on you from all angles with more force because you're more dangerous than Darryl was."

"But I haven't done anything to anyone. I haven't threatened anyone or taken over anything."

Fran looked at me for a while, probably thinking, He still doesn't understand. "You don't have to *do* anything. You represent a threat. You have the potential to destroy."

"But I haven't . . ."

"The fact that you have power and the potential to use it either way makes you a dangerous person."

By this time I was grinning. I could not see myself as the danger she made me out to be. There was still a long way to go before I could consider myself as a threat. I needed more support.

I had not reached one of the most powerful factions in the school. I spoke to Mr. Davis, president of the Parents' Association, and requested permission to speak at the meeting that was coming up. He said that I could. The only available time he gave was at night, coinciding with the indoor Borough Championship track meet, but I accepted.

Meanwhile, in my classes I saw and felt the deadness and boredom of the school. And although as a result of my involvement I got only one or two hours' sleep at night, I was glad that I had something to do to take me out of the abyss that I saw other students in. It was an overwhelming down for me to see musicians going to class after class, practicing and practicing behind closed doors and being let out to perform only two or three times a term. This bothered me because they could have been inspiring other students in culturally deprived schools. They could have been in the ghettos playing for the children or even right here on the hill in Morningside Park, playing for Harlem—for the kids outside during the warm months. Children from neighboring public schools did get to come in and hear the rehearsals—probably one of the worthiest accomplishments of the Student Government during my involvement.

Most of my teachers understood my situation but told me that although I submitted all the assignments, they really couldn't give me as high a grade as my work warranted because I missed too many classes.

The day the Parents' Association meeting finally came, I had to go to the Manhattan Indoor Meet after school. It had been almost two months since I had seen Mr. King—almost two months since I'd told him that I wasn't going to miss any more practices. I wasn't sure if I was still on the team. When I got to the armory, I saw my friends. After about an hour of pleading, I got permission from Mr. King to run. He said, "It will probably do you some good to get whipped in the same event you won last year. You're supposed to be defending a title, remember?"

I was angry. All through warm-up I was psyching myself up. I never resented anything that Mr. King said to me. I respected him and knew what he was asking from me. I wanted nothing more than to be a champion—one that he coached—but the time was not there.

We were at the starting line. Bang! We shot down the straightaway and into the turn. Two guys were in front of me. I'd get them on the second lap. The gun lap, I moved out in front, began to push, pull away, but I could feel it—the strength wasn't there. I closed my eyes for just a second, opened them, and saw a Brooklyn Tech guy in front of me. I made one last effort but couldn't do it. I placed second. Mr. King said nothing to me, just put the silver plaque in my hand. The psychological defeat lingered. Always in my mind, if, if, if only . . . but I had no one to blame but myself. That I never came last but felt victory snatched from me was like a slow mental death.

I sat through the meet and watched our team snatch medals left and right. When the outdoor season came—there was no question about it—we'd be in the front for the championship.

When you're a senior, it hits you that you're going through

the cycle for the last time, that as each scheduled championship meet passes, it pushes you nearer to your last high school meet. When you realize this, all your energies are exerted in every race; you feel like it's the last one of its kind you'll ever run.

After the meet I took the subway up to Lynn's house to wash up and have dinner before the Parents' Association Meeting. She was one of the most beautiful girls I had ever known. We had seen each other intermittently throughout the year. All through the summer I had written her letters. At one point I even wanted to marry her. Now we were just close friends.

There was such a difference between what I felt for people personally, in terms of love, and what I felt for them politically. On the one hand, I loved her, very much; still it was students like her I despised the most. She was one of the most intelligent people in the school, yet she didn't participate in anything but her own personal affairs, never giving a thought about using her brains to help other people.

In all honesty, I hated those students who lived for getting high grades. I hated them because they never took their behinds out of the classroom to confront the problems they complained about. They analyzed and criticized the way everybody else was struggling but did nothing themselves to make things better.

After dinner, I spoke to Lynn for a while, thanked her parents for the hospitality, and made my way back up to Harlem. I got to Music and Art at about 8:30 and sat in the back of the auditorium until 10 when I was finally given a chance to speak. I got angry, asked them how would they like it if their child were in my position, not doing homework, up here in Harlem at 10 P.M.—not getting home until 3 in the morning because they were up here speaking to some parents. After a seemingly endless series of apologies by the parents, I began my speech:

Much of what I have to say is negative and subjective because up until now you've heard only the positive side, which the administration has always fed you . . . They publicize the white lie and submerge and negate the Black truth. This is done to keep you uninvolved in internal affairs. You remain complacent—coming to the school for coffee and cookies but never once really probing into the filth that we live with here every day . . . Unlike the picture presented to you tonight, the lunchroom is filthy, over-crowded. The library is not open for students who want to study during lunch, and even this auditorium, which seats over a thousand people, is not available . . . The Student Government is powerless.

It is the administration who invites disruption. Repression gives birth to frustration and aggression . . . If we had influence, at least some influence, as much as you do with the administration, then there would be no need for "subversive" activities . . . You can't see the apathy, the stagnation. The students must be given a chance to further their creativity outside the classroom curriculum . . . I am not leveling an attack against the administration as much as I am asking for your support to see that justice be laid down.

I said nothing about the drugs I saw circulating in the school * or about the undercurrent of racial polarization.

---

* According to a New York City Police Department press release of Tuesday, February 17, 1970, in 1969, 12,700 people between sixteen and twenty were busted by New York police for using dope. This was an increase of 65 percent over the previous year. Board of Education Curriculum Bulletin No. 16, "Prevention of Narcotics Addiction and Substance Abuse" (pp. 19–20), gave the following instructions to all teachers:

When a teacher is concerned about a student who he thinks may be a user of drugs or an abuser of chemical substances, he should refer the case to the principal.

[To make teachers inform more efficiently on their students, the Board of Education has also provided additional instructions:]

The day-by-day behavior of all pupils should be carefully observed by all school personnel. Any marked deviation from normal behavior should be viewed as a possible clue.

Records of observations should be entered on the pupil's health card or on the health envelope.

All necessary data should be relayed to the immediate superior who should refer to others as the need arises.

Those who normally supervise play areas, lavatories, stairways, locker rooms, and other places where pupils congregate should be given additional training in the area of drug abuse. Unused rooms should be locked.

A careful check on attendance should be made, not only by the official teacher, but by each subject teacher. A record should be kept of pupils leaving the room; lavatories should be carefully supervised at all times.

[They're even watching you when you take a shit.]

Klein went directly to the microphone and stated, "Never has the school been slandered so politely." He went on to apologize for my entire speech. Klein was under so much fire that he started lying his head off about the "wonderful school spirit" and a "girls' track team." There were shouts of disapproval from the parents. I was storming back to the microphone but was held back by some parents who tried to calm me.

"Take it easy. If you go up there with your temper now, you'll turn the people who are supporting you, against you."

They walked me to the back of the auditorium and sat with me while the parents voiced support for the students, pledged to do whatever was necessary to help. After about three hours of parliamentary debate, they passed a motion to have students at all their meetings.

Parents, when organized, can be the most potent force that a school administrator has to contend with. Organized parents don't take very long to get things changed in a school or to have an unwanted administrator removed. One letter from an angry parent is enough to make some administrators go off on a tangent to remedy things before their goose is cooked.

The meeting was over at about 1:30 A.M. I gained so much support from the parents that many invited me to their homes to discuss the problems. Some parents even formed small groups, and I spoke to them until all hours of the morning.

Only once was there any animosity between myself and a parent. It seems that this man had read an article about my suspension last June. He said, "One thing that really impresses me about you: you're not like those other Blacks who irrationally talk about separatism."

This is what I began to hate most in white people—as soon as you let down your defenses, started talking to them and showing them you were human, they'd exploit you. Things

---

Teachers should investigate when pupils arrive in taxicabs or cars or begin to wear sporty or expensive clothes, especially in the low socio-economic areas.

There should be a close relationship between the school principal and local police in all matters that relate to law enforcement.

that they would never dream of saying in front of the more militant brothers and sisters, they felt at ease to shove down my throat because they saw me smiling in their presence. When this man said that to me, he might just as well have had a brush with white paint and shoved it in my face. I told him:

"At this point in history it's more irrational to talk about integration than separatism. Did *you* try to integrate with the Germans in World War II? I'm not a separatist. I know that Hasidic Jews advocate separatism just like Black separatists do. Black people wear red, green, and black, colors of nationalism, of liberation. Hasidic men wear big black hats and long black coats; you'd think *they* were advocating Black power. Even though Hasidic Jews are a small minority in this country, they make you bourgeois Jews feel guilty, don't they? They are living symbols to remind you of what you are —an Uncle Tom Jew."

In fact, the Jews did try to integrate with the Germans, to become German Jews. They thought of themselves as Germans first and Jews second. Even up to the point where they entered the gas showers, they didn't know what was happening to them as Jews. When they got released from the concentration camps, many of them went right back to Germany.

I could understand why my comments made this man angry, but he also was insensitive and had abused me by demeaning my people.

I continued to meet with parents. We discussed everything from racial polarization to drugs and the Cultural Exchange Program. One mother even offered a van to help transport musicians from our school to other schools. All during this time I had lost contact with the student body. It used to surprise me to find that many parents were more receptive to what I had to say than their children were. I learned a lot about parents and their fears, many of which came from meetings with school officials and PTA bulletins with "Letters From the Principal's Desk." Administrators always built up violence within the high schools as a reason for repression and resisting change. Administrators don't want parents in school because with them around, it would be harder to create illusions of utopia in the midst of dungeons.

Every time I met with the parents I learned more. All this information, I felt, would help me in one way or another to design a uniform program to confront the Board of Education.

Contrastingly, in school Klein caught me walking into the building one day, ordered me into his office, and demanded that I stop meeting with the parents. I told him that I wasn't representing the school or anyone but myself and that he had no jurisdiction over my actions outside the school. However, he seemed to feel that he did and showed me a copy of a resolution up for adoption called Emergency Suspensions by School Principals. Among other things, it stated that the school principal had emergency power to suspend a student from school "when he determine[d] that the overt behavior of that student prevented the orderly operation of the class" or "present[ed] a (clear and present danger) of physical injury to school personnel or students."

It was a subtle threat. I don't know who he was trying to kid. I was now in Darryl's shoes—secure because I had enough "potential" to bring down a whole lot of pressure on him—and he knew it. With support from the parents, I was invulnerable to his arbitrary powers.

Only one thing bothered me. I began to feel uncertain inside, like the rug was being pulled out from under me, like I thought I had been drinking water, but it was actually wine. I was going on borrowed time. I developed a chest pain that started coming and going, then started coming more than it was going, and each time it came it took longer to go.

Andover

KLEIN WAS ON my back for the volume of by-laws he lent me, and I had no intention of returning it to him. One of the things high school students and prisoners had in common, it seemed, was that they weren't allowed to see law books. The only time that the rules and regulations were ever shown was during the trial, and so you broke rules you didn't know existed. How could you defend yourself when you were already tried and convicted of a crime you didn't even know about? The majority of students had never seen the rules that controlled their lives.

I was going down to disrupt the City Council again. I wasn't going to let the Council meet in peace until they dealt with the educational system that institutionalized racism, that oversocialized us to a point where we stopped questioning orders, contained us, and left us helpless and unable to make independent decisions. I wanted them to look at the overall picture of students flipping out on drugs, unable to cope with the system. With all of the problems going on, the Board was trying to pacify us by sending us to conferences out in the country. I felt that it was my duty to attend and disrupt these meetings. I would do so until either the advisors were ousted or the organization was destroyed. I felt that students must control their own organizations, for only then could we truly represent ourselves.

When I got down to the Council meeting, many students were happy to see me, telling me how wonderful the Moratorium had turned out. I laughed and smiled right along with them—it was not a pretense so much as it was a feeling that these smiling faces soon would look frustrated and confused when the students came to grips with themselves and understood how they were being used. If they didn't understand, I'd soon tell them.

The advisors saw me and said nothing. This was a psychological game. I saw it happen during the demonstrations at Music and Art. After each demonstration the school was immediately repaired; the next day it looked like nothing had been accomplished to shake the power structure, that nothing had changed. The expected result was that you considered your efforts futile and gave up.

I decided right there that I was going to stick around. I realized that if I wasn't there constantly disrupting and challenging the Authority, no one else would take the initiative. The students on the Council weren't radical *or* conservative. They were just there following orders, so-called leaders of tomorrow.

As usual, Castka took the floor. He showed slides of the conference location. When he finished, I started in, "What has the conference ever accomplished? Nothing, absolutely nothing. He's trying to put us out to pasture on a farm."

Almost immediately, Castka, Sullivan, and DeMaio were upon me, yelling at me to stop causing trouble. All of us were surprised by their outburst and got on the defensive.

After distributing information materials, Castka told us that the purpose of the Welling Conference was to plan a program for the 1969–70 school year.

"What happened to last year's program?"

"Shut up."

"Freedom of speech is—"

"Shut up. *I'll* tell you when you—"

"You'll tell, hell!"

The meeting was cut short. Castka angrily told us that we had to elect a chairman for the conference and an acting chairman for the City Council. I was elected to both positions. It looked like Castka and Sullivan were having fits when they realized what had happened—that I was *their* baby now.

We arrived at the Hudson Guild Farm in Andover, New Jersey, on Saturday sometime around midday.

SATURDAY

1. ARRIVE AT THE HUDSON GUILD FARM
     If the weather is clear— leave your luggage on the grass outside the main house
     If the weather is rainy— put your luggage in the main living room of the main house

2. RECEIVE YOUR ROOM ASSIGNMENT
     Proceed to your room and make your bed
     Take whatever you will need between now and 4:00 P.M. with you to the barn. LEAVE NO VALUABLES IN YOUR ROOM

3. RECREATION TIME
     Walk to Big Rock; walk to Bear Pond; walk through the farm

4. GENERAL MEETING IN THE BARN
     Reports from the discussion groups
     Square dancing
     Dancing

     Camp Fire and Sing

     Return to the dining room for a "late snack"

5. RETURN TO QUARTERS
     Lights out

Many of us were rejuvenated by the chance to feel real grass beneath our feet and to breathe clean air. Guys were planning to meet with girls during the night. I also momentarily lost sight of the reason in our coming here. I began to take interest in Judith, a sister from Jackson High. She was about my height, and her eyes were a light brown, like her hair. She was one of those girls you felt good talking to—you knew you didn't have to put on any airs with her. I could spend hours, days on end talking to her. No girl ever made me feel as good as she did. I felt so gooood. But several times I felt urged to tell her that I was sexually involved with white girls. I wanted so much to know how she would react to me if she knew that. I weighed this, decided not to take the chance because I wanted her too much to risk losing her. I wanted to see her after this conference.

"I want to see you again."

She was hesitant, about to say no. Please don't.

"Please don't. You don't understand how much you mean to me."

"Oh boy," she said, smirking. I laughed.

She meant so much. I really wanted her, at this moment, more than anything else in the world. Please.

"*Please* Judith, give it a chance, let me see you."

She answered with a solemn look, "I'm engaged." Shit.

"When are you getting married?"

"Maybe June."

"Judith, I can't tell you how much . . ." I couldn't tell her how much I needed the love of a Black woman.

She started laughing again. "You don't even know me."

"It only takes time. I want you now, can only want you more—can only grow closer to you in time."

"I'm engaged," she said sternly.

"Can we do things before you get married?"

"I'll think about it."

I sincerely wanted her, but always on my mind were those Black girls at Music and Art who hated me, called me a Tom because of Vickie. Their incessant cursing of me had so warped my thinking that I actually thought about taking Judith up on the hill to M & A so they could see that I didn't worship white women. This was sick: in my mind I was exploiting her, thinking of using her as an ornament to prove I was Black. How could I be this insensitive and live with myself?

I would see her four times after this conference. Each time I hurt myself a little more because I truly loved her and realized that it could last only so long. Never did I bring her anywhere near the hill. I didn't have to prove anything to anyone.

By nightfall almost every guy had a girl. Some overenthusiastic girls had small groups of guys chasing after them in and out of the woods and behind the barn. The more sedate students, all three of us, were reading comics and drinking coffee in the kitchen.

What was happening here was obvious. All of us had been in the crowded, filthy, noisy city, and now we were in the woods. We were like animals set free from a zoo. The planners of the conference conceived it as primarily an opportunity to give city kids a chance to get out in the country. As for political planning, it was a joke. In two days over a hundred students who didn't even know each other were supposed to formulate a uniform and relevant program for 275,000 high school students. Again we were being deceived. It was not our program. It was designed intentionally by the Board of Education to fail.

During breakfast one of the so-called advisors announced that we should split up into smaller discussion groups. In opposition I said, among other things, "We must remain united in one body so that our decisions can be uniform and relevant to all of us."

The advisor got angry at my attack on them and the language I used. She started screaming back at me, appealing to everybody to see that I was leading them to make the same mistake that people had made before. She tried to convince them that more could be accomplished in smaller groups because people would be less inhibited and would participate more effectively.

In response I looked at the students and jokingly said, "I'll bet many of you are really afraid to run this show on your own."

The advisors were so angry that they stood there huddled together like wet chickens, watching the delegates march off toward the barn. Only a few chumps remained behind to ask for guidance.

As the day went on, I found myself in a whole mess of trouble. My plan of having one large meeting was failing. We had been arguing and cursing for the best part of five hours. The students I called chumps had finished their resolutions; we didn't have a sentence to show.

I felt all alone, tongue-tied, as again and again I tried to make them understand that the by-laws had to be the major target, that without revision of the by-laws, nothing would be changed. I was almost fanatical in my plea for them to understand that the by-laws had to be rewritten. I felt like a madman nobody understood, that I was speaking to deaf and blind people or zombies, that I was speaking a foreign language they didn't understand. The entire room was filled with people who just sat in silence, staring at me sweating and ranting. I felt that I was breaking down inside, that my mind was going berserk.

People started putting me down. One student shouted out, "I don't see why Reeves has got us concerned with his problems. If he's got some kind of trouble with his principal, that's *his* business. You know, Reeves was that guy who got suspended in the papers last year. He's probably trying to get revenge on his principal."

Shit. It was a long story. How could I get it across? I was pissed off. Mad.

"What the fuck you mean *my* problem? I'm not talking about me-Klein-Music and Art, I'm talking about the whole goddamn high school system. I ain't talking about me-Klein-my so-called suspension. I'm talking about what it all represents." I felt a throbbing in my brain. I couldn't finish what I was saying because I got dizzy and sat down, wiping the sweat from my eyes.

I was a wall being demolished brick by brick. I felt their eyes on me through the quiet in the room. Finally a girl's voice broke the silence. "The advisors said that this was going to happen, and we turned our backs. I think we owe them an apology." I then heard people leaving.

When my senses came back, I saw six people waiting, still willing to stick it out with me. It was a bittersweetness, a feeling of realization of the difference between friends and support. So often I confused the two. I would always remain indebted to my friends who stayed with me in spite of my shortcomings.

We talked for a while and formulated succinct resolutions on college guidance centers—to be funded by the City—revision of the by-laws, establishment of a Cultural Exchange Program, and student-controlled organizations. After the meeting I went straight to bed.

I pushed open the door to my room. Two girls were standing before me.

"What do you want?"

"People are saying things about you."

"Oh, like what?"

"Why don't you apologize to the advisors? It might ease a lot of tension."

"I don't apologize to people who spitefully use me."

"They haven't used you."

"I'm not giving them a chance to! You don't seem to realize that consciously or unconsciously, they are instrumental in perpetuating institutionalized racism. When they manipulate and deceive, they destroy the confidence that you and I have that things can be done in peace. There has never been peace. They don't allow us to make decisions by ourselves. We graduate still dependent, still unable to determine our own lives. Look what they've done to your minds—made you feel *guilty* about being independent . . ."

Both of them looked at each other as if to say, He's hopeless. "Everybody here is on your side—that is, most of the students. But you just have to let up some time, compromise here and there. The by-laws should be our major objective, but if people don't see it that way, you can't shove it down their throats. People have different priorities and, besides, nobody has ever *seen* the by-laws."

"I'll see you tomorrow," I said in a low tone.

I had failed. I'd asked these people to have faith in me, and it hadn't worked. Although I had not dominated the discussion, my insistence that the by-laws be given priority annoyed them. I saw myself sweating and ranting, surrounded by blank faces desperately trying to understand, becoming frustrated not because of my uncompromising attitude, but because they could not identify with the repression I was talking about. It was only too obvious that none of them had ever stepped out of line, had ever opposed any authority and been oppressed. My inability to get them to identify with the problem tied my tongue, reduced me to repeating, "If only you could see." The bureaucracy had been so successful in indoctrinating them that they failed to see the suspensions, expulsions, and arrests of their fellow students. It was selfish and short-sighted of them to say that my problem was an arbitrary suspension. It was everybody's problem. It happened to a lot of people. They could not yet perceive their principals and schools as I saw them—as dictators and colonies. But I hadn't known any different either before I was suspended and repressed. I was trying to save others from having to go through the process. Why did people have to wait until the crisis hit before they found out that channels to deal with them fairly weren't there?

I had to laugh at myself for wondering that. After all, I had gone through two separate and distinct thought processes, one that had developed Black consciousness, the other a colorless student awareness that saw disruption, but went further in search of the motivation for the disruption. Many of the students hadn't been jolted into any new kind of consciousness. How could I condemn these students for not identifying with the general problem? I'd made a mistake. I had expected others to automatically share my basic assumptions and experiences.

Consequently, these students reacted to me in much the same way that I had reacted to my pressure—reject it, proceed with what is clear to me, with what I have experienced, with what I believe. No amount of speaking, ranting, or pleading, I realized, would ever make them see the universal problem. They had to experience for themselves the frustration and fruitless process of working peacefully in the system. My forcing it on them only obstructed their vision—made them unable to see that I was an ally, not an adversary, a friend, not an enemy.

The student mind didn't have to be revolutionary or conservative; it needed to be a mind always willing to look for the MOTIVATION behind the actions of groups or experiences the person had nothing to do with. It was like the process of developing a "Black consciousness." That means that no matter where a student came from, he or she would not only focus on the problems within their immediate institution but could also identify with the struggles of students in other schools and would feel responsible for taking up the cause as if it were his or her own. Isolated struggles are no more than that, and so an arbitrary suspension was dismissed as "his business." The group then proceeded to talk about soda machines.

This realization made me see the necessity of refining my approach. I couldn't continue to go around cursing and putting people down. The only time I'd put it straight was when it was the plain truth. I would have to be discreet.

Those students who had come to my room said that despite everything, I still had a chance. I was lucky and thankful that they were giving me a second chance.

The following day I chaired my two sections without incident. At the large meeting I read the cumulative report and apologized to the students.

We had a student forum coming up at Music and Art. I initiated the Cultural Exchange Program by inviting five representatives from other schools to share their problems with us so they could realize the necessity of unity throughout the city in order to benefit all students.

The Issue

ONLY A FEW DAYS after the Andover Conference, on October 30, 1969, *The New York Times* carried an article entitled "Text of a School Board Resolution on Student Rights." * The document referred to was the Board of Education's resolutions on "Rights and Responsibilities for Senior High School Students." The Board's explanation, in part, for this so-called "Student Bill of Rights" was "to make students responsible for their conduct" and expand "the range of their responsibilities." It was meant to "foster an atmosphere of trust." And yet who had formulated this resolution, this Student Bill of Rights?

The Board of Education's document grew largely out of a memorandum prepared by lawyers of the New York Civil Liberties Union and presented to the Board of Education. The original document, while not embodying all of the NYCLU's proposals, did provide some real guarantees for students' rights. However, during the summer of 1969, the Board

---

* See Appendix B: Board of Education's Bill of Rights.

of Education conferred with the Principals' Association. The
Association officials were unanimous in their opposition to
any broadening of student power. Not only did the boys in
the Principals' Association reject the original draft on Student Rights, they also formulated firm, fascist guidelines to
handle student dissent.* A remarkable, confidential document reprinted in the *High School Free Press,* this guide to
counterinsurgency cut off healthy criticism, reduced active
participants to passive observers, and maligned legitimate
criticism as open attacks on the school structure.

The Board of Education, in concert with the High School
Principals' Association, proceeded to water down the original
draft, and even this weaker bogus resolution was not acceptable to the High School Principals' Association. Ultimately,
the comic strip guidelines (published in *The New York
Times*) were accepted. During this entire process, no student
organization was consulted. The Bill was not written by students, not amended by students, and not passed by students.

Virtually every section of this document included a qualifying phrase that permitted circumvention by principals.
Actually, this bogus proposal was merely a restatement of existing rights already upheld by laws and courts, already broken
by principals in New York and other states throughout the
country. While superficially granting us our Constitutionally
protected rights of free speech and assembly, the limitation,
"so long as they do not interfere with the regular school program," left a vacuum for administrative interpretation. The
"Explanation of the Bill" states: "In no way does it diminish
the legal authority of the school and of the Board of Education to deal with disruptive students." There was no question
here about who was going to define "disruptive." Clearly,
while allowing students certain limited rights, the resolution
negated the concept of student self-determination.

These token resolutions came only after militant actions by
high school students in the spring of 1969. This document
failed to reevaluate or exchange power within the educa-

---

* See Appendix C: Confidential: For High School Principals Only.

tional system. The principal was still free to exercise arbitrary and discriminatory power.

The educational bureaucracy had taken it upon itself to grant rights that were not even within its jurisdiction. Despite a statement issued in 1968, by Dr. Ewald Nyquist, the Commissioner of Education, principals still continued to suspend students for wearing dungarees.* If this insignificant "right" warranted suspension, why were we to believe that other rights would not warrant harsher punitive action? Moreover, while enumerating the so-called rights and responsibilities, the document failed to provide any realistic channels through which reforms could be achieved peacefully, within the system. Such vague phrasing as: "to participate in making decisions," "to share in formation of school policy," "to discuss . . . and assure implementation" were evidence of the Board of Education's lack of honesty. Nowhere in the document were there outlined powers to assure implementation of anything.

This document of liberal deceit continues in the tradition of bureaucratic lies. In no way does it confront the fundamental problems facing thousands of high school students. It is totally unresponsive to the needs of Black, Puerto Rican, and lower-income white students who have been channeled into inferior vocational high schools. It has failed to confront drugs, racism, inadequate college guidance, police repression, community control, intimidation through unfair grading and academic record-keeping, discriminatory and arbitrary power of principals, and powerless student governments. It deals puritanically with censorship of obscene and political material found on school property.

Just who is to determine what constitutes obscenity? Even the Supreme Court has difficulty grappling with that question. And what materials promote racial or religious prejudice? A high school principal can and probably will decide that an occasional four-letter word makes an underground

---

* According to *The New York Times Encyclopedia Almanac* 1971 (p. 536), the major issues resulting in demonstrations were general disciplinary rules and dress codes.

paper or leaflet obscene or that the advocacy of Black power is an endorsement of racist attitudes.

The section on journalism requires that school newspapers be governed by "responsible standards of journalism." "Irresponsible standards of journalism" usually means that a student newspaper has published an article critical of the administration. Many school officials are willing to listen patiently to student demands. The problem is that when the action is taken, those demands are invariably ignored. The High School Principals' Association said: "Where militants demand a hearing on a transient issue, they must submit an agenda and their recommendations in advance, allowing time for consideration and consultation. TRANSIENT ISSUES MAY DIE STILLBORN."

Students are not viewed as people. We are merely functions, statistics that are filed in computers. At one point in American history it was legal to view Black people as property. Students are also viewed as property from nine to five. The student's function is to learn, occasionally questioning what he is learning, but not to an extreme. The slave's function was to pick cotton, occasionally resting, but not for too long. The owners would kill slaves who tried to *learn,* to understand their position. Today, we see the same thing happening on college campuses, where students who challenge the foundations of this nation and the American Creed itself get maced and teargassed and murdered.

Being Black we suffer the most, get cheated the most, are born to fail. There must be a confrontation, but first an understanding among ourselves. There must be a plan, some course of action, so that we can win instead of lose. Those who stick to the script, who accept indoctrination as education, get by without ever being able to examine the process of their education. Those in the educational bureaucracy who oppose change are paranoid. Afraid of becoming anachronisms, they are already anachronistic.

The Board of Education's Bill would be the unifying factor I needed—the perfect issue, the one answer to many questions. Shortly after the Bill of Rights appeared in *The Times,* Nathan Brown, Acting Superintendent of Schools, sent me a letter informing me that the Board of Education was planning to organize a citywide high school council "to [advise] the Superintendent and his staff on all matters affecting the education of high school youth." He request that I select three representatives from the City G.O. to be on the council. The first meeting would be on November 7th. Everything started to fall in line, and a plan for confrontation began to emerge in my mind.

Downhill

ACT FIRMLY AND WITH CONVICTION. THERE IS LITTLE TO
LOSE. TRY TO ISOLATE THE LEADERS. TAKE APPROPRIATE
FORTHRIGHT ACTION AGAINST THEM.

High School Principals' Association

I WAS RUNNING WILD on optimism. At the beginning of the
year things had looked pretty bad. Unintentionally, the
Board of Education had united many different groups of
people by giving them something in common to hate. Even
though the resolution had been published in *The Times,* the
majority of high school students remained ignorant of the
issue being launched in their name. The law required that
the Board hold a public hearing before the resolutions were
adopted. Even this was a sham because the decision had already been made. The "public hearing" was never publicly
announced—news of it got around by word of mouth.

It couldn't have been mere coincidence that the Board of
Education had picked that time to organize a citywide high
school council, "to advise the Superintendent and his staff on
all matters affecting the education of high school youth." This
move was timed to coincide with their proposed so-called student Bill of Rights. They were using a strategy of co-optation.
The students on this council would be used by the Board of

Education as a front to justify half-truths and repressive actions, and to lend legitimacy to resolutions they formulated without consulting students. The Board would say: See, look here, we have students on our committees.

All of my mind-searching and optimism blinded me. I had no idea of how detached I had become from Music and Art. I couldn't see that nothing was as it had been, that I was being buried alive and didn't know it. I persistently kept after my primary goal, which was to expose the Board's so-called Student Bill of Rights and to promote the Cultural Exchange Program.

At first I complied with Klein's red tape. He barred me from using school facilities; he even denied me one minute to make an announcement about the Cultural Exchange Program. When I insisted that, as "the democratically elected president of the student body," I be given a chance to address my constituents, he refused, then changed his mind. He told me that if I got the Black Security Council, ASPIRA, the Student Union, and Women's Lib to sign a statement permitting me to speak, and not demanding equal time, that I could use the microphones.

I went through this obstacle course in spite of the fact that when I had defended him and condemned the fires, I never needed permission to speak out, but I expected this. The school and everything in it belonged to him and to no one else. I didn't have the time or the energy to get outside help the way I had for the October Moratorium. Besides, I still had commitments to SDS for using their printing machines and sound equipment.

It was like sending a sheep into a wolves' den. I spent most of the day begging my enemies to sign the paper. I had once vowed that I would never ask them to do anything for me. Now I had to swallow my pride, which was painful for me. I grew to hate Klein more than I had ever hated anyone.

The Black Security Council was having a meeting. When I walked in, there was silence. All eyes were on me. The hatred in those eyes was so obvious that even if I were a blind man I could have felt it. Mr. Flout, advisor of the BSC, was in the front looking at me wondering what the hell does he want? I would later see this same Black man—who denounced me as a Tom in front of the Security Council and behind my back —at a party with a white girl. I would see him having an affair with a white girl, but it was done outside the school. Inside the school he was Mr. Black—a phony! But at this moment there was only one thing on my mind—to get the frigging paper signed.

I walked up to him. "I have to get your permission to use the microphones."

He didn't even look at me but looked at the floor and smiled, smirked. The whole Security Council burst out in laughter. I could feel my nerves getting tense, my teeth clenching. I wanted to stuff the paper down his throat.

After the laughter subsided, he looked up and said, "I can't sign that."

"Well, who can?" I shouted.

He walked around me, as if I were a post, or a chair, and didn't answer my question. I was growing angrier. I could feel my hands shaking. I turned and looked at the Council. "Can anyone here sign this?" There was silence. I got looks from people who wanted to spit in my face.

I slammed the door, locking the laughter behind me. Turned down by my own people, called a Tom, I had been humiliated, shat upon, stepped on. I was so angry I thought I was getting an asthma attack. Halfway down the hall I saw Russell, head of the Council, and Manny, son of the most outspoken Black parent at Music and Art.

"Can either of you sign this?" Russell was kind of a cool dude. He had a naturally low, muffled voice. It looked like it wouldn't take much to provoke him into kicking your ass. He never spoke to you, always gave you a speech. Manny was one of the most intelligent brothers in the school. Next year these guys would be seniors. Klein would have to deal with them. They read the paper together while I looked on hoping they'd sign it.

Russell reached for his pen, looked me dead in the eye. "Having problems with the man?"

I didn't answer, only took the signed paper from him. Both of them knew that Klein and I weren't friends. It was only the Black girls on the Council who still hounded and cursed me. To them my unforgivable sin was Vickie, a white girl, a girl I now loathed. My patience with this pettiness was slowly running out.

When I showed the paper to Klein, he was astonished. Obviously he expected me to fail with the odds stacked so high against me. Klein now went back on his word. He said that the matter would have to be referred to the Consultative Council. I kept my cool. I couldn't attend the Consultative Council meeting because I had to chair a meeting of the G.O. City Council Elections.

After fifth period Sarah, Gladstone, Karen, and I took the subway down to the High School of Art and Design. On the way down I thought about my situation at Music and Art. I had been cut off from the student body. None of the things I thought about were materializing. The optimism existed only in mind. I needed a plan of action and a base from which to work without interference from the administration. I would infiltrate the City Council—become a candidate for some office.

When we reached Art and Design, the meeting was already in progress. Swartz was handing out leaflets. He was running for president. I went over to sit with the Black reps from the High School of Fashion Industries. Before I had said a word to them, they declared, "You've got our vote."

Castka called the meeting to order. I went back to sit with Sarah and Gladstone. Swartz came running over. He pulled a chair up and whispered in my ear, "Do you want to run on a ticket with me?"

"O.K.," I whispered. However, I forgot to ask him what position.

"Pssst, what position?"

"V.P."

V.P.?

"Hey man, why don't *you* be the V.P.? Let's switch the order. I need some white support." There was nothing he could say. I had an established name in the Council and really didn't need to run on a ticket to get white support. Gladstone and I started laughing.

The election procedures were spelled out by Castka. You had to be nominated and seconded. You then had the opportunity to make a one-minute speech and answer questions for another minute.

Three people were nominated for president; the other two were white. They spoke for three minutes and answered questions for at least a minute. When my turn came, Castka held on to the microphone and allowed me to speak for thirty seconds and to answer one question: "To what extent would you jeopardize your present position as president of Music and Art by devoting your efforts to the City Council?"

In my mind I pictured a little Black boy laughing on the ground, rolling all over, laughing. I could hardly keep a straight face. Jeopardize my present position? What a joke.

"I will relinquish my position as president of Music and Art to serve under the will of the Council, if asked to do so."

The infiltration was complete. I was elected president of the New York City G.O. Council and was not asked to relinquish my position at Music and Art. Swartz was elected V.P.; Valerie, a sister from Fashion Industries, was elected corresponding secretary; and Bonnie, a nice gal from Madison High School, was elected recording secretary. A typical division of labor between the sexes.

The next day at Music and Art the noose started to tighten. The school newspaper printed my article pleading for student unity in the face of administrative repression. The headlines blaring my name spelled disaster for me in a school where people were restless and needed something to attack—something big. I could feel the envy from all corners. "Looks like our paper is a *Don Reeves Journal*." But absolutely no one said anything about the content of what I had written. They made me feel as if I had set my own name up in bold print.

I spoke to Fran in the morning. I could feel the pressures

mounting more and more. Fran suggested that I quit before it was too late.

"Why should you keep pushing if everybody is putting you down?" And again she said, "If Darryl couldn't succeed, you know it's hopeless."

I couldn't accept her advice. I was going to stick it out all the way.

In my art class, even Mrs. Winston, whom I had always loved and who always loved me, began to put me down.

"You can't say that there's nothing going on here. People are going to classes like they should. You're a troublemaker. You have absolutely no right to say that there's apathy here."

Politically, I rarely took Mrs. Winston seriously. In fact, I liked having her scream at me. She was a good person who always put more out for people than she got back. Every morning she came in at least an hour before school to help students. She was one of a handful of art teachers who I considered dedicated and sincere. Mrs. Winston even sent a letter home to Mom Reeves telling her to buy me an alarm clock so that I would get to school on time. In my junior year I had worked on the *Yearbook* staff with her. But now she seriously got angry with me, condemned my views, and insisted that I read some book on demagogues, because, she said, "That's what you are, a demagogue."

I paid absolutely no attention to her scolding; in fact, I laughed it off.

I had virtually stopped speaking to parents after school because they were getting too impressed with me as a "Black boy who could articulate" and were not acting on my pleas for help.

Fineberg began interfering in my personal affairs. My breaking up with Vickie had left me free to see my old flames and have a ball. During this time Vickie had gotten close to Fineberg. Seeing them together reminded me of the saying, "Misery loves company."

Sometimes it would get to me. I'd come in and see Vickie moping around school. The Moratorium had momentarily nourished her ego, but it was over. She now was where she had always been—alone, with no real friends of her own. I felt bad inside because I knew that no matter how much I hated her and no matter how much she despised and envied me, in no way could it be compared to the envy and jealousy the students around school had for me. Of course, Fineberg was only too happy to see Vickie and me on ice with each other. But that wasn't enough. She started working on girls that I was seeing, trying to turn them against me. She'd meet with one in the morning, another at lunch and so on, and tell them all sorts of lies about me and reveal my other relationships to them. It was no vague rumor; everyone in the G.O. office knew that this was going on. Now it began to hit home. She was using gutter methods of ripping me off.

Fineberg, a woman I had once trusted, who gave me the first book I ever read from cover to cover, had turned into a two-faced devil. A fucking grown woman, old enough to be my mother, she was carrying on like a jealous sixteen-year-old girl. Ever since the first day of the term, she'd been trying to get David, Karen, Vickie, and me to bend to her will. As far as I could tell, the main thing in her life seemed to be running that office her way, trying to manipulate other people's lives. (Some readers may think it's nasty of me to say that, but the point is, there are thousands of people in education who just don't belong around students.)

A number of times she took it upon herself to tell me what to do, contending that in my speeches I always exaggerated issues. When I wanted to inform the parents that none of the fire extinguishers in the school worked, Klein stopped me. I insisted that the parents should know. Fineberg always said that I was creating the "cause and effect." At one time it meant nothing to me, because I didn't understand the meaning of the term. *The New York Times'* editorial on Malcolm's assassination said that he turned "many true gifts to evil purpose . . . had a ruthless and fanatical belief in violence," and was killed by someone who came out of "the darkness he spawned." In other words, what *The Times* tried to say was that Malcolm's preachings were the cause of his own death— that he created the cause and effect.

It incensed me to hear that Fineberg was spreading the word about me. When I was denied the right to speak freely, she used class time to malign my objectives, to turn people away from me, and to convince them that I was inciting unwarranted disruption. I tried to use bulletins to reach the student body with my side of the story. The administration locked up the supply rooms. Fineberg lied to me, told me that the school had run out of paper. All of this stemming from her little office on the first floor. Over what? The same pettiness and filth is used to crush and blacklist people in "the real world" outside high school.

I stormed into Klein's office and shouted, "I want to have a meeting with you and Fineberg now." I only caught a glimpse of the astonishment on his face because I had left to get Fineberg. I could take all the political repression, but I wouldn't stand for any of this shit of interfering with the lives of innocent people, and those who worked with me. I got David, Susan, Terrie, and Fineberg. We went into Klein's office and sat down around the table.

"I want you to tell this woman to stop messing around with my personal life." I was so angry I was stuttering.

Klein just sat there smiling. Fineberg sat back, pouting, frowning, squinting from behind her red-tinted horn-rimmed glasses.

David, Susan, and Terrie sat in silence. Klein said that he wanted to know the details.

"The details of what?"

He said smiling, "I want to know the details before I take action."

"What action? All I want you to do is to tell this woman to stop messing around with my life." I was practically screaming.

It soon became clear, watching the grin on Klein's face, that he had no intentions of reprimanding Fineberg. They were cohorts in a conspiracy to shut me up. Klein had me where he wanted me. This was a bogus meeting. I was acting purely on emotion and impulse. I had set myself up and had gone to the wolf pleading for justice. My mind was destroyed. I felt nothing but hate, spreading through my body. I saw what was happening but could say nothing; things were moving too quickly. I was taking a beating physically and mentally, just pushing on borrowed time. It was a test of strength not to capitulate. I would find some means of reaching the students to let them know exactly what had been going on.

I was the only one who felt the pressure. It was brought down from the outside on my head alone, but it seemed like the whole world around me felt it. I had never thought it possible that I would be made into a symbol of common hate.

It was at this time that the distinction between friends and support became clear. I called a meeting of all the students who worked in the government office. David, Karen, Terrie, Gladstone, Susan, and I met behind the stage in the auditorium. We all knew why we were there. All of us had gone through the process. We shared frustration and repression; we had a common enemy and discriminator. Tomorrow, November 7th, would be our last chance to communicate with the student body as a whole. Only with the support of all the students could we confront the administration and fight the repression. We would have only forty-five minutes to reconstruct and articulate two years of sustained injustice, half-truths, and repression. Five students from other schools had already been invited to speak at the forum, which meant that our time would be cut even shorter than we anticipated.

At first the discussion was spontaneous and undirected. David was going crazy: "Fuck'em, fuck'em, walk out, quit. We don't need all this shit. Let 'em run the damned school . . . their school . . ."

Gladstone broke his silence. He said in an accent familiar to both of us, "I can't see why? You treat Klein like he's responsible for everything, dat's wrong. You charge de mon wid society's problems, dat's why he don't know what to do . . ."

At one time Gladstone and I used to think alike. We

started out together trying to get uniforms for the track team. Now there was a gap between us. I knew where his mind was at—mine used to be there. He saw Klein as just one man doing his job. Gladstone had no way of understanding the paranoid psychology that the High School Principals' Association was based on. He failed to see how brilliantly deceptive and manipulative Klein was. (He had even served as an intelligence officer in the Army—he told me so himself.) Gladstone had yet to go through the process himself.

After an hour of discussion, the decision had been made to take over the assembly. The government had become intolerable, unresponsive to the needs of the people, and repressed by a dictatorship. The decision was made using the Board of Education's own so-called philosophy:

THE EFFECTIVE STUDENT ORGANIZATION REQUIRES AN ATMOSPHERE OR CLIMATE THAT ENCOURAGES STUDENT PARTICIPATION AND INVOLVEMENT THEMSELVES . . . STUDENTS . . . WORK INSTINCTIVELY FOR THE OBJECTIVES THEY BELIEVE . . . THEIR PRESENT WELL-BEING AND THEIR FUTURE WELL-BEING . . . EACH STUDENT BODY MUST CHOOSE ITS OWN FORM OF ORGANIZATION . . .*

The circus would finally come to a close tomorrow morning. The organization was not effective because it wasn't controlled by students.

Around fifth period word leaked out. Within minutes David, Karen, Vickie, and I were rounded up and brought down to Klein's office. Klein wasn't grinning now. This was the first time that Fineberg had let things get out of hand. She was trying to outdo Mrs. Shapiro. Mrs. Shapiro couldn't keep up with us, but Fineberg always got the goods on us. The meeting was brief. Klein said that the forum would be can-

---

* "You and Your Student Organization Get Involved," a pamphlet published by the New York City Board of Education, August 1969, pp. 8–13.

celed if all of us didn't promise to end it on time, at 10:49 A.M. We made the "official agreement."

At the end of the day I went into the G.O. office to pick up my books. I was heading out the door when I saw Vickie approaching. I was torn between love and hate. She came over to me. I wanted to hit her across the face, but I couldn't. She tried to start a friendly conversation. I didn't reply to anything she said. I was trying to put it out of my mind: I loved her. I wanted so badly to tell her to fuck off, but she looked so humble and solemn.

She looked so damned humble. She was so young, and yet she looked like a middle-aged woman who had just gone through labor pains. We were on the subway going home when she turned to me and said, "I've learned." Tears started to fall from her eyes. Trying real hard to be cold, I started looking around the train, at the floor, at posters, at anything that would keep my eyes off her. Then she broke out crying. I started to get nervous. People were looking at me as if I had done something to her. Finally, I gave in, placed her head on my shoulder.

It was this seemingly instinctive, symbiotic impulse that brought us together at that particular moment. We had devoured each other while being consumed ourselves. In my head flashed a myriad of recognitions, all of which condemned me as a fool for picking up with her again. Here I found myself consciously submerging the truth, clinging to the lie. Buddha said that if you hate god in anger and raise your head to spit at the heavens, the spit falls right back in your face.

She said, "My father is a bigot . . . He said that I'd turn my back on my family but bow down to any black nigger who came along."

"Do you think he'd mind having me for a son-in-law?"

We started laughing, but she abruptly resumed her solemn posture: "I can't go home unless they accept you . . ."

I sat in silence for a while. Well, I certainly wasn't bringing her home with me. Francis didn't too much care for this interracial stuff.

A number of times when I had been under pressure, I'd gone to the airport.

My mind was drifting off, thinking of how many times I'd been there within the last two months, and at that point I asked Vickie if she wanted to go.

It was about 9 P.M when we got to Kennedy. We went to the International Arrivals Building and stood there watching people coming in from foreign countries. I always looked out for the college students. It was fun to watch how the customs officers would practically tear their luggage up looking for drugs. Guys who looked respectable—that is, wore ties and jackets—were hardly ever searched. Whenever I saw a guy being searched, I'd start banging on the window trying to attract his attention, then I'd smile and give him the peace sign.

The later it got, the less congested the airport became. We went over to the TWA building. It was virtually empty. All during this time we avoided talking about the split between us. Instead we talked about Fineberg. She told me how Klein and Fineberg were messing me over. It was about one o'clock when we fell asleep. We slept on the couches in the terminal for about an hour. But I couldn't stay all night.

"Man, I'm tired and hungry. I need a shower . . ."

"I want to call my parents."

She went into the phone booth and called her mother. She left the door half open. I started laughing again. "Let me speak to her. Let me say hello."

As soon as her mother got on the phone, the yelling and screaming started. I stood outside, listening to them yelling at each other. When they finished, Vickie came out grabbing my arm.

"My father knows you're with me. We'd better get out of here."

"Why? What's happening? How does he know I'm with you?"

"He's calling for the police."

"I got to call my mom." I went to a booth.

"Mom? Mom Reeves, this you, right? This is me, this is you, right? I'm coming home . . . with a girl."

"O.K."

O.K.? It was almost a letdown not to have Mom screaming at me.

The subways and busses were running slow.

When we got to my house, Mom and Vickie sat on the sofa to talk. I was hungry and went into the kitchen to eat some pork chops. Francis came downstairs. I knew what he was going to say.

"Who the white girl belong to?"

"Hey man," I said jokingly, "she's O.K." He just smirked, took a bite of pork chop, and went back upstairs.

The phone rang; it was Vickie's father. I got nervous and didn't know what to say. I told him Vickie was with me. She got on the phone yelling again. I don't know what was wrong with me. I felt removed from the whole thing, like I was supposed to be involved, but wasn't. I felt like I was observing a drama. She got off the phone, said that she wasn't going home, and had told her father not to come for her until morning. A couple minutes later her father was rapping on the front door. It was old bald eagle himself, red in the face. Mom told him to have a seat. As soon as Vickie came downstairs, bald eagle started screaming. Mom and I were spectators. I sat there trying hard to understand what was going on. He said that he didn't care what Vickie did with her life, but she was upsetting "my wife." Why didn't he say "her mother?"

Finally, they both left. Mom closed the door, and without even saying a word to me, she started back upstairs.

"Hey Mom, aren't you going to say anything?"

There was something wrong. I could feel it, something wrong with Mom Reeves.

"Are you mad because of what happened?" She turned around and came back downstairs.

"I feel sorry for you. I don't want to tell you what to do with your life. But I don't think that she's the right girl for you. She's terribly confused. Her parents don't think much of you. Everyone I've talked with seems to feel that it would be harmful for you as a Black man to have a white wife . . ."

"But—"

"Now, just a minute. I'm not saying it's wrong, but reason it out for yourself. As rich as those people are, you can just bet they don't have time to give her any attention or love. She's using *you* to get that attention. Now, you know that you'll never be able to satisfy a woman like that. I didn't raise a shit." She started raising her voice. "You lower yourself as a man when you try to get in with those Jews, and you know they don't want you. As confused as Vickie is, I can bet she'll be with you one minute and gone the next. As soon as she gets the attention she needs, you're going to be dropped. You know there's any number of nice Black girls out there. If your relationship with this girl ends tonight, you should go upstairs and pray, thank God for small mercies."

Demonstration—Klein—school—students—envy—jealousy . . .

I was confused, couldn't think, couldn't even see straight. There was just too much going on.

Mom Reeves stood up.

"You know what time it is? Are you going to school tomorrow?"

"Yes, I have to," I said, holding my head.

"When's the last time you had a full night's sleep."

"I'm O.K."

"I spoke to Miss Fineberg. You've been pushing day and night without food, without rest."

"What's Fineberg have to do with it?"

"You're on drugs, aren't you?"

As hard as I tried to convince her that I wasn't on drugs, I don't think until this day she's believed me. All the facts were there against me. I hadn't been sleeping or eating, and I was losing weight, talking to myself in the dark. Fineberg had turned my own mother against me. The thought never left my mind that my own mother had taken that bitch's word over mine.

Man Alone

IT WAS FIFTH PERIOD, and I had called for a takeover of the school. David had resigned. Klein had called our parents and told them that we were inciting riots throughout the school. There was chaos. Over seven hundred students were following me all through the building. I was looking for a place where we could assemble. At that time I would let everybody know why we were demonstrating. Nobody knew what was happening. People were asking me questions, and I just kept repeating, "Wait—let me say it one time." We went through the locker room and assembled in the small gym which quickly got overcrowded, then to the big gym, but that too got overcrowded. I told everybody to meet outside. There was a sit-in on the first floor. I went outside and told everybody to come back inside. We marched on the auditorium but were met by Klein and teachers blocking the entrance. The tension was mounting. Where to go? What to do? I was looking for a place to assemble, without interfering with other people who wanted no part of the demonstration. But I had already disrupted everything. Finally, we converged on the cafeteria. People swarmed onto the tables. There had never been so many packed into the cafeteria at one time, Everybody was waiting for me to say something. Mr. Drexler, my art teacher, was guarding the microphones.

"Open the box," I shouted.

"No, Don. Please, I can't. I have my orders from Klein."

"Tell him I beat you up and took away your keys."

"Please, Don I can't. I can't do that."

"GODDAMN IT GET TO HELL AWAY FROM THE FUCKING MICROPHONES!"

I jumped up on the stand and began pounding on the microphone box—pounding and pounding, spraining my hand. Soon Mr. Beller, from the attendance office, came down and opened the box. In my blind rage I was thinking about the repression, Fineberg turning my mother against me, the lies, the begging, ass-licking, ostracism, deceit, manipulation, last night, Moratorium, criticism, common hate, Bill of Rights, confrontation, pressure, pressure, pressure. It was in my mind, enclosed in my mind. I made the mistake. I let it out.

I began thinking out loud. I was talking wildly, as in a delirium. Everything that I had been holding back now rushed out, unrestrained. I wasn't even conscious of what I was saying. I just saw hundreds and hundreds of people staring at me, then feverishly applauding, smiling and laughing. Looking down at Sarah yelling at me to stop speaking because we were late for our meeting at the Board of Education, I felt dizzy—felt needles pricking my brain—which made my eyes see darkness. I stopped speaking.

I had told everyone that I was going down to the Board of Education, that if they wanted something done to let me know, I would go over Klein's head and present the demands to the Acting Superintendent of Schools, Nathan Brown. Everybody seemed bewildered. Russell forged his way up to the stand to let me know that the Black Security Council "supported the actions." At last, I thought, unity. Suddenly there was Abzug, the girl I had defeated for the presidency, the girl who I felt psychologically could not accept being defeated by a Black person, on a chair screaming at everyone, telling them that I was ego-tripping, that I'd called the demonstration to ego-trip. But her voice was muffled by the noise. Another girl started screaming, "Where were you last year? Why weren't you sitting in then?" Sarah began screaming at me to come on or she'd leave without me. Again I asked the people if there was anything they wanted done. This time I got a few hard-pressed suggestions, all concerning the Student Government. I told them that I was going to resign. Someone fired back, "But if you resign, who will lead us?" This pathetic remark met with wild applause of acclamation. I was motionless. Had I been the victim of my own skepticism? Had I been imprisoned in negative thoughts— surrounded by a small clique of resentment and jealousy?

I thought everybody was against me. Who would lead us? The question had been put to me. I couldn't handle it without appearing to be on an ego trip. I got down off the stand and ended the demonstration. Sarah and I left for the Board of Education.

All the way down to 110 Livingston Street, she was telling me that I had made a mistake in taking over the cafeteria.

At the Board meeting I didn't get a chance to present the demands. Nathan Brown came in, made a speech ("We're glad to have you kids here . . ."), and left. The main topic of discussion was Franklin K. Lane High School. Dr. Selig Lester, Deputy Superintendent, and my boy, George W. Castka, Assistant Administrative Director of high schools, were among the few Board officials present.

The issue at Franklin K. Lane was the same as that all over America—racism. Lane was still burning from the past spring, and the Board was in a bind. The students had thrown lighter fluid on a teacher, set his clothes afire, and sent him to the hospital. There were numerous incidents of beatings and sexual assaults in and around the school. No doubt countless incidents went unreported for fear of reprisals. In response to the racial conflict at Lane, the Board sent police to occupy the school. In March, 1969, security guards were sent into fourteen high schools in a supposed attempt to prevent violence. Applicants were required to meet certain physical and medical requirements, but no formal education was required. These guards were given clubs and the authority to use them to suppress dissent. Accepted applicants received a thirty-hour training course, covering in depth secondary school organization, Black and Puerto Rican History, narcotics identification, and self-defense. Principals contended that the guards were working out well.* Up to this point no educational approach had been taken to resolve our problems. The security guards were another manifestation of the Board's paranoid, repressive attitude. Instead of receding, the racial insurgency at Lane began to erupt again, and the Board needed a way out. Plainclothesmen hadn't worked; undercover agents dressed as students hadn't worked; parent patrols had fallen apart. The Board now turned to us, the students on the Council, and urged us to go into Lane and "stimulate racial harmony."

I couldn't help but laugh to myself. They actually wanted me, who had just disrupted a whole school, to go into another one and make peace. They had no way of knowing what had gone on at Music and Art. But it was evident that we were being used again. The Board of Education was largely responsible for nurturing the racism at Lane. The whole goddamned society was responsible for the problems there. The student violence was just a by-product of the Board officials' way of life. Not once during the entire discussion did the Board officials give any reasons for what actually started the racial confrontation. They only sought methods to repress the insurgency. From this room the decision had been made to send police into high schools. I saw it. I was there.

I had always wondered what kind of mind would actually send police to beat fourteen- and sixteen-year-old students.

* "A Report on New York City High Schools," p. 6.

The possibility of brutality never entered their minds. They couldn't see it. Their paranoid minds saw only one thing: a problem; saw only one answer: repression. I listened but said nothing. I was just waiting for the opportunity to be sent into Lane. Finally, we received the authorization. The Board called Franklin K. Lane's principal, Morton Selub, and informed him that we were coming. At Lane we would meet with members of the Afro-American Club, the Third World Coalition, and the principal.

Sarah and I took the train into Brooklyn's East New York section and switched to the QJ going into Queens. It was a dark, rainy, muggy day, and the school was located near a cemetery. It was massive compared to Music and Art. There was a field in the front surrounded by a high prison-like fence. Up the street we could see small groups of police huddled in circles, near paddy wagons. The whole atmosphere was one of impending violence. The school looked like an armed camp. All of the police were wearing helmets and swinging clubs.

Until now the thought had never occurred to me that I was walking into a school where Blacks and whites were at each other's throats, and here I was coming up the block with Sarah, her long blond hair flowing in the wind. I almost started to laugh. In my mind I was constructing all kinds of scenes—of Sarah being attacked or raped, of my trying to fight off the attackers or my being stabbed. But I looked at her, and she was calm and confident.

As we approached the door, two helmeted policemen stopped us. I showed them our pass from the Board of Education. We were escorted to a room with about fifteen white students. These students couldn't have been any older than I, yet they were haggard, defeated, and frightened. You could see it so clearly in their faces. While waiting for the principal and Afro-American Club to show up, I started sketching their expressions.

Eventually the principal came in. I asked him where the Afro-American Club was. It was obvious that practically no one had been informed about the meeting. Other students from the school convinced him to leave before the brothers came, and he did.

When the brothers arrived, I had to go through the harassing, haranguing ritual seemingly reserved for all "outsiders" to their immediate group. There is a dichotomy that exists between outsiders and insiders. No chances could be taken, any outsider might easily be an undercover agent. However, Klein had done me a favor when he suspended me. He gave me a name and consequently credentials as a victim of oppression—a brother. I told them why members of the City Council were sent into their school. I told them that we were being used, but that we also needed the information they had, as evidence against the Board of Education.

They began their story. They were still fighting over the seventeen demands of last year. The demands were needed for "survival." During the month of October a conflict arose between Blacks and whites. The situation culminated during the week of October 27th when racial fights spilled into the streets. Ronald Green had been arrested for assaulting a police officer. He was pushed through a supermarket window on Jamaica Avenue. The principal later informed us that the pig also went through the window with Green. Reprisal: five white girls' hair was set on fire. As early as January, police were called in to ward off assaults on teachers and students. One teacher suffered burns, a broken nose, and compound bruises. Seven police had been brought in, but now there were at least ten on every floor, two guarding every exit. In fact only one exit remained open; the rest were chained shut. If there had been either a fire or a riot, over five thousand students would have to make it out through that one exit.

What caused this confrontation? The situation was the result of a dispute between whites and Blacks over the display of the African Liberation Flag. A white teacher objected to the replacement of the American red-white-and-blue with a red, green, and black flag. The African Liberation Flag had been put up in the African studies course and taken down by a white teacher.

All this time I couldn't help thinking that this was where I belonged, somewhere at the bottom, where people were embroiled in trouble, where I could do something worthwhile. Music and Art had softened me. But this was real. These people had to learn under these conditions of brutality, of racial strife, of oppression. In the room, Blacks and whites were arguing over seventeen non-negotiable demands, talking about the way the pigs were busting the heads of the brothers and sisters. The pigs had to go. A sister with a rheumatic condition had been beaten by police in the cafeteria. The students claimed they had heard the cop say, "I'll teach you, Black bitch." Police were on duty in the lunchroom. At times, cherry bombs went off causing chaos and more police brutality. We then argued over the ratio of whites to Blacks brutalized. The Black students had charged the principal with being responsive only to the white community. In their words: "The pigs are here to beat us upside the head and protect the white kids."

The meeting broke up. Sarah and I and a few white students went to see the principal. But he refused to meet with members of the Afro-American Club—he wouldn't even let them enter his office. Sarah and I took issue with this, but the principal made it clear to us that it was *his* school. He explained to us that the Student Government had broken down, that there were really no legitimate channels for reform. He refused to recognize the Third World Coalition or Afro-American Club as representative groups. We then urged him to rebuild the Student Government by permitting the student body to hold a democratic election. He refused, contending that an election had already been canceled.

"Whose decision was it to cancel the election?"

"Why, mine, of course."

"How can you ever get legitimate channels if you don't permit democratic elections?" Sarah had put the question to him.

He failed to answer. Instead, his assistant now intervened: "What do you kids know about anything? *We're* the professionals. We've been trained in this sort of thing . . ." He went on denouncing us. I sat listening and thinking, watching his mouth moving. There was absolutely no communication here.

This school was a microcosm of America. This man, who blocked out everything we were trying to say, represented the so-called Establishment, desperately trying to "understand the youth." The principal—blunt, tactless, inarticulate, and all-powerful—represented Adult Authority. The Black students attacking each other and attacking whites represented the embittered masses on the streets who mug and murder to avenge society's injustices. The brothers and sisters here failed to confront the real issues of class status and political repression. They lost the opportunity to confront the source of their problems because of a preoccupation with hating whites and vice versa. What was happening in this school happened all over America, not only in the high schools but on the streets. There wasn't one element here that couldn't be found as the basis for any number of race riots that America has witnessed within the last five years.

To say that the students were not at fault is not to condone the burnings and bombings, but to understand the underlying reasons why violence was inevitable. Were there any attempts at internal communication before the police were brought in? No. Were there any attempts at communication now? No. Many of these students came from slums and sat beside whites who came from "communities." It's like trying to get back at something, but you don't know exactly what it is, just that it's responsible for your position. You try to kill the first thing you can lay your hands on, the first thing that you associate with the problem. And so the real culprits escape, those who sit far away in plush, green-carpeted rooms making decisions that spell REPRESSION, never communication. They never try to reason and understand why a problem exists. The students at Lane were wrong for brutalizing each other. This slow disintegration was a prelude to total destruction.

The Board of Education created the police state here. The Board of Education pitted the white community against the

Black community to justify the necessity of a police state, in a so-called institution of learning. Hundreds of kids in this school were on drugs. One of the student demands was that there be community rehabilitation centers set up to treat known drug addicts. But the Board's response was negative. Instead, teachers were now working as informers for the police. Plainclothesmen now sat in classes among students, pushing dope to make contact with other addicts. What happened when dope was presented to an innocent student? Who took the blame?

Why aren't trained medical people sent into the schools? Why is it always police and more police? It is an atmosphere of professional incompetence and administrative repression that nurtures student rebellions that destroy $200 million worth of public school property in one year. Meanwhile the principals spend their time preparing booklets on counter-insurgency. Instead of trying to uproot the problem, they cultivate it.

After the meeting with the principal, I spoke to members of the Afro-American Club again. They were planning to present their complaints to the Board of Education at the hearing coming up November 12th, on the proposed, so-called Student Bill of Rights. We exchanged addresses and promised to keep in touch.

It was getting late and had started raining again when Sarah and I left. We were waiting for the subway when she asked, "Do you think we accomplished anything?"

"Of course not," I replied. "Who the hell are we?"

I felt compelled to tell her I'd been afraid at first. Yet she never once showed any sign of nervousness. I said, "Thank you," and kissed her.

When I got home, Mom was waiting for me. She, along with David, Karen, and Vickie's parents, had been called up to Music and Art. She said that everybody was against me. I couldn't accept this. "What about my friends?"

"Everybody said that what you did was wrong," she said sternly.

I went upstairs and called David.

". . . Don, TURN IT LOOSE, QUIT! Fineberg and Klein got you cornered. They got all the girls in the office against you. They even got your own mother against you. The students are against you—you can't win. TURN IT LOOOOSE."

On the phone it sounded like David was going crazy. I called six people after that and each time found myself in deeper trouble. Teachers were saying that I led the students around like fools, some students claimed that I was on an ego trip, and still others said that I started trouble and ran away. I called Fran and spoke to her. She confirmed everything.

Malcolm wrote in his autobiography, "I never dreamed that they were going to try to make it appear that instead of inoculating against an epidemic, I had started it . . . hating me was going to become the cause for people of shattered faith to rally around." *

No matter how wrong I appeared to anybody else, as long as I was able to identify with a similar situation that occurred in Malcolm's life, I knew that I was on the right course. I became a scapegoat for hate and frustration.

Articles appeared in the school newspaper shooting me down from all sides. I was labeled as being everything from a phony to a liar. Klein sent letters to all the parents, whether or not their children had participated in the demonstration, so I made even more enemies. As for the few teachers who supported what I was doing, they also received letters from Klein asking them to report to his office bringing their Delany books, so that he could discuss their "amazing success in discouraging student participation in disruptive activities."

Brilliant as ever, Klein took advantage of the situation by permitting students who hated me to print lies about me. The underlying purpose was obvious. These articles would be shown to the parents, and of course, I would lose their support. It was important that these articles be written by students and not by Klein himself. It would more easily convince the parents that I was not to be listened to. Klein had to read these articles before they were printed. I wasn't even allowed

_____
* *Autobiography of Malcolm X*, p. 299.

to make a rebuttal. Nobody, absolutely nobody, said anything on my behalf. Every newspaper in the city had covered the story of my suspension. Over five hundred people supported my reinstatement, and yet nobody took issue with the lie that I had not been suspended.

The school newspaper had printed mild comments compared to those plastered throughout the school. Nobody was on my side. They hated my guts; and for the first time the hate didn't come from the Black Security Council; it came from white students. It came from the same people who didn't have the guts to confront Darryl and speak out against his actions. I was always approachable and open to people—too open at times. Nobody was afraid of speaking their mind to me. But Darryl was unapproachable and feared.

I had read political science books which explained this situation. I understood that as soon as the force behind the threat of violence that made white liberals afraid was removed, there would be absolutely no need for me, and in fact, with my new views, I would be a threat to the calm. Because I understood the reasons why things were happening, I could stand the pressure. Not one of the white students who now denounced me and said that I should be burned, ever had had the courage to openly criticize Darryl.

But as the days dragged on, the expressions of hate became almost intolerable—someone even placed a noose up on the bulletin board with my name printed in the middle. Every day there came more lies, more criticism, and after a while, people I didn't even know would just walk up to me and tell me how much they hated me, how much they had always hated me. Even Black students whom I had never got along with spoke to me and told me that they couldn't figure it out. Hassan Adeeb, who had helped me get elected, said that at first he thought the whites were just jealous of me because I was growing bigger than the school. But now he couldn't understand it.

Then came another problem. Eva, who had helped me through academic problems in English when I was a sophomore, asked for my help. It came as a surprise to me that anyone should still want my help. The problem was that my history teacher, Miss Thal, and another teacher, Miss Vrable, were being fired. When a department chairman takes a personal dislike to new teachers who haven't taught for three terms and therefore don't have tenure, the chairman can fire them without giving the union or Board of Education reason for his decision. In this particular incident the department chairman had not even been in the school during the probationary period of these teachers. Only the principal had the power to override the decision. We took this case to the Consultative Council. Eva and I had "morality" on our side.

Klein made it clear that this was not a matter that was within the jurisdiction of the Consultative Council. The truth was that a principal usually doesn't want to override the decisions of his department chairmen because it might start a "conflict." Administrators tend to have a loyalty for each other that cannot be broken. If students had the same understanding, it would be great. The law ought to be revised so that a teacher is hired according to ability rather than for a personality compatible with a department chairman's. This whole incident only further demonstrated the ineffectiveness of the Consultative Council.

After the meeting I apologized to Eva for not being able to do anything. She hesitated before responding, as if thinking about a problem, then said, "I had the wrong impression of you." I felt good hearing that at least one person knew that I wasn't the bastard I was made out to be. I went down to Moratorium headquarters and ran off a leaflet explaining why the demonstration had failed and asking that they look for the *motivation* behind the disruption and not at its failure. I also urged that they pay more attention to the Board of Education's Bill of Rights. But it was like trying to soak up an ocean with a sponge. The confrontation wasn't against Klein or Fineberg; it was against the system responsible for what they represented. When hate, resentment, and jealousy set in, reason and rationality have no meaning. Nothing that I could

say would change anything. The odds were against me. I was
Black, called an Uncle Tom, an anti-Semite, and I had a Jewish girlfriend. How could I possibly stand up in front of an
assembly of two thousand and tell them that I blew my cool
because someone turned my mother against me? How could I
tell them that I was angry because some woman was messing
up my personal affairs, affairs with white girls, at that? I was
so mad, but there was absolutely nothing I could do.

Fineberg called me into the office to talk to me about the
leaflet. I told her to get her hand off my property and that if
she was the first white person I'd ever met, I'd be justified in
hating every other white person who ever crossed my path.

Then I was told to report to Klein's office to discuss my
leaflet. He asked me if I really believed in what I had said. I
told him I did. I had a pain in my chest that really started
hurting. I opened my shirt and reached for my heart. Klein
was startled, "Are you O.K.?" I told him I was. He then asked
where I thought racism had its roots. I told him in the homes.
I told him about my education at Knox, how free it was of
racism, how American schools institutionalized racism by
using standardized lies and projecting an image of Black
people as beasts and three-fifths human. We spoke for a good
while and when we were through, he suggested that I "make
use of the psychiatric help in the school."

At first I was angry to hear him say that, but a few days
later I went to see the psychiatrist. It wasn't really because of
Klein that I went, but by this time, so many people had said I
was crazy, I was beginning to wonder myself. So there I sat,
waiting for him, in the emergency room.

Legally, the Board of Education is responsible for students
while they're in school, for any injury. Yet students complained about the medical care. In this room, the nurse would
examine a broken knee and diagnose it as a bruise. They
weren't allowed to administer anything more than hot water
bottles and rubbing alcohol.

When the psychiatrist finally came in, he smiled, "You're
Mr. Reeves."

"How do you know my name?"

"I heard you speak the other day." He paused. "I can't really do anything for you."

"What? I haven't even said anything."

"Well, you see, uh, the other psychiatrist, Dr. Rosenbaum, spoke to a girl the other day. Vickie. I believe she had something to do with you . . ."

What the hell is going on? "Well, what happened?"

"She told him everything."

"Everything?"

"I'm afraid so, and, uh, I really can't get this deeply involved because we're here with the school's permission. If it was outside, it would be a different matter."

I went to go find Vickie.

"Hey, what's the matter with you? I just spoke to the psychiatrist. You told him everything. You're crazy, you know that?"

"Well, he promised he wouldn't tell anyone."

"He already did."

"I'm sorry."

■ ■ ■

On November 12th, the Board of Education hearing at the Fashion Institute of Technology ended abruptly. The five members of the Board—Murry Bergtraum (soon-to-be president), Seymour P. Lachman (author of the Bill of Rights), Mary Meade, Isaiah Robinson, Joseph Monserrat (then president of the Board), and Dr. Nathan Brown (Acting Superintendent of Schools)*—all walked out on the hearing. They did not answer any of the complaints presented by the students at Franklin K. Lane.

On November 13th, the Consultative Council voted not to suspend me, and that night I wrote Klein a letter. In it, I said, among other things:

---

* The racial composition of the Board seems fair and ideal, but does the color of a person's skin completely determine his thinking? Of course not. The thing that really matters is what these people in positions of power think and do.

Mr. Monserrat, President of the Board of Education, Dr. Nathan Brown, Acting Superintendent of Schools and other people you work for do not understand that the real problem is their system.* Issuing a suspension guideline or a Student Bill of Rights does not deal with racism and inadequate education throughout the city. Board of Education officials will never learn about the problems that exist in their system if they continue to ignore valid questions, dictate laws, and leave meetings when their presence is essential for constructive planning . . . It is clear that if the Board of Education continues to dictate laws without hearing the views of the parents, teachers and students, such actions can only lead to continued unity and militancy on the part of high school students in conjunction with aroused parents and radical teachers.

Klein received this letter and called a meeting with Karen, Vickie, Fineberg, and me. He said that he wanted us to put our signatures on the letter I had written. Why should he want our signatures? The question entered my mind, and I'm sure Vickie and Karen were wondering the same thing. Nevertheless, we signed the letter, and left his office. By midday Karen sent Klein a four-page brown-nosing letter, requesting that her signature be removed from the letter, and saying that I no longer represented the views of the students. At this point the thought occurred to me: What is Klein going to do with that letter? And then a funny thing hit me.

I remembered numerous times when I had given Klein my speeches and writings and he always had a xerox copy made. Then I remembered Walter Crump's suspension and the file that Klein had on Walter. From here on it was quite clear that a file was being made on me and possibly on the others. I in turn started to compile a file on Klein.

I sent Klein a personal letter requesting to be excused from meetings not stated as my responsibilities in the Student Government constitution. I told him I could no longer trust him or Fineberg.

Klein replied with a public campaign letter in which he put himself in the sun and made it look like I was copping out. He sent his letter to the president of the Parents' Association,

* Of course they understand.

Fineberg, and the Student Council. Now I was done for good.

My ideals and opinions had become unpopular, and instinctively the administration knew that it was time to get me out of the way. It really wasn't a question of my political views. I just had too many personal enemies and personal problems that everybody knew about. The students had wasted all this time and energy criticizing me. When I was gone, then what? The problems would remain the same. As for Klein, his school was on the way out. All these other schools, like Franklin K. Lane, at one time were just as peaceful as Music and Art was now. But because of the methods high school principals used to crush students trying to inoculate against a disease, the germ grew until it was uncontrollable.

■ ■ ■

It was January 1970, and the last time that I would address the student body as a whole. From the rostrum, I peered over my wire glasses, looking at the same students who only eight months before had given me the vote of confidence. While watching them file into the auditorium, my mind reconstructed past vistas of demonstrations, elections, forums, fires, speeches, negotiations, and friends, and Darryl. As I began, the crowd hushed. I quoted Malcolm X: " 'Sometimes, when a person's house is on fire and someone comes yelling fire, instead of the person who is awakened by the yell being thankful, he makes the mistake of charging the one who awakened him with having set the fire.' " * To the brothers and sisters I said, "And, some of you who have been calling me a Tom, I think we got too many people running around here with 'Afro-heads' yet with processed minds."

While they were offended, they loved it. I hit even harder at the so-called white revolutionaries: "We got too many warm-weather revolutionaries, with thin, white skin. We got too many people around here who read Guevara, wear green

---

* Malcolm X, *Malcolm X Speaks,* ed. George Breitman (New York: Grove Press, 1965), p. 45.

jackets and dungarees, and then claim to be revolutionaries, and yet who don't even understand the meaning of revolution, the basis of it, or its timing in history."

I understood Malcolm's definition of revolution and realized that none of us were willing to sacrifice anything that would even come near to fulfilling the meaning of that word; it would involve bloodshed—not self-defense but *offense,* not Afros, green jackets, daishikis or fist-raising, but guns to overturn the system. "Do unto your oppressor before he does unto you."

I told the traditional teachers who denounced me: "Many of you teachers who have blended into the walls over a number of years, only see change as meaning an increase in your salaries. You define all protest as violence because you're opposed to change."

I finished my speech by saying, "If you still believe that I've become an egotistical, power-hungry demagogue, I can only say that I wish the same things for you as you wished for me." I had committed one unforgivable sin—thinking out loud—and it made me an outcast.

I rejected the Afro-Americans' cultural revolution because they were in no position to dictate any norms or formulate morals for Blacks who never felt cultural deprivation. I had witnessed for myself during the initial stages of the Mideast crisis that the Jews gathered money and materials for Israel, while these so-called brothers and sisters remained idle, not supporting Egypt, playing cards, and partying.

Julius Lester pointed out that, "To talk militantly and to act militantly are not necessarily revolutionary." Rallies were becoming commonplace, and the revolutionary rhetoric all too redundant. The so-called anti-war movement had got caught up in impressing itself with how many people were on the streets; it became a numbers game—headlines for *The New York Times* and the *Daily News*—nothing more than a reactionary stimulus. We demonstrated against the war in Southeast Asia, to free the Panther 21 and Seale and eleven political prisoners, for ecology, to celebrate Malcolm's birthday, to protest the assassinations of Kennedy and King, and soon more murders at Kent and Augusta.

There had to be some way of organizing all the students for an all-out confrontation with the source of their problems. But the bureaucracy had been so successful in brainwashing the masses of students that they failed to see what was happening to their minds every day. They never once examined the educational process that taught them. Even while we demonstrated, we were still being controlled. We never initiated any action; we always reacted to one. Even at the height of our militancy, we were still reactionaries because of the system. We bypassed the "insignificant problems" to tackle the "important international struggles." We couldn't even crawl before we wanted to run. And this is why we always failed. We demonstrated against the "big things," but never did we seriously devote any time to end any one specific problem. We failed to see that the struggle against racism was a long-drawn-out battle and that many other collateral fights were involved.

The only platform I had left to work from was the City Student Government Council, representing 275,000 high school students—technically. The organization had a Mickey Mouse reputation. It was historically useless, merely a high school leadership circus. But whenever revolutionary or militant groups took to the streets, the Board of Education always justified its lack of response to the militants because the "Council was the truly representative group for students." Therefore, I would transform the Council.

I realized that the masses of students were not militant, and they believed in the viability of the system almost as strongly as I had. I would wage a campaign to make them see reality. I started to write down all the ways in which the administration repressed students and all the things that students needed during a crisis.

Then I submitted a list of accomplishments within my tenure and a letter thanking everyone who had helped me. (Those articles were never printed and no reason was ever given.) I realized that the administration had set an image for me that it wanted everybody to believe. So I had to be stifled. Finally, I came to an understanding with myself. I didn't hate Klein. I just lost all respect for him. The thing that I resented most in the way he put me down was that he used my relationship with Vickie against me. He knew how Black students felt about me because of Vickie and, through Fineberg, how much many white students hated me for the same reason.

In the end I felt we were two opponents, that he was the victor of an empty war in which I had been beaten. I chalked it up as a learning experience. As for Klein, drugs, racism, and flunking school—all these things would soon be out in the open.

I was just passing through.

Runnin'

It takes all the running you can do to stay in the same place.

Lewis Carroll

I STARTED RUNNING AGAIN. The cross-country season was almost over. There were only two big meets left, the Manhattan and City Championships. Mr. King wasn't even speaking to me, and I was no longer co-captain. None of this really bothered me, except that I had let him and the team down.

It was good to be back with the team, sitting in the locker room, jiving around and making jokes about each other. There was John ("The Smoke") Crews calling me "Uncle Don," Calypso Coop, still my friend, and old chicken-faced Matsoukas calling me a "washed-up politician."

We started regular workouts at Van Cortland Park in the Bronx. I was really out of shape. During practice I must have stopped at least ten times—I just couldn't get my second wind. We had time trials, and Tony was beating me consistently. Mr. King never even bothered to look at me when I finished, and I felt like I had to do better only to please him. I can't see why this man always got me upset. I respected him and always wanted to do well for his sake. Mr. King was a champion—all of us knew it. He was reliving the days of his prime through us, and we were letting him down. I began to punish myself at workouts, trying to cram over three months of practice into five days. Finally, I broke ice and beat Tony, but I must have looked like a fool coming down the finish, hopping for at least twenty-five yards because I had a cramp in my right leg. But this, I could tell, got Mr. King even angrier. By beating Tony after so little practice, I was destroying his self-confidence. Mr. King didn't have to say anything to me. I knew this was a crime. I stopped trying to beat Tony. Instead I concentrated on developing stamina and ridding myself of that damned chest pain.

Our team won medals in the Manhattan meet, but nobody was really satisfied. We had poor times. Vickie showed up afterward. She really got along well with the guys on the team, and it was always a good feeling to have your girl watch you compete—sort of gave you a little incentive.

The last cross-country meet of our senior year was coming up. Tony and I were the only seniors on the team, so this race meant a lot to us. We started working out together, running as often as we could, on Saturdays as well as Sundays. In school we didn't go to gym. We went outside and ran around Morningside Park and through Columbia University. As we developed more stamina, workouts naturally became easier. Before, we used to stop and rest, but now we talked and joked while we ran. We moved in rhythm, and never once did our legs lose their strength. It was such a beautiful feeling to be getting back in shape again, away from that hell up at school. Running in the rain, running in the sunshine, just running and running and feeling your legs grow stronger, your body more powerful.

Mr. King started to talk to me again. All the other coaches had been watching our team work out. Music and Art was expected to be victorious.

Finally the day came. We got up to Van Cortland early Saturday morning. The locker room was filled with a Ben-Gay aroma. Athletes from all schools were getting ready for the meet. After massaging tense muscles, we found ourselves on the line looking up and down at each other. Over two hundred of us dressed in golds, greens, reds, and maroons. We looked across the field at the narrow opening of the cross-country path half a mile away. Beyond that narrow opening lay two miles of track that had to be ripped off. Bang! I moved out, pulled out, reached the opening before the pack. For the first time in a major cross-country meet, I was out front. I could see Tony not too far behind with competitors all around him. I tore on up the hill, across the bridge, up the hill and down, going faster and faster.

Never had I felt such freedom and fulfillment before. I was actually in a position to win. While running, I had constructed the finish in my mind—the crowds surrounding the last stretch, Mr. King smiling, and me, me alone in sight coming down the straightaway. I could taste this victory, feel the wild expectations running throughout my body. I looked back and saw no one, absolutely no one. I was alone, all alone, listening to the rhythm of my breathing, looking down at the ground moving beneath me, not feeling pain, wanting to sing. The rays of the sun sparkled through the foliage. There were no sounds from nature; only me striding over the ground. I stopped.

I started laughing: I don't know why; I started laughing out loud. I was in front and could win, but it was only a question of time, more time than my patience could permit. I was tired of running—not physically tired, just tired of running over the same path, the same hills. I had just wanted to know what it felt like to be out there, number one, with hundreds of other legs and lungs behind me—just once I wanted to have this feeling. I soon caught sight of other runners. At first I started to run again, but the momentum was gone, and I really didn't care, so I stopped and started walking back toward the start.

On the way back I saw all those I had led. I saw Tony and gave him the high sign: "Kick their asses, man." Soon I caught sight of a little white guy, the last man—not by any means built to be a runner. I stopped at the hill and waited for him. I was tempted to ask him how he felt, why he was still running when he had no chance of being anything but last. But I stood there in silence listening to the rhythm of his breathing. When he passed, I sat down on a log and watched some ants on the ground—two little fuckers were carrying this fly. Next thing I knew, maroon pants with Tony in them were in front of me.

"What happened?" I asked.

"I'm tired of running over this path, man."

I smiled, "Me too."

Both of us started walking back to the start, laughing and clowning around all the way. The last big meet, and here we were walking backward.

I never in my life saw Mr. King so let down. He said absolutely nothing.

PART V

MOVING OUT

Requiem For Miseducation

I sit on a man's back, choking him and making him carry me, and yet assure myself and others that I am very sorry for him and wish to lighten his load by all possible means— except by getting off his back.

Tolstoy

NOT ONLY WAS I starting all over again, I was running backward. In school I was catching hell from everybody. I was being messed over from so many sides that I found it difficult to trust anybody. I was so bitter that outside my immediate family, there were only a handful of people that I had any respect for.

I trusted only Vickie and told her it was essential that she not violate my trust. It's important to have at least one person you can rely on, one person you can totally expose all of your emotions to without fear of that person using this knowledge against you.

While I did not at any time actually hate white people, the incessant animosity from white students in and around the school and intimidation from Klein forced me into a situation where all I saw was white people attacking me. It became clear that as long as I had Vickie, whites would feel free to say whatever they wanted to say about me—without the fear of being labeled racists. If I were truly a "Black man" in the popular sense of the phrase, that is, if I damned miscegenation and stood solely with my people and for their liberation, none of these whites would have had the courage to use me as a scapegoat for their own racism and frustrations. But I was not part of the Black community with Vickie around. It is unfortunate that at this point in history, the interracial affair has been given so much attention within the Black community—to the point where it serves to affirm "manhood" if a Black man condemns it. That kind of criterion reminds me of the days when ignorance guided people to think that certain women possessed satanical, supernatural powers, which made them witches to be burned at the stake.

It is difficult to say this in light of the knowledge that white people lynched, burned, and tarred the bodies of Black men who dared even look as though they desired to taste the white man's forbidden fruit.* But outside of this issue there was an even more important problem facing the Black community, one that would inevitably create internal strife and a cutback in what little gains had been made. It was the battle of individualism, the aggregate of qualities which distinguish one person from all others, vs. conformity, the impermeable shell of group identity. Because of the pressures to conform within the Black community, individualism and conformity have become dilemmas that many Black people have had to face, and in some cases succeeded in evading, with a view of human nature that frightens them. As the pressures to conform increase, the cohesiveness increases, but at what point does it become dysfunctional? When it serves only to reinforce comfortable beliefs and to limit people and ideas incompatible in that group's immediate sphere of interest. An individual must be free to do what he wants as long as he doesn't harm

---

* Ralph Ginzberg, in his book, *100 Years of Lynchings* (New York: Lancer Books, 1962), gives a nine-page partial listing of approximately five thousand Black people lynched in the United States since 1859. The book contains about three hundred newspaper stories of lynchings of Black people by whites, many of which are related to incidents between white men and Black women and white women and Black men.

other people. Any element that restrains those freedoms becomes an infringement on that individual's right to be a free
human being.

For so long it has been the white man who has set himself
up as "Bwana," the white settler who determined the freedoms of the Black natives. Whatever Bwana said, the natives
did—even though they wanted to kill him. What the natives
often failed to do was to let Bwana know that they were willing to do more to get their freedom than he (Bwana) was
willing to do to deprive them of it. In this way, as long as
those natives existed only as a group, they were easily controlled, for Bwana knew that if their spirits remained alive as
individuals, it would be totally impossible to control them.
Whoever thought the day would come when the natives
would echo Bwana's orders to one another?

During this time of isolation, I started hanging out in the
school's kitchen in the morning, talking to the cooks, and in
the afternoons I'd go see Arthur, who ran the elevators. Having so many people hate you makes the few friends you have
more valuable. Being an outcast, I was able to share and feel
the resentments of those at the bottom, the invisible beings we
never hear from. Being down there in the kitchen made me
think about the factory and people who work with their
hands. It made me realize that education is a luxury that few
people are fortunate enough to get. At the same time, so-
called educated people look down on those who work with
their hands. They don't realize—rather they refuse to acknowledge—that if everybody suddenly had to survive in the
streets, the people in the schools would be the first to die because they aren't prepared at all to confront reality. It is as
Cleaver pointed out, that what many of these so-called educated people have lacked physically, they have tried to replace
with their minds. Therefore, they have assigned the appela-
tions of superiority to the mind and inferiority to the body.

The cooks, especially Doris, always had a lot to say. There
was always this argument over respect. The cooks wanted to
be respected as live human beings. People, no matter what
jobs they maintain, want respect. Where there is no respect, it

is harder to maintain any dignity as a person. And also, when you have lost all respect for authority, the odds against you standing up against that authority mean nothing.

The times when I used to talk with Arthur, the elevator man (who was off in another world most of the time), I learned a lot.

Arthur and I met in a very strange way. Students aren't allowed to use school elevators without a doctor's note and an approval from the school administration. One day I tried to sneak a ride to the fourth floor just when Arthur decided to check everybody's pass. He started hollering at me and told me to get off his elevator. I screamed back, "What do you mean, *your* elevator?" I could see that I had struck a very sensitive nerve in him—it was his pride. Arthur just looked at me. I stood outside the elevator, looking at him and the people inside. Arthur slowly pulled the door closed. I felt very bad about the whole thing and approached him later to tell him I was sorry. In a short time we became very good friends. The thing that amazed me about Arthur was his knowledge about people and, again, this thing of respect. His whole life was that elevator—it *was* his. By just watching the people and listening to what they were saying, he had acquired a kind of wisdom and intelligence that often astounded you, caught you off guard because you just couldn't conceive of Arthur knowing anything but who got mugged on 125th Street and Amsterdam Avenue.

These people who stand around and watch things see a lot and have so much to say, but nobody ever asks them anything. Between Arthur and the cooks, school became bearable. I got free lunches from the cooks and free advice from Arthur. I wasn't taking advantage of the cooks; I just believed that all students should get free lunches.

Arthur really shook me up one day when he asked me what I was learning in classes and why I was never there. It really didn't make sense for me to be going to classes anymore, just filling up space and taking up time. While the courts were failing to dispense justice, the schools failing to educate, America hiding the truth, and the military manipulating its wargasms, we were sitting in classes discussing the lessons of man's past mistakes, the same mistakes we continue to make today. I had stopped going to classes and had begun to read books that had relevance to my life—that is, I was reading about today, what was happening right now. Eventually I just cut out of school. I had acquired enough experience and made enough mistakes to be successful, at least to a degree, in building a movement to confront the Board of Miseducation.

I didn't even ask myself—what were the consequences of leaving school? I just looked at my situation and figured I didn't have too much to lose. In English we were reading two plays, *Hamlet* and *Macbeth,* and learning how to spell. In math, Miss Lane already understood that I was there only because it was a college requirement. I wasn't learning more than just enough to get by. I sat in the back of the class watching Wysnesky, a student who was a magician. All during class I'd sit and watch him doing card tricks, pulling coins out of his ears, making silver dollars disappear.

In art appreciation I was learning how not to appreciate art. We learned about Fra Angelico, Michelangelo, Tintoretto, Giorgione, Titian, Raphael, and Da Vinci, all of the Renaissance period, and very briefly of other periods in art. You would think that Europe was the only place on the face of the earth where art existed. Up until then I knew nothing of African art. And it is safe to say that if the Black Security Council had not demanded that attention be given to African, Asian, and other art cultures besides the European, the teachers would have remained quite content with leaving things the way they were.

In ceramics I worked almost a month on the bust of a slave in pain. Mr. Veres put the thing in the kiln, and when he took it out, the damned thing wouldn't stand. It just kept falling over. But it never broke, so I renamed it "The Head That Wouldn't Stand."

History had much to offer, and I spoke to Fran for a good

while about taking a temporary leave of absence. She gave me a list of books that I would need to keep up with the course work. I got the names of students in my other classes and arranged to call them from time to time to find out what was going on, when I had a test, and so forth. As for my attendance record, David, my official teacher, didn't too much care for the system himself, so that was no problem. In crafts I was far enough ahead of the class to remain safe for a while.

I left primarily because I believed that anybody who was aware of the inequity and the counterproductive effects of the educational system had an obligation to use whatever abilities he or she possessed to abolish it.

■ ■ ■

There is no accommodation made for the increasing number of students who are not responding to existing programs. Most administrators pride themselves on the achievements of their best students, which is natural since these "achievers" raise the school's prestige, records of scholarships, and number of admissions to good colleges. And it's tough shit for the rest of us.

Most of the attention is given to the "achievers" while the "underachievers," unprepared from elementary school, are not able to deal with high school programs. The demographic shift in the city's population—the Black migration and white exodus—has changed the composition of the student population, and the reaction to date from administrators is that they resent this changing composition because it lowers the standards of their schools.

But there are other questions and problems that need answers. Any time one school has a graduating class of 513 students, of which only twenty did not go on to college, and you have citywide figures like the ones mentioned on page 82, you know something has got to be wrong. Somebody is getting shortchanged, and somehow it's being done intentionally. Whenever such large numbers of failures are involved, the entire onus cannot be placed on the students. The large majority of dropouts and those who received the general diploma—which is a worthless piece of paper—were Black and Puerto Rican.*

"To get a good job, get a good education!" Everybody's heard that, and yet just look at the obstacles confronting the working-class student. First, many students are unprepared from junior high school, so they are unable to take advantage of the high school programs. There is no accommodation made for those who are learning at a slower pace. Those who are benefiting from the programs are placed in special classes aimed at getting a "good education." They are prepared for the next step, the SAT and PSAT college admission tests, which measure cumulative verbal and math aptitudes of a student and are used as criteria for college admission and placement.

Middle- and upper-class whites love to talk about how high their college board scores are and complain that Black students are getting into college with low scores, which worries them. The truth of the matter is that these college admissions tests are constructed intentionally to screw the Black student and, in general, the working class.

Most Black people are poor. Only 25 percent are in the middle class—that is, have white-collar occupations, a high school education, or middle-class income, compared with 60 percent of whites.† In most cases Black students throughout the country are receiving inferior educations in overcrowded schools with obsolete equipment and inexperienced or disinterested, salary-secure teachers. Fighting discrimination and deprivation, a black person coming from a ghetto into a school is in an alien world. How the hell could these college admissions tests be given without the results showing Blacks and lower-class whites always lagging far behind in "achievement"?

---

* The general diploma will be abolished in 1973, and the same academic diploma will be given to everyone. This change was initiated only after militant demands were made by Black and Puerto Rican vocational high school students.

† *Changing Times, The Kiplinger Magazine,* July 1969.

These tests don't measure anything for the Black student. The one or two gifted brothers and sisters who are able to transcend the limitations of their low socio-economic background and successfully achieve comparable scores with high-income whites, are used as scapegoats by those who argue that college admissions tests are valid and not out to deprive thousands of lower-income people of a college education.

The simple truth is that giving more Black people a chance to get educated takes up space that could be filled with whites. And yet whites still argue among themselves that the requirements shouldn't be relaxed for middle-class Blacks because "they are no different from middle-class whites." Colleges started opening up to qualified Black students only after those who never would have the chance to see college doors took to the streets and told the white Establishment that it's freedom for everybody or freedom for nobody. Even the violent aftermath of Martin Luther King's assassination brought about scholarships for Black students.

A few token Blacks were admitted under the quota system, and yet whites still complain that *all* Black people are getting into colleges just because they are Black. There was never any sincerity on the part of the institutions of higher learning when it came to admitting Black students—it was done as a show of good face. It was just like Malcolm said, whenever you get a new administration in the White House, the first thing they do is to call down the Negro Leaders and invite them for coffee, to show that the administration's O.K.

All the elements are clearly against us. These college admissions tests don't measure our intelligence; they measure the ruthlessness of a system responsible for this situation that knowingly continues to uphold these methods of testing as valid criteria for admission to colleges and universities.

The beneficiaries of this inequity cannot be reasoned with because they harbor only a self-centered and elitist opinion about the problem. They see the problem in relation to themselves and not those who are the victims. It would take long hours of persuading to make them understand that it is not the victims who are responsible for their situation, that the full blame should be placed on the structure of the educational system for perpetuating this heinous crime. The only time these tests won't count is when they are not given. The deal made between high schools and colleges should be ripped off so that everybody can get some education. All of the commissions on civil disorders have found that the typical riot participant is a high school dropout. As Malcolm often said, "It is a system that crushes people and penalizes them for not being able to stand up under the weight."

It is clear today that if this downhill channeling of Black and Puerto Rican and lower-class white students continues at the present rate, America will lose its chance to engage in a bloodless revolution. The colleges must change their admissions policies to conform with the restructuring of the high schools—high schools must develop new programs to prepare students who are not being reached by existing programs for college entrance. In other words, high schools must implement and restructure existing programs that will lead right into college instead of the present system of unrelated prerequisites that lead up to and stop at college. The *independent* attempts made by colleges and universities to accommodate those students who are unprepared to handle their work have failed primarily because the colleges alone cannot change this situation. It's just like a tree—it doesn't grow from its branches but from its roots, and this is where the change has to be made. It is a question of reevaluating the existing programs as far back as elementary school. Unless changes are made from this level, very little can be accomplished to change negative social attitudes at the college level.

Education should be the answer, but it is not. The economic gap between whites and Blacks is tremendous. According to another *Time* "Situation Report," a Black man who completes four years of high school earns less than the white male who finishes only eight years of elementary school. The Black man with four years of college has a lower median income than a white male who has only four years of high school. And a Black family often has to have two or more workers to earn as much as a white family with one member at work.*

The failure of the school system to educate Black, Puerto Rican, and working-class white students has been documented. And the economic discrimination in this country has also been documented. The curriculum is not geared to the interests of New York City's high school students. No school system can be considered to be doing its job when 63.5 percent of an original class either leaves school by the senior year or fails to get passing grades.† The problems underlying this crisis have a lot to do with the mentality of those running the school system. The most salient example of these destructive attitudes was reported by the U. S. Department of Health, Education, and Welfare.‡ A High School Principals' Study Seminar was conducted in which the stated purpose was to "describe and analyze the occupational psychology of New York City high school principals and its relation to the emergent problems of urban high schools." They hoped, by focusing on the person most directly involved in high school administration, to locate the key problems of the high school as seen through the role of the principal. They also set out to examine any contradictions and misconceptions standing in the way of adequate responses to problems of urban secondary education. Their major finding was the "defensiveness" of principals whose main concern is with "holding the line against encroachments on their authority within the schools and defending the system, their careers, and themselves from outer attack." According to the report:

A rhetoric of professionalism is used to justify claims of expertise and demands for autonomy . . . New issues and arguments must be ideologically absorbed, refuted, or evaded . . . They thus

---

* *Time,* April 6, 1970.
† *Report of New York City High Schools,* p. 2.
‡ High School Principals' Study Seminar, Arthur J. Vidich and Charles W. McReynolds, February, 1969.

become defenders of the status quo at the very time that the maintenance to their claim to professional expertise and educational leadership requires that they respond creatively to the crisis which challenges them.

In some schools people come right down to the point of graduating, only to find out that they didn't have the requirements either to graduate or to get into a college. Other students are transferred to night school (which later I found out was against the law) if certain procedures were not followed. New York City has never met the State Department of Education's recommended ratio of one licensed guidance teacher for every 250 students. There is no uniform guidance system. Some students sit on benches for hours, days, and even months before they get a few minutes of "guidance."

It's an entirely different reality from what the television would like an uninformed public to believe. Such programs as Room 222 are lies. They show all teachers as friendly and understanding, and all students with problems which are ultimately solved by teachers running around after school hours, going into students' homes, offering a helping hand. They show a principal who never calls the police to beat up the little, shiny-faced Negroes in the school and who says his door is always open. Many people really believe that shit when they see it on TV.

The city should establish and fund college guidance centers that would be open to all students who want advice on college admission. As for the grading system, its destructive effects have already been proven. What it has done more than anything else is to develop a code of academic cheating. The current grading system doesn't help the student to see where he is either weak or strong; it is a comparison of students to *other* students. Grades should be eliminated. If people insist on having something to replace them, a system of credit evaluation based on a student's real performance (not on slanted IQ tests) could be instituted. Any immediate transition to a new system cannot be expected to work without difficulties.

But I suppose it is a difficult thing to ask that teachers have the students' best interests at heart. Many corporations use grades as a hiring criterion; colleges and universities use them for admissions standards. There should also be an independent study program for senior high school students. By the time most students reach their senior year in high school, they realize the worthlessness of most of what is being put before them and what they are *required* to do. Students must be free to leave their classrooms to confront the world they are expected to live in, to become conscious of the real world. The current events—Vietnam, Laos, Cambodia, nationwide racial polarization, international struggles—aren't part of any curriculum. If they were, it would be relevant. The academic community waits decades until relevance has passed and then teaches what has already happened as history. Overcrowding may one day force the independent study program into effect.

It's crazy that people should spend the first sixteen years of their productive life in school. There should be some period in high school when students are not required to come to school and are able to work and read a certain amount of books of their own choice. After this period of a semester or even a year, a discussion or creative writing program should supplement the independent reading period. I am aware of the fact that jobs would have to be available and that there would be difficulties with students who don't like to read.

However, jobs *can* be found, and there *are* many students who could only benefit from such a program. Once we were outside of the school, the institutionalized perspective instilled in us would crumble, and through working with people of all temperaments, races, and nationalities, we would acquire a broader scope on life, the world, and our position in it. It would be a time where we would have the freedom to straighten our minds out—to find out "Who am I?" (That sounds funny, doesn't it? Well . . .) I know that such a program is better than sitting around in some stuffy room verbally pussywhipping some outdated novels and melodramatic poems (no matter who wrote them).

Oh, I almost forgot something: what will we do with the

teachers while all the students are out working and reading? Let them have a coffee break?

If the independent reading program was conducted during the senior year, this would only free more English teachers to teach the lower grades, which could be split up into fewer students per teacher, providing more contact and comfort for both the students and teachers. It is from one extreme to the other; at the outset, like all methods of radical change, it will probably fail. We have never experienced such loose structure before. We have been, in a sense, spoonfed since birth. We are unable to deal with independence. But if the correct methods are applied for the changeover, the program can be functional.

■ ■ ■

I wanted to see if things I had heard were true—about schools where ceilings were put on grades, where no matter how good a student was, he got no higher than an 85, or where some schools were funded on the basis of IQ test scores, where ninth-graders were given sixth-grade IQ tests so that they could get high scores.

The records show thousands of illegal suspensions and disciplinary actions. The principals violate the law. The police enforce the principals' violation of the law, and the student is always the victim.

Sometimes the educational system makes an attempt to become relevant in the form of a one- or two-day seminar or conference. On that day we would discuss anything from drugs to ecology, from race to revolution. These discussions might come right after a U.S. invasion of another country, after the assassination of some prominent figure, or on the eve of an anti-war demonstration. What you would try to solve in one day was probably the result of decades of neglected problems. And the discussions that are held on that one day should have been held 365 days of the year. It manifests either ignorance or insincerity on the part of those who organize these one-day crusades.

The central issue is the autocracy that the Board of Educa-

tion has vested in the principal. When the autocracy is threatened, it is protected by the police department.* With regard
to the drug problem, we see that the high schools have become wide open to the selling of drugs. The source of drugs
is not the high schools, yet because of corruption and the
unwillingness of the city government to crack down on the
big suppliers of drugs, such as the Mafia, the high school
student is subjected to prison-like conditions in order for the
Board of Education to claim that something is really being
done to cut off the supply of heroin; this is a pretense that has
misled the public to support the Board of Education's violation of the constitutional rights of students. High school students are not the suppliers of drugs; they are the recipients
from well-organized dealers whom the police should be
cracking down on instead of brutalizing sixteen- and seven-
teen-year-old people. Any time a school has set one day
aside under the banner of "Drug Prevention Week," it is a
trick to deceive the public that something is being done. No
problem, especially not narcotics addiction, can be solved in
one day or one week or by having teachers act as informers
to the police department.† Only a program of rehabilitation
is logical and necessary.

Even at demonstrations police intervention must also be
questioned. The public never sees the months of student frustration due to administrative procrastination. The defenders
of the status quo don't want anything changed. Protest is always met with police repression based solely on the discretion
of the Board of Education.

Unfortunately, teaching in high schools is not considered a
desirable profession. Some intelligent people who could make

---

* According to a Formal Opinion of Counsel No. 67 in the N.Y. State
Department of Education, Division of Law:

Police authorities have no power to interview children in the school building or to use the school facilities in connection with official police work, and the Board of Education has no right to make students available to the police for such purposes. Police who wish to speak to students must take the matter up directly with the parents. Police can enter the schools, however, if they have a warrant for arrest or search, or if a crime is committed on school property.

† Board of Education Curriculum Bulletin No. 16, pp. 19–20.

excellent teachers don't want any part of the bureaucracy of rules and regulations. Other intelligent, empathetic, and well-qualified persons who would like to work in the public schools are unable to get around the obstacles erected by the Board of Examiners (who would sooner hire an American who has taken a few courses in Spanish to teach that language, than a native speaker who has a little difficulty writing perfect English).

Let me, for a moment, apply a bit of faulty logic. If teachers were placed in the situation that students find themselves in, what would their complaint be? In a nation that is ostensibly based on capitalism and competition, why shouldn't teachers also be forced to compete with other teachers, as students are forced to compete with other students? Almost invariably, those teachers who had established rapport with their students would find their classes overcrowded while those who were inefficient and unable to communicate would be left alone. Naturally two wrongs don't make one right. However, this does illustrate what teachers would have to go through if they were in the students' position.

Which leads to another point. Since records are kept on the performances of students, why shouldn't there be records kept on teachers, written by students for entering students to look over what students thought about teachers in the past.

The HEW Study on Principals revealed what has been known all along: that the desired student is polite and respectful of authority—he accepts school learning as important. The principals view the school as a smoothly functioning organization of personnel and materials in which teachers teach and students "achieve." Neither the rationale of the school nor the authority of its staff is questioned. The best students go on to college while those who fail or lose interest know and accept that it is their own fault and quietly take their appropriate place in the job structure. These so-called professionals want total conformity. But, the challenge presented to these professionals by troublemakers and non-conformists is one they have a *responsibility* to confront.

(None of this love it or leave it crap.) Today the space program is already contemplating orbital stations while the school system is moving backward. There are minimal gains being made—every city has a well-publicized demonstration project—but very few children benefit from them.

The community from time to time gets behind a principal and against the students to use any means necessary to suppress the very problems the principal helped to create. Any time one man in charge of a school is interested solely in maintaining the illusion of stability and that man intimidates students who are trying to reveal the true situation of the school, it is a crime. Any tampering with college files, keeping letters, or using unjust disciplinary procedures is also criminal.

The school newspaper, like the mass media, reinforces those values and demands of the institution it functions in. The media create opinion. But the school newspaper can do more than create opinion. It can be used to spread propaganda, as well—especially where the parents are concerned. The principal realizes this. He will use any vehicle that he can to promote himself, to maintain his position, to ward off any and all forms of threats to his security, power, and prestige.

I saw this for myself in the newsletters to the parents. The illusion of stability was maintained and comments referring to the principal were prefaced by, "under the progressive leadership of . . ." When parents find themselves working closely with the administration, they sometimes cannot resist taking advantage of the opportunities afforded to those who support the principal. Supporting the principal on any and all fronts, especially if they have a child who intends to go to college, is to the parents' advantage. But in the process of doing so, if truth and justice are sacrificed, they have been accomplices in a criminal act.

How can anyone with any degree of intelligence see all of this and more and say, "Well, I already know that" or "It's always been that way," not only accepting that position, but remaining a complacent onlooker? If students would categorize themselves intellectually and examine their academic environments, their relation to society, their place in it, and the track they had been placed on even before they were born, they might, find themselves in one of two positions: (1) That of never having known poverty, hardship, or a struggle for survival. Their world is one in which books tell them virtually all they know, so that they "think too much and feel too little." Their grades are the only thing that mean anything to them. Their "credentials" are all important and nothing else is. (2) That of having been born to fail and having become aware of that. These students must take on the task, with what little they know of the world, and fight to abolish those conditions they find intolerable. Those who have no respect for grades constitute a threat for the grade grubber. Through the system of grading and competition, students have been indoctrinated from birth. Even today we find people begging for competition, to outdo someone else. They are not necessarily concerned about themselves—so long as they know someone is under them, they feel O.K. They are terrified at the idea of someone else also getting ahead. They are terrified of people who don't believe in the same values (those of grades) that for all their school lives they've been fighting for. The process is so effective that it is often irreversible. That's the way many people think—they define their personal success in terms of what other people think or acknowledge as "success."

■　■　■

I looked back at my past involvement in the Student Government and learned from my mistakes. I had been too preoccupied with not alienating people. My greatest mistake was to lose my cool, to allow my emotions to govern my actions. Having Vickie at my side during meetings and forums didn't help matters any; it only invalidated everything I had to say in the eyes of those who listened. As for the City Council, I had been using the wrong approach. Both Castka and the Council could be used until a coalition of the victim groups was formed for an all-out confrontation with the Board of Education.

If the Board of Education maintained that the Council

represented 275,000 high school students, I would use their claim to expose the inadequacies and injustices of the educational system. It would be difficult because I knew only too well how high school students scorn anything titled Student Government. And also how many of them could not believe that anybody working in the Student Government would be able to repel the pressures of co-optation.

The City Council provided me with a base and audiences in forms of conferences and seminars, none of which were ever taken advantage of by other students who had been in the position I was now in. I would attend as many conferences as possible. Wherever groups of people were, I'd be there exposing them to a different point of view, different from the one being presented by the Board of Education, the United Federation of Teachers, and the High School Principals' Association.

The City Council wasn't militant and would never be militant. Most of the representatives from the predominantly Black schools had already walked out of the Council stating that it had nothing to do with Black students. And at this point I had only a feeling of what I was getting at; my thoughts were still unclear.

I was through with nonviolence. I wanted a confrontation with the Board of Education, but not one that was merely disruption for disruption's sake. There had to be no loose ends. I knew only too well how the Board of Education publicly exploits violence, the criminals, and rebels without programs. Students like these have no program, no political objective, no objective, period. The Board often *uses* those types to strike fear into the minds of both parents and students so that they will support the Board's policies of arbitrary repression.

I had to know at all times what effect my speech and my appearance would have on people. I had to know not only what was needed for today, but also what the future would demand. There had to be some lasting purpose to the confrontation which I saw necessary.

My final act of involvement at Music and Art was to submit an article for publication in the school yearbook, entitled
"Music and Art—A Closed Society?"

To get something published, you had to submit the article
to the *Yearbook* staff. They decided what should and should
not be printed. I had turned in my article six months ahead of
time. It was censored by the assistant superintendent of
schools, Abraham Wilner, and by Klein. The article mentioned no names, nothing slanderous, or obscene. It even
complied with the Board of Education's standards. Klein objected to the article being published because, in his words,
there was "no counter opinion as strong as his represented in
the book." The teacher in charge of the *Yearbook* at first
took issue with this and told me that they would have my
article printed and slipped into the book, at the last moment.
But she crumbled under Klein's intimidation. She told me
that Klein had even threatened to fire the printer if he printed
my article. Once again Klein had taken my property, dupli-
cated it without my permission. In fact he gave me back the
xerox copy and kept the original.

On December 22, 1969, the *Yearbook* staff wrote an in-
troductory statement for my article, stating Klein's reasons
for prohibiting it and their position that seniors should not be
denied the right to read it for themselves. Six months later, a
few days before graduation, I received a letter from the
teacher in charge of the *Yearbook* staff telling me that *they*
were sorry that their minds were changed so late and that I
had every right to be "annoyed and angry." She said that,
after rereading the article several times, discussing it with the
Yearbook staff and others, everyone was in agreement that at
that particular moment it did not seem "relevant enough" although she thought it was "relevant generally." She went on
to apologize for leading me to believe it would be used and
then "so precipitously" having the *group* change its mind.

Even though my article wasn't included, I knew, because
of that incident, that what I had written had more truth behind it than anyone wanted to face. I said that:

One cannot despise Music and Art. On the contrary, there were those of us who stood in support of our school when it was burning. Those who had been used to retain "normalcy" ultimately discovered that they were being manipulated and deceived; trust lost can never be restored. It's only a question of time before this school falls like all the rest.

Notes On A Black Stripe
In The American Flag

Integration. The word has no real meaning. I ask you: in the racial sense in which it's used so much today, whatever "integration" is supposed to mean, can it precisely be defined?

Malcolm X

OTHER THAN a few periodic checks at school, to take tests and work on my paintings, I was free. The City Council became my new base of operations. Just around the same time that I was pulling out of school, I received a letter from the New York State Association of Student Councils, inviting me to a District Presidents' meeting to be held in Albany. I had already made a commitment with WNYE–FM "Speak Your Mind," a New York radio series, and was undecided on which invitation to accept. It was a question of numbers, of how many people could be reached. I thought about it for a while and decided that going to Albany would be a better idea because at present, I still had no solid program.

We were in a car en route to Albany to attend a District Presidents' State meeting. Me, a "president"—what a joke. In the car I was struck by the variety of white people. Rarely had I come into contact with a white person who wasn't Jewish. In fact, up until this trip I had always sort of believed that the majority of white people in this country were Jewish. The people in the car with me were White Anglo-Saxon Protestants and Catholics, elites, economically and politically.

Melzer, the only Jew in the car, reacted to my presence as if I was the first Black person he had ever seen. One look at where he lived caused me to assume that, in his high socioeconomic class, he didn't come into contact with Blacks very often, not even maids or gardeners. It just seemed typical of white people, that whenever a Black person was in their presence, they always brought up some topic pertaining to race. Melzer cited the suppression of Black history and one "classic example": A poster depicting the charge of Teddy Roosevelt's Rough Riders up San Juan Hill shows the men as all whites. "Yet many blacks were up there," he pointed out. He now proposed a solution to compensate for the injustice that historians and journalists committed against the Blacks who played a major role in molding "the gallant American past."

His proposal was that a "black stripe be added to the American flag running from the end of the field of stars to the bottom right-hand corner intersecting the red and white stripes." The black to illustrate "the role that Black Americans played in bringing our nation forward as the greatest nation on earth." His ignorance and arrogance angered me. His overall presentation was one of: Now that we've given you a stripe, what *more* do you want? But this was a typical situation; it was America out in the open. At Franklin K. Lane, Black people took down the American flag, cast it aside, and raised the black, red, and green colors of liberation. And yet here, sitting right beside me, was liberal America, offering one black stripe to compensate for four hundred years of oppression, of emasculation, of subjection to a system designed to teach us to hate ourselves, to erode our intelligence, and to prevent independence. To agree to the inclusion of a black stripe in the American flag is to be identified with the slaughtering of the people whom this land originally belonged to, the Indians. White nationalists took the land from the Indians and reduced them to creatures living in rusted hulls of automobiles on "reservations."

When we arrived in Albany, it was night and snowing. It was beautiful; there were huge homes, nice streets, and everywhere it was clean. They left me at a house with some of the whitest people I've ever seen.

I am free on the racial question. I believe, as Malcolm did, in a society in which people can live like human beings on the basis of equality. I am against all prejudice, but I couldn't help noticing the vast distinction between whites I had known in New York City and those in Albany.

This environment was Southern, at least what I conceived a Southern environment to be. I stayed with Mr. and Mrs. Toomey and their eight children—Mary Beth, William, Nancy, James, Margaret, Joseph, Paul, and Maura. Mary Beth, the oldest, was sixteen and Maura, the youngest, was five. To me they seemed like one of those Thanksgiving Day families. Almost immediately I was on the defensive and pre-judging them, the personification of lily-white America.

I was more conscious of my Blackness than I had ever been. Mr. and Mrs. Toomey hadn't even spoken to me for more than ten minutes before they left me, a complete stranger, in their home alone with their eight children. I didn't understand this. In fact, I was shocked.

It began to dawn on me that I had been living and fighting in a very small and isolated environment. As for this "distinction between whites," there was a difference between WASPs and Jews. These people were White Anglo-Saxon Protestants. I had always heard Jews using the term "WASP" but never tried to find out what that word actually meant. I had been paranoid in meeting these people because of all the stereotypes I had unconsciously accepted as facts.

Their children wouldn't give me a moment's rest. Margaret, nine, and Joseph, eight, played with my clothes. They got dressed up in my shirts and pants. I ate with them and waited for Mr. and Mrs. Toomey to return.

When they did, I expressed my amazement that they had

trusted me alone with their little children. Mr. Toomey sat down to talk. Right off we started to discuss the racial situation in Albany. So far, on this visit, I had not seen any Black people. I remembered that during the anti-budget-cut rally last year, I had seen many Blacks living around the State House in slums. In a moment of Tomism, I decided to bring up a conversation I had overheard in the car. I said jokingly, "I hear you're having racial problems over soul food."

He said that I shouldn't have said that, it was typical of ignorant people to single out the only seemingly insignificant part of the Black struggle and ridicule it. "Whites have always been catered to—they take it for granted. Spanish people, Chinese people, Jewish people all have certain foods that they like and prefer."

We then started talking about confrontation and here again he was telling me that "it is always the protest of the minority that confronts and ultimately forces the majority to capitulate, to change, and adopt new laws." Either this family didn't fit, I didn't, or they were very unusual people. My mind was wandering, from the hell of Franklin K. Lane, to the superficial racial harmony of Music and Art, and now to a new America. It was new for me because I had known none other like it.

Later that night I went upstairs and started writing about my feelings and how it was impossible for Jews to call themselves white, in the same sense that WASPs considered themselves white. In Brownsville I had always referred to Jews as a race, but there was no such thing as a Jewish race.*

---

* Clyde Kluckhohn, in his book *Mirror for Man* (New York: Fawcett World Library, n.d.), pp. 87–88, says:

To classify human beings as a race on other than a purely biological basis destroys the proper meaning of the term and removes even the support provided by the one-sided biological argument. Here, "the Aryan race" is a contradiction in terms . . . The Jewish race is equally a misnomer because there is a great diversity in physical type among those who practice or whose parents or grandparents have practiced the Jewish religion and because the physical stereotype which is popularly considered Jewish is actually common among all sorts of Levantine and Near Eastern peoples who are not and have never been Jewish.

Jews have mixed so much with

I remembered the parents I had spoken to. Once I had been invited to dinner in a Jewish community. I went to discuss the methods Klein and Fineberg were using to silence me. In the middle of the discussion the topic shifted, and we were talking about Israel—at least they were. One lady said, "I'd love to be there, in a land where everybody is Jewish." I listened to a girl who had gone to work on a kibbutz describe the feeling of being an Israeli, with a new pride in themselves as Jews, in Judaism. She said, "It made me proud to be a Jew and more conscious of the fact that I was a Jew because I had never really felt like a real Jew." I asked them, "Do you feel like one people because you are Jews? Do you, in Israel, look upon each other as Jews first? I mean, what is it that holds you together?" The girl looked at the table for a moment, stared off in silent thought, then replied, "It wasn't so much that we were Jews—our lives were at stake."

Their lives were at stake. Israel was a part of them, gave them a sense of new pride, of Jewish consciousness. The victory in the Six-Day War of 1967 was a psychological boost for Jews. In that same year in Chicago, Jewish radicals broke with Black militancy when they walked out of the conference refusing to support Black demands—including one demand that called for a resolution condemning Israel as an imperialist aggressor in the Middle East.

Many Jews have not been able to get over their years in slavery and the Nazi holocaust. The building of the State of Israel, the wanderings of the Jews since their dispersal two thousand years ago, and the horrors of Nazi ovens are parts of history that Jews seek not to forget, but have made central to their culture. No one can deny the significance of always being aware of the events that unify a people. The Jewish

---

the varying physical types of the different countries in which they have lived that by no single physical or physiological feature nor by any group of such features can they be distinguished as a race. Huntington regards them as a kith, like the Icelanders, the Parsis, and the Puritans. That some Jews can be identified on sight is due less to physically in- herited traits, than as Jacob says, to "those emotional and other reactions and conditionings which take the form of distinctive facial behavior, bodily posturings and mannerisms, sentence tone, and temperamental and character peculiarity" which can be traced to Jewish customs and to the treatment of Jews at the hands of non-Jews.

community, family structure, synagogue, philanthropic and fraternal organizations are all forces which have held the Jewish consciousness together while assimilation, or Americanization, absorbs the Jews into the fabric of American society. The Jews' upward mobility, to a large degree, is due to their commitment to education. For Jews, the 1950's supposedly marked the close of racist quota systems in American colleges. On March 1, 1971, *Newsweek* reported that the proportion of Jews in colleges was twice that of the general U.S. population. And the proportion of Jews enrolled in graduate and professional schools was triple that of students in the general population. Although Jews accounted for only 3 percent of the U.S. population, they provided more than 10 percent of all American college teachers; at elite Ivy League universities such as Harvard, Jews represented as much as a third of the faculty.

It appears as one reads through American Jewish history that the Jewish Establishment has always looked out for the newly immigrated Jews who constituted a social liability to established American Jews. And from this, one can easily understand the resentment Black people reserve for Uncle Tom Negroes who realize that their status, economic security, and livelihood are derived from a segregated system geared to keep Black people at the bottom—even when they think they're on top. They enjoy life at the expense of others.

White Christian Americans claimed that, once they became aware of the brutality practiced against the Jews and the full horror of the Nazi ovens in Auschwitz, they found it far more difficult to tolerate many of the petty forms of anti-Semitism that had long been a commonly accepted facet of U.S. society. This of course is a hypocritical statement. Professor Stanley M. Elkins of the University of Chicago, author of one of the most brilliant studies of slavery in the United States (*A Problem in American Institutional Life*, published by the University of Chicago Press in 1959), pointed out the parallels between the way Nazi concentration camps changed the personalities of prisoners who survived and the way in which slavery in America altered the personalities of Black people brought from Africa and molded the character of Black people born here—that Sambo, the dumb, lazy, shiftless Negro, was a reality. So damaging had slavery been on Black people that its effects are still present today. The Black man was reduced to a boy, a child dependent on the white society, who controls life or death. Elkins in his study said that the most striking aspect of the concentration camp inmates' behavior "was its childlike quality." He said that the childlike behavior had so damaged the prisoners' minds that they identified with their SS guards, accepted the Gestapo's value system, even sewed uniforms to look like them, imitating their mannerisms, absorbing their German nationalism and anti-Semitism even to a point where Jewish prisoners became anti-Semitic. And Malcolm X has said that the worst crime the white man has committed has been to teach Black People to hate themselves. Elkins wrote, "to all these men, reduced to complete and childish dependence upon their masters, the SS had actually become a father-symbol . . ." It was clear to me that America was a hypocritical, colonial power, that nowhere in history has there been any other group of oppressed peoples who love their oppressors as much as Black people. No other racial or ethnic group of people have tried harder to integrate into the system and been met with more brutality and social degradation than Black people. When desegregated school systems were legalized by the Supreme Court in 1896 establishing the "separate but equal" doctrine in the case of *Plessy v. Ferguson* (I say this with a smile), it was a third of the battle won. Prior to this, some states had laws forbidding *any* education for Black people. Justice Henry Billings Brown, in declaring the Court's opinion on the separate but equal doctrine, said: *"If one race be inferior to the other socially, the Constitution of the United States cannot put them on the same plane."* * (Emphasis added.)

An underlying factor in this question of desegregation is

---

* 3. Id., at 163 U.S. 543, 16 Sup. Ct. 1140, 41 L. Ed. 258.

miscegenation. I truly believe that the White Citizens' Councils and many other white Americans see this as the real issue. And yet what other race has watered down more races than the white race?

To just about every psychological brutality that the Nazi regime practiced against the Jews and other prisoners, American slavery shows a parallel. And so every trait or piece of evidence like IQ scores, which the new breed of intellectual racists use to support their claims of Black inferiority, are only the crystallized effects of four hundred years of slavery at the hands of the white race.

It has been asked before, and it still puzzles many—why is it that the Jew and the Black man are not one? Historically it is only logical that the two groups should be united. Is it as Baldwin says: "the Jew has been taught—and, too often accepts—the legend of Negro inferiority; and the Negro, on the other hand, has found nothing in his experience with Jews to counteract the legend of Semitic greed." I saw that during the New York teachers' strike, Jews were traumatized by the resentments between Black parents and Jewish teachers. And because my life in America had been conditioned by this resentment, I naturally came to regard the Jew as the True White American. Jews I had known thought of themselves as Americans first and Jews second. There was nothing religious about them. We, my friends and I, even joked about it. My friends took Rosh Hashanah and Yom Kippur as seriously as I did Halloween.

Charles E. Silberman, author of the highly informative and prophetic book, *Crisis In Black and White,* says that, "For in truth there is no 'white American'; there are only white Americans." The Jews had blended in with the WASPs, the Italian-Americans, the Irish-Americans, the Polish-Americans. All of these groups have different views on sex, education, religion, etc. These ethnic groups brought about more racism because they had inward, reinforced, inherent prejudices, and were physically segregated in "communities" which preserved their identity. Ethnicity to a large degree influenced their behavior. These white groups are segregated, even from one another. So just how or with which group is the Black man supposed to integrate if all these groups practice exclusivity and have in common an inherent assumption of white superiority and black inferiority?

I believe that Malcolm's analysis of the situation is correct, that it is really no longer a question of Black people forcing ourselves into a society where we are not wanted but of our building our own community in such a way that our own social group becomes more desirable and we no longer have to look outside our race for people with whom we feel more comfortable. "I believe," Malcolm said, "that if we migrated back to Africa culturally, philosophically, and psychologically, while remaining here physically, the spiritual bond that would develop between us and Africa through this cultural, philosophical, and psychological migration, so-called migration, would enhance our position here, because we would have our contacts with them acting as roots or foundations behind us." *

Frederick Douglass, the great Black abolitionist, said more than a century ago, "We are here, and here we are likely to be. To imagine that we shall ever be eradicated is absurd and ridiculous. We can be remodified, changed, and assimilated, but never extinguished . . . We shall neither die out nor be driven out; but shall go with this people, either as a testimony against them, or as an evidence in their favor throughout their generations."

I suppose so much has been said about race in this country, of the oppression of Black people and Jews, that it has been reduced to a cliché. People often tend to become less sensitive to atrocities when they are amid comfortable surroundings. Their intellect searches only for a counterargument to a story describing a crime, rather than trying to perceive or to place themselves in the victim's environment or state of mind so that they may truly feel his anguish, the pain, and hate.

---

* *The Last Year of Malcolm X,* (New York: Grove Press, 1965), p. 45, The position of Malcolm X stated at a Haryou-Act Forum in Harlem on December 12, 1964.

Among the many things that I had yet to learn, something that I had passed over in history was that German Jews were a product of intermarriage. Jews had made greater contributions to Germany than the Germans themselves had. With Hitler's rise to power, German Jews were used as the scapegoat to rally support for the so-called master Aryan race. In a sense, it could be said that intermarriage had weakened Jews. When I later found this out, I could more clearly understand why Vickie's parents hated me, why Jewish parents, in general, fear the marriage of their sons and daughters to gentiles.

I saw how the Jews flocked together out of necessity, developed their own community and sense of Jewish consciousness—to a point where they thought themselves superior to other peoples. Why was it ominous for Black people to demand community control over schools in their neighborhood when whites were controlling their schools within their communities all along? I could see it clearly now, how necessary it was to develop a sense of cultural consciousness and exclusivity like the Jews. It was necessary for us to deal with our internal problems, and the best way to do that was through education. Not just plain "education," but education of self and education where you can siphon out the useful from the useless, the good from the bad, the truth from the lies. Black people need an education that will destroy all the effects of slavery, lifting them up as independent men and women who no longer unquestioningly follow the individuals the ethnocentric media acknowledge as their leaders.

I was also coming to realize that America's technology and wealth had permeated and were taking possession of the land that I loved and identified with as freedom, escape from America. Jamaica's currency was now dollars and cents.

Like so much of the Caribbean, Jamaica was being absorbed by America. The tiny island has been exchanged between two colonial powers, Britain and America. But there is no difference. "I distinguish," says Osagyefo Kwame Nkrumah, "between two colonialisms, between a domestic one and

an external one. Capitalism at home is domestic colonialism."
It is precisely this "domestic colonialism" which has enabled
the Europeans and Americans to control the Caribbean to
the extent that the true natives of the sun are called "aliens"
in their own land. There was no escaping because America's
presence was felt everywhere; it was like what they used to
say about the British Empire—it was so big that the sun
never set on it.

I had gone to a school that stood for the values of Scotland. I had been torn to a point where I had no sense of cultural identity with either Black people here or in the West
Indies. I could identify only with Malcolm, a man physically
dead but spiritually alive. There was no getting around it:
there was one element that predetermined my freedoms, gave
me hell because of the color of my skin—the white power
structure.

One of my problems up to now had been that when I met
white people like the Toomeys who were not racists or white
supremacists, I made them the norm. But, while there have
been white people who have had more courage to stand up
for the rights of Black people than Black people themselves,
these whites are the exceptions. Those whites I knew not to be
racists would remain my personal friends, my personal business. Yet collectively, whites, by circumstances or intent, are
oppressors of Black people. At the same time I saw that
people aren't always oppressed on the basis of skin color—
sex, class, and ethnic background are also big factors. Regardless, I now realized it was my duty to use all of my energies to
serve the community that I belonged to. My relationship with
Vickie was not a consideration in my mind. I made no attempt to reconcile the reality of my personal situation, of the
possibility of my marrying Vickie and having children whose
minds would be just as fucked over as mine was—unable to
be assimilated and yet aware that assimilation was taking
place.

It was getting late, but when I got into bed, I couldn't
sleep. Bill, the smallest boy, wet his bed and came over to

sleep with me. He was so young. I wondered if he would be so loose with his company when he grew up.

In the morning the so-called District Presidents' meeting was held in the library of a Catholic all-white girls' school, called Mercy High. There were about fourteen of us, and I was the only Black person. The president of the State Association was a tall, saintlike, slender, blue-eyed, blond-haired Baptist. Our host was Natalie, president of Mercy High School. She was, without question, very beautiful, but I was trying to avoid any more problems. I kept to myself and just sat and watched what was going on.

I found the conflict between Jews and Catholics to be interesting. I had never known one existed. It was here that for the first time I heard Jews referred to as a minority group. I had to laugh because this was a strange thing for me, coming from New York City, where there are more Jews than anywhere else in the world. In New York City the ethnic composition of a school is listed under: White, Black, Puerto Rican, and "Other." All the Jews are put under the white category. When I told one of these Christian guys that I went to a school where over 60 percent of the student body was Jewish, he replied, "Jesus Christ, I couldn't stand going to a school with that many Jews around me." I was going to ask him if he would say the same thing if there were that many Black people, but I anticipated his answer. The thought just never occurred to me that Jews were still subjected to pressure and name-calling like Black people.

I learned that the Catholics felt that the Jews in the Board of Education were seeking to destroy Catholic schools through abolishing state aid for them.

My beliefs about the educational system were reaffirmed. In various districts the racial polarization was due largely to the structure of the community and system. Some schools were 80 to 90 percent white; in others the same ratio held for Blacks. Hence, de facto segregation right here in New York State. All along I had been under the impression that this kind of thing existed only in the South. Americans draw the line at the prospect of closer association with Black people. Witness the controversies that arise over desegregation and Black people moving into white neighborhoods. Smaller cities have fewer central high schools, and because the school has to draw students from the entire city, racists call the result "forced integration." But even inside the schools there is segregation—separate entrances and separate lunch tables, for example. In most of the schools I visited, students told me that this was true.

During the lengthy discussion, my mind was wandering all over, comparing the Andover Conference to this one—quiet, controlled, chaired by parliamentary procedure, and no ranting or raving. But the concept was still there, the game was still being played. As intelligent as these kids sounded, they formed a New York State Association of Student Councils and then arbitrarily declared themselves leaders of New York State. I couldn't help but laugh at us meeting here in the library as so-called leaders of the state, formulating policy for students who didn't even know of the existence of the organization. But it is students from organizations like these that the Governor and the State Education Department and the legislature call upon to "represent student opinion." Furthermore, I realized that ten or fifteen years from now it would probably be guys like these I'd have to go ask for a job.

When it came time for me to give a rundown on the New York City situation, they listened to me as if I were telling them a fairy tale. I told them how the students organized themselves for the Moratorium, about Franklin K. Lane, suspension procedures, arrests, racial conflicts, and all the rest. When I was finished, they spoke about the difficulties they would have if they tried to organize on such a massive basis. I thought New York City students were apathetic and disorganized, but these upstate students presented serious problems of lack of incentive or interest, and a conservatism that seemingly made organization impossible. The more they spoke of their problems, the more I realized how advanced

New York City was. We had underground papers, leaflets, offices, one Board of Education to deal with, one organization that comprised the ninety-one high schools; we were in New York City, opinionmaker for the rest of the nation. It was just a question of pooling all our resources.

We later began to discuss other problems, and the issue of civil rights in schools was totally neglected. It was the feeling of the group that it didn't pertain to them.

I asked why? They said their schools and "districts" were all white. I asked them if any of the people in their districts or schools ever intended to go to college or to leave New York State. They would eventually come into contact with Black people, and people have a tendency to react negatively to things they can't understand. (I knew this to be true about myself.)

I brought up the Cultural Exchange Program again. The educational system, I explained, was so structured that many Black, Puerto Rican, and white students rarely had the opportunity to see a multi-racial group produce anything constructive. By transporting our musicians from Music and Art to elementary, junior high, and high schools, we would be promoting cultural understanding and an incentive to many upcoming musicians. My suggestion to them was to revise their curriculum to involve the study of Afro-American, Jewish, Irish, and other such ethnic groups in terms of their art, music, and literature. These factors would be put into a historical setting and studied "primarily" for music and art. I had to say primarily for music and art so that they wouldn't react with a forced integration attitude. I said it would be called Ethnic Humanities. Ethnic Studies would be approached from a sociological and historical point of view, and this would be one of the ways of interpreting their views and problems.

I felt so close to the root of the problem and yet had no power to do a damned thing. The system is man's strongest creation: it is self-perpetuating, its complexity is amazing—integral parts, veto groups, political and apolitical strata.

The system is all fucked up, but saying it doesn't change anything. Trying to pretend that the system has "lied" and that you've caught it "lying" is a waste of time. It's no lie: these problems are all planned out and executed by people who *know* what they are doing. I was used and got angry because of it when I should have understood that I couldn't expect to change the man's system without him trying to stop me. I didn't see that before, but saw now that "by any means necessary" applies to both sides.

During the final minutes of the Conference, I kept looking at Natalie. I'd be talking, then just glance her way. At times we stared at each other. And it was just something that was understood, that we were attracted to one another. She was so unlike all the other girls I had known. I suppose it was that she lacked that New York City superficiality. Just then I didn't feel any sexual attraction toward her although I was conscious of how beautiful she was. I didn't even speak to her, but I wanted to let her know everything that was bothering me, all my inner thoughts and insecurities, because she looked like a person I could trust. I had trusted Vickie, but I don't know if it was her age or culture that made her unable to deal with the dilemmas that were now facing me. Vickie was a girl, and Natalie was a woman. Natalie asked me for my address so that she could get in touch with me about the Cultural Exchange Program, and I gave it to her. In the months that followed we developed a very strange relationship in which the most important thing that I learned was that where a woman looks to a man for strength and security, it isn't wise for him to let his defenses down for a second, to reveal personal insecurities. This has nothing to do with male chauvinism. An insecure person often looks to another person for security; if that person fails to meet those expectations, then he is dropped. It was as simple as that with Natalie and me.

After the Conference a guy I was talking to told me in private that the advisors and other students were relieved when they found out that "I didn't want to burn everything down." That statement left me with mixed feelings because on the one hand I realized his thinking was a response to the new Black militancy, which I saw as serving only a reactionary function and following a policy that would inevitably mark its own destruction. But also, I felt he put me in an Uncle Tom context. In other words, I took his words to mean—You're not like all those *other* Blacks. I told him that he should understand one thing: "Because I talk to you doesn't mean that I want to join you: understand that."

On the way back home another student from New York City gave me a resolution on students rights submitted by students in California. The document had a lot of legal terminology and seemed to fall short of giving students real power—adults had helped write it.

Insurrection

It is not always necessary to wait until all the conditions for making revolution exist; the insurrection can create them.

Che Guevara

IT IS THE UNDENIABLE TRUTH that throughout history, violence has been the chief means of social change, and also that the threat of violence, the rhetoric of violence, has been a catalyst to peaceful reform. Of all our studies, history best rewards all research. Through the interdependence between those working in the system and those outside the system, violence and peace are interrelated. And it is the lesson of our times that only when the victim groups organize *themselves* will they be able to win their freedom. In cases where those at the vanguard, the victims of oppression, have fought and been repressed, the laws are liberalized in the aftermath. But the chief beneficiaries of the sacrifice of life or effort made by those who have fallen in the struggle are ultimately the non-participants, the complacent figures.

What is clear is that the educational system is involved in a conspiracy to miseducate masses of Black and Puerto Rican students, and that the people in positions of power plot and scheme to crush and penalize those individuals who even before birth are doomed to failure. When people in positions of power remain unaccountable for their power or actions and make arbitrary decisions that may jeopardize the security and future and violate the rights of live human beings, it is necessary for this power to be brought under control or eliminated.

To teach the true history of this nation is to ask for revolution. In our high schools the free exchange of political views and thoughts is not tolerated or is limited to after-school discussion, and controversial speakers are locked out of schools.

Meanwhile, our schoolbooks tell us that the only time we will be fit to govern ourselves is when we are exposed to all that can be said in favor of the educational system and all that can be said against it.

Throughout history there are people who have fought for liberation, and along with this struggle are those who oppose freedom. The names and faces change, but the ideas remain the same. Because men involved in penology are overexposed to sadism, their attitudes and behavior patterns change. They become cold and indifferent beings, conscious of only one thing, moving upward in command over other men. Then, too, they acquire preconceived notions of the behavior patterns of individuals. The same process exists in the Board of Education's hierarchy where men in positions of power sit down among themselves and plot, scheme, and crush live human beings. (See Appendix C.) As long as those in positions of power are incompetent, corrupt, and resistant to change and they play on the human instincts of fear, envy, jealousy, prejudice, and insecurity in order to divide and conquer, violence is inevitable.

The historical attempts at peaceful change escalating from sincerity to frustration, to violence, to disillusionment, to withdrawal and nonparticipation are countless. Rules are made to be obeyed, not challenged. To obey rules that are intolerable, unjust, and repressive is to voluntarily submit to oppression. The system is self-perpetuating and will allow all forms of criticism and threats to its security, but the reality has always been clear. That any time a system is truly threatened by an element, it will move without regard to life or justice to crush the source that threatens it.

Up to now there had been no citywide organization that could speak for the new awareness of high school students. Up to now all insurrections were sporadic and unplanned. The nature of disorders is such that when trouble breaks out in one place, the issue could touch off waves of rebellions elsewhere. But if these rebellions were uncoordinated, it would mean only more brutality and repression. For too many years we marched on our own schools, not realizing how far away from the real problem we were.

Whenever a union has a grievance, as the teachers did in 1968, over one school district, the union doesn't strike only that particular district—it strikes the entire school system: everybody gets penalized. And we are so foolish as to believe that by setting fires in bathrooms or taking over rooms in our individual schools, we are actually accomplishing something of importance to all students! The teachers had a contract and a union to support their position. The provisions which they claimed were necessary for their survival and "professional dignity" were used to justify the barring of over a million students from attending classes. The teachers broke the Taylor Law, which prohibits strikes by public employees. Although one need not agree with the law, the actions taken by the UFT were illegal. Those high school students who had to take Regents' examinations in the year of the teachers' strike were instructed to sign their names to a lie that they had received forty weeks of regular study. And yet, before every Regents' exam, you are told: FRAUD IS A MISDEMEANOR. Any union or group of people who find, after exhausting all the peaceful channels, that no agreement or settlement of their grievances is arrived at, have only one of two options left: to strike or engage in militant actions to bring about a settlement.

We justly accused the educational system of disseminating an irrelevant and wholly inadequate education. However, when *we* broke away—walked out on this "education"—it was always we who suffered. We always lost because we gave up before we understood that winning takes time, sacrifice, and endurance. We lost because the educational system that we deemed irrelevant and inadequate still functioned in our absence in links of requisites—Regents'-SPAT-SAT-CEEB— finally admission to "higher education." If we lost one link in this chain, we suffered. If we walked out and endured until the links were destroyed, there would be no chain to hold us. You have to be willing to accept the consequences. When teachers, auto workers, or any union goes on strike, the membership always remains united to win.

The Board of Education had accidentally united wide varieties of people by giving them something that they could hate, a bogus Student Bill of Rights. The Board's resolution was a trick to mislead the public into thinking that reforms were being made when in reality, what they had done was to restate laws that already existed.

My primary interest in this Bill of Rights was to secure the right of Black and Puerto Rican people to control the schools in their communities. I envisioned the schools being governed by democratic boards where the people from the community (of each school) would have control over the affairs that affected the education of their children. Only in this way could Black people build social dignity and lift themselves out of the economic trap. All those other upstate ethnic groups controlled their schools. Jews, here, controlled the schools in their community. The history, the heritage, the self-knowledge had been denied to Black children, and as long as these teachers, who were unable to relate to the needs of the Black student and Black community, were in control of the schools, there could never really be a strong Black collectivity. More than once, in words and unconscious deeds, I had seen for myself that many of the Jewish teachers expressed sympathy for the poor and also a view that they were inferior and could not really benefit from the education they were receiving. Never once would they blame themselves.

Education is both the content and prerequisite for the careers of many high school teachers who entered the school system during the Depression. The cultural value which they place on education is far different from that Black people place on it. And this creates a conflict within many of these white teachers, between their sympathy and desire to teach and their resentment toward what appears to them to be a lack of respect for education by Black people. Of course, this conflict is really an inability of the white teacher to understand that there are enormous problems intrinsic to being Black, living in the real world, and then being placed under house arrest from nine to five in an artificial world run by theory and not blood, sweat, and tears. Apart from the emotional side, Dr. Martin Deutsch, Director of the Institute for Developmental Studies of New York Medical College, found that differences between Black and white academic achievement may be due to environmental factors which the ordinary measures of class do not take into account. His studies are intensive and much of what he has to say should be put into practice immediately on a larger scale.* Besides opening the way for many people like Deutsch to come into the school system, not just on an experimental basis but on a large scale in the regular program, this bill could help produce many other important things—human rights for high school students and provisions to make up for the inadequacies of the educational system. And most important, by including unmet demands presented by other militant groups, we could form a coalition of the victim school groups to confront and defeat our common oppressor.

I saw now that there had already been attempts made at peaceful reform, and most of them had failed because of those who controlled the system. I thought of organizing only the victim groups and taking over the Board of Education of

---

* Charles Silberman in *Crisis in Black and White,* p. 270, writes: "In one instance Dr. Deutsch tells of a student in one class he was studying who had the habit of enclosing himself in a closet for fairly lengthy periods of time. The more psychiatrically-oriented members of his staff were ready with the usual Freudian explanations until Deutsch took the trouble to ask the child why he did it. Seems that this was the only time during the day when the student could have any privacy and could enjoy the feeling of reading in solitude; home was crowded and noisy."

New York City. Nowhere else in the country had it been done before. Unlike the previous year, Black people did not need to be at the vanguard—it would be better if these white groups went down and got their heads busted because only then would there be public attention paid to our problem. With this Bill of Rights as our program and a takeover of the Board of Education as our strategy, the whole country would focus its attention on the problems facing the 275,000 high school students of New York City. With our demand that the schools be run by the community of each school, all over the city various Black and Puerto Rican communities would voice their support for us. The takeover itself would serve only as a vehicle to opening up widespread discussions among teachers, parents, and students.

There was a problem, and that was the negative effects of a student takeover. It could produce more repression and public condemnation: the media had characterized virtually all student demonstrators as psychopaths.

When adults sit home and watch televised student demonstrations, the heralded "generation gap" becomes a reality and the students are viewed as a collective entity—not really human. When these adults ask, "What are the students protesting about?" it is not really a question, and they do not really expect an answer. They make this statement with the feeling that there *is* nothing to protest about. The unfortunate part about this is that *some* people who are protesting don't really know what they are protesting about, or they use protest as an outlet for inner frustrations, an excuse to escape exams in the spring. But the Establishment makes *them* the norm.

One good example of the media's role is the way it inflated the takeover of Willard Straight Hall at Cornell University in 1969. It sought to dramatize only the very presence of Black students with guns on campus. Only a picture appeared; no explanation was given for why they had the guns, and no mention was made that the guns were unloaded and brought into the building *after* the occupation in view of the threat of outer attack from whites on the campus.

Yes, the takeover was possible and my being president of the City G. O. Council and also member of the Citywide High School Council would help. This Council was composed of the acting superintendent, the deputy superintendent, five assistant superintendents, all kinds of executives, government researchers, and coordinators, the chairman of the United Parents' Association (UPA), and three students from the City Council. In all, the council had twenty-six members. I was the only Black face. The Council, of course, was advisory, and it was quite easy to see what the Board was doing. The Council was used to record policy statements by the top superintendents; nothing was ever resolved, and every remark made by Deputy Superintendent Seelig Lester or Assistant Superintendent Jacob Zack was written into the minutes—to have the Board on record. Nothing that anyone else had to say was written into the minutes. It was a sham, a deception that something was being done when nothing was being done.

However, by going to the Board regularly, I saw how a takeover by about five hundred students could easily be accomplished. Up to then, the Board of Education still didn't have an adequate security system.

I began to compile papers on the injustices of the educational system so that I could get a program together. I called Vickie up to tell her to meet me over at City College in the morning. We began writing the student Bill of Rights. Other groups had written student resolutions before, but they didn't plan any solid action; they only wrote them up on paper and left them there. On the same day that Vickie and I began writing the Bill of Rights, Sarah said she wanted to help.

At a meeting of the Steering Committee of the City Council, I met Raynetta, a sister from Walton High School; Larry, from George Washington High School; Louis and Eileen from John Dewey High School. All of them were interested in working on the Bill. Swartz included sections from the New York Civil Liberties Union's Resolution on Students Rights.

Castka sat in on the Steering Committee meetings when we were working on the Bill. He assumed that when we were finished, we'd just give it to him like Swartz had done the year before, and no one would hear about it again. As for the students, I never discussed with them my personal intent for writing the Bill; it had a dual purpose, and I was sure that my motives would be unacceptable to them.

Through the grapevine word started getting around that students were writing this Bill of Rights and what's more, it was coming from the Mickey Mouse City G. O. Council. Miguel, from the Third World Committee at City College, and Bob, from the Student Mobilization Committee, also of City College, showed up at one of our meetings.

With the decline of sds, the Student Mobilization Committee was the most well-organized group—that is, when it came to getting people out on the streets for Moratorium demonstrations. smc is a class-collaborationist organized front of the Socialist Workers Party and the Young Socialist Alliance. Its stake in the formulation of the Bill of Rights was clear. In fact, the reason the Bill of Rights was attracting so many groups was that it was one of the few groups to organize around human rights. The smc people were being suspended from school all over for leafleting. And as public opinion began to shift toward the right, the anti-war movement lost the Board's sanction.

As we started to include some heavier stuff in our resolution, we decided that we could no longer meet on the premises of the Board of Education. At first we held meetings on weekends in a run-down, abandoned supermarket, and then we got a better place—City Councilman Carter Burden's run-down storefront office (at least it wasn't cold inside). We worked hard on the Bill, discussed it thoroughly so that each of us was familiar with all the concepts and reasoning.

We were all convinced that the high schools are analogous to prisons. To see the similarity clearly you only have to pick up the newspapers or any material dealing with disturbances in jails and then substitute a few words. For example, you can make the following substitutions:

prisons	=	high schools
criminology	=	educational psychology
penologists	=	school administrators
inmates/prisoners	=	students
warden	=	principal
guards	=	teachers

I tried inserting these substitutions (italicized below) into what George Jackson wrote about jails in his book *Soledad Brother:*

The textbooks on *educational psychology* like to advance the idea that *students* are mentally defective. There is only the merest suggestion that the system itself is at fault. *School administrators* regard *high schools* as asylums . . . But what can we say about these asylums since *none* of the *students* are ever cured. Since in every instance they are sent out of the *high schools* more damaged physically and mentally than when they entered. Because that is the reality. Do you continue to investigate the *students?* Where does the administrative responsibility begin? Perhaps the administration of the *high schools* cannot be held accountable for every individual act of their charges, but when things fly apart along racial lines, when the breakdown can be traced so clearly to circumstances even beyond the control of the *teachers* and the administration, investigation of anything outside the tenets of the fascist system itself is futile.

Nothing has improved, nothing has changed . . .*

We felt it was imperative that the structure of the high school be changed so that such an analogy could not be made. The conditions in high school will continue to worsen or may eventually become uncontrollable because those who have the power to effect change misguidedly use that power to confront symptoms rather than causes. That is why there is rape, stabbings, and racial violence within the high school classrooms.

There were now thirteen people working on the Bill of Rights, all of whom were high school students. The resolution itself had been written by Sarah, Vickie, and myself. We used

* George Jackson, *Soledad Brother: The Prison Letters Of George Jackson* (New York: Bantam Books 1970) p. 30.

the following resources in the formulation of the High School Bill of Rights:

1. The United States Constitution
2. "Academic Freedom in the Secondary Schools"—American Civil Liberties Union
3. Proposal of the NYC G.O. Council
4. Resolution on Rights of Senior High School Students—NYC Board of Education
5. Recommendations to California State Board of Education—California Association of Student Councils
6. Afro-American Student Association 17 demands
7. New York High School Student Union Demands
8. Women's Rights—NYC High School Women's Coalition

At this point the draft was still crude. I started working on an explanatory statement and confidential strategy for taking over the Board of Education.

I had spoken to various informal parent and community groups in the Bronx and in Brooklyn. I wanted to find out how willing and ready they were to support our actions. At first they were skeptical, but over a short period, they became more receptive to the idea.

In December all of us had to stop work on the Bill. Swartz, from the Student Mobilization Committee, took a leave of absence from City College, and I had to go back to school to take some tests, prepare for college interviews, and get some business straightened out.

I went up to Music and Art, picked up some mail that had been left there for me, got a track and field profile (a record of events and best times) from Mr. King, and in the morning took a Greyhound bus to Hanover, New Hampshire, for an interview at Dartmouth—a college in the middle of nowhere and no place for me. The next day I cut out for Harvard. I spent the day with Kenneth, one of my stepbrothers.

I felt good up at Harvard, the closest I'd ever been to the

Ivy League. Kenneth and I spoke about my grades and PSAT scores.

"That bad—uh, well, I don't suppose they count those things anymore."

We laughed, but it wasn't funny. I was interviewed by a Black admissions officer who said I didn't have anything to worry about, I should be up there next year if I did well on my SAT's.

When he said that, I knew that the decision had already been made. The night before the SAT's I'd stayed up all night speaking at a meeting. In the morning, I came in, answered a few questions, and fell asleep.

Back in New York City, work on the Bill had all but come to a halt, as it was winter. Students never seem to want to demonstrate when there is snow on the ground. But June was only five months away.

■ ■ ■

I received a letter inviting me to a conference in Ithaca, sponsored by the Richard Ford Associates, a group of educational consultants. The conference was to be held at Ithaca College. Fineberg was also invited. We went up on the same plane, sitting next to each other all the way up, but avoided talking about anything that had happened in school. Before the conference we went into a bookstore where I picked up two books, *Castro's Cuba* by Lee Lockwood and *Venceremos: The Speeches and Writings of Che Guevara,* edited by John Gerassi. Fineberg offered to pay for them. I'll never forget it. She stood there, looking at the books, and told me, "Che Guevara was irresponsible."

At the conference I saw how the government gets its information on students. This conference wasn't set up to help us, the students. You could look at the guest list and see that they got a bunch of high school students together with principals and doctors, teachers and research people, and that the information wasn't going to help the students—in fact, we'd never see what they did with the tapes or film. Where do you think these "crisis intervention people" get their information on how to handle student dissent? But something else was also happening here.

With the recent high school rebellions, newspapers and magazine articles began to reflect the growing conflict between students and educators.

The students know what's going on. Why get us to talk to each other? Why aren't the commissions for youth openly attacking the educational system for its atrocities against politically oriented students and minority groups? The commissions have enough evidence in terms of reports of the laxity of laws by the Board of Education. They should be in business to be working themselves out of a job. The plain fact of the matter is that, like the war, continuing student crisis was good business. Most adults can remember what high school was like when they were there and hopefully could become sympathetic to what is happening now. The problems haven't changed much—the only difference is that students today have more guts to speak out about them. Capitalistic foundations, such as the Ford Foundation, work day and night pouring thousands of dollars into the hands of people for the purpose of "studying the problem." Of course, it is not unusual that an organization, or foundation, or commission, or whatever is out to maintain the status quo will always find methods to keep itself in power. At the same time students lose out. Hundreds of students continue to graduate with an inferior education; hundreds of students graduate into a world where they can't survive as human beings and become "social liabilities."

Hundreds of students attend discussions, summer rap sessions, and conferences, and leave high school with the false notion that these commissions and organizations will help the students they left behind. Even though many staff of many research teams attempt to get a representative "ethnical and geographical cross-section of students" to participate at their conferences (if they attempt to get students at all), they seldom *employ* minority groups in their corporate structure.

Many of the problems high school students protest or talk about to make either the society or some ubiquitous adult authority aware of are already known by the authority, and the protest serves only as momentary news to the public—as is evident in the media coverage of student protests the last five years. Almost every adult commission in the country exploits the crisis facing students. The State Education Department, in 1968 and 1969, held numerous two- and three-day workshops supposedly to get youth to communicate, to bridge the generation gap. In three days they wanted students who didn't even know each other to find answers to problems that had accumulated over decades. And of course, these conferences are always publicized so that the public will be under the impression that something is being done.

There seemed to be no getting around it: the student is being studied, exploited, and picked apart from every angle. In a sense, this book exploits me. It represents a compromise.

When the conference began, I found myself in a situation that was getting out of hand. For some reason that was really never quite clear to me, some white people love to have Black people curse them, tell them what devils they are. And I knew that during this time when Black militancy was on the upswing, there were many opportunists among Black people who played that role. They told white people that they were butchers and racist devils, and white people clapped and loved to hear it. White people did not fear these pseudo-revolutionaries—though they did fear Malcolm X. They were nothing but militant Uncle Tom Clowns.

James Baldwin wrote about this phenomenon extensively as did Richard Wright, Ralph Ellison, and others—all of them knew Black people had these skills to perform to the white man's amusement.

At the conference I made a few comments. I told them that there were other students who should be in my place speaking to them because they were closer to the real problems than any of the people who were invited to speak. I was thinking about the students at Franklin K. Lane. At the end of the conference, the group was asked to make comments about the discussion. One man got up and said, "What we should have had was a big Black militant, with the green jacket, jeans . . . who'd foot-stomp, tell us what it's like to be Black and how white people have oppressed Black people."

I kept my cool. I wasn't there to entertain anybody.

Hagood At The Hilton

THE UNITED PARENTS' ASSOCIATION had chosen Music and Art as the high school with the "most advanced" consultative council. I couldn't see how it was possible. Music and Art's Council couldn't even get bicycle racks or hire back the teachers who had been unjustly fired.

Ken Hagood, a Black lawyer, and Ed Levin, an educational consultant, both from Cornell University's School of Industrial and Labor Relations, were responsible for setting up a model demonstration of the consultative council for the United Parents' Association Convention at the New York Hilton. I was the lame duck president of Music and Art.

The people on the Consultative Council had a meeting in Klein's office with Mr. Hagood and Mr. Levin. Klein was worried about my participation in the conference because he didn't want any "dirty linen washed in public." Mr. Davis, president of the Parents' Association, backed him up. There was no way in the world for me to have the opportunity to get up in front of two hundred people and not expose Klein and the ineffectiveness of the Council. I didn't have to say anything at this moment. The teachers and parents got so uptight about something going wrong that they started to discuss which topic they'd bring up, and what would and would not be said. Finally they decided to scrap the script and let things happen naturally.

On Saturday morning Barbara, Owen, Karen, Vickie, and I showed up at the Hilton Hotel. Vickie had invited her parents—that gave me a really uncomfortable feeling. The platform on which we were to be seated made us look as if we were going to be examined like fish in a bowl. We took our seats with me sitting where I could look directly at Klein. Mr. Levin opened the conference by explaining that the purpose of the demonstration was to show parents the effectiveness of the Council. To begin with, Owen was elected to chair the meeting. They had tried to elect me so that I couldn't participate in the discussion. Then the floor was opened to topics for discussion. Klein and Davis brought up some wishy-washy issue—I don't even remember what it was. All I knew was that they were deceiving the parents. I said that we should discuss real issues, like the arbitrary firing of the teachers, the Bill of Rights, or drugs in the school. But everybody voted against discussing the topics I brought up. Man, I was angry: everybody in the room knew it, but I sat there quietly. A few minutes before the end of the meeting, I took the microphone and told the parents that this was a sham, a cover-up, that the Council was powerless and ineffective. I told them about the real problems. They applauded but obviously weren't listening to what I was saying. (Nobody applauds for a problem.)

When the meeting was over, I turned to Vickie.

"Why'd you go along with them?"

"If I had gone along with you, my parents would have said that I didn't have a mind of my own."

"You know, you're really a child, Vickie."

I went over to Karen and Barbara. "You realize this was a put-on."

Karen looked at Barbara and sighed, "Oh well, I just didn't want a confrontation."

Owen came over to me. "So what would we have accomplished if we had discussed a real problem?"

"You'd show the parents what's going on in the schools."

"So is that really all that important?"

"In itself no, but it's the truth. Look at these people. All of them came here for a free meal and a cup of coffee. It's nothing but a social gathering."

I sat down by myself at the table while everybody else was filing out. Owen stood over me. "Well, what do you think will work?"

"A student coalition so that we could get the power to do something."

"That's not realistic."

"It is," I said sternly. I could feel how on edge I was, losing my cool. Owen left, and I sat there alone in the room. Suddenly Mr. Hagood, the Black lawyer, came from behind.

"Say brother, looks like you have a problem—nobody's on your side." I looked at him: Bourgeois, I thought. He put down his card in front of me and told me if I ever needed his help to call him. He walked out, and I ripped up his card. I was mad at the world. I got all the way downstairs before I realized that a lawyer might be a good thing to have when we got busted down at the Board of Education. I ran back upstairs and picked up the pieces.

The following week I went up to Mr. Hagood's office on West Forty-second Street right across from Bryant Park and the Fifth Avenue Library. I wanted him to look over our Student Bill of Rights. It was raining heavily that day, and I got drenched.

I entered Mr. Hagood's office, and his partner, Mr. Howard, told me he wasn't there, but I could wait. Mr. Howard gave me a kind of funny look and went back into his office. (People get wet when it rains—right?) Finally Mr. Hagood showed up.

"Reeves," he said smiling. "What's up?"

We went into his office. I was grinning like an idiot. I just couldn't get over the fact that these were two Black lawyers. I mean, I'd never been around any Black people who were in "bigshot professions." Mr. Hagood sat down behind his desk and looked at me staring and grinning at him.

"What's the matter with you," he said smiling.

"You're a *lawyer.*"

He smiled, and looked at me as if to say, Damn, where's this guy from?

"Mr. Hagood, I want—"

"Hey man, stop that Mr. Hagood shit. My name is Ken."

Damn, I thought, where's this guy from?

"Ken, uh, I want you to look at this. It's a list of demands that we're going to present to the Board of Education."

It took him a long time to read it.

"This is pretty good. Who wrote it?"

"Me and a couple of friends of mine. What do you think of the first two sections?"

He looked up at me, then down at the first two sections.

"I was just about to tell you, you'll never get the first two sections. That's community control."

"I know it, but the community people are willing to support us."

Hagood put the Bill down and asked me to tell him specifically what I had in mind.

I told him that the Board of Education had written a Bill of Rights for students without their even knowing it, that it didn't confront any of the problems facing high school students, that Black and Puerto Rican people should control the schools in their communities, and that only a takeover of the Board of Education with a large number of white students would focus public attention on our problem. I told him that all last year Black students had been in the vanguard making legitimate demands and that the Board of Education publicly maligned their objectives and made it look like a racial confrontation.

Hagood looked at me for a while without saying anything and then asked me how I planned to get students into the

Board. I told him that around one o'clock lots of people file in and out of the Board for coffee and lunch, and there is no security. Groups of five could easily get in unnoticed.

He burst out laughing. "Well! I see you've got it all figured out. Reeves, do you realize that people could get *hurt?* I mean *seriously* hurt?"

"It's the price of revolution."

Again Hagood looked at me, at the window, at the floor, not saying anything, just thinking, and smiling.

"Why don't you meet me for lunch tomorrow. Leave the Bill with me—I want to look it over. Hey, one last thing. Do your friends know about this takeover?"

"Not yet."

"Man," he started to laugh. "Just don't say anything until we get things straightened out, O.K.?"

"O.K., but can I ask you a question? How much are you going to charge for helping us?"

"One dollar."

"You serious?"

"Yeah, can you afford any more?"

"No."

The next day I met him down at the Brass Rail with Ed Levin. I felt kind of uneasy around them. They were wearing suits, and I had on the same old green shirt and jeans. Ed had to leave early, but Ken and I discussed the Bill and my strategy for almost four hours. He pointed out a number of things that I'd never taken into consideration—like somebody getting killed and who'd really be responsible, me or the pigs. He said that I'd be playing into the Board's hands, and turning the public against the student movement.

Ken was a labor lawyer. He told me that if I got the coalition organized, a general strike would be better than a takeover. I told him that students were unwilling to strike for more than a day. He responded by telling me that unless I made an attempt to sit down and talk with the Board of Education, I wouldn't be justified in calling them unresponsive and repressive.

In the days that followed the conversation I had with Ken,

I became more and more influenced by what he'd had to say. I still believed that a takeover was the best solution, but I decided to try his way first.

Ken and I developed a real close friendship in a very short time. Up to this point I had never had a partner, a close friend, a guy that I could sit down and talk to. And Ken was the first man who ever called me "brother." I'd never thought something like that would ever really mean anything to me, but it did.

He told me a number of times that in so many ways, I was like him when he was a young guy. He said that he didn't have anyone to show him things. In time we got to be like brothers, always clowning around on the streets and doing things together. He showed me a whole new world where Black people lived in fancy apartments, ate in costly restaurants, danced at the Playboy Club, and enjoyed living, instead of barely surviving. I began to realize that as a child I had always looked at the Jewish community, at their doctors, lawyers, teachers, and bigshots, but never were there any Black people around of equal stature.

I went with Ken to his appointments, and I listened to every word of his conversations with clients. I saw that in many instances they, he and his clients, would bullshit each other, bluffing and tactfully avoiding questions that they didn't have answers for. And as I kept sitting in with Ken, my vocabulary increased, and I adopted many of his debating tactics. I don't think that I can put into words how much Ken meant to me or how much he helped me. He temporarily dropped his practice to work with the students. At night we went to all kinds of fancy restaurants. We would bullshit each other for hours and talk about all kinds of things: people, Black women, white women, law . . .

Apart from Ken, the two men who had had the most effect on my life were both Muslims—Malcolm X and Muhammad Ali—and I began to realize how important the Muslim philosophy of image was. I had been surrounded by so many white faces that I began to believe that wearing a clean shirt or clean shoes was wrong or square, and that "image" was a question of personal ego building. But now I realized that, especially today, the Black man has a responsibility to set himself up as an image of dignity, of manhood, of cleanliness to inspire other younger brothers, encouraging them to lift themselves up and be men. I had noticed while reading Malcolm and looking at pictures of him that his hair was neatly combed, his appearance clean. And there I was, dressing to suit the image of the white generation's concept of what the new Black militant should look like: unkempt, unclean. If white men wished to dress in women's clothing and to make themselves look like their ancestors did in caves, that was their business. I didn't have to follow them. I'm sure that if Hagood had looked like I had, I would have left his card ripped up in the ash tray on the table.

I began to borrow more and more money from Hagood. He really gave it to me because he knew that I couldn't pay it back. I bought shirts and ties. Mom Reeves was only too happy to see the change in me and bought me a brown three-piece suit. In a few weeks I had the appearance of a college graduate. It meant little to me personally, but as I began to attend more and more conferences, the results were always positive. Black parents always felt proud and had respect for me. Then too, by discussing things with Hagood I became less rhetorical and relied on facts to back up whatever I had to say.

The times that I went back to school to take tests, I just didn't seem to fit in; somehow I felt too old.

Now there remained only one problem: Vickie. I loved her, and it was only a question of time before Hagood would have to meet her. I told her to meet me in Ken's office one afternoon.

Ken was sitting behind the desk.

"Ken, this is Vickie, we've been seeing each other for over a year."

He looked at me, at Vickie, at the floor, and then replied, "Hello," with a smile.

Now everything was complete. But at first, he'd always pressure me and in private tell me about statutory rape and what her father, as a lawyer, could do to me.

I started to tell everybody about Ken. Every now and then he'd ask me to start going to school again, but I preferred hanging around the office and reading his books.

In late January work on the Bill of Rights picked up again. We started to have meetings in Ken's office. Swartz, Sarah, Gladstone, Raynetta from Walton, Wheatman from George Washington, Tempkin from John Dewey, Chaney from the Student Mobilization Committee, and other people all got together to discuss setting up press conferences, meetings, negotiating teams, picketing, and the strike.

I had had enough bad experiences to know better than to get caught up in optimism. The time had come for me to analyze some cold facts and to look beyond what was happening in the present and into the future. I wasn't a student of politics, but I had been burned too many times before to go rushing blindly into "the fire this time" again.

Hagood, a labor lawyer, was accustomed to negotiating with a strong, organized union behind him so that a strike threat supported his position. With only four months before the end of the school year, the high schools could not be organized to bring about the support we'd need to carry out a union strike. At this stage the City G. O. Council had only a handful of potential allies—people who understood that little could be done through peaceful means considering the makeup of those in power at the Board of Education.

I also had to anticipate the inevitability of my becoming an unpopular figure in the Council, just as I had become unpopular at Music and Art. But if I became unpopular because of my political views, that was O.K. because at least it would mean that an opinion existed where there had been none. If others presented counterarguments and countersolutions to my program, then it would be healthy because minds would be working.

The militant coalition would be a more difficult task. The

coalition would have to be comprised of groups who hated one another, who had different political philosophies. I already realized that once the coalition was formed, a vote would have to be taken to determine who should be at the head. I would abstain from the leadership role and be primarily one spokesman for the coalition; in this way, if the coalition fell apart, I would have a personal following and reputation that would enable me to continue spreading the concept of student self-determination. The same thing had happened to Malcolm. He split from the Muslims, but because Malcolm was a spokesman, he acquired a large personal following that enabled him to advocate his policy of Black nationalism independently.

Because of the time factor it was impossible to organize juniors to carry on where we would leave off—in the event that we failed. The coalition would have to be loosely organized, yet ready to move, to strike on a few moments' notice. To accomplish that, the most important members of the coalition would have to be arrested and suspended students in addition to those students from schools that were currently involved in insurrection.

Again, the closest problem was Vickie. What Darryl had told me was true. It seems that very few people, Black or white, have respect for a Black man who has a white woman. I could see that the white groups who were just getting involved in the coalition didn't respect me as a "Black man" because they knew about Vickie.

You see, it's a strange feeling, but you grow accustomed to it after a while. When whites approached me, not knowing about Vickie, I could tell that they were intimidated, inhibited about saying certain things about me and certainly anything about Black people that might put me on the defensive. But once they knew that Vickie and I were together, it was only obvious that this fear of me as a Black man was gone, that they'd say just anything around me, about race, things they wouldn't normally say around a brother who had nothing to do with whitey. Having Vickie, in a situation like this, was a handicap. And after discussing the situation, Vickie and I made an agreement that our affair had to be carried on in the strictest privacy. But even then we had problems.

■ ■ ■

One day Vickie and I planned to cut school. For some reason, my interest in films was aroused and I wanted to show her some movies I'd taken in Jamaica. She mentioned that she also had some films from her vacation in France and some from her childhood.

"Really, your childhood?" I exclaimed. "Hey, I want to know what Jewish upbringing, what Jewish culture is all about."

So the next morning we went to the supermarket, bought all kinds of fruit, and split for my pad—after Mom Reeves left for work.

We played around in my room before watching the movies. (I'd tacked this sheet up on the door.) After we fucked, we fell asleep and then woke up and fucked again and started to watch the movies. I was sitting there fascinated as she pointed out all her relatives. I mean really fascinated because I knew about only two of my uncles, and three of my aunts—nobody else. But she knew everybody. I had to ask her, "Do you think your folks are going to disown you because of me—"

Just at that moment there was a bang on the door. It was Francis.

"What do you want?" I shouted.

"Mom's comin'."

"Oh shit! Hey Francis, get the ladder up by the roof." I jumped out of bed, reached for my pants. "Vickie, you better get dressed, go out to the roof, and down the ladder!"

Unknown to me, my two cousins next door, Delsie and Elaine (who couldn't stand Vickie because she was white), had already told Mom Reeves that she and I were upstairs in my room.

Mom Reeves was rushing up the stairs, Vickie was out on

the roof, and I was sitting on the bed, listening to laughing outside and not knowing what was going on.

Mom pushed open the door, gave me a hard right across the face, and cried out, "Traitor!" And without even looking for Vickie, she walked out.

"Traitor?" I thought. What a strange thing to say! I couldn't figure it out.

Meanwhile, Vickie was stranded out on the roof. Delsie and Elaine had moved the ladder and were out in the backyard laughing at Vickie crouched on the ledge behind the smoke stack, trying to keep out of sight.

I heard the laughing, opened the window, saw what was going on and pulled Vickie in. "Well," I said, "if this had happened at your house, I'd probably be dead."

I told Vickie to wait in my room while I went downstairs to speak to Mom. But I couldn't find her; she was gone. I realized that she'd left so that I could get Vickie out without embarrassing her, and that's probably why she didn't look for Vickie on the roof.

Vickie and I got our coats and split from my house. I never asked her how she felt having to get out on the roof—I mean what it did to her mind to have to go out the back door for the first time.

And the problems never ended. One night I was home watching the *Hideous Sun Demon* on TV when Vickie called. She said her parents weren't home and wouldn't be getting back until late. She wanted me to come over.

"You crazy?" I said. "What if something happens and they come back early and catch me there?"

Then she started reminding me of things I had said to her about life not being worth living unless you take risks, etc.

I had a fifteen-speed bicycle, and I rode over to her house and left it in the backyard. I went in through the back door. We stayed in the kitchen for a while, talking, playing, and kissing. Then we went to her room, got undressed, and into bed. Despite everything that I ever said against Vickie, I could never say that she wasn't sexy. We fucked and fucked and fucked until I fell asleep. When I woke up I almost had a heart attack: Vickie was gone. I had no way of knowing whether or not her parents were in the house. I didn't know what to do. I didn't want to move or make a sound, so I hid under the blankets—Man, if I never prayed to God before, I sure as hell made up for it that night.

A couple minutes later I heard footsteps coming downstairs. It's her father, I thought—he's got a gun—I'm dead. No, it was Vickie.

"Vickie! How the hell could you let me fall asleep? I'm getting out of here now!" So I got dressed and rode back home. It was about three in the morning. A few minutes after I got in bed, Vickie called, and we talked for the rest of the night. And it didn't happen only once—her phone bills were higher than most people have to shell out for rent.

Free love is great if you don't have to pay for it.

Debating The Man

The following is a verbatim transcript of a WCBS/TV News broadcast in a series entitled "Public Hearing," aired at 11:30 a.m.–12 noon on May 10, 1970 (Channel 2, New York).* The discussion topic was high school students' rights. The participants were Walter J. Degnan, president of the Council of Supervisory Associations, and Donald Reeves, chairman of the High School Students' Rights Coalition. The moderator was WCBS/TV News Education Editor Robert Potts.

ANNOUNCER: From WCBS-TV News, in color, Public Hearing, fact finding inquiries into opposing sides of major public issues.

Today's topic: High School Students' Rights. The moderator of Public Hearing is WCBS-TV News education editor Robert Potts.

ROBERT POTTS: Good morning. New York City high school students are organizing to try and negotiate a new bill of rights. One strong faction wants student control over all student activities, and student participation in running the high school.

---

* Transcript of debate reproduced with permission of Columbia Broadcasting System, Inc. Originally broadcast May 10, 1970, on "Public Hearing."

Professional staff groups have tended to resist any incursion of students into areas regarded as the province of the educational professional.

We have with us representatives of both sides of this argument. And they are Walter Degnan, the president of the Council of Supervisory Associations, the organization that represents school principals and other supervisors. And Donald Reeves, chairman of the High School Students' Rights Organization, and president of the city-wide Students General Organization.

Mr. Reeves, why in your view do students in high school need a new definition of their rights?

DONALD REEVES: Well, the Board of Education, I believe in December, published their student bill of rights. And it was merely a restatement of things that already existed, and in no way tried to grant students their constitutional rights.

Their bill was not formulated by students, it was not voted on by the students. And, in all honesty, it was not a bill designed to give students the opportunity to change things peacefully within the system.

The bill of rights that we have authored in the Coalition, through the City Council, is one that outlines the constitutional rights of students that are granted in the United States Constitution. And it confronts the problems of drugs, of racial polarization, and a number of other problems, that the Board of Ed's document left out.

We're also trying to protect students from such arbitrary power that was used by principals at Franklin K. Lane, when they created a police state in that school, or the forty-one arrested and suspended students at Cardozo High School, or principals who still continue to censor student work, and to arbitrarily discipline them.

POTTS:Mr. Degnan, I'm sure that you are not opposed to rights for high school students. But where do you draw your line, as far as the demands being made by Mr. Reeves group is concerned?

WALTER J. DEGNAN: I'm very glad you said just what you

said, because your initial statement upset me. We certainly are not opposed to student rights. We have always consistently held that students should be—have a voice in the operation of the school, and they should be concerned about all the things that are important to them. And that we've also felt that as they became older in high schools, that there are more things that could be given to them for decision than in the lower schools.

So there isn't a principal in New York City who feels that students should not have rights. The problem is one of definition.

Now I think Mr. Reeves will accept the fact that he's been criticized for not truly representing the students of the city. He's accused of taking over the February 18th meeting of the General Organization; and there's been a lot of correspondence from his own colleagues about how that was handled.

And I think, essentially, that what he is trying to do is to state things that students cannot accept.

Now, for example, we know that schools are an agent of society, and we know that the rules are set down by society. And we know that a principal is not, in a sense, the boss of the operation. He carries out directions from the Board of Education. And he also has the responsibility of bringing to maturity youngsters who are not ready for the sort of thing that perhaps Mr. Reeves would like to have them do.

For example, his platform states that there should be a liaison board created, made up of ten students, four teachers, the principal, and five parents. And this board should have absolute control of what happens in the school, taking away from the principal, if you will, the authority that has been vested in him, the responsibility that's been vested in him, through society.

And this, of course, I think is something that is completely untenable. We might argue that students might decide that there'll be no homework, or there'll be no tests, or we won't take certain courses, even though they are prescribed.

And I think in a way we are approaching a situation

where, perhaps comparably you might think of a medical school, where medical students tell those who teach them that they're not going to take certain courses, let's say in anatomy, because they feel they don't need that course. Well, obviously, they are not going to become very good doctors if that sort of thing happens.

So I think that, however you think about this, that basically the responsibility given to the experienced, trained principal, who spends many years learning how to do this job, is something that has to be respected.

And, further, let me say that, you know, the students change every three or four years. And, quite obviously, what one group might want in one year could be quite different from what they might want, another group might want in the next year.

And I think, in effect, that this is the kind of thing that is causing a great deal of trouble.

POTTS: Mr. Reeves, before you respond, might I just ask you, do you recognize that there should be some kind of executive authority in a high school?

REEVES: Without question. But, you know, I'd just like to answer Mr. Degnan's statements.

POTTS: By all means.

REEVES: First of all, I'm glad that you've taken this position already, because I'm much more relieved. I thought that you would be well informed on this issue of student rights, and my position on it. But obviously you aren't.

The second thing is, you said something about principals not being against student rights. I'd like to point out that before the Principals Association even discussed the bill with myself, or any representative from either of the groups of which I'm the head, the Principals Association came out with a statement deploring the student bill of rights.

They said that the bill was formulated by outsiders who were seeking to overthrow the high school system, and to take over the total high school community.

Now that bill was written by three high school students.

And the only prerequisite for negotiations was that we had "peaceful" negotiations with the Board of Education.

You further went on to say that I have been accused of not representing the students, and that I controlled a meeting of the City G. O. Council. I would like to tell you that I'm chairman of this meeting, and that the meeting was chaired according to parliamentary procedure.

The only complainant or the major complaintive in that case was George W. Castka, a non-student, a member of the Board of Education. Now he was the one that said that that meeting was railroaded.

I'd like to point out that the City Council is an organization comprised of ninety-one high schools. And if you have five letters within your possession stating that they are against the actions taken at that meeting, then that is very unrepresentative of the city's high school students.

Further I'd like to say that the City G. O. Council is in no way the representative group for the students in this city. And that's the purpose of forming a coalition, so that we can represent a broad spectrum of students, regardless of their positions on the student bill of rights and whether they wanted to work within the system or not.

Now you went on to say that students want to run the school system, and so forth. The liaison board is not comprised solely of students. We also wanted parents to have some voice in the school community.

I'd like to point out the reason for this, was that recently there's been this mass hysteria about the drug problem in the high schools, and about the racial problem. And all along the school community, through the principals, have excluded parents from coming into the schools and seeing what is actually happening in those schools.

Therefore the drug problem escalated, the racial problem escalated. And then, finally when students (*sic*) demanded the right [for parents] to come in and see what was going on, you blamed all of [the problems] on the students.*

---

* Which is blaming the victim.

DEGNAN: Mr. Reeves, I would remind you that two years ago, I think it is, the Board of Education established an official policy which said that every principal was to have an advisory board made up of teachers, parents, and students. And these boards have been meeting with principals regularly.

Now quite obviously they're interested in the drug problem, of course. This is a matter of major concern for everybody. But I think you will recognize that I didn't make up the liaison committee as you have outlined it out of thin air. And certainly it is overweighted, in terms of the fact that you have ten students, four teachers, one principal, and five parents.

REEVES: That is again erroneous, sir. That is an equal number of students to parents and teachers. Another thing that I think we have to get straight here. The bill that we have outlined is negotiable in all points. That means that we did not set down some things, saying that you have to take it as we have outlined it. Our wish is that we negotiate.

Now if you find imperfections in that bill, then we're willing to compromise on them. You're talking about an advisory board. I'd like to say that Music and Art was selected by the United Federation of Teachers as having the most advanced consultative council.

Now at that time, when I was president at Music and Art, I sat on the board. And I would like to tell you that that board is ineffective, and just another buffer zone to just cut off student unrest altogether.

It happened with the student government. These things are all advisory, and they still do not provide students with any legitimate grievance machinery.

DEGNAN: Well, Mr. Reeves, I think there are several things we should put in perspective. First of all Mr. Lachman on the present board, as you know, is quite sympathetic and receptive to any discussion concerning student rights.

They've also liberalized the so-called bill of rights for students to a point that I think makes good sense. But I think you're failing to recognize that, when a school operates, it operates as a professional operation. It requires people who know exactly what they're doing.

Now the fact that in one school you think that a certain advisory board didn't work out, that's quite possible; that's perhaps the weakness that all human beings suffer from. There are things that work well in one place, and not too well in another.

But this whole concept of doing business in the way you suggest, and in tying the hands of the responsible head, the legal head of the school, I think is something that we must come to grips with, and that your committee has to recognize this.

Now I think there's one other thing here that should be said, and that is that there's ample evidence that the students, the G. O. Council, rejected the statement of rights as you outlined them. As a matter of fact, they took action after the February 18th meeting, in which they repudiated our committee.

They said there were some college people on it, they represented the Student Mobilization Committee. And they said they have no right to speak for us. And they also accused you of not allowing the duly elected representatives from various high schools to express themselves. They said that you packed that meeting with people who didn't belong there.

Now I think there's one other thing that you may have met in the course of your discussion, and that is a reference made to the *Student Mobilizer*.* And I think it was dated February 8th, and I quote from it. "The high school bill of rights . . . but the important starting point for us is that we approach the high school bill of rights as an antiwar organization whose interest is in securing the rights of high school students to fight against the war."

Now, you signed that.

REEVES: That's not true, again.

DEGNAN: Well, you signed it.

REEVES: No, I didn't. Is my signature on that paper?

DEGNAN: Your name is on it.

REEVES: Is my signature on that paper?

DEGNAN: Well, I'm no—I assume—I'm not going to . . .

---

* An anti-war newspaper.

REEVES: I know, but before you continue—see, you're throwing many erroneous accusations that are . . .

DEGNAN: This is the paper, Mr. Reeves.

REEVES: Yes, that is the paper. But I'm sure you've seen Nixon's face in that paper also, you've seen statements made by him . . .

DEGNAN: I'm not concerned at the moment about any one thing but this. That this was issued on May 8th. And the meeting that you're accused of rigging came about on May— or rather, February 8th, the meeting followed on February 18th.

Now I know that a good many of the representatives put these two things together. And they said, in effect, that if a bill of rights is to be expanded, if we're to do something different from what we've done, we can't do it in the context of an antiwar movement. It has to be broader than that.

Let's hope this war will not last during our lifetime. And to assume that this should be timed to that, I think is another reason for the kind of rebellion that you've experienced in your own group.

REEVES: That's not true. You see, again you're trying to create mass hysteria by throwing out a lot of accusations. Now, number one, I was going to approach you as being somebody that was poorly informed. But since you've taken the stance that you've been correctly informed, I'm going to tell you some of the things that you have stated are wrong.

Now if this council—first of all, I am the president of this council. I in no way determine who shall come into the meeting, and who should not.

POTTS: You're chairman, now, of the city-wide General Organization Council.

REEVES: Number two, if I've been accused of doing this— and I am not sure that you can produce any evidence to back that up—I'd like to state that, on all points, it was passed by the City Council, as only the representatives in the City Council can vote.

Now unless you can produce some evidence as to my having a gun and forcing them to do this, or for my having a belt and beating them and telling them to do this, then produce it.

Number two, is that I would like to get back to the principal and his power, because, number one, you were not present at any of these G. O. City Council meetings. Your information was fed secondhand by George W. Castka, who is the advisor to the City Council, and in effect the controller of the Council.

I'd like to point something out about this Council, that it was set up by the Board of Education. It in no way has any power over school activities. The City Council has never benefited the students in any way.

And, to get back to what I was saying before, I cannot understand why you're trying to say that I'm having any hassles with the G. O. City Council, because I'm not. If I was, then I would be impeached, and I am still the president.

Now as for this principal, I have to make you understand that we're not—I am not only talking about student rights, I am talking about human rights for high school students. I'm talking in the context of democracy, as opposed to a dictatorship.

I see a lot of advisory councils set up in the schools in which advice can either be accepted or rejected. Now that cannot happen in a democracy, where people vote and regardless, only one man makes the decision.

I would also like to point out that the incidents at Music and Art last year, in which the principal refused to negotiate with the students there on demands to include black history in the curriculum, to try and get more black teachers in that school, where you had a staff of a hundred and ten teachers, only two of which were black—at George Washington High School, where the parents and the students tried to set up some kind of a—to make up for the inadequacy of the guidance department by setting up a grievance table—the Board of Education permitted them to have this, and then reneged on that agreement and created a police state in that school.

Allen Hodges, who is the vice president of the school, was arrested for trespassing on George Washington property. You also had the same situation at Franklin K. Lane, in which I may point out that I was called down by the Board of Education and asked to go into that school and speak to those students about the problems there, where the Board of Education had created a police state, rather than trying to talk to the students and find out what their problems were.

At Cardozo High School, because a principal feels that students screamed in his face, he has found it necessary to arrest forty-one of them, to drop charges for the other 35, and keep the other five students still facing court cases.

Now these are things that are happening within the high school community. I think that if the decisions were arrived at, not by one man, but as you said, by people who know what they're doing—namely, the parents, the students, the faculty, and the administrator of each school—that it would be more democratic than allowing one man to arbitrarily control the school.

DEGNAN: Well, Mr. Reeves, let's take one thing at a time. I agree completely that in a democracy there should be an opportunity for everybody to be heard; and no principal in this town has ever voiced any other point of view, to my knowledge. As a matter of fact, I don't believe he'd be worthy of the task if he did so.

REEVES: A lot of unworthy principals.

DEGNAN: But let me ask you a few questions. We don't allow children to vote when they're thirteen years old, because they're not ready for it. There are many things that you're asking for that students at the high school level are not ready for.

As a matter of fact, I pointed out before, they're not ready yet even at a graduate level to make serious and important decisions. Now . . .

REEVES: What is the purpose of a high school? You said that they're not ready . . .

DEGNAN: Well, the purpose of a high school is to help

young people to mature, to grow to effective adulthood. And we, in doing that, we have a dual purpose. We try to bring out their best talents, and secondarily, in doing that, we bring them to the level of participatory democracy, whereas as adults, they can exercise their full constitutional rights.

REEVES: All right then.

DEGNAN: No. I want to.

REEVES: May I just answer that?

DEGNAN: I haven't finished my statement . . .

REEVES: You see I asked you that for one purpose.

DEGNAN: Yes, but let me finish my statement. I think you will recognize, that as I said facetiously before, you would not have them vote in the national election at the age of 13, and if you agreed to that, you certainly wouldn't have them do this at the age of ten. What I'm saying is this: that young people at the high school level are not prepared to make decisions even if this were possible. And society has structured schools in such a way that this was not the intent of schools at all.

Let me say this too. Is it true that you disrupted—you and some others in this group—disrupted the last meeting of the Board of Education, with epithets and all sorts of things to the point that the President had to dismiss the meeting?

REEVES: . . . I did not disrupt it.

DEGNAN: No. Let me finish.

REEVES: I'm answering you . . .

DEGNAN: I'll come back to you. You can answer me after I finish. Is it true that there have been firebombings? Is it true that in various schools—is it true that in Washington the place was broken up only two or three days ago? Is it true that there is an element of violence, and, if you like, something that goes beyond this order, that has to be contended with?

Society has to do something about this.

POTTS: Mr. Degnan, are you contending that those incidents you referred to are the work of high school civil rights . . .

DEGNAN: No, I assume, I think rightfully, that people are encouraged to do this through the kind of loose thinking that I think some of our young people are involved in.

Now, when a principal calls in the police, he does it for—the protection of people around him, the youngsters who are in his charge. He has no option. He can't call a committee meeting and say to students, what shall we do? He has to move quickly or somebody gets hurt.

We've had enough illustrations of that in this city to recognize the fact that it is not a viable kind of thing to have people get together the parents who weren't there, teachers who were busy in other parts of the building—to make a determination for the person who is charged with responsibility.

Now, in every instance, every instance in this city, where the police have come in, they have come in over the reluctance of the principal. This is the last thing in the world that he ever wanted to do. But there is a time that you must. To protect life and limb. And this I think is something we better learn. Violence will get none of us anywhere. And I think we've got to—right at this moment—think in terms of stopping that sort of thing, and then go on with the dialogue which you refer to, and as a matter of fact, you know, if I didn't believe in dialogue I wouldn't be here talking to you about this. I believe in it. And I believe that the Board of Education does. But it ought to be done under the kind of circumstances where there cannot be the kind of criticism that is made today. When people get violent and do things that are beyond the law, obviously dialogue breaks down under those circumstances.

REEVES: OK. Well—once again this mass hysteria of violence and so forth. I mean, it's become so stereotyped for superintendents and principals to use in front of the public. I'd like to say that personally, I believe I've been consistent, if you've been covering me, Mr. Potts, and if you've been reading articles in the papers that I have—I have said, we wish to negotiate peacefully with the Board of Education, and in no way have I advocated any violent action within the schools.

However, I will tell you that in one point in my high school career I used to believe totally in non-violence. Now, I'm not saying that I would use violence now, but I'm trying to say that in no way would I hinder students from using it to achieve whatever demands they have. Because, through non-violence, I have been thwarted at every step I tried to take. See, I issued a bill of Rights that is negotiable in all points. I've expressed the hope to negotiate peacefully with the Board of Education, and here I am receiving this kind of animosity from you and all these erroneous accusations in front of the public. I'd like to state also that what good is a system, which after four years of education, a student is not able to control his own student organizations?

You see? This is an anemia of your system, if students are incapable of making any sort of decisions. Also, it strikes me as being kind of funny—if what kind of a parent would really want a student not to be able to make his own decisions during that four years. The only time that a high school actually now—that is of course if his parents don't pamper him and use him as a puppet—the only time that a high school student has a chance to assume some kind of responsibility is when he's applying to college, and when he has to decide what kind of college he wants go to, financial aid and so forth. And in a high school . . .

POTTS: Mr. Reeves, I'm going to have to break in on you now. Our time on this broadcast is growing short. I'll ask you both now for a summary, beginning with you, Mr. Degnan.

DEGNAN: Well, I'd like to say that I agree completely with Mr. Reeves that dialogue should continue. I think our Board of Education takes this position. I think too that it should be pointed out that Mr. Reeves is a very able young man, and he has accepted responsibility here, and I've great respect for the fact that he has. But I do think that he ought to do his best to get this done within a framework that's possible. And again, I would say, perhaps above all, Mr. Reeves, that a repetition of the Board meeting and you were there, I understand, ought not to take place. We ought to be people of good will; we ought to try to do the very best we can to extend student rights as far as we can.

POTTS: Mr. Reeves.

REEVES: I'd like to state that at all Board of Ed. meetings I spoke in the time slot that I was appropriated with, and that every peaceful effort that I have tried to take in regards to the Board of Education, I have been thwarted, the bill was deplored by the Principals' Association after ten weeks of requesting peaceful negotiations with the Board.

We have been denied that right.

As a matter of fact, after those ten weeks, we had not even received a letter from the Board of Education.

I'd also like to state that there are things in our bill which I hope that the people watching this program will read. We have included things that promote racial harmony, that confront the drug problem, and the fundamental problems facing the high school community.

And I'm sorry that you've had the impression through your informers that I am a violent person and we've been advocating violence . . .

DEGNAN: No. I was never told that, Mr. Reeves, not at all. I have no informers. I read the paper and I read what comes to my desk.

REEVES: Well, you know what the papers . . .

DEGNAN: And I understand what students are about. I have students in my school who are in your council. So I'm not a . . .

REEVES: But you see, you've never met me before . . . you've given people the impression. . . .

DEGNAN: No, I haven't met you before. I have deliberately stayed away from the meetings that you speak of because I don't think that this is the place for any principal to be . . .

POTTS: Gentlemen, at this point we must thank you for being with us on Public Hearing tonight to discuss the topic: high school students' rights and the politics thereof.

Our guests have been Walter J. Degnan, the President of the Council of Supervisory Associations and Donald Reeves, Chairman of the High School Students Rights Coalition.

This is Robert Potts, WCBS/TV News, good afternoon.

Calling In The Troops

WE WERE RACING against time. The Board of Education scheduled a second hearing on their proposed Bill of Rights for the 26th of February. The City G.O. Council was scheduled to meet on the 11th, when our Bill would have to be approved to make it officially representative of the City's 275,000 high school students. Ira Glasser, from the New York Civil Liberties Union, and Steve Bernbach, from the National Conference of Christians and Jews, began to attend our meetings. Both the Civil Liberties Union and the NCCJ circulated information about our efforts to get the Board of Education to negotiate.

The Coalition now had a negotiating team comprised of representatives from the City G.O., the Student Mobilization Committee, Afro-American Students' Association, ASPIRA, the Vocational High Schools, Women's Liberation, and four openings for schools engaged in confrontations. We knew that no single student organization could be representative of all the high school students, and we made it clear that no agreement would be made until a vote of approval or rejection had been taken by all the City's students. The central negotiating team was comprised of those groups that could deliver significant numbers of students for the strike force.

The Coalition's specific intents was to involve in the negotiations the following: the United Federation of Teachers, the Council of Supervisory Associations, the High School Principals' Association, United Parents' Association, United Bronx Parents' Association, Public Education Association, the New York Civil Liberties Union, Afro-American Students Association, High School Student Union, the underground high school newspapers *Free Press & New York Herald Tribune,* the New York City G.O., NYC High School Women's Coalition, the New Coalition (radical caucus of the UFT), NYC Moratorium Committee, ASPIRA, the Third World Committee for Solidarity with Vietnam, vocational high schools, and Project Justice.

Our Bill involved parents, teachers, students, and administrators. Presumably, all of us should have been able to sit down and work out an agreement acceptable to everyone— an agreement that would be put to a vote by the City's 275,000 high school students.

The Board members have always contended that they are out to deal with students in an adult manner; yet when it comes to the reevaluating or exchanging of real power, they always maintain that students are incapable of making independent decisions. Hence, we could only expect that the Board of Education would denounce the Coalition and accuse us of not representing *all* the students. Yet the United Federation of Teachers doesn't represent *all* the teachers; the United Parents' Association certainly doesn't represent *all* the parents. And the Board would continue, in its tradition, to use the media to gain public support enabling them to abstain from dealing with us "in good faith" and using the spurious argument that we didn't represent *all* the students.

The major issue in our Bill was the establishment, in each of the City's ninety-one academic and vocational high schools, of a twenty-member School Liaison Board whose decisions would be final, absolute, and binding on the parents, students, teachers, and administrators. As the SLB was presented in the document, it was easy to prove that such a Board was unworkable. However, our point was to argue the necessity of replacing the principal's autocratic rule. Anyone can check the New York Civil Liberties Union's files and see that the record on the high school principals is marred by hundreds of violations of the law, directives from the Commissioner of Education, constitutional rights, and even their own laws. And in each case you can see that where a student is determined to exercise his constitutional rights, he must be prepared for a court fight. Even if he wins, there is no assurance that another student in another school will not be penalized for the same problem the next day.

Short of revolution, what is needed to revise the educational bureaucracy systematically is a uniform resolution to change administrative behavior and social attitudes. High school positions provide security for the insecure. And the intrusion of democracy into the school system is a threat and open challenge to the security of the high school principals and the Board of Education. Members of the Board are not elected.

Anyone who is in a position of power in a democracy is in a constant state of insecurity. That's why in unions the leadership use all kinds of undemocratic methods to cut off any encroachment on their power or position. The Board of Education will never submit to voluntary, binding arbitration because that means a loss of autocracy. And even where there appears to be "impartial mediation," it is often a deception because the Board itself selects the "impartial mediator," and you *know* what that means.

Our Bill outlined a fundamental change in school structure. It would enlarge the decision-making role to include the students, the faculty, the parents, as well as the administration of each school. This concept is in line with our overall idea of the school as a democratic community.

Decisions should be made by the community on a representative basis. Therefore, students must always have their fair share of voting representatives at any decision-making meeting. The administration represents the smallest interest group so should have a proportional vote. That protest occurs when decisions are made affecting people who are not consulted, only points out the necessity for reform of the present dictatorship in the schools to a democratic structure. Students must also be free to control all facets of students' organizations.

In addition, students must be at liberty to express themselves without intimidation in the classroom or with college files or behavior records. They must also be free from discrimination and have the right to due process.

News of the formation of the Student Coalition spread quickly throughout the city. I received an invitation to speak to the Public Education Association, and a few parent groups had begun to support the Coalition.

On February 11th, the City G.O. Council held its first meeting on the Student Bill of Rights, at the High School of Art and Design. I had a difficult time explaining to the members in the City Council why it was necessary for us to pass the Bill as quickly as possible. Time was against us—the public hearing was only fifteen days away.

Our first meeting ended in chaos, and the only thing that was accomplished was the unanimous rejection of the Board of Education's entire resolution. Another meeting was scheduled for the 18th. That gave everybody enough time to study the proposal and discuss it in their schools.

At 2:15 in the afternoon of February 18th, the City Council met again to consider the proposed Student Bill of Rights.

There was an unusually large number of G.O. faculty advisors in the audience. I had invited the Student Mobilization Committee to sit in. They had difficulty entering because Castka and Sullivan were complaining about "outside groups."

It soon became clear why so many faculty advisors were present. They were busily supplying their student cronies with advice on procedural tricks to waylay the meeting. (I guess some students will do anything to get graduation awards.) I told the students to split up into discussion groups according to their boroughs. Discussion on the Bill would last for about forty-five minutes, and after, we were going to take a vote. Castka said I shouldn't have invited Student Mobe, as they were outside militants, and that he and the Board of Education *owned* the Council, so until things changed, I'd have to do things his way.

I left him standing there screaming at me and walked around listening to the discussion groups. All the way in the back of the auditorium sat an Art and Design "Leadership Class." They were "observing" the meeting. By the time the discussion groups had ended, I was already hot, tired, and frustrated.

The action began. The Student Mobe and other people wanted to participate in the voting, but the Council people said that *they* were the official representatives, and no one else should vote. There were more complaints—that I was rushing things, that the Bill was too extreme, that these out-side groups shouldn't be present at the Council meeting. Then the Mobe people began to criticize the Council people. I tried to keep order, but as my knowledge of parliamentary procedure was for shit, I let Weisman from Student Mobe chair the meeting—he knew how to handle it and was right there.

Immediately the Council people accused me of letting an outsider chair the meeting. I resumed control—time was running out, it was almost 4:30. I told them that we'd have two speakers representing the pro's and con's of the Bill. A handful of people started walking out, but the majority remained.

I explained to the Council that the Bill was negotiable on all points and that nothing would be agreed upon without a vote of approval by all the students. I admitted that certain sections of the Bill were merely negotiating ploys and that we had asked for more than we knew we were going to get. And I pointed out that the very extreme sections that violated laws and contracts were included solely to expose the parents and other outside groups to some of the problems we faced

because of legality and contracts not involving our best interests. Another speaker got up and said the opposite of everything I had said. The discussion came to an end, and a vote
was taken on the individual sections of the Bill of Rights. The
entire Bill was passed, by a majority vote, as presented to the
Council.*

Up to now there had been no contact with the Board of
Education. Yet almost instantly, the Associations of High
School Principals and Supervisors as well as individual administrators went to *The New York Times*—deploring the
Student Bill of Rights. The so-called educators said that the
document was "the work of a small group of extremists and
outsiders seeking to gain control of the high school system."
The president of the High School Principals' Association said
that the draft "appeared to be the work of college students
and some persons outside the schools." Walter Degnan, president of the Council of Supervisory Associations, called it "a
very extreme and foolish statement on the part of extremists."

Because of their collective paranoid mentality, the Council
of Supervisory Associations came out in the news denouncing
a Bill of Rights that neither the public nor students outside
the Council had ever seen.

Ken, who was now officially the New York City G.O. Council's lawyer, sent a letter to the Board of Education requesting that they set a date, time, and place for negotiations
within ten days of the date of his letter, February 23rd.

Later that day I received a phone call from Leonard
Buder, of the *Times* Education Department. He wanted
a copy of the Bill and an interview with me. The principals
had attacked the Bill, and the paper wanted our side of the
story.

Vickie and I went over to the *Times* office. On the subway
she was acting very strange.

■   ■   ■

---

* See Appendix D: The Coalition's Student Bill of Rights as passed by
the General Organization City Council, February 18, 1970.

"O.K., what's wrong?"

She hesitated. "Come on, come on, come on," I said in a matter-of-fact tone.

"They'll probably want to interview only you," she replied in a low voice.

I felt bad inside and didn't know what to say to her.

When we got there, Buder called me into a little office and told Vickie to wait outside. Man, I knew she was mad. But what got to me even more was that Buder knew what was going on. Anyway, he wrote the article on the Bill,* and I was interviewed by Paul Montgomery.†

Whenever people read demands that have no explanation or appear to be very extreme without carefully considering the rationale behind those demands, they almost invariably react negatively.

Of all the proposals in the Bill, the twenty-member liaison board received the most attention. "In blunt language," Fred Hechinger pointed out in his article "Why Johnny Wants to Run the School," ‡ such an arrangement would "spell not a student voice or even student power, but virtually total community power . . ." But he had sense enough to realize that "it can readily be argued that this proposition, because it is so extreme and so easy to prove unworkable, may be little more than part of the negotiating mechanism. Only Hechinger saw that ". . . a revolutionary ploy, then a modus vivendi, might well emerge from the Board's and students' separate proposals." As for the school officials, they charged the City Council—the organization they had always recognized as the legal representative voice for the city's students—as "not reflecting the sentiments of the majority of high school students." They also viewed our proposal as "part of a new campaign by high school and college militants to sow discord in

---

* Leonard Buder, "City Students Ask a Voice on Policy," *The New York Times,* February 24, 1970.

† Paul Montgomery, "Student in the News," *The New York Times,* February 24, 1970.

‡ Fred Hechinger, *The New York Times,* Education section, March 1, 1970.

the schools . . ." They even questioned the legality of the
meeting at which the Bill was passed. (One might ask why, if
the Board of Education is so concerned with legality,
students are denied their legal rights.)

It is absurd for the very same people who are denying students their rights to cry loudest about an alleged denial of
rights at their meeting. The assertion that the G.O. Council,
in passing the rights proposal, did not reflect the sentiment of
the majority of students boils down to nothing more than
principals claiming that students do not represent students.
Representatives of the Board of Education complain about
the way students run their meetings, and the principals determine which students represent students. At the same time students are strictly forbidden even to listen to faculty meetings
—which are always held behind closed doors. The principals
meet behind closed doors. The supervisors meet behind
closed doors. The Board of Education meets behind closed
doors. And yet the Board of Education by-laws prohibit students meeting without a faculty advisor. Therefore, we would
have to take our meetings outside the school structure.

The media had given us extensive coverage, and I started to
get mail from many people, young and old, asking what they
could do to help. I got letters from teachers, students, and
parents all over the country who were happy to see that at
last students were no longer going to go through the high
school system of arbitrary restrictive rules, petty regulations,
silently swallowing their hate and making it part of them.

I got letters inviting me to speak to all kinds of groups—
like Phase III, an organization consisting of interested people
and parents of drug addicts. Most of the mail concerned
drugs and asked me to make students aware of drug rehabilitation units, etc.; I did, however, receive one negative letter.
Someone wrote:

I wanna enlighten you. The USA is the only country in the
Americas that allows an idiot like you to demand "rights" and
garbage like that!

Only in a permissive society like here in the U.S. can clowns and jackasses who think they're bright carry on as you do!

I didn't have time to reply to letters—things were moving too quickly. Some nights I didn't even go home but stayed in Manhattan organizing and planning with other members of the Coalition.

The Board, faced with the prospect of a true coalition of G.O. and militant groups, was trying to sweet-talk the G.O. back into the fold. Dr. Lachman, author of the Board's Bill, sent a letter to Ed, chairman of the Council's Students' Rights Committee, requesting that he get another committee together to meet privately with the Board. Lachman was trying to divide and conquer the students. He knew that other groups were involved in the Bill of Rights struggle. The one thing Lachman didn't know was that many people on the City Council were also members of the Coalition. In fact, Ed was one of the nine students who originally helped put together the final draft of the Bill.

Because the Board's only response to our offer of peaceful negotiations was one of divisiveness, we decided to call a press conference at the Commodore Hotel and state our objectives publicly. Ken and I had a long talk before the conference. He told me not to let the reporters pressure me into talking about violence.

Sitting in that crowded room, looking face to face at all those cameras and microphones, sweating under the hot lights, I couldn't help but feel inside that I was getting all this attention only because it was unusual for a Black guy to be doing this. But my personal feelings had no place in what I was doing; just as long as I got my point across, that's all that mattered.

Ken, Weisman from the Student Mobilization Committee, and I sat up front. I made an opening statement explaining the basis of the Coalition as an opportunity to be more responsive to the needs of the city's high school students. I read a list of the fifteen member or supporting groups involved in the Coalition, told them that the Board of Education's Bill had been rejected earlier, and that we had sent a copy of our resolution with a letter stating that it was up to them to "respond to our peaceful actions."

The questions came: Violence. Violence. Violence. Violence. Is the Coalition militant? Are you going to use violence in the event that the Board doesn't respond? Up to now I hadn't even opened my mouth. Most of the questions on violence came from the *Daily News*.

Many questions concerned the School Liaison Board. I had said it at least a hundred times—"It's negotiable."

The following morning I was in Ken's office checking out the conflicting coverage we'd gotten at the press conference. In an editorial (February 25, 1970), the *Daily News* said that the coalition had "drawn up a sweeping list of demands that amount to a blueprint for student takeover of the schools . . . the GOC *manifesto* would just about abolish all restrictions on student behavior . . ." *The New York Times,* along with three other papers (*Village Voice, N.Y. Post,* and *Long Island Press*), supported our position that to deny out-of-hand validity of negotiable proposals would be to foster frustration and revolt.*

During this time the Coalition became too dependent on the media. I don't think I can adequately emphasize the overwhelming psychological effects the mass media have on groups that are able to create opinions and make impressions far out of proportion to their own size. I actually forgot for a time that the media only create opinion—they don't build a movement as easily as they can (and often do) destroy movements. Ho Chi Minh, for example, got a lot of coverage for his movement in Indochina, yet he didn't call any press conferences. The difference between the reality of revolution and romanticized Hollywood concepts of it is in itself an explanation for why movements in this country are inevitably doomed and always in need of a martyr to kill or imprison in order to revive the revolution from the dead of the past year.

---

* "The Students' Voice," *The New York Times,* February 25, 1970.

It is the media's function as an accessory of the system to destroy revolutionary movements by diluting, overexposing, and making shams of valid causes and martyrs and so-called leaders. The people on the Left have been made to look like idiots, clowns, misguided children. On television and in the movies, the so-called revolutionary youth culture in this country has been commercialized and made into a subject of comical debate by many. When a real danger is present there will be a news blackout, and rumors, lies, and distorted information will begin to circulate. No one will know whether these things are true or false (something close to the information we receive through the media about the war in Indochina will become the norm until the danger has passed). Up to such times, the media will freely publicize the freaks, print their books, interview them on television and radio, and of course feature them in *Playboy* magazine.

When I started working on a speech for the next day's public hearing on the Bill, Ken had me water it down at least four times. I told him that once other people had watered down my words and what I now thought of them. We got into an argument but eventually worked out a compromise.

On February 26th, the public hearing was held on the Bill of Rights at New York City Community College's Center Auditorium. Seven hundred people turned out for it. The police were outside and inside and behind the doors peering through the glass. The members of the Board sat on stage. On the desk was a red buzzer. Each speaker would be allowed to speak for two minutes. After that time limit the Board would ring the buzzer and cut that person off no matter what he was saying. Questions were never answered. The Board just sat and watched. The people often screamed and carried on, but their voices fell on deaf, dumb, and blind individuals.

The meeting was rigged so that students, whom this issue concerned the most, were scheduled to speak late in the afternoon after the Board's supporters had spoken.

Meanwhile the Coalition's people were busily circulating leaflets, urging everybody not to disrupt the hearing. Parents from the United Bronx Association were screaming: *"Re-spalde nuestros estudiantes, ellos solamente están deman-dando por sus derechos humanos y civiles en las escuelas públicas"* (We support our students. They are merely de-manding their civil and human rights in the public schools).

I went outside to look for Ken, but he was nowhere in sight. When I came back in, I was confronted by a group of guys who looked like they were going to do me in. They sur-rounded me, and one guy stepped forward.

"My name is Ralph. We from Samuel Gompers Vocational High School, and your Coalition doesn't represent us, and you haven't got any right to say you represent the students if you don't represent the vocational high schools. We sent a letter to Dr. Lackerman [sic] denouncing the Coalition, and we told him to read it before you spoke. You going to get hurt if you don't keep your mouth closed about how you represent the students."

Shit. I looked around, saw that he probably wasn't kidding about beating sin out of me. "Well listen. We've included de-mands that all of us want. If you've checked the Bill out, you can see that your rights are included. You're joining with the enemy. They don't care about you. You know what people think about the vocational high schools. Well, I'm trying to make them see you deserve respect. Why don't you join the Coalition, become a spokesman for your group?"

We spoke for some time, and in the end Ralph and his boys saw it my way. They withdrew the letter from Lachman.

Members of the Afro-American Students' Association were getting restless, and I knew that our people had better get a chance to speak before the action began.

When it did we received support from representatives of the Public Education Association, Urban Coalition, United Black Front, Free Yippie, School Defense Network, *Village Voice,* Harlem and Brooklyn Fight Back, Poly Tech, United Bronx Parents' Association, and the New York Civil Liber-ties Union.

When our people had finished speaking, I delivered the

Coalition's statement telling the audiences what we thought of the Board of Education and its lack of responsiveness to student problems. I told them about the Bill that the Board came up with without even consulting the students. Then I told them about the Coalition's resolution:

The basis of our resolution is democracy . . . The power now vested in one man—the principal—must be exchanged with a truly representative school board comprised of an equal number of voting students to teachers and parents—our bill is negotiable, but if you turn it down completely, our actions can only be based on your reactions.

After my speech, the Board refused to let other students speak. The crowd of seven hundred students and parents got angry. There was total disorder, chants, and shouts. Paper planes began to fly. People seized the microphones and cried out that the real problems were illegal suspensions, oppression of minority groups, and poor handling of the narcotics problem in the schools. One aide to the Board was hit in the head and knocked down by a dry-cell battery thrown during the disorder. A few parents got up and accused the students of "biting the hand that feeds them." Paper planes continued to fly, fists were raised to the chant of "Power to the People." And then a vocational high school student marched up and down the aisles with a battery-operated bell, buzzing at the Board and screaming, "This is what your education has taught me!"

There were other sporadic outbreaks, and finally some kids from the Afro-American Students' Association seized the microphones when a fat woman from the Queensboro Federation of Parents' Clubs said, "Youngsters ought not be allowed to destroy the educational structure."

The Afro-American Students' Association read the list of their seventeen demands, which included protests against dope-pushing in schools, general diplomas, and Regents' exams. The speaker looked at the Board and said, "You people got to learn to respect us—else you gonna die." The entire audience gave the Black Power clenched fist and shouted "Power to the People! Off the Pig!"

The president of the Board tried to say something, but a squadron of paper planes flew across the room, and the meeting was officially ended.

Two days after the hearing the Coalition held its first open meeting at the Washington Square Methodist Church.

Over two hundred people showed up, but I could count the number of Black faces in the audience on one hand. That was strange, I suppose, the victims not being here. But there was a more important problem: we were still splintered. In concept, in theory, everything indicated our strength, but we were disorganized and weak. The Student Mobilization Committee had too much control over the Coalition in terms of meeting places, organization, etc.

Our objective today was to approve a negotiating team. Ken stressed the importance of unity in labor negotiations, but his approach was too academic and turned off those ears that are accustomed to militant rhetoric.

While the composition of the negotiating committee was being discussed, the Afro-American Students' Association opened fire. Angel, a suspended student, took the floor and told us:

There would *be* no high school Bill of Rights without the ASA. We all got our heads beaten in at Lane last year. We don't have to *read* about it; we were *there*. We gave birth to you. We're your mothers and fathers . . . it's human rights you have to fight for. If you don't, you're behind the times. And address yourself to your parents' needs, too. They know what the problems are even more than you do. They know drugs are a big problem. Do you? Do you think you represent all the students? Well, you don't. How many of you snort dope? [No hands.] And how many of you have ever been suspended?

Angel then turned to me.

"Who is at the head?"

He was now going to sound off on me, but from past mistakes I knew his game. I told him to finish what he was saying and sit down. He turned around facing the audience, picked up a copy of the Coalition's Bill and ripped it up. "This," he said, "is what the Board will do to you."

Another student stood up and fired back, "We don't represent all the students—it takes time." The meeting broke open in the usual revolutionary dialogue—the soothing, masterly oratory that we substitute for the reality of our situation.

Why is it that as oppressed people each of us, each group, seeks to claim the source of liberation in a manner in which we resent and try to destroy other groups fighting the same battle and maybe winning where we have failed? It is always good to bring out strong points at meetings and constantly question the strategy. We need a sectarianism that brings out points to build the movement, to sustain the movement's life, not destroy it.

Most of the ASA leadership had been suspended and arrested in the spring of 1969. The ASA all but burned down the Board of Education, yet their demands had still not been met. But what of these other groups that had previously made demands that had not been met? Why was it that they had not actively joined the Coalition? The adult groups who supported us had done so only in words, but nothing more could be expected because this was not their fight—it was ours. The only explanation that I can see is that there was resentment toward this Coalition because of the mass publicity we'd received and the appearance that we were making progress. Many groups had written up demands, but to date none had reached the stature that we had. They had been struggling for years, the Coalition only a few months, yet it had received extensive coverage in the English, Spanish, and radical press for a number of weeks. The reality of our situation was becoming painfully evident. These other groups resented the speed with which we had taken over the struggle. They even wanted us to fail.

That day, for the most part, had been a success. The Coalition was alive. The students were the only force that could destroy this movement. We had the Board beaten. They could send the police, they could even send the National Guard into the high schools, but they couldn't hurt us because we wouldn't be there. We would strike until our demands were met.

FREE THE NEW YORK 275,000

It was the best we could do for a slogan . . .

It was ours and indicative of most *generalized* sentiments characteristic of people who find the schools repressive. However, there are many inmates who find prison tolerable, even desirable. Like lost fish surviving in a tiny bowl of water in the corner of the room, they wish only not to be disturbed and to be fed when they are hungry. The overshadowing problem of the student movement is that there is no class consciousness among students. Ultimately, our problem always is trying to stick together.

Itinerant

IT WAS NOW NECESSARY to show the Board of Education that the Coalition was not just a disruptive element that could be easily ignored. We had tried to deal peaceably but had failed to make any inroads, and so we felt justified in striking the system. Members of the Coalition got on the streets and started organizing and leafleting. Only the schools where agitation was openly apparent could be organized on such short notice.

In the midst of all this, Buder wanted to see me at *The Times;* something had come up. When I got down to his office, he showed me a letter from some parent at Music and Art, criticizing the paper for supporting me. Included in the letter were articles from Music and Art's school newspaper denouncing me and my activities at the school. I just wanted to get free of that fucking school. Buder said that he wanted an explanation, said that he'd been taking my word up to now, but if these articles were a true measure of the way students felt about me, *The Times* would have to support the principals and Board of Education. I tried to tell him that I hadn't always been the way I was then. I went home to get some notes to show him what had happened up at Music and Art and how I'd been framed. I also brought along what I could hardly believe—my speeches supporting Klein and the system in general. I found speeches where I had even *lied* to defend Klein. It was then that I became conscious that I had gone through a transition, that I was a different person. And from that point I started to put dates on just about every piece of paper that came into my hands. I made little random notes of four and five sentences of things that happened day to day. I was sure that this movement concerning the Student Bill of Rights was or would one day be an important part in the high school struggle throughout the country because in high schools only the students have absolutely no power and only over the students does the principal have total control. Sooner or later the students would no longer permit themselves to be used as scapegoats during school budget crises, teachers' strikes, etc.; they would one day form a union to protect their own interests.

It is even the hope of some that public education as it is presently structured will be destroyed. Many people—doctors, students, teachers, and parents—who had been pushed out of the school system were beginning to set up free schools, based on community control, that would educate students and not process them. The problem of sporadic violence would spread to uncontrollable proportions in schools where rigidity and stagnation are rampant because nothing was being done to treat the causes.

Education is the foundation of a society. Much progress made in a society is due to the education or intelligence of its members. To a large extent economic barriers are set up to the degree or level of an individual's education, which is, of course, omitting discrimination. When people realize that they've been shortchanged in education and are doomed to failure and misery for the rest of their lives, they may logically place the blame on the public school system that determined their destinies. They may even join in the struggle being waged by today's school inmates.

I started doing a lot of traveling, trying to build support for our movement. First, I went down to 125th Street for an interview with the *Amsterdam News* to make a rebuttal to derogatory comments about our Bill made by Robert Mangum, State Commissioner on Human Rights. The Commissioner is Black, and he had taken time off from his high-paying position of power to go on TV to ridicule and malign the objectives of students trying to get their human rights. As for a debate between us, Mangum replied, "He'd have to have a degree before he could speak to me." I know that his words angered a lot of people, and it had nothing to do with me. Look at the millions of dark-skinned people in New York City who don't even have a high school diploma (which is not to say that they are stupid), whose human rights are violated every day, and yet this so-called protector of their human rights had the gall to say on nationwide TV that "you have to have a degree before you can speak to me."

But this is typical of Mangum's attitude toward all too many Black people. Why, for years Black and Puerto Rican people have been on the streets protesting to "Dump the Division of Human Rights." They realize that the division is nothing but a buffer to block the people from reaching Governor Rockefeller.

I went up to George Washington High School. That was a victim school.

As far back as February 2nd, parents and students went to the man who was the principal at that time, to request that a table be set up in the lobby to receive student complaints concerning scheduling and guidance. GW has a population of 4,500 students—twice the capacity that the school was built to hold. Out of a class of 1,500 students, only 300 graduated with academic diplomas. The acting principal of GW, following the directives in the High School Principals' Manual on Counterinsurrection, sat on the demands for over a month. The parents got wise, tired of waiting, and began to demonstrate. On March 6th, Deputy Superintendent of Schools, Selig Lester, granted the table and everything the parents asked for. On the same day GW's UFT Chapter Chairman told all the teachers to leave their classrooms for a sit-in in the cafeteria. The Acting Principal quit on the spot.

Again it is apparent that the teachers penalize everybody when their own interests are at stake. All the parents wanted to do was to make up for the inadequacy of the GW guidance department, but the UFT denounced them, and then claimed that the parents wanted to take over professional functions of guidance and consultation. When the teachers walked out, leaving over four thousand students sitting in their classrooms, everything came to a head and students took to the halls.

When the problems of a school reach the newspapers, it usually means that the peaceful channels have been exhausted. It happened at Erasmus Hall High School, Thomas Jefferson, Franklin K. Lane, Music and Art—all over the country. Now the mass media would soon be focusing on George Washington High School. Publicity had misled many into believing that the Coalition had organizational strength since our policy was to support the victim schools, just like the UFT does for its locals. Allen Hodges, vice-president of GW, joined the Coalition. However, you didn't even have to be there at GW to know what was going on—to know exactly why the UFT pulled off an instant sit-in. Just look at this—the Deputy Superintendent of Schools issues a directive to settle a dispute, and teachers react by walking out of their classrooms to sit in in the cafeteria. The Board of Education renegs on its own agreement because of pressure from the UFT. Now, should the parents and students put their confidence in the Board of Education?

You hear administrators and teachers saying parents should be involved in the school. Parents are apathetic. Parents aren't involved with their kids. But the reality of the situation is that it is not in the school officials' best interests for parents to be involved. The longer parents stay away from the school, the longer the UFT, Board of Education, and Council of Supervisory Associations can get away with dispensing a wholly inadequate education and covering up the problems which they themselves create.

On Monday, March 9th, the teachers filed in, punched in their cards, and went to sit in for the remainder of the day. Acting Superintendent of Schools, Mr. Irving Anker, took back the table and replaced it with one to screen people coming into the building.

GW had made the news. They weren't saying "Black students" anymore; it was now understood that the word "militants" meant Black students. The white students were "radicals" and the parents were "dissidents." I think that was very clever of them, not coming right out with what they wanted to say.

Shortly after GW erupted, Cardozo High School, located in the heart of a Jewish middle-class section, with an enrollment of 4,200 students, 700 of whom were Black, broke out into a political controversy over ten demands. The students demanded among other things that "all racist teachers be excluded; all police and special agents be excluded from school premises; all students that have been expelled or suspended be reinstated; all students, when brought to trial, be tried in student courts, by a jury of their peers; the addition of Black literature . . . justice and peace." The Black Students Union had met fifteen times with the principal; their appeal to implement the ten-point program was "cut off, postponed, and put off for another time." * The BSC openly stated that "it was not a racial struggle but a student struggle in which it became necessary to confront the administration because of his stalling tactics." The principal quickly moved to publicize the dispute as a racial issue and told the Jewish community that *their* children would be protected by police who would be stationed in the school.

---

* "Where militants demand a hearing on a transient issue, they must submit the agenda and their recommendations in advance, allowing time for consideration and consultation. TRANSIENT ISSUES MAY DIE STILLBORN."

High School Principals' Association

Finally Michelson, the principal, called another meeting with twelve students in a school conference room. As soon as they started to get down to business, Michelson told them the meeting was off until tomorrow. The students refused to postpone the discussion. At this point thirty other students entered the room. Michelson claimed he was held captive and had thirty-five of those students arrested.

The details of the incident at Cardozo High School were carried in the *Long Island Press.**

One of the suspended students said:

"We feel the white students of this school have got to learn that the stereotype of the black man isn't true.

"Our problem is that there is not communications between the black and white students in the school."

"The black kids can't relate to the curriculum being taught," another stated.

"We have many racist teachers in Cardozo. They don't know anything about black people and they don't try to learn."

"One teacher said to me, 'You people shouldn't even be in this school.' We have just one black teacher in our school and no black administrators."

Three suspended students said they haven't been disrupting the school, but rather have been the ones who have been "cooling it."

"We've been talking a lot of students out of raising hell and doing damage to the school," one said. "And, we're not just talking about the black students. I've had white students tell me they would like to put bombs in the school.

"We want the best possible education we can get, but they're not giving it to us."

"We didn't do anything disruptive on Monday. I would say we were suspended strictly for political reasons."

Another said, "There is only one black history class offered. As a result, most of us can't even take it. The course is being taught by a substitute teacher who volunteered for it.

"I spent several hours with a grade advisor here and was told to forget about my first choice of a college. I want to go to the State University at Old Westbury, which is an outstanding school of social studies.

---

* "Cardozo Suspensions Lifted, But Police Will Stay," *Long Island Press,* March 18, 1970.

"We were all under the impression that the advisors were to help us, not hinder us. It seems the advisors aren't interested in seeing black students go on to college."

"They suggest to the brothers that they go in for a trade. They say they can make more money. But they don't encourage any of us to become something more than laborers."

The suspended students said they were not disruptive Monday. They said they had asked a teacher to move his class to an empty classroom so they could use his room for a meeting.

"We asked for the room and we were given it," one of them said. "We didn't take it over like the principal said."

The principal adamantly refused to withdraw his criminal charges against five Black students who took part in the take-over. The Defense Counsel for the Cardozo 5 sent a letter telling Joseph Monserrat, president of the Board of Education, that the suggestions presented by Jacob Zack, the man in charge of all high schools in New York City, and Assistant Superintendent Wilner were unacceptable for obvious reasons. First, Mr. Zack suggested that there was no problem of self-incrimination or double jeopardy since "students can always proceed with suspension hearings and remain silent." Second, the suggestion was made that the "students accept transfers to other high schools until the disposition of the criminal charges."

In plain words the first suggestion is that the students stand mute while criminal charges are made against them. Similarly, the second option contains an implication of guilt and a predetermination of the truth of the principal's charges, without affording the students the opportunity of a fair hearing as required by law. And also, the relocation of the students to another school would preclude their reinstatement at Cardozo, even if the evidence at a hearing were in their favor.

The Defense Counsel for the Cardozo 5 made a plea to the members of the Board of Education that the principal withdraw his criminal charges so that fair suspension hearings could proceed at once. The charges were not dropped; instead a date was set in May for a hearing at Kew Gardens Criminal Court in Queens.

Parents and students in victim schools like George Washington and Cardozo were so involved with internal disputes to exercise their rights that it was impossible to get them involved in a citywide struggle.

When a white institution takes in one Black face it brings in a whole world of problems.* These white schools in which Black students find themselves were never structured to meet any of the needs of the Black community. One Black student in a white class finds himself in a position where people look upon him to speak for the entire Black population of this country.

But the problem with victim schools is that they carry on isolated struggles that serve the immediate needs of only a few. If only it were possible for all of us Black students and white students to unite and confront the source of our problems, the Educational System, then our struggle would be more meaningful, in terms affecting the lives of thousands if not millions of people.

On Thursday, I went up to Schenectady, New York, to be part of a TV cast of upstate principals and students who'd be discussing the role of the high school principal. I don't think that at any time I saw a better example of how afraid principals are of losing their power and becoming managers of the school, rather than autocrats. The more I listened to the problems facing upstate students, the more I realized how far along New York City really was. These upstate schools are moving at a slower pace. Dress codes and smoking lounges, dances and basketball games are still their major concern.

It's criminal to see what high schools can do to the mind.

---

* In *The New York Times* of March 23, 1970, Bayard Webster wrote in his article "Fieldston School Seized in Demand to Add Blacks":

It was one of the first instances in the country where minority students in a private preparatory school actually took over a school building. The students' action, accomplished with no violence and no property destruction, was in protest against the failure of the school's board of governors to act on long-standing demands for more Black students, teachers and advisors, more Black school employees, and the *integration* of the Black and Latin-American experience into all curriculum levels. Hours later the faculty agreed to recommend to the board of governors that the school add ten minority members to the enrollment.

One student actually felt that the principal's letting him clean up the lunchroom was "student control." And one principal had the best idea on how to handle dissent that I've ever heard; he said that the underachievers and troublemakers should be taken away from "the other kids." I guess this point of view is held by many so-called educators; witness their success in the legislature to win approvals of resolutions to increase the number of suspension days. They want total conformity. It's the "underachievers and troublemakers" that make these educators *earn* their pay, and yet they don't even want to deal with the problems that they have a professional responsibility to confront.

That next Saturday the Coalition held its second open meeting, this time at Hunter College. Again there were very few Black students at the meeting. The Coalition as I had envisioned it was still not a reality. Our Coalition existed in name only. The composition of our membership was primarily white and committed to Moratorium organizing and nothing more. The Afro-American Students' Association had died out politically and were now turning toward cultural movements around the same time that Afro Sheen and Soul Soda were being introduced in the ghetto.

Even though I had invited representatives of the Student Mobe to sit in and speak at City G.O. Council meetings, they refused to let me speak during their major meetings for fear that I'd convert their membership to the Students' Rights movement. To a degree all of us, the SMC people and myself, were playing a political con game. I worked with them only because of their organizational strength. The SMC owned its printing machines and was financed by outside sources. Being president of the G.O. City Council meant absolutely nothing because the Board of Education *controlled* the Council. Necessity forced me to form an alliance with a stronger group. And this was a mistake. The SMC had our mailing lists, and when we first formed the alliance and assigned duties to people, their members were placed in the positions of the treasurer and publicity manager. By holding these key positions while I was traveling, they were turning the Coalition's membership into their membership, to fight their struggle, which was to fill space at the next monthly peace parade. They had one interest: to build their organization. All their energies were directed to that end.

The night after our meeting at Hunter College some other students, teachers, administrators, and I went down to Channel 5 Metromedia Television to tape the David Susskind show. In the beginning of the program we were in a vacuum of racial rhetoric—all under Susskind's direction. He didn't know anything about the high schools—all he could talk about was violence. He took advantage of the overemotional student panelists. He got them to scream at him, "Don't you understand us?" And the cameras rolled in for a close-up so that America could see just how crazy high school students are. Susskind understands his audience and uses them against panelists. Can you imagine what the reaction was when a brother approached the microphone and said, "We gonna have to start bringing our guns to school"? Susskind must have repeated the brother's words at least six times. At one point he said that students were mindless amoebas.

Susskind represents, at best, a wishy-washy white liberal. He is at the extreme, worse than the epitome of the principals that I speak about who are not interested in dialogue, who are mere tools to uproot the worst in peoples' prejudices and hatreds.

A few days later I was in Albany spending the week with Natalie. Actually, I had received a letter inviting me to be part of a regular student group in Albany that Ewald B. Nyquist, State Education Commissioner, was establishing to assist him in dealing with educational affairs. The invitation was nothing but a free ticket to co-optation. That's one of the many things that the system does to pacify those who step out of line—they try to buy you off or appoint you to some funky position so you'll be content and keep your mouth shut. And when you get older they just put a bullet through your head. My purposes in going up to Albany were to get information, publicize the Bill, and speak to Ewald about his boys in New York City who were violating the law and his directives.

I spent a few days with Natalie before the conference. I gave her the bust that I had made in school—"The Head That Wouldn't Stand." Natalie was one of the most beautiful girls I'd ever known. She was the kind of girl you'd just want to hug and never let go, but she'd always push you away and let you know that you had to let go. I liked her, but I didn't love her as much as I did Vickie. Vickie and I were part of each other. We were going through changes together.

Anyway, I got a few days rest and went to see Ewald. The Commissioner and his Task Force on Student Affairs had organized a "cross section of New York State's students to make us think that we were "educational consultants" and would be "involved" in State Education Department affairs.

We arrived Sunday afternoon, all fourteen of us. I was the only senior. Schnell, a young college student, was in charge of the operation. He explained the role of the Student Advisory Committee (SAC). Apart from "advising" the Commissioner, we were supposed to make available to him "a greater resource of information."

After the orientation session we had a chance to question the Task Force. Of the thirty-six groups that the Commissioner had advising him, this ad hoc committee was the only student group. The Commissioner himself was never directly involved in any kind of school dispute. And there wasn't one Black or Puerto Rican Bureau Chief in that whole State Education Department. The Student Advisory Committee's main function was to discuss the previous meeting's agenda and plan one for the next meeting. It was made clear to the students that the advisory group's function was "strictly up to the Commissioner, since [we] belong to him technically."

After the question period with the Task Force, there was a second group discussion with Bureau Chiefs and Task Force in the Regents' Room.

Once I saw what the Regents' Room looked like, I just couldn't resist the temptation to go buy a big White Owl cigar. Up until then I'd never smoked in my life, but this scene was such a circus that I couldn't help joining the act. The Regents' Room had a long brown table like the ones that big corporate executives meet at. I decided that I was going to sit at the head of the table and be the president of GM. Right before the meeting I lit up and started choking. I didn't even know how to hold the cigar properly. With my elbow resting on the table and the cigar pointing up in the air, I almost burned my hair off.

All the Bureau Chiefs of the State Education Department were present. Each of them was to give a short rundown on the functions and progress of his department. Afterward we, the students, could ask questions.

The Commissioner said that he really hadn't given any thought about when the committee would actually be functioning. Aside from this we asked why New York is the only state that still has Regents' exams? A Bureau Chief got up and replied, "Regents' exams are good indicators of effective teaching. In fact, Regents' are responsible for the high quality of education in New York State." When we asked how was it possible for other states to teach their students effectively without Regents', the same Bureau Chief got up and equivocally replied, "Well, in no other state have there been equivalent testing methods."

I then asked the Commissioner about the kind of guidance program the state has. He said that the Department covers eight hundred school districts—with a five-member staff.

Can you imagine that, New York City—over ninety-one high schools, hundreds of elementary, intermediate, and junior high schools with 1,120,000 students, categorized as being *one* school district, to be covered by a five-member board supposedly in charge of checking on a total of eight hundred school districts? I'm sorry that I didn't ask how much money these people were being paid.

Nyquist held a press conference. I was elected spokesman for the student group but said absolutely nothing about the committee or Nyquist. Instead I publicized the Bill.

Even though the conference was scheduled to go for another day, in the middle of the night I packed my bags and left for the train back to New York City. I had better things to do than sit around and be part of a political ploy. The State Education Department paid us to go up there, and that's why many of the other students who knew the committee was a farce went along with it. We were being bought off. Maybe I shouldn't say this about the Commissioner, but I only know what my experience tells me. Students are often sucked in and fooled when they meet people in high positions who tell them that they sympathize with their situation and appear to be positive toward change and progress. But the truth must be measured in the reality of their deeds, and not just by their words. A man in a position of power can say virtually anything; the flexibility is there, simply because he has power. At no time would I take the word of any of the people in the State Education Department because there has been nothing in my experience to make me believe that what they say is true, that their intentions are in the best interest of the public.

I was down at the train station when I realized that I had only fifty cents in my pocket and no ticket to get home. I called the Toomeys. They drove out to the station and loaned me some money. We talked for a good while because I had missed my train.

I got back to New York City very early in the morning. I had just enough time to go home, get my spikes and shorts, roll up my suit and stuff it in my black bag, and head straight for school. I had to take an English test first period. I got to school on time, but slept through the test. In fact, I slept through all my classes. After school I had to go to track practice so that I could show Mr. King that I was still in shape and was ready for the Borough and City Champs in May. I was beat, hadn't had a bite to eat all day, but I ran three miles, did a couple of baton passes with Tony, and ran a few 220 sprints. After practice, Vickie and I went down to the Fifth Avenue Hotel. I had to make a speech to the Village Independent Democrats with Basil Paterson, who was campaigning for

Lieutenant Governor. I went in the bathroom to get into my suit and wash the dirt off my hands and face.

Ira Glasser from the New York Civil Liberties Union introduced me. I went to the rostrum and started my speech. I was on the second line when I started to get dizzy; the lines were moving all over the place, then my head felt numb, and I felt needles pricking my brain—everything was getting dark. I started to pass out. I said, "Excuse me," and passed out.

There was a doctor in the audience. He and I went out for a walk around the block.

"I'll bet just about everybody in that room thinks I'm on drugs."

The doctor looked at me with a smile and said, "To be honest, the thought had crossed my mind. But I've been watching your movements, and you appear to be in control of yourself."

"I'd better go back inside."

"Do you need a ride home?"

"No, I'd better go back inside and finish my speech because if I don't, I know it will never leave their minds that I'm on drugs."

I went back to finish my speech and explained the difficulties with organizing our April 15th strike. They donated almost $200 toward our effort.

Ira Glasser drove Vickie and me home. We dropped her off and headed for my neighborhood. Glasser and I joked about my fainting, and we got into a light discussion about Vickie's parents and me. When he dropped me off, I stood there in the street thinking about the whole thing back at the hotel. Vickie hadn't even made a move to help me. That thought hadn't occurred to me until then. I mean, I just naturally expected her to be there, but she wasn't.

I went inside and sat in the kitchen reading *The New York Times*. Mom came downstairs to speak to me. She was angry about the amount of time I was putting into the Bill of Rights and said that I didn't even have time to be with her and Francis anymore. It was a difficult situation, consciously knowing that I was neglecting the only two people in the world who would always be on my side, no matter what happened, to take up a cause that made enemies out of my closest friends and people I didn't even know.

■ ■ ■

On Friday, March 27th, the Coalition announced plans for a students' strike. About two hundred people showed up at the SMC's Union Square Office, but the door was locked. Many people went home and about fifty of us went over to the Alternate U. building—at Fourteenth Street and Sixth Avenue. Ken showed up about an hour later.

I'd been able to get Ralph, from Gompers Vocational High School, Allen, from George Washington, and some other brothers and sisters to attend Coalition meetings. The "rainbow coalition" was becoming a reality. However, I'd gotten into too many personality clashes with members of the SMC —Weissman and Chaney in particular. Both of them just seemed to have this obsession with bringing large numbers of people out on the streets for their Moratorium demonstrations. Just about everybody, Ken, Sarah, Vickie, and Ralph, had advised me to take more control over the Coalition because the SMC was running the show. I knew that this was true, but there was no other organization that could supply the machinery that we needed to confront the Board of Education. We found ourselves in a position where we saw all that was going on, but we were unable to do anything about it. I relied heavily on Ralph and Allen for strike support.

When the meeting got underway, we started to argue about a strike date, and everything broke open. The SMC started to run a political con game. They wanted the strike date on April 15th, the same day as the Moratorium. It was obvious that the Bill of Rights movement would get absolutely no coverage if the strike were held on that day. Ralph opened up: "Who you think you trying to kid? You jive-assed motherfuckers—"

"Hold on, Ralph!" I said. "Listen, Chaney, when we started this struggle, I told you that we weren't interested in a one-day strike. All power to your Moratorium movement because it's finished. As long as you keep bringing people out into the streets, and no results come out of it—it's only a question of time before your numbers dwindle to zero. There are only two months left in the school year and the citywide strike is nowhere in sight and—"

A guy from the Panthers interrupted.

That's why they call you HIGH SCHOOL KIDS, 'cause you can't get your heads together. Here you are, arguing over which day you gonna strike when the Man wakes up every goddamn day, plotting ways to bust you upside the head. I want to call your attention to the most important problem—the number one maneuver on the part of the fascist power structure—the attempt to murder Bobby Seale in the electric chair. You high school kids got to become part of national struggles and forget all this high school shit—that can't get the get-go, understand? You all should go back into your schools and organize against the fascist power structure . . .

He went on for about thirty more minutes, and as soon as he stopped, we started arguing again. My position on having the students' strike before April 15th had no strength, so when the vote was taken April 13th and 14th were scheduled as dates for rallies and pickets at the Board of Education. April 15th would be the major strike date. The SMC had everything so sewed up. The 15th would be cut in half. The idea was: "In the morning we'll strike for the Bill of Rights; in the afternoon we'll strike against the war." Shit, a half-a-day strike. A farce. But that wasn't all: the morning strike wouldn't be held at the Board of Education; it would be held at City Hall. I just didn't have enough people to support my position. The SMC always had large numbers of people from their organization supporting them. The City Hall strike was a setup. It would only be convenient for the Moratorium people to organize all the demonstrations going on in Manhattan and lead them down to Bryant Park. There'd be anti-war speeches. There would be an estimated 25,000 people at the rally. The Women's Coalition and Gay Liberation Front both jumped on the SMC bandwagon, leaving me with only the handful of people that I started out with—and all of them said that I had been used, and were unsympathetic.

I didn't blow my cool but weighed my options. The possibility was still there that I could find enough victim schools to organize for a takeover of the Board of Education. But that seemed unrealistic at this point. There had been a wave of bombings in the city and around the country. Just about all public buildings in the city had increased their security forces —especially the Board of Education. I elected to go along with the April 15th demonstration, but I'd get students from victim schools to speak all over the city wherever a crowd gathered and in this way, try to extend the demonstration into another day, or on that same day, April 15th, try to get as many people as possible to go over to Brooklyn to the Board of Education for a massive demonstration.

The meeting ended and we were at odds with each other.*

Things were in a mess. The City Council had closed itself off. The Board was lying in public, stating that they wanted to sit down and talk with us, yet we received no word from them. All I had left was the feeling that I couldn't give up because everything I saw—the principals violating the law, the faculty advisors manipulating the students, students manipulating other students, inadequate education—it all pointed to only one thing. The seemingly insurmountable obstacles to solving any one of these problems didn't mean that it was wrong or foolish to use all energies and any means available toward eliminating them.

Until April 15th, we—that is, what was left of the Coali-

---

* "The new left is not monolithic. Quite the contrary, it is composed of many view points and of many divergent groups. If it seems unified at the moment of confrontation, the unity is deceptive. With time, and under pressure, cracks will appear and caucuses surface."

High School Principals' Association

tion, Ken, Gompers High School, Allen, and me—would have to bluff to make the Board of Education think that we were still well organized and able to pull off a strike. The most effective way to pull this bluff was to call up the *Daily News*. We figured that they'd twist anything. We said "negotiable" and "peace"; they printed "manifesto and militant."

Wipe Out

On Thursday, April 2nd, I went to school. I was embarrassed to find out that the Center For Marxist Education had people up at Music and Art distributing leaflets about me speaking at their forum the next day. I didn't feel bad about speaking there, but I knew that, as often happens when musicians and artists are constantly trying to distinguish themselves, the resentments against members who gain recognition are intensified. Not one teacher or student had anything to say to me except, "You're getting your face in the papers." The only one who approached me and talked about the Bill of Rights and the content of the articles relating to it was the shrink.

I remember that many of the art teachers got upset over a statement that I had once made in the newspapers when I was asked what I thought of the art courses at M & A. I had said that I found them to be a big letdown. The teachers took issue with me because they claimed I hadn't been in classes long enough to make that statement. They couldn't see that I wasn't in art classes just because I had expected to be doing and learning more than I was.

I had had the best art teachers in the school ever since my sophomore year. I can't possibly claim they didn't know anything about art. All I can say is that by the time I got to be a senior, I practically hated art. It was unfortunate that I had such negative feelings at this time because I had Mr. Drexler for fine arts. Mr. Drexler was an artist in the truest sense of the word. I am by no means an art expert or critic of artists, but I can say that what running was to me—the food, the water I needed to live by—art was to Mr. Drexler. He really tried to get us to love art. He'd tell you where there were exhibits all over the city, show you books and magazines of paintings and drawings. He'd try to get you to feel art, identify with the forms, colors, and textures. But unfortunately, he was seldom successful. People like me had already been fully crushed before Drexler got to us.

As a practical matter, more than half the graduating class of Music and Art turn away from the arts and seek some other field of study; many never even pick up a brush or instrument again. I think it's criminal that this happens. I don't think that anywhere in the city, state, possibly the entire country, there is as talented a group of young people as at Music and Art. The evidence, judging by the net results, speaks for itself—the school is stifling creativity.

When Klein got hold of one of the Marxist leaflets, he called me into his office, looking troubled. "Donald," he said, examining the leaflet, "I'm concerned about you." I knew what he was getting at. I was supposed to be this innocent deaf, dumb, and blind student who was getting sucked into all kinds of subversive groups and being used—he could identify with that.

We had a very brief talk, and I went to a few classes. It was a good thing that I had come to school that day because Karen, for some reason, was in the G.O. office, checking the minutes book to see if I had been "officially" elected as representative to the City Council. If she had found what she was looking for, she was going to have me impeached as president of the City Council. I laughed when I heard about that, but when I spoke to Gladstone, he laid it straight on the line. Castka, Fineberg, and other citywide advisors were in fact meeting regularly to find a way to have me impeached as president of the City Council. Karen (to my surprise), Ralph, a House Nigger from Aviation High School, and some white students from Queens had formed a caucus to kick me out.

The first thing I started to do was to write a letter of resignation, but I tore it up. I discussed the situation with Ken and Vickie, and we all agreed that it was a healthy thing if the Council people took initiative to organize themselves to do *anything,* even to impeach me. But I just couldn't see why it had to happen again. Why couldn't they see that I was insignificant, inconsequential to their real problems. When I would go, I'd be gone; what would be accomplished? The problems would remain.

I was in school when the call came informing me that the City Council was meeting at Art and Design. When I got to the meeting, the agenda had already been made. There were at least ten G.O. faculty advisors present. There were only thirty-three of the ninety-one schools represented. I could see that the only people present were those who had voted against the Bill and who had not been there when it was passed—a setup. Castka had even invited Leonard Buder of *The New York Times* to make sure that the story made the news.* A fixed agenda, a stacked meeting. I could see Castka, De Maio, and Sullivan standing around the only other Black face in the room. And for that split second, my mind reconstructed the scene from last year with Fineberg and Klein standing around me while I denounced Darryl, and, as two Black people, we fought while white people looked on. And now here it was again, but this time *I* was looking at the House Nigger.

It's important to understand this situation. If the City

---

* "Students Split on Policy," *The New York Times,* April 5, 1970.

Council just had white people denouncing me it would have had racial implications, but by having a House Nigger as not only the leading spokesman but the only spokesman for the group of whites against me, they made the job look more or less clean. As for Ralph (who was Puerto Rican), he thought he was involved in a power play, and that after I was gone, he and the House Nigger would move in.

Adults must realize that students do not compose a homogeneous group, incapable of individual thought or dissent with each other. We are people, live human beings who often disagree with each other.

I opened the meeting. There were charges that I wasn't representing the City Council, that they didn't want to form alliances with college students, that I was working with outside groups. None of this made any sense to me. In a few months just about everybody in the room would be a college student. And just what was an "outside group"? Outside to whom or what? And if I *was* working with so-called outside groups, it was on my own time and had nothing to do with them. I did, however, tell them that I was a spokesman for the Coalition, not the City Council. But it was clear that nobody was here to listen to what I had to say.

The House Nigger waved his hand to be recognized. He came to the front, made a speech telling the Council (rather, appealing to their egos) that they were the representatives for the 275,000 high school students, that we shouldn't work with outside groups and that the City Council should be at the head of the Coalition. He received applause.

One girl had taken the Coalition's Bill, revised out the part about the student liaison board, and put the name of her school as the group who wrote up the Bill of Rights.

Throughout this time I watched the advisors smirking at me. I could say nothing, but inside I was in the dumps. Everything—truth, justice, morality—was on our side. Yet right here the students who had never organized on any front organized to destroy the only issue that ever gave their organization any significance, the only issue that truly could affect the lives of 275,000 high school students. The advisors at one point were laughing at me as I told the Council about the State Education Department, George Washington High School, Cardozo, Lane, and our right to strike. The Coalition wasn't part of the City Council; they couldn't be at the head of what wasn't theirs. But I said nothing. I waited for them to make the move to have me impeached. When they were all finished attacking me and criticizing the Coalition, I asked them what they wanted to do.

There was silence. People were looking around at each other. Nobody wanted to make the move. I saw Gladstone smiling at me, trying to hold back his laughter. They didn't have the guts to do it. Instead, the House Nigger got up and told the Council that they should detach themselves from the Bill of Rights and appoint another group to work on another Bill during the summer. I told them it wouldn't work because by that time the Board would have already passed their resolution. Besides, they knew the truth—not one of them was going to give up a second of his personal time to work on any Bill of Rights, especially not during the summer. Nevertheless, they cut themselves loose. They put their trust in the Board of Education.

These people didn't impeach me, and I didn't resign because that's what the Board wanted. As long as I was president of the City Council, the Board couldn't say I was unrepresentative because the Council was the Board's organization, the one that they had for so long held up as the legal representative voice.

When the meeting ended, I spoke to Buder. He knew what had happened and told me that we'd "missed the boat." The students in the Council had betrayed themselves.

I could now work only with the Coalition. We would have to get ourselves organized to strike the system. I would say that our main problems were time, money, and space—a building or just a room of our own. The Coalition was a volunteer-type operation that demanded too much of an individual's time with little or no results in return and too many risks, like suspensions, arrests, and black-mark notations on confidential records. With these risks it's only natural to understand why at its zenith the Coalition never had an active membership of more than ten students and no more than two hundred followers. In addition, we didn't have a central location where we could meet regularly and were always on the run—day and night.

The only thing that we had going for us was the Coalition's reputation, which could still be used to pull off the threat that we were going to shut down the high schools unless the Board agreed to negotiate with us.

On Friday, April 3rd, we called a press conference at the headquarters of the National Conference of Christians and Jews. I told the press that we had no other recourse but to strike. As expected, the *Daily News* flavored up our statement by saying that "a 'nonviolent' coalition issued an ultimatum: . . . 'Give us a greater voice in school affairs or be prepared for massive demonstrations and a shutdown of all the city's high schools.' "

Later that night I spoke at the Center For Marxist Education and tried to enlist more support for the Coalition. Membership in the Coalition was open to all students of all races, all political beliefs, even suspended or arrested students as long as they were of student age. I explained why the Moratorium strategy was ineffective. A general strike would paralyze America. The Moratorium could pressure Presidents into resigning but neither the Republican nor the Democratic Party had presented a platform for immediate total withdrawal from Vietnam. Aiming solely at the President wouldn't get the desired result. The war wasn't run by one man alone, but a complex of government, military, and business interests. Until anti-war demonstrations were directed at all the fronts that created Vietnam, nothing would be gained and nothing would be done to prevent America from continuing her "mistake" in Indochina, starting another Vietnam in some other part of the world.

I asked them to demonstrate on a front where we could

win. No educational system in this country can endure a sustained students' strike.

The next Friday, Vickie and I went down to the Civil Liberties Union to get some paper. Even though we knew nobody was going to show up, we wrote up a leaflet announcing a citywide demonstration at the Board of Education. I was going to leave a few leaflets in and around the Board in the hope that they'd think a strike was coming.

Every day I grew angrier and angrier at the Mobe. From the very beginning they had been draining all the Coalition's resources to build their one-day strike. What it all boiled down to in the eyes of the Afro-American Students' Association and vocational schools was that whites couldn't be trusted and that I was a fool for thinking it was possible. They were probably right.

We printed about three hundred leaflets: STRIKE THE BOARD OF EDUCATION—APRIL 14TH AND 15TH.

Vickie went home and I took the train down to the Board of Education offices where I threw the leaflets all over the place, in the lobby and even the elevators. On Monday, April 13th, Ken, Ira, and I went down to the Board to see the president, Monserrat. He said that he wanted us to call off the demonstration. I don't know what kept me from laughing, but I told Monserrat that I'd called it off, threatening to call it on again if we failed to reach a settlement by the end of the month. Ken, Glasser, and Monserrat laid down the ground rules for negotiations. Monserrat was quick to state that he didn't want to keep minutes on public record.

In the end an agreement was reached. The Coalition would have representatives from ASA, SMC, Women's Liberation, ASPIRA, United Bronx Parents' Association, Public Education Association, and HSSU. The City Council had boxed itself out of the issue.

Ken pointed out that principals had been disciplining students who had been trying to publicize the Bill of Rights, and that the Board of Education had a responsibility to permit discussion in the high schools on an issue that affected all high school students. Monserrat got on the defensive and said, "I'm meeting with you only to take back rhetoric to my colleagues." And the discussion was over.

On Tuesday, April 14th, my friend Ed and I showed up at the Board in the morning. There were police all over the place. The Board had swallowed the bait and called for the police to hold off the demonstration they anticipated would be there because a few leaflets had been left around the streets.

Ed and I formed a picket line and soon three other students joined us. Five people showed up to FREE THE NEW YORK 275,000. The Board even sent a photographer down to make sure our faces were on file. The police sent for reinforcements. It was a sad scene, I can tell you. Five high school students picketing in the rain, over a hundred cops watching you and laughing.

That night there was a meeting of radical groups at Union Square—where the Mobe was sponsoring a symposium. I showed up to make one point.

The SMC was nothing but a bunch of ass-licking, class-collaborationist phonies who understood nothing of alliances with minority groups for the purposes of furthering political objectives, other than holding *peace* parades. They would invite practically anybody to speak at their rallies as long as that person could attract support. They lied and deceived just like the people in the system they condemned as fascists. Their view of revolution was a slogan, a cliché. If people like those who were in the SMC were in power tomorrow, I'd leave the country. The SMC not only betrayed the Bill of Rights movement, but if any one student organization could be singled out as being the most harmful to the morale of the movement in general, the SMC would be way out front. They absorbed weaker organizations, squandered their resources, manipulated people within their own ranks, and attempted to silence any opposition to their methods of operating.

In the middle of the speech to the SMC, a thought occurred to me to lay down a challenge. "If you are true revolutionaries, then you'd have the guts to take over the Board of Education tomorrow morning rather than listening to speeches and clichés." I could tell that everyone in the room was fired up. The SMC people were giving me these dirty looks, and the people in the audience were smirking and looking down at the ground. I walked out and didn't give a shit what they thought.

I got home at around two in the morning, but the phone wouldn't stop ringing. Vickie called, Mr. King called, and then Steve called saying that there was going to be trouble tomorrow. There were plans being made to disrupt the rally if Lindsay showed up, and it would be wise if I also wasn't on the platform. As soon as I got off the phone with him, someone from the Moratorium committee called up to make sure I'd be at Bryant Park. Tomorrow would either make or break the sustained student strike.

On Wednesday, April 15th, I waited alone at the Board of Education for almost two hours, and nobody showed. A few blocks away at Borough Hall, about two hundred students gathered for the anti-war demonstration. It started to rain, and we started to march, across the Brooklyn Bridge and over to City Hall where we'd join up with that demonstration. Once across the bridge, we were met by disorganized crowds of people. The City Hall rally wasn't scheduled to start for another hour; in the meantime people were all over the place carrying buttons and posters and shouting: JOIN THE REVOLUTION, BUY A BUTTON. Brothers were selling Panther papers and liberation buttons (you know how uptight you get when you don't pull that quarter out of your pocket), and I was running all over the place trying to find a bathroom —guess I was overexcited.

I found Ralph who showed up with a huge crowd of vocational high school people. I thought it funny, watching Ralph and his friends. All of this demonstrating stuff was new to them, and they just wanted to see Ralph get up on the truck and say something—anything, just as long as he said something.

The SMC had rented a truck with sound equipment. Ralph

and I took it over. He spoke about the problems in the vocational high schools, but the people were unattentive. A
member of the Panther Party showed up and spoke about
people organizing to free Bobby Seale. He read Eldridge
Cleaver's manifesto.

By this time thousands and thousands of people were in the
streets. It was chaotic. People were running all over, carrying
flags and posters, and following crowds. Some little kids were
carrying an American flag and being chased by anti-war
people. The police were running after the anti-war people. At
Battery Park a poster-sized replica of a 1040 tax form was
burned. At the Internal Revenue Office only twelve blocks
away, pacifist and folk-singer Pete Seeger along with William
Kunstler and Dave Dellinger was speaking to crowds, calling
out for action. This was supposed to be the year for it. I
looked across the street and saw many disaffected city government workers sitting on benches: just another lunch
break. I stopped and wondered about the thoughts that were
going through their minds as they watched the thousands of
us on the streets. Many of them just folded their arms or read
the newspapers, got up and made their way through the
crowds and back to work.

You know, sometimes I wonder. When you look at it ob-
jectively, just why the hell should anybody listen to us? In
the summer we play frisbee and blow balloons, sing songs,
and smoke grass. A day comes and we organize, we listen to
speeches, most of which we've already heard. Then we march
to block traffic or anything we can, there is blood spilled—
usually our own—nevertheless *we* are placed behind bars.
The *day* goes, the protest is over. Yet we expect people to dis-
mantle their working mechanisms for what? And from whom?
From us?

I left the City Hall area and took the subway up to Bryant
Park. I went across the street and up to Ken's office.
"Reeves," he said hanging up the phone. "What's happening?
I just had the Board on the phone. They're afraid that you're
going to bring some people down there."

"Nah, nobody's going down to the Board. Can I have some of your calling cards?" I took about ten and put them in my pockets.

"What are you doing that for?"

"Just in case I get hurt. I want them to call you."

We talked about my speech. He wished me luck, and I went over to the Fifth Avenue library where all the speakers were supposed to meet. In the back of the library, hidden from the view of those on the streets, stood squads of police in riot gear. I looked at them for a while, their sticks, their guns, their uniforms, their faces. I went inside and down into the basement with the other speakers.

Inside I had no way of knowing what was going on outside. Not only physically but also mentally, I had been so deeply immersed in my efforts to build a citywide struggle for human rights for high school students that I had failed to see another theme developing.

Mayor Lindsay was under attack for the campaign of extermination against the Black Panther Party in New York. Militant groups charged that Lindsay's appearance was an insult to the Panther 21 who were languishing in prison as a result of an outrageous frame-up by the police. It was also an insult to Lee Berry, one of the Panther 21, a Vietnam veteran kidnapped from a Veterans' Administration Hospital, thrown into solitary, beaten, and denied medical attention until he now lay in a coma, near death, in the Bellevue prison ward. With a few phone calls, Lindsay could have obtained the proper medical attention for Lee Berry, stopped the frame-up of the Panther 21, and guaranteed the Panthers their constitutional and human rights.

An anti-war movement unrelated to Black self-determination, an anti-war movement not in solidarity with peoples of all struggles, collapses under the weight of its own racism and opportunism.

The time came. Neither Kunstler, Dellinger, nor Afeni Shakur showed up; they refused to speak on the same platform with Lindsay. I now had a clear way ahead of me. There were over 25,000 people outside—a large segment, if not the largest segment, were high school students.

Along with four other people, I was being escorted to the podium. The others weren't speakers, but readers of the names of American soldiers killed in Vietnam. I had long since given up symbolic protest. The people that this reading of Vietnam dead was supposed to reach had no feelings, no morals.

I was almost in a trance; I couldn't believe that the opportunity was right before me to build strength and support for a demonstration at the Board of Education. The sun was beating down brightly as I stood behind the podium looking out at the crowds and colors and flags and banners and black people, yellow people, white people, thousands of bodies covering every inch of Bryant Park and pouring over into the streets. There came a shout "Free the Panther 21!" and "Off Lindsay!" I was startled. I tried to speak, but some people up front had a bull horn that was making a ringing sound.

Then there came a rush—some radicals had fought their way onto the terrace behind the library and tried to take over the podium. I was at a loss for words and just stood there watching. I turned around just as a huge chunk of dirt came flying through the air toward my head. I caught it and threw it back in the face of the guy who'd thrown it. Those people up front were determined to reach the podium. They made a second rush. I watched as the guards threw chairs, and fists started to fly. And I saw clearly, as if in slow motion, a fist connected with some guy's jaw, and his whole mouth seemed to fall apart. I couldn't speak. I couldn't bring myself to say anything; I remained in a daze.

It was just a strange feeling of watching these people fighting beneath the podium and thinking of tomorrow or tonight when the demonstration would be all over, when nobody would be here, and the podium and the park would both be empty—then what? I was looking at the clash, listening to the cries of "Revolution Now," I was thinking of being high up in the sky looking down on the crowd. I'll bet that the farther away, the higher you got, the smaller we looked. I thought of Jamaica, of China, of Russia, of what must be going on in other parts of the world while we were there in that park.

Kunstler finally made his appearance. The crowd was still trying to take the podium. I came out of my trance and started screaming, "YOU MOTHERFUCKERS, YOU MOTHERFUCKERS, YOU MOTHERFUCKERS, YOU GODDAMNED MOTHERFUCKERS, DEFENSE LAWYER WILLIAM KUNSTLER IS HERE." Kunstler got his hearing. He spoke for the Panthers, attacked Lindsay for remaining silent, and said, "Resistance is everything short of revolution." In the midst of his speech, factions broke out. "Revolution Now!" "Peace Now!" came the reply. When Kunstler was finished, the podium was stormed and taken and destroyed.

I sat on the terrace until late evening, almost nightfall. The park was virtually empty. I watched as a few demonstrators picked up discarded leaflets and other debris and built bonfires. The police showed up, threw me out, and closed the park. I went home, and for the first time in over a month, I got a full night's sleep—there was just about nothing else I could do. I had been at the right place at the wrong time.

A few days after the demonstration I went up to Teachers College at Columbia to be part of a panel to discuss Fred Wiseman's film *High School*.

It was a really bright morning, windy, a really thrilling feeling. Before I met Vickie I picked up the mail, five letters. I opened each one, from the University of Pennsylvania, Harvard, Georgetown, George Washington, and Hunter College —all regretting to inform me that the Committee on Admissions was unable to approve my application for admission. Shit. I knew that if Mom saw them she'd say, "See what I told you. Why don't you go to school like everybody else and keep your mouth shut." Just about every day she told me that.

I put the letters in the garbage. That left only two places— Dartmouth and Cornell. The thought of going to school for four years at Dartmouth College gave me the shivers. The only difference between Dartmouth and Siberia was the political ties: eternal snow, no girls, four years of masturbation, and enough free time to count all the pores on your body. I figured that my chances at Cornell weren't too good, so I just forgot about the whole thing.

At Teachers College that day we saw *High School,* and I just can't see how they let Wiseman into the schools to get those scenes. Wiseman has got the overkill, the socialization, the authoritarianism all on film. He missed the political scene, but even without it, he's got it.

My discussion on the panel concerned primarily things that happened to me at Music and Art. I told them that I might like to write about those experiences, and after the conference, Verne Moberg, from Pantheon Books, gave me her card and said that if I was serious, to give her a call.

On Thursday, April 23rd, Percy Sutton, Manhattan Borough President, issued a press release urging the Board of Education to rescind its decision on the George Washington High School dispute. The Board of Education had rejected community involvement at George Washington High School and had issued its orders unilaterally, without the courtesy of even momentary consultation with the scores of people who participated in forty-two hours of mediation conducted by the president of the Board of Mediation for Community Disputes, Ronald Haughton. The Board would not submit the dispute at GW to voluntary binding arbitration. The parents felt that this "unilaterally determined so-called settlement shows the contempt that Board feels for parents and students." There was no settlement. Here again the Board of Education attempted to deal with a crisis by a public relations trick. The Board's "settlement" did not have the consent of all parties and was not agreed to by the community.

"It was precisely," said Percy Sutton in his press release, "this absence of community and parental involvement in George Washington High School in the past that originally led to the school's educational stagnation and physical violence. By *imposing* a settlement . . . the Board of Education has blocked the way to meaningful participation by the parents and the community . . . The Board has pandered to the interests of the UFT and the school's administration and dealt a cruel blow to the interests of the students, parents, and the community."

Around the same time that the Board of Education rejected community involvement at GW, Albert Shanker, president of the United Federation of Teachers, was back on the scene threatening to shut down the schools if he didn't get what he wanted for the paraprofessionals, a newly enrolled group of union members.

Largely Black and Puerto Rican, the paraprofessionals were hired with Federal antipoverty funds to assist regular teachers in the classroom. Many of the paraprofessionals came from the ghetto and some hadn't gotten as far as high school in their own education. They were earning barely enough to live on—$2 to $2.25 an hour. The paraprofessionals joined the UFT, and immediately there was Albert Shanker, the Great White Hope, threatening to close the schools down, depriving younger Black and Puerto Rican children of an education so that the wages for his new members would be raised. The Federal Government should have given these people that money.

Personally, I feel that it was a stupid move for the paraprofessionals to join the UFT. That's just why Black and Puerto Rican people never get anywhere—they always want to live in somebody else's house. What I mean by this is basically what Malcolm X said in regard to Black people building and expanding their own little business so that eventually Black people would be in a position to employ other Black people, instead of disgracefully picketing and boycotting white people's business trying to get jobs from them. Why couldn't the paraprofessionals have organized their own union? Why didn't Black lawyers help them?

Before joining the union, the paraprofessionals were in a unique middle-man bargaining position. Any UFT strike would have been hurt if the paraprofessionals had abstained from it. No, they made the mistake of joining the UFT and, in the Black tradition, becoming wholly dependent on the white power structure. As *The New York Times* editorial put it, "The speed with which Mr. Shanker has started brandishing his familiar strike club makes inescapable the conclusion that his prime purpose is to polish up the tarnished image he acquired in the Black and Puerto Rican communities by the Union's fight against community control in the Ocean Hill-Brownsville strike two years ago." * That's exactly what he was doing, and the paraprofessionals were caught in the middle.

All over the city, the Board of Education was violating the law, even their own laws, and misleading both students and parents into thinking they were trying to work out problems "in good faith." Now the Board, unable to get their Bill of Rights passed during the hearings in November and February, scheduled yet another public hearing, but no announcement of the hearing was made. However, the various community groups involved in disputes with the Board over violation of agreements heard about it anyway through word of mouth and turned out at the April hearing in full force. The mass media were also on hand to cover the story. Leonard Buder was there from *The Times*. Ken and I were in the crowd. And unknown to all except the Board of Education were some surprise guests backstage behind the curtains.

Trouble erupted twenty-five minutes after the meeting started. Various community leaders stopped making speeches and started demanding that their grievances be heard and their questions be answered. All five members of the Board of Education remained impassive as the parents, who at first had quietly asked for answers to their questions, started screaming at the unresponsive ears of those in power. Monserrat ruled a woman from District No. 6 "out of order."

"Let her speak! Let her speak!" people shouted from the audience of four hundred. I turned to Ken and said, "They're doing it wrong." I ran up to the front and jumped up on the

---

* *The New York Times* editorial, April 23, 1970.

tables in front of the members of the Board. The audience, startled, became silent.

People, brothers, and sisters, this is nothing but a sham. You can scream until your tongues fall out of your mouths. These [I pointed to the Board] are nothing but wolves, public relations con artists, and you are sheep, dumb enough to believe they're here to give you justice. So don't waste your time. Brothers and sisters, look at these men. They represent nothing but castration: a Black man who is nothing but an Uncle Tom; a Puerto Rican so-called president of the Board of Education—nothing but a kitchen Spic; and these Jews who have exploited your communities for centuries. And now, all of you are dumb enough to bring your complaints to the same people who created them. Remember what Brother Malcolm said, "You don't bring your case to the criminals—you take your criminals to court." And this is what we must do tonight, forget these fools. We're going to have our own hearing—for the people. ALL POWER TO THE RIGHT PEOPLE!

Bergtraum, vice-president of the Board, and the others left their seats and stood huddled in a group, giving their stories to the reporters. I kicked over their tables, got the community people to come up on stage and voice their complaints. It was beautiful.

I stood there sweating, feeling really good inside to see the community people working with each other, organizing to support each other's disputes. Then suddenly a parent involved in the table dispute at George Washington got up on the stage. Most of the audience was from George Washington, so everyone was emotionally involved with what she had to say. For over forty-two hours they had bargained, and the Board had violated the settlement that was laid down by a mediator that the Board itself had called in.

As the meeting got more and more heated, more students started to climb up on tables. One ran backstage. A parent went after him, pulled the curtain back, and there stood over two dozen pigs, ready to move. There was a deafening silence when the people saw the blue uniforms, black sticks, and riot helmets. No one ran or shouted. All of us just looked at the members of the Board.

Everyone was motionless. A voice rang out, "Oink! Oink!" and broke the silence. There was no violence. Quietly we filed out into the streets and went home. It was night and raining. I looked for Ken but couldn't find him. I had no way of knowing that he and Monserrat had left to discuss setting up negotiations.

I was alone on the subway platform, looking at the tracks, thinking. I felt uneasy over the speed at which I had been able to take over the meeting and how quickly the people had placed their confidence in me—a complete stranger. People could be led too easily, and I felt this was dangerous to their own security. What if my purpose had been purely agitation, disruption for disruption's sake? Their legitimate grievances would have been invalidated by their following unstructured militancy.

It is of the utmost importance that community people engaging in any kind of militancy or protest be fully aware of what they're doing. They should know who to trust and who not to trust, who to follow and who not to follow. They should realize that the system will use plants to stir up tempers in the community so that it can legitimize police repression to muffle the voices of the people. Most of all, it's essential that we *learn* from our mistakes (and from theirs!) so we can *make* the education system accountable to the people.

Daylight

KEN AND I HAD BEEN UP all night talking about Fanon,
Baldwin, Cleaver, and Vickie's father. The following morning
I had to go to Randalls Island for the Manhattan Relays. I
wasn't feeling tired or anything because I was on the high:
that's when you don't get any sleep, for a week or so—all
you've got is this pent-up energy that stays with you for a
time, then you start spiraling downward. The possibility of
having a nervous breakdown does exist, I suppose.

Mr. King wasn't mad at me for a change. Well, he was
never really *mad* at me. It's just that I had a habit of letting
him down.

Torrence, Tony, John, and I were in good spirits, and for
the first time we had a few spectators from Music and Art. It
was a sunny day with a brisk wind coming every now and
then. The four of us started warming up, rubbing muscles
with Ben-Gay, stretching, and jogging, and of course, we
took the usual leak before the meet.

We were put in the third heat. From where we sat on the

grass I could see Vickie, Mr. and Mrs. King, and Music and Art people. Tony and I watched the first two heats; the competition looked pretty stiff.

Finally they called us. We took our places. I started getting nervous. The gun sounded, and Torrence did his quarter in third place, John took the baton and gave it to Tony in fifth place, and then Tony made a comeback, running neck and neck for first place. I was standing there on the line watching him come round the turn with that other guy on his shoulders. I started to shake my hands, loosening up. I looked at the other guys beside me, who I'd be running against. I saw Mr. King with his arms folded looking at me. "DON!"

"Shit I'm sorry man." I hadn't been paying attention to Tony coming down the straightaway. I got a bad handoff, but by the turn I was way out in front. It was thrilling. I felt good, moving as I had never moved before.

As I sprinted up that back stretch, I could hear the crowd cheering. The other guy was far behind; I couldn't even hear the sound of his feet or breathing. I was covering ground and not getting tired, only stronger and stronger. I rounded the turn and could see that the closest man to me had not even finished the straightaway on the other side. This was the race. I was running for daylight, my fastest time, and almost started to smile as I burned down the last stretch and into the tape. "Music and Art, Music and Art, Yeah, Yeah, Yeah . . ." I shouted. Man, I felt good, and Mr. King came running down grinning like a little kid. I slapped Tony five. Torrence came running up: "Yoooo, Don. Can I get it?" I slapped him five. John "The Smoke" Crews was jogging around the place singing "Number One, Number One."

I left the meet before they announced the results. Although we had won our heat, it didn't mean that we had placed in the meet. I naturally assumed we hadn't. I left immediately after for a conference in Albany, not knowing that we had won the meet, the gold medals, and plaque. When I later found out what had happened, I was elated, of course, even though they'd lost my medal. When I asked Mr. King to show me the plaque he told me Klein had it. I went up to Music and Art, took the plaque out of Klein's office, and gave it back to Mr. King. I told him, "Klein doesn't deserve this—you do. You're the only person who has taken any interest in us." Mr. King took it, but said that he had to return it. I got mad and told him, "Burn my half before you do."

My times were getting faster and faster despite my not going to practice. Every time I ran it would just blow Mr. King's mind. He'd say, "If you came to practice, you could be something, Don, but you just keep playing around."

On the day that they had the Manhattan Borough Championships, I was especially nervous because I'd be running against a guy from Stuyvesant who everybody said could beat me.

It was a real hot day out at Randalls Island. Vickie and I went jogging outside the stadium. We were jogging on a big grass plain surrounded by the river. When we finished jogging, I lay down to do some sit-ups, and Vickie sat down to watch. I was lying on my back thinking about what a tough race it was going to be. When I turned my head, there was Vickie sitting with her legs wide open. I could almost see through her little flimsy yellow panties. I laughed and pulled her close to me, and we started kissing. Then both of us got on our stomachs, beside each other. I was looking at her, at the grass, and at the little earth insects. And from the ground my eyes surveyed the grass plain and the surrounding river. My eyes made a wide sweep, and I caught sight of four athletes from Boys' High jogging down at the far end of the plain. They were running in wide circles. Every fifteen minutes or so they would pass the spot where we were lying on the grass. When they passed us a second time I rolled over on Vickie. She started laughing. Her blouse came unbuttoned, and I opened it more and started fondling her, and we fucked. It was fast. It had to be. We got up before the four guys passed us again. Vickie said, "It sure beats jogging." Sure as hell did.

We went back into the stadium, and I was placed in the

first heat. The starter came around with the upside-down pop-sicle sticks, and I drew lane one.

At the starting line I was trembling. Mr. Bowdie, Mr. King's friend and track coach at Hunter, was standing near to me and whispered, "Be cool man, be cool."

Bang! We were off. When you're in that first lane on a staggered start in the quarter mile, it seems like you've lost the race even before you've begun to run. I began to pull away from the others. I thought I was alone, but on the turn there was the guy from Stuyvesant making a big kick. My legs were longer than his (otherwise he would have taken me), and I leaned into the tape for another victory. I was really happy. Mrs. King said it was beautiful, and Mr. King was happy too. I ran over to Vickie.

I said, "I think we should fuck before every race." She gave me a playful punch on the chin. The results came over the loudspeaker, and I was shocked. There was a tie for first place. "Tie for first place!" I screamed. Mr. King said it was no tie, but if I had gone to practice the guy from Stuyvesant wouldn't have been anywhere near me for the judges to call it a tie. So we had to flip a coin for the gold medal. I won.

In the triple jump I was placing second. A tall, lanky-legged fellow from Stuyvesant was just about jumping out of the pit. Actually he was placing first with the same distance I had placed second with in my junior year. And of course, there again was Mr. King—"If . . ."

I had one jump left; after that the meet would be over. I shook my hands, my legs, took a couple deep breaths, and promised God that I'd always pray to him if he just let me win this little thing. I looked down at the pit and all the people surrounding it and tore down the straightaway and fouled out. "Noooo jump," the judge yelled.

A Show Of Hands

No one has clean hands, there are no innocents and no on-lookers. We all have dirty hands; we are all soiling them in the swamps of our country and in the terrifying emptiness of our brains. Every onlooker is either a coward or a traitor.

Frantz Fanon

PRESIDENT NIXON GOT ON TV and rejected his own Nixon Doctrine in Southeast Asia, escalating the war from which he had promised to disengage. His decision was based on the same explanations that the government has given from the first days of America's "mistake" in Southeast Asia.

Three days later I was in Albany standing in the lobby of the State University of New York, reading a leaflet, thinking that by now everybody should have learned that America doesn't give fair trials. We learned that from Sacco and Vanzetti and the Chicago 7. As for the leaflet itself, I thought it strange that things like this went on all the time. Only two years ago there was a massacre in Orangeburg in which three Black students were killed and fifty others were injured, for trying to desegregate a bowling alley. And in Birmingham, Alabama, four years before Orangeburg, four Black children were killed in a church when a bomb exploded, and one boy was killed from a shotgun blast.

I went up to the student lounge to get a coke, and the next

thing I knew, crowds of students started to pour into the building; something was happening, a demonstration. I listened closely. They began to speak about the murders of the four students at Kent State University in Ohio and American troops in Cambodia. SUNY seemed so isolated. For the two days that I'd been there, I watched the students going to classes and playing frisbee. Now all of a sudden they were talking about striking. I was thinking that in New York City probably no one heard anything about the killings at Kent State. There was a show of hands to strike the university.

Two days later I was on the train back to New York, reading articles about how the murdered students were all white, All-American. It was then that I realized what was being done, and I couldn't believe that this country was so sick, so blatantly racist. The mass media were trying to show white America that the guns had been turned on their own children, so (now) it was time to protest.

In New York City, all over the nation, there were rifles and roadblocks, demonstrations and strikes. Spontaneously universities and high schools began closing down to step up protests against the war and repression and to avenge the Kent Four. The Black community was not at a loss for descriptive words. We have had leaders from within our own ranks who have told us to "let our blood run in the streets" so that America would be appalled by her own brutality against the dark man; that strategy of ignorance had been going on for almost four hundred years, and the desired response has not been received to date. The murderer of Medgar Evers goes unpunished. Julius Lester put it in his *Revolutionary Notes:*

Maybe one day the nation will go into mourning when poverty penetrates the skull of a poor man and shatters his brain. Maybe one day the flags will be lowered, the schools closed, and a day of mourning proclaimed when the pain of every morning's sunrise makes the heartbeats of Black mothers stumble through the bare kitchens of their lives.*

* Julius Lester, *Revolutionary Notes* (New York: Grove Press, 1969), p. 112.

In his highly informative sociological study of Black people in the United States entitled *Black Americans,* Alphonso Pinkney states that:

. . . during the summer of 1964, in Mississippi alone, white Christians bombed or burned thirty-four Black churches. These churches had long been sanctuaries in which Black people could be immune to outside intrusion. These and hundreds of other similar acts of violence, including the murder of ministers, have led Black people to question the notion that nonviolence and love disarm one's adversary.

Four days after the Kent State massacre, criminal charges against seven Black Panthers who survived a Chicago police raid in December, 1969, in which two Panthers were killed, were dropped after the prosecution said that there was insufficient evidence that any of the defendants had fired at the police. Twelve days after the Kent State massacre, six Black people in Augusta, Georgia, were shot in the back and killed, over seventy-five people were injured. Governor Lester B. Maddox, who ordered the National Guard to shoot to kill, called the riot a "Communist conspiracy."

Barely two days had passed before a 28-second fusillade killed two Black students and wounded twelve others at Jackson State. Reports of earlier sniper fire were totally unsubstantiated, and the Administration in Washington engaged in political maneuvers to discredit the findings of its own commission.

Almost immediately after the murders at Kent State, public schools were closed down in memory of the students killed. This was never done when Black lives were involved. I was in the president of the Board of Education's office when Black students and Black parents were outside demanding that the schools be closed in memory of the students killed at Jackson State. Left alone, the Board would not have made the decision to close the schools at all; it was merely a political maneuver to save face.

In New York City, the Graduate Center of the New School

for Social Research became the base of coordination for citywide strike activities. All over town, high school and college students were in the streets—it had the appearance of revolution. But as soon as school officials started to remind high school students that Regents' examinations were right around the corner, the crowds started to grow smaller and smaller. Regents' examinations safeguard the system against strikes, among other things.

I felt ambivalent about all of this. On the one hand I saw the necessity of action, but questions kept running through my mind. If we were able to mobilize so much manpower and machinery against such major national and international struggles, then why couldn't we do the same to end the universal oppression that we face every day? Is it that in major struggles people's consciousnesses are already sympathetic to the cause, and they are readily able and willing to lend their bodies? Or is it that in these major struggles nobody fears the consequences because of the security provided by the involvement of large numbers of people? Would our objective to get U.S. troops out of Indochina be accomplished just because there were a few days of disruption? And how do you support people who are already dead?

I, along with some college students, was invited to appear with Edwin Newman on an NBC Special relating to the killings at Kent State and the invasion of Cambodia. We spoke briefly about these issues and spent most of the time discussing America's historical adhesion to violence. As H. Rap Brown put it, "Violence is as American as cherry pie."

Thousands of people turned out at the West Side Memorial Chapel to see the coffin of one of the four killed at Kent State. There was a show of hands, of peace signs.

I *feel* that in the souls of the white left there is a strong *belief* that the American government will work for them, too. They hope that those watching their actions in the struggle against overwhelming and indescribably cruel odds, will have pity for them and will be appalled by the brutality being inflicted on the flower children. They hope they will change their minds and join the lines for PEACE NOW, to give it a chance.

I feel sorry for them because there is no pity for them. Many thousands have gone freely to spill their blood, to hold candles in the cold, singing "We Shall Overcome," to hold the barricades, yet the odds continue to grow more cruel and the *pity* has long since been all dried out. The spirit that keeps the *kids* going, keeps them trucking and alive, is what makes me happy, although I think they are fools for not fighting fire with fire.

I went up to George Washington High School. All over the school and in the streets and on the roofs were police in riot gear; it was an armed police camp. About fifty students stood enclosed behind police fences, protesting. A brother and I were standing on the sidewalk watching, contemplating whether or not it would be wise to go up and join the line. I looked at the school, at the inscription on the cement (George Washington), and at the police and the Black students huddled in front of the school. It passed through my mind that the days of slavery and contemporary slavery show interesting parallels.

When a policeman came over to us and told us to get off the sidewalk, we refused. Three of them came over, and we were taken to the back seat of a police car. They didn't even inform us of our right to remain silent. I said to the other guy, "What do you think they're going to do?"

"I dunno," he shouted.

"Look." I saw a crowd of brothers coming toward the police. Next thing I knew, the guy beside me had opened the car door and was gone; I bolted after him and we ran down to the subway. I headed for home.

That night there was a meeting in Queens concerning the criminal hearings for five arrested Black students at Cardozo High School.

Community people hate outsiders coming in and telling them what to do, and taking over the leadership of their struggle. However, I couldn't help but get into an argument over the necessity of community people joining and helping

other communities facing similar disputes. I could understand their reluctance since they had struggled all year to get
the charges dropped against five students at Cardozo. Everyone was tired and wanted only to confront this last problem
of the evening.

Communities confronting the Board of Education face a
common discriminator and therefore should unite on the
basis of what they have in common, just like any other union
does that has gained respect from its members. Only when
Black and Puerto Rican communities reach a point where
they understand the necessity of *organizing before the crisis*
will they be in an effective position to support their children
and schools within their communities. White communities
meet constantly and always keep in contact with the administration—that's why you find that during a dispute a single
letter from the white community has more effect than six
months of demonstrating and jail sentences reserved for
Black people who dare demand a voice in their education.
Our problem is that we get organized on the spur of the moment and always fall apart in the end. We have to be in a
constant state of readiness. We have to remain as one all the
time before the crisis. Then too, Black communities do not
often exercise the power of the ballot. And we wonder why
white communities with fewer people get better treatment, in
terms of transportation, construction, and sanitation. We
have failed to organize ourselves as a political threat, despite
the rhetoric that makes us think we have. Black people
who understand this political process have a responsibility to
be in the communities showing those of us who do not know
how to look out for our own interests, what it is we must
do.

In the morning I went down to the High School of Performing Arts. Only yesterday 250 students from this school
invaded Music and Art to debate their demands with Klein,
who was now principal of both schools. (The two had merged
to form the Fiorello H. LaGuardia High School of Music and
the Arts.) I was in the school's run-down cafeteria trying to

get support for the Cardozo 5 who were facing criminal hearings that morning at Queens Criminal Court. Klein sent his ace troubleshooter, Fineberg, to see what was going on. She acted as if she had caught a little boy stealing cookies from the kitchen. She was mad. My job was done here. I split, went back to Queens.

I had never been inside of a courtroom before, but it's all part of going to high school nowadays. There was a huge turnout; over a hundred people filled the room. Michelson, the principal at Cardozo High, sat up front, by the judge. There were four guards (three big white pigs and a burnt chitlin). Behind the judge, inscribed on the wall were the words IN GOD WE TRUST. The guards were pushing everybody around, taking away newspapers, and throwing people out of the room. I sat behind rows of angry Afros. The Cardozo 5 entered the room, and silently clenched fists rose into the air. The guards almost had a fit. "Put those hands down," they shouted.

Then the trial. The lawyers were superb. They were all volunteers. Despite what I had known to be true about supposedly fair trials for political prisoners, I sat there unable to believe that I was in a court of law. Everyone heard the judge's comments. It was so obvious by his intervention and remarks that he supported the principal's position. I was wondering why he didn't openly state that he was making himself counsel for the principal. That little baldheaded motherfucker sat over there by the judge as if they were brothers. I kept looking at those words IN GOD WE TRUST.

The Cardozo 5 stuck it out together because if some had taken lesser penalties, the others would have been left with more serious charges. They fought it together and got off with minor violations and a $25 fine, that is, after almost an hour's debate between the lawyers, defining such terms as criminal trespassing. The five students, though not criminals, would have a criminal record. At the end of the trial, clenched fists rose into the air again. One hundred voices closed the case: "All Power To The People!"

Over two hundred students in nine Queens high schools were arrested in the closing months of the school year for a variety of offenses, most of them stemming from peace and student rights demonstrations following the Cambodian invasion and the Kent and Jackson State killings.

When they demand knowledge of their history and culture, Black students realize they are being crucified and find themselves in court asking for justice from the same people who have legalized brutality against them.*

Weeks passed before tempers started to cool off. Things calmed down for a while and business as usual resumed its momentum. One morning I decided I'd make a quick run up to Music and Art. Vickie usually met me at the subway. It was a regular day. I even had my stuff for track practice after

---

* *Time* magazine in a "Situation Report" (April 6, 1970):

Whites often assume that civil rights acts and court decisions have made law the black man's redeemer. In practice, many blacks see the law as something different: a white weapon that white policemen, white judges and white juries use against black people. Indeed, blacks are clearly underrepresented in law enforcement and overrepresented in crime and punishment. Among the facts:

Law Enforcement. Blacks make up 38% of the population in Atlanta, 27% in Chicago, 39% in Detroit, 40% in Newark and 63% in Washington, D.C. By contrast, the proportion of black policemen in those cities is 10%, 17%, 5%, 10% and 21% respectively. Of the nation's 300,000 lawyers, only 3,000 are black—one of the smallest black ratios of any U.S. profession. Of the Government's 93 U.S. Attorneys, none is black; the most recent (Cecil Poole of San Francisco) has just been replaced by a white. Thurgood Marshall sits on the Supreme Court, but of 459 federal judges, only 22 are black. Among the country's 12,000 state and city judges, only 178 are black. As for prison

administration, California is a good example: 28.6% of the state's inmates are black, but all 13 prison wardens are white.

Crime and Punishment. Blacks are arrested between three and four times more often than whites, partly because police stop and search blacks far more frequently than they do whites. This is only partly rooted in race prejudice: blacks probably commit more violent crime than whites—partly because the black population has a far higher ratio of youths who mainly commit such crimes. Most of the victims are black. Example: black women are 18 times more likely to be raped than white women, and usually by black assailants.

Once caught, black suspects are more likely than whites to be jailed rather than bailed, more likely to be convicted than acquitted, and more likely to receive stiff sentences. Of the 479 condemned men now on death row in U.S. prisons, more than half are black. According to many experts, one factor in this disproportion is poverty: few black defendants can afford skilled lawyers.

school. I got down to the subway only to find crowds of people standing outside. Police were all over the streets, and there were traffic jams. Nobody on the bus knew what to think. Maybe somebody had been shot—a robbery, a car accident?

I got off the bus and headed for the subway. I was late. I got to the entrance but it was closed. "What happened?" I asked. A cop told me there'd been a train crash and people had been killed. Vickie. I ran through the streets, through the crowds like a madman, trying to find Vickie. I was so nervous, so afraid that she might have been among the dead on the train. I called her home—no answer. I called the school, her father's office—no answer. I called the Police Department to find out who was on the list of injured and dead people—but they wouldn't disclose the names to anyone but relatives. I called up again, saying that I was her father. I almost got away with it, until he asked, "What's her name?"

"Vickie Ginsberg."

"Would you please say that again," came a cynical reply.

"Vickie Ginsberg," I shouted. I heard him chuckling.

"You're Black, aren't you."

I thought only Vickie's father could tell the difference between a Black and white man's voice. I shouted back over the phone, "You're a fucking racist pig!" and hung up. I was breathing heavily and didn't know what to do. The same thing had happened when Bruno, my turtle, died. All during his life I was never quite sure how I felt about him. The dog bit his head off, Bruno died, and only then did I realize how much a part of me he was.

I went to the hospitals in Queens, first to St. John's and then to Elmhurst.

I was waiting in the lobby, feeling like an expectant father or a husband whose wife was dying. I sat beside this Puerto Rican man who was in the same situation. He was looking for his wife. He said to me, "Are you also trying to find your wife?" My wife? I thought about how wrong I'd treated her, how much I doubted her feelings for me. The Puerto Rican man and I left the hospital together. He had gotten word that his wife was safe, but there was no word about my wife.

Late that afternoon I was walking back home, dejected. I was going over to the bus stop, crossing the street. And then suddenly I heard her voice. I smiled. God, what a relief. I saw her running toward me. It was like a scene in a movie, all played out.

Black Caucus

KEN HAD GOTTEN ME an invitation to a "Crisis Retrieval Conference" in Ann Arbor, Michigan, but he couldn't make the same flight with me. As it happened, Julio Rodriguez, consultant to the president of the New York City Board of Education, was also going to the conference and wound up sitting next to me on the plane.

Almost instantly, Julio and I got into an argument. I guess his conscience must have been bothering him because for no reason at all, he tried desperately to prove that he wasn't *really* a part of the Board of Education, part of the public relations tricks, repression, and programmed miseducation. I guess because he was a Puerto Rican in such a position, he was especially sensitive to other Black and Puerto Rican people's identifying him as part of the problem and not the solution.

"Boy," Julio said, "you're real bitter; you're a very bitter person." I just sat there looking out the window, listening to him shoot off his mouth. He finally came out of his bag and asked me, "What could be better than the system we already have? And what has your revolution got that will benefit me?" The questions he asked only revealed how integrated he was into the system, how fully a part of it he was. Black people concerned with revolutions, unlike white people, don't have to convince each other that our programs are better for the society.

Often white radicals and revolutionaries who are deeply involved in "The Struggle" are cut down by conservatives who ask just basic questions about what will be different after the revolution? What is going to make my life different from nine to five? And won't you still educate my children toward political ends to stabilize your new revolutionary society? But no white person with any degree of intelligence will go into the Black colonies in this country and ask these "challenging" questions because most Black people haven't got anything to begin with—they would have no trouble telling you how their lives would be improved by a victorious struggle. For whites, it's a question of looking at what is already established and asking, What could be better than what we already have? Julio was asking the same questions that you'd expect a white man to ask. Although I know this might seem funny, coming from me, I felt that Julio felt threatened by a Black struggle because his wife was white.

I was the only high school student at the conference and the youngest person. All kinds of crisis-intervention people and research assistants from Harvard and the University of Michigan were there. David Selden, president of the American Federation of Teachers, Preston Wilcox, of Afram Associates at 125th Street in Harlem, and Art Thomas, former director of the Model Cities Education Program in Dayton, Ohio, were among the many big-name people at the conference.

Every minute was a learning experience for me. It was mostly from traveling and attending conferences and discussions like these that I learned, increased my vocabulary, and became more and more conscious of how much more I had to learn.

Seven of us were put in Room 1407. Art Thomas and I

were the only Black people in the room. In fact, there were only five Black people in the entire conference. Everything that was said during discussions would go down on tape. Where was this information going?

I was really impressed by Art's brilliance and was astonished to find out what had happened to him in Dayton. He had been appointed by the Superintendent of Schools, Wayne Carle, to the position of director of the Model Cities Education Program. Yet while performing his duties, Art was unilaterally fired by the Board of Education on the recommendation of Superintendent Carle who, prior to the Board's action, had improperly dismissed Art.

The decision to fire Art came after he had tried to avert imminent racial violence precipitated by the Board of Education's abortive attempt to deal with charges by the U.S. Department of Health, Education, and Welfare that the Dayton school system was in violation of the Civil Rights Act of 1964.*

In Art's legal brief it was explained that the Board transferred a group of Black students from the Model Cities neighborhood to Strivers High School in a white middle-class neighborhood. But the transfer took place without adequate preparation of the school, students, or community. This is typical of the way in which the United States Government is handling the integration program for schools. All the sociological and statistical commission reports coming out of Washington concerning court-ordered desegregation plans that involve reassigning students to different locations have said basically that those schools still segregated have experienced little or no trouble whereas the newly integrated schools have hosted violence and continued disruptive activities. However, most of these reports fail to point out clearly why it is only natural that anything designed to promote racial equality in the United States of America will be opposed by the very racism that has been institutionalized in this country from the very start.

---

* [42 U.S.C.A. 2000 (c)] All statements relating to the dismissal of Arthur E. Thomas were taken from the legal brief filed on his behalf.

Tocqueville said that, "There is a natural prejudice that prompts men to despise whoever has been their inferior long after he has become their equal." It was the *law* of the United States that made the Black man supposedly "inferior." The ability to enslave a people does not mean the slaves are inferior. Witness the Jews: two thousand years of oppression—and yet they had made some great contributions to Germany and now to America; they are wealthier and better educated than most of the population of this country.

It has been documented that initially few Black people ever came over here of their own free will. As slaves we were brought here and given less care than was given to animals or plants. Black women were infested with the seed of their white masters, and the little white/Negro offspring were set free. The Civil War was fought not over the issue of Black people; rather, it was a dispute between two white groups that resulted in a technical emancipation of the Black man. But he *did not command* his freedom. And to me this has essentially been The Message that Malcolm preached during his lifetime: that the Portuguese, the Dutch, the Jews, the Irish, the Poles—all white immigrants, even those from countries America fears the most, communist countries, have been able to come to this country and get full citizenship, full human rights while Black people in the twentieth century are still singing "We Shall Overcome." This has happened only because of what one could call the immigrant theory. As one group comes in, another group moves up from the bottom; in turn that group that just came in supposedly waits until another group comes in before it can move up. Everybody has moved up and is gone—except Black people. We're still at the bottom because the white power structure has always been in the position of determining our progress, or lack of it.

What had happened to Art Thomas was nothing short of denial of equal legal protection on account of race. In Dayton the first week of the 1969 school year began in a racial holocaust. At Strivers, the situation escalated into fighting between Black and white students. People were beaten and chased. Art was ordered to go to Strivers and attempt to cool the situation. When Art got down there, he saw Strivers in the midst of a violent racial confrontation. He went to the principal, who told him that he could not guarantee the safety of the Black students. Art then led the Black students out of the high school and away from the danger threatened by armed students and a hostile crowd. Shortly after the Black students' removal, the crowd reached proportions of several hundred white persons carrying firearms, chains, steel pipes, and other weapons. In his legal brief, it states that "for this act, Superintendent Carle, acting without consulting Thomas, the Board, or the Council which selected Thomas, suspended him from all his duties."

Art was discriminated against because of "his functionally effective use of the kind of language which sociologists have recognized as the cultural 'norm' in the Black ghetto," for repeated assertions of racial pride and racial identity, for intense personal involvement with Black children. He was also discriminated against inasmuch as they were "specifically attempting to punish him by restricting his access to those children and discharging him for going to the aid of Black school children at Strivers High School when no other official of the Dayton school system would respond to the crisis." Thomas was suspended without pay, restricted from his office, and forbidden to enter any public school building. His assertions of racial pride were characterized as part of a "conspiracy to secure Black control of the schools" with "Thomas himself as an inciter of riots."

Recently *The New York Times** carried an article about groups in Dayton distributing pamphlets warning that integration brings "forced busing, that in turn brings crime, extortion, rape, cannibalism and an increase in interracial sex." The attitude of the Dayton white community toward integration is characteristic of most racist white communities in America.

---

* "School Heads in U.S. Beset by Disruptions," *The New York Times,* April 4, 1971, p. 1.

During most of the time that Art and I were in the room, I was taking notes on things he was saying. There was no getting around it—he knew what he was talking about. Of all the things he had to say, one thing stuck out most in my mind; he said that "the child can be oppressed as hell and still look to his parents for love. So you have the internal contradictory emotions—love and hate at the same time. The child may act irrationally because who, after all, can he turn to but his parents? The child may do all the things that the parents disapprove of in order to annoy them or get their attention and love . . ."

I was thinking about Vickie when he said that. She was in that situation, but she had me to turn to. Was she turning to me only to annoy her parents, to get their attention, their love? I didn't know, but all too often she tried to make me feel that she was the one taking the greater risk in our relationship. Although I never let her know that I had practically divorced myself from my mother and brother because of their feelings about her, she always made it a point to let me know about all of the conversations she had with her family, friends, and relatives over her Black boyfriend.

Later that night Ken, Art, Preston Wilcox, two other Black representatives, and I met to organize a Black caucus. We started discussing the conference and its purpose, and at the end of our discussion it was only too clear that all of us were being exploited. The information was going one way. They had selected Black people who happened to be leading struggles in different parts of the nation, assembled us here in this conference, and tried to scoop out *The Souls of Black Folk*. They wanted to know what Black people think, why they act the way they do. Are Black people going to assimilate, or are they becoming more militant and unwilling to take what the system has given them? These questions weren't designed to help Black people but to preserve the white power structure. They wanted to know what it is that makes Black folks tick before they blow up. The conference was so structured that there would never be more than two of us in the same room. White groups remained constant so that they got a chance to hear all of us in teams of two. They had us rotating. The information that we would be giving out would not go back into the Black community or help us in any way. It would be sent to the White House. Preston Wilcox demanded that if there was any publication resulting from the conference, the royalties be sent back to the Black communities— if not, there would be nothing to write about. They didn't agree.

The conference atmosphere became more heated. At this time I felt even prouder to be a Black man. I watched Ken and Preston and Art plan out a psychological strategy of what we would and would not say, how we'd approach the whites and reinforce each other's position.

The conference entered into a new phase. Although Julio was Puerto Rican, instead of joining the Black Caucus, he felt threatened by it. In fact, the only two Black research people who were part of the organization sponsoring this conference had white wives and were also reluctant to join the Black Caucus. As for me, inside I felt free and in no sense threatened. I felt free and they didn't because they were crumbling under the weight of society's condemnation of interracial marriages. They felt both ashamed and guilty.

The following days of the conference were marked with more racial put-downs than I'd ever heard in my entire life. Ken had this poor guy from Harvard in the room and was already laying it on the line to him.

"Listen, Hagood, if the revolution came today, and it was Blacks on one side and whites on the other, are you trying to say that even though you'd be outnumbered and I came over to help—you'd shoot me?"

"Fucking right, I'd shoot you!" Ken broke up laughing, which got the guy from Harvard all upset.

The people who sponsored the conference had not counted on this happening. Nothing was going according to plan. In one room there was Art telling another research man that "our thing is organized. The pimps and prostitutes have their territory more checked out than the President . . . Watts and Detroit weren't planned, yet what happened there was more dynamic than all the years of SCLC and civil rights hearings—it put Black folks on the map . . ."

At lunch they got a Black speaker who was working with the white administration during the racial crisis at the University of Michigan. They called it the Black Action Movement—BAM! As for this Black guy, we gave him all hell for working with the whites.

I was overwhelmed, partly by a lack of sleep but also by a feeling of pride such as I'd never had before. I felt real good because it was the first time that I had been accepted by men of my own color. For once, I wasn't on the receiving end of the hate. I put people down mercilessly without regard to their feelings. I used the same put-downs that had been used on me—I was dishing it out for a change. (That's how damaged my mind was. That's what being exposed to prolonged hate can do to a person.) By this time I had realized that most people didn't hate me because of my views, but simply because I *was:* I existed. But in addition, those people up at Music and Art hated me because I did what I believed in, and they were afraid to do the same.

After the Black guy finished speaking and sat down (Art *cut* him down), I went into a rap, and the whole room fell silent. I talked about the way these young Black guys shuffled through the system, out for all they could get. No one could believe that I was saying this. The Black guy looked at me with an angry frown: "Are *you* referring to *me?*" I told him that I had once read in an article that when a person says something that gets under your skin, then it's directed at you. What isn't part of you, doesn't bother you. After that, tensions were so high that the program had to be cut short.

That night the guy who'd organized this so-called Crisis Retrieval Conference invited the entire group to his house. We drove all the way out in the woods to his huge ranch-type house that had a front lawn big enough to build a track field on. Ken said, "No wonder this guy is *concerned.* He's looking out for his own ass." That was the truth for all White America. From the time God led Black people to the promised lands of Harlem, Watts, Brownsville, and Bedford-Stuyvesant, drugs have been reaching epidemic proportions within the Black community. As soon as the little Kelloggs' Kids —the children of white America—started to smoke, shoot up, and nod, America cried, "My God! Something must be done." Riots, too, had shown Black people that they were only destroying their own communities, and they realized that their militancy would be more effectively heard if they struck at the heart of the white communities. When that started happening, a whole nationwide bureaucracy was immediately erected supposedly to deal with the "problems." A maze of crisis-intervention commissions, urban studies programs, and police public relations programs resulted in response to the threat white people felt—not in sincere response to the needs of the Black community. It is unfortunate but true that in the experience of all too many Black people, whites have extended a helping hand only when it has been convenient for them to do so, only when it benefits *them*.

The tense racial dialogue continued the next day. Ken and I took an early plane back to New York City. This conference really opened my eyes to a lot of things about my relationship with Vickie and the expertise with which the white power structure manipulates the Black masses. Why, they had even paid the Black consultants less than the whites.

After the Detroit conference, I received an invitation from Art to speak at the Students' Rights Center on Germantown Street in Dayton, Ohio. When I arrived, I was picked up by Art and a reporter. I spent about an hour answering the reporter's questions in the airport restaurant. On the way to a hotel later, the newsman gave me a rundown of the Dayton situation. The community was segregated, with Black people and white people separated by bridges and rivers. There was only one integrated school—"a model institution" called Colonel White.

At the hotel Art hurriedly rapped down the conference

schedule, and then he said with a smile, "You know us niggers is loyal to the man. You ever look in the Dayton phone book? Look down the list of people named Abraham Lincoln and George Washington—all of them are black! Why, we even got a black Patrick Henry!"

Art left for the airport to pick up two women from the New York Civil Liberties Union. One of them was an author of an anthology of high school student expressions. While Art was at the airport, some brothers showed up. I can remember the names of only two of them: James and Donnie.

Donnie Moore was raw truth: Black, intelligent, a fire-brand. Art meant as much to him as Ken meant to me. Donnie had been a pimp. He went to summer school "only to time the janitors and check out their whereabouts at certain periods. Donnie had a long record of trouble: in the sixth grade he was arrested for gang-fighting, and in the eighth grade, for beating up twenty girls who had attacked him. In the ninth grade he was suspected of stealing cars and turned out not to have been involved. He had been arrested on suspicion of narcotics violation, which was false, and for violation of curfew. Because of his involvement with the Black Student Union and Art Thomas, Donnie was intimidated by the principal and teachers at Dunbar High School who tried to keep him from continuing school. On a whim, one teacher wouldn't let him use school materials and equipment. His school activities were limited, and he was even put off the varsity basketball team. Donnie told me of a white man who carried a "billy club" at all times and threatened to beat his "black ass" if he didn't keep his nose out of other people's business. Donnie had sold stolen goods to this same man. One day in the halls of the school, the white man approached Donnie, intending to beat him. Donnie whipped out the pistol and "put the motherfucker up against the wall." The white man was influential and went free. Donnie—seventeen, Black, and poor—was booked.

We spoke for hours. He had been repressed and exposed to more psychological tactics used by the administration than

any other high school student I knew. He had been arrested
and intimidated by the police and school officials. For two
weeks he was on trial in his school, "without ever being invited to attend, either to ask or answer questions." One day
he stormed in on his trial and "told the jury where it was at"
and ripped off a copy of the Dayton Student Bill of Rights.
"Anyone can see," Donnie said, "that this so-called Bill of
Rights is intended for the Black section—'no gambling, no
drugs, no alcohol . . .' "

"Are there a lot of drugs around here?" I asked.

"Hell, no!" he snapped back. "Most of the drugs are in the
white section, in the white schools. You can't get the shit anywhere but from the white section."

When Art got back, he had the two women from the
NYCLU with him. I wondered what a sister was doing with
this white woman. Actually I knew that the NYCLU didn't
have a Black lawyer and *used* those Blacks that they did hire
to go into Black communities, dig up information, and then
came out with a report or a book with royalties to fill their
pocket. I didn't blame the sister for working with the NYCLU.
They had done some good things, but not nearly as much as
they could be doing if they made no secret concessions what-
soever to the Establishment. In fact, I have a lot of respect for
Mr. Aryeh Nier who heads the CLU in New York City, but I
feel that there's something disingenuous about the whole operation. In the end, however well-meaning these white liberals
might be, they're really more interested in their own comfort
than the well-being of the people they're supposedly helping.

Anyway, the woman who published the anthology of student expressions was having breakfast with me and Art the
following morning. For some reason I just felt that she resented something about me. I didn't know what it was. For
no reason at all, she said, "The Board of Education sure has
kicked your ass." I thought it was an odd thing to say if supposedly we had a common enemy. I said, "Well, maybe if I
write about it, they won't get away with it."

"Ah," she said disdainfully, "the whole thing will be dead
by the time *you* write a book."

Now I was mad inside. The NYCLU got fucked over nine out of ten times by the Board of Education; their victories were nothing short of legal ironies, getting students readmitted once they got arrested or expelled from the very institutions they found intolerable. I didn't say anything to her. The thought never occurred to me until later that all this resentment toward me was coming down because I believed in students fighting their own battles, writing their own books, and organizing their own groups for legal defense (like the Coalition), rather than relying on what's already *established*. I suppose she thought I was trying to take the bread out of her mouth. After all, how else are these people paid if not from continuing student crisis and the inability of students to pull themselves up by the bootstraps to suffer *the consequences all people must suffer if they truly want their freedom more than their oppressors are willing to oppress them?* Yes, I could understand her resentment. Here I was only seventeen, Black, a little high school student, preparing to write what might be a book and telling all other students *Do everything for yourselves.* And here she was with her Harvard degree, capitalizing on and exploiting students dumb enough to let themselves be had, fighting among her peers who are pushing other works similiar to hers on the market, making sure that their books didn't have the same crap she compiled in hers. When she most clearly made her feelings known right after my speech to the community people from the Black section of the Dayton area, I went off on a *truth* tirade. I should say that even I wasn't aware of how much hate I had in me against whites, Jews in particular. I completely lost control of myself. She had said:

"Reeves is at an integrated high school in New York that doesn't have half as many problems that he talks about and he himself hasn't had any problems there . . ." She continued molding an image of me by implication that I was a token Negro, well off, just spouting the same crap as everyone else was in her position—that is, not really feeling the repression of high school, yet telling the world: *The schools are like prisons.*

Even people in the audience were madder at her than I was. I shouted:

". . . to hell with these whites . . . racist pigs . . . we can build our own communities . . ." She opened her mouth to say something. A sister yelled, "Don't be putting down our Black men." I felt good inside to hear that. Then the brothers and sisters roared "SPEAK, BROTHER. TRUTH!"

I continued. "You take your money to bring people from outside of your community to tell you how bad it is and *you* live in it every day. You bring me—even though I'm your brother. I'm still a stranger from outside to tell you the things that Donnie or all these other brothers right here in Dayton could tell you . . ."

The conference was cut off after I spoke.

It is typical of most communities and audiences concerned with high schools to hear panels related to the institution, panels that don't express the opinions of the person most victimized, the high school student. I think the adults have run far away from the students, not talking to them but talking *about* them while not really *knowing* what's on *their* minds. I don't mean people like me or those who you hear from in books. I mean those who can't express themselves as well as others might. The kernel of truth that the oppressed and inarticulate are able to give, whether you like to hear it or not, is more valuable than all the analytically edited dialogue put forth by the omnipotent professionals.

Only a few days after the Michigan conference there was another conference in New York at, I believe, the Biltmore Hotel. The Board of Education had hired the firm of Cresap, McCormick, and Paget to advise the new community school boards on how to be effective with what little power they had. Black communities had abstained from participating in the voting in these elections, and as a consequence, the Jews and Catholics were in control in many districts—even though they didn't represent a significant part of some of the community's population over which they supposedly had control.

Cresap, McCormick, and Paget had invited various community people to advise their advisors on the problems in the community. In the beginning they requested that each of us give his or her idea (in two minutes) on the model decentralization plan. Two minutes to come up with the perfect solution to problems that professionals in Washington, D.C. haven't been able to solve in over four hundred years.

When it came time for me to give my model idea, I told the community people, instead, what had happened in Detroit, and how this conference wasn't much different. Why should Black and Puerto Rican people who have been working in the community and who understand their people and problems, voluntarily give their information to white people who don't know anything about the ghetto, so that they can come in as "experts" in Urban Affairs and tell Black people what their problems are. We know what the problems are.

I turned to the Puerto Rican lady next to me and asked her how much she was being paid to come here and give these people the information she had. She was getting paid the same as I was, $25. I then turned to the white lady sitting next to a white man and asked them how much they were being paid, and they said $100 each. Everyone on the panel saw clearly what was going on. But what happened was beautiful. There was no division among the people on the panel even though we were being paid different sums of money. We turned against the source of our problems—the people who created the division among us—and demanded that everyone be paid the same amount. Normally, there would have been fighting among the victims of the exploitation while the culprits watched. It was a question of capitalistic exploitation and division along color lines.

Later that night Ken, Gladstone, and I went to a cafe on Broadway. Gladstone ordered a Tom Collins and Ken his usual Martini Tanquery. We started to talk about interracial sex when Gladstone said to me, "Man, if you saw three white girls on one side of the street and three sisters on the other side of the street, you goin' with the white girls."

"Bullshit!"

"Man, I know you," Gladstone said. "When you were a junior—remember all those white girls . . ."

Ken was laughing. I said, "Hey man, listen to me, listen . . . Gladstone was in the stuff too."

"Ah man," he said, "I was just following you until I got my head together. But listen now: if you goin' to be a *success,* why not take a sister along *with* you?"

Ken intervened and started to talk about the reality of the situation: how the interracial thing affects social mobility, how other people look at it, how some sisters destroy Black men—and the reverse—and how essentially an interracial relationship involved a risk that could bring about a great deal of harm psychologically if it didn't work. He kept talking, but he didn't say anything directly about Vickie, and neither did Gladstone. I had a feeling that they were trying to tell me something about her, but I didn't try to find out. Instead I told them of relationships I had had with sisters—how I'd really flipped over this Cuban chick who went and got pregnant by some other guy, and Ramona, who left me and became a prostitute. I told them I'd had enough bad experiences to say I wasn't having anything to do with sisters anymore. But I knew in my heart that if Judith, the sister I'd met at Andover, wasn't going to marry someone else, I'd marry her. For the few days that I'd been with Judith, I felt how much closer we were because we had a common experience. There are just so many things a white woman cannot understand about a Black man, so many things only a Black woman *can* understand. But unfortunately it isn't as simple as this. A union between two people is a very personal thing—it transcends all because that's the person you'll be living with for a long time. It cannot be broken down into race or religion—only the minds and their common experiences are important. Everything I told Ken and Gladstone I based on how much I thought of Vickie. I didn't take into consideration her Jewishness. I only thought of the common experiences that we had shared since I had known her.

Ken, Gladstone, and I talked until very late at night. To

everything I said, they presented a counterargument but never, for some reason, would they deal specifically with Vickie and me. Instead they generalized and hinted that Vickie's experiences with me were not necessarily as meaningful to her as they were to me, that I had an obligation to live up to the expectations of other Black people, and that it might not be such a bad thing if Vickie and I broke up. The discussion ended on that note.

It was almost six in the morning and I had to get into Queens, pick up my track stuff, and get back over to Randalls Island for the City Champs. I asked Ken to come because he didn't think I could run. I knew I could.

Ken met Vickie and me at Randalls Island. It started to rain, and I just couldn't keep my eyes open. I had about six cups of coffee, but I still couldn't keep awake. The rain started to let up but it was a dark, drizzly, miserable day. I had to triple-jump first, but I had to wait for a long time because I'd fallen asleep on the grass while waiting to be put in a section. They just gave me a chance to get in at the last moment.

Ken, Vickie, and the rest of the team were standing around the pit. I stood there on the runway trying to psyche myself up. I saw Ken smiling, probably thinking I was going to mess up. I tore down the straightaway and fouled out—ran through the pit. On my second jump I almost missed the damn pit; my glasses flew off into a mud puddle. I was looking real bad, and Ken never stopped smiling. "Listen man," I said, "I'm a champ, I tell you." Ken just looked at me.

"Sure, I know, but these guys are jumping pretty far into the pit. Maybe if you could get at least one foot in the pit, the judges might give you some credit."

That broke me up. I said, "I'll show you, you mother."

By this time the other athletes had set a tough mark, and whoever else didn't pass that mark wasn't even going to be counted in for the finals. It was my last jump. Ken ran up to me and told me to keep my legs in the air a little longer than I'd been doing.

I was gone, striding down the runway, faster and faster. Bang! I hit the board, I was sailing through the air, I let out a scream, "Shiiiiiiitt!" and landed—just above five feet away from the qualifying line. I felt like shit. And there was Hagood standing over me smiling.

"Well, I'll do better in the relay," I said. But I didn't. Our team placed second.

I messed up the last meet.

The last meet signaled the coming of the end. In school they were already giving out *Yearbooks*. A funny thing happened. Originally, all the pictures had been taken in color; however, in the *Yearbook* the color photos had been reversed to black and white, giving the white students a tanned appearance while most of the Black students looked like tar babies. I mean, we looked black as sin. But the funny thing is that all those people who'd been running around all year talking about how proud they were to be Black and how Black they were—once they saw those pictures, they wanted a refund.

I took my book around to all those teachers who'd helped me, those who from time to time had sat down and spoken to me about personal things that I didn't see or understand until later. I wanted to get their signature.

I took my book to Mr. King. He signed it. After he was gone, I looked at what he wrote: "Good Luck to the champion who never was."

A New Trust

All men would like to be God, but there are some who are not prepared to admit the impossibility.

Bertrand Russell

IN THE MIDDLE OF JUNE, a few days away from graduation, the Board of Education set up a negotiating session at the New York Hilton Hotel. The entire hierarchy of the New York City educational system was present. To mention a few names: Albert Shanker, president of the United Federation of Teachers, Walter Degnan, president of the Council of Supervisory Associations, Blanche Lewis, president of the United Parents' Association, Joseph Monserrat, president of the New York City Board of Education, Dr. Seymour P. Lachman, author of the Board of Education's Student Bill of Rights, and some superintendents (whose names are not even worth mentioning).

On our side, whoever wanted to come. The Coalition had long since fallen apart. But if we (Vickie, Sarah, Julie, Allen, Ira Glasser, Ken, and I) hadn't showed up, the Board would have had an argument that could always be used against students. However, we were present, and I'm sorry we didn't bring a tape recorder so that you could draw your own conclusions.

We showed up with the purpose in mind of negotiating a Bill of Rights; the same intent was not shared by the other groups. Mr. Monserrat quickly announced himself chairman of the session. He discussed the events of the past school year and expressed the hope of establishing "A New Trust" between the Board of Education and the students of New York City. However, what the Board of Education had done was to tell the three groups involved different stories as to why we were here.

Before the discussion began, Albert Shanker walked out. (Here's a man who claims he's interested in dialogue.)

It soon became clear that the Board of Education's intent was not to negotiate a Student Bill of Rights, but openly to declare valid their Bill which had been put to a vote by the legal representative body for New York's 275,000 students and rejected. Furthermore, during the summer of 1970, the Board, in concert with the High School Principals' Association, abolished the City Council. All those students who'd placed their trust in the Board were just washed away. This was underscored by the fact that the Board had already prepared slides of diagrams on how they intended to present their Bill to the 275,000 students, using homeroom time for discussion. Julio Rodriguez handled the projector. But this, too, was a deception, a lie. The Board never had any intention of permitting student discussion on their dictated guidelines.

The question was put to the body—How can you ignore our attempts to work within the system, to use legal channels, and to express a wish to negotiate our Constitutional rights? A representative from the Council of Supervisory Associations replied, "Students have no legal rights."

The double messages and unreasonable emotional behavior should give parents grave doubts about the men in charge of the lives of over a million students. These men should be held accountable to the public and subjected to public censure. There should be some questions as to their mental fitness to be controlling the lives of children.

At the end of this discussion, in which nothing was accomplished, the president of the Board of Education promised that further "negotiations" would be set up during the summer. Only a few days after this statement was made, on June 30, 1970, Irving Anker, Acting Superintendent of Schools, issued the Board's statement called "Rights and Responsibilities of Senior High School Students" to all superintendents, principals, directors, heads of bureaus, chairmen, and local school boards.*

On July 7, 1970, *The New York Times* carried an article entitled "City Issues Code For High School." The Board explained that the policy was to establish a "New Trust."

On July 9, 1970, in a press release, the New York Civil Liberties Union attacked the Board of Education for

unilaterally issuing its statement on Students' Rights and Responsibilities . . . at the same time the Board and representatives from the High School Students' Rights Coalition were engaged in negotiations on these very issues . . . Once again the Board has confirmed the students' belief that their so-called rights are granted and withdrawn at the sole discretion of the Board of Education and that any appearance of student participation in such decisions is a cruel hoax . . .

WHAT DOES THIS ACTUALLY MEAN? What about the people in positions of power who trample all peaceful efforts, violate the law and their own agreements, deceive the public, use everything at their disposal to hide the truth about the system and themselves, and label as "subversives" all opposition to what they stand for, to what they are doing with the lives of over a million children? What other recourse do we have when these people in the adult authority use undemocratic means to retain their status and obliterate all criticism, all efforts at change?

Yet all that I had written and said to older people about the conditions crushing those who cannot bear the weight was simply an attempt to shock them into realizing that this could

---

* See Appendix B: Board of Education's Bill of Rights.

be happening to their sons and daughters. I hoped they would become appalled and rise up to oust the devils who go on committing crimes without being punished.

So much blood has been spilled and flesh torn from the bodies of defenseless Black women, men, children who try to show America what a cannibal, what a sick country, it really is. Thousands have died, yet we are still not free of this *promised land,* this prison without walls where we live in misery, poverty, and hate. Better all of us pick up guns against the oppressors than go down unarmed.

For years administrators and teachers have said that students are rebels without a program, psychopathic and unreasonable. But these arguments were totally washed away in the instance of the Coalition's efforts to negotiate with the Board of Education. We had a program. And we were so adamant in our efforts to arrive at a joint settlement that we actually said our Constitutional rights were also negotiable. To these actions, the Board of Education's response was to lie, manipulate, divide, and crush those seeking legitimate change. Of course, I knew that this would happen long before it did, but that was only speculation; the possibility of victory was still very real. The Board of Education behaved so predictably! In considering the Board of Education's methods of counterinsurgency in crushing the Coalition, we must realize that such practitioners of counterinsurgency are, in the words of I. F. Stone,

like men watching a dance from outside through heavy plate glass windows. They see the motions but can't hear the music. They put the mechanical gestures down on paper with pedantic fidelity. But what rarely comes through to them are the injured racial feelings, the misery, the rankling slights, the hatred, the devotion, the inspiration and desperation. So they do not really understand what leads men to . . . take . . . gun in hand . . . to challenge overwhelming . . . odds rather than acquiesce any longer in humiliation [and] injustice . . .*

---

* I. F. Stone, *In Time of Torment* (New York: Random House, 1967), pp. 173–74.

The principles on which counterinsurgency is based usually necessitate the perpetuation of the very conditions that breed popular discontent: witness many of the commentaries written by UFT president, Albert Shanker in the Sunday education section of *The New York Times*. "Too often counterinsurgency does no more than enable one petty dictator or another to suppress the progressive [and positive] forces . . ." * for change in a system that is recognized as undesirable and intolerable by everyone with any degree of intelligence.

I strongly believe that only the students can turn the system around. And they must use any means necessary to do so. No longer can the system say that we are mindless insurrectionists without a plan. We have had all too many programs and all too many lost causes. Only a united front can win, whether it be militant and aggressive or a passive mass withdrawal.

* The Committee of Concerned Asian Scholars, *The Indochina Story* (New York: Pantheon Books, 1970), p. 77.

Graduation/Liberation

IN FIFTEEN DAYS we would have citywide and Regents' examinations. I had bought a review book in English comprehension, and every night I used it as if it were a Bible. It seemed like only a weekend before the Regents' came around.

WARNING: SENIORS WHO FAIL TO SETTLE PART OR CURRENT BOOK ACCOUNTS OR WHO FAIL TO RETURN TRANSPORTATION CARDS CANNOT BE CLEARED FOR GRADUATION. NO TICKETS FOR GRADUATION. NO PLACE IN GRADUATION CEREMONY. NO DIPLOMA. NO FINAL TRANSCRIPTS TO COLLEGES. ANY UNSETTLED ACCOUNTS WILL INTERFERE WITH YOUR GRADUATION.

Miss Lambert, my English teacher, said that if I passed the Regents', she would consider passing me. At the same time she told another student that if he failed with a sixty, she would pass him. Fran told me that Lambert was after my ass because I annoyed her. People started telling me stories about Lambert, how her father was mugged and killed by a Negro, how she hated Malcolm X, how she ridiculed Eldridge Cleaver's works. Everything that I had written about in her class had to do with either Malcolm or Cleaver.

On Tuesday, at 9 A.M. during the English comprehensive, I sat in back of Vickie. I wished my glasses had been stronger. Now and then the proctor would glance at me, look at the way Vickie was seated, assess the situation, and ask her to sit up and move her desk. And I got the look of "I'd better not catch you eyeing her paper again." On part two of the exam I was on my own. Suddenly there was Vickie's hand with a yellow sheet of paper with what appeared to be the short answers. My heart had already been bothering me before the exam. Every vein in my body froze as the proctor came striding across the room. I felt sure that she had seen the action. Luck, someone behind me was told to sit up and move his desk farther back—tough luck for him. Without unfolding the yellow paper, I stuffed it into my pocket, signed my exam, and bolted out the room, down the hall, and into the bathroom where, after taking a well-deserved leak, I flushed the paper into oblivion.

On Wednesday at 9 A.M. we were given the American history exam. I had not attended a full class of history in over two months. Whenever I came to school, Fran and I would go outside and rap. After school she would give students cram lessons. In two days we had covered the entire term's work. Fran did some of her best teaching in the halls and stairways after classes. Later on in the week, Miss Burak told me that I had passed the Regents', but that there was still no word about the English. I worried about Vickie, but fortunately she just made it over the line.

I wanted to find out what mark I got in English. I called Lambert and said nothing about the test. Instead I asked her how to go about getting a publisher for a book even though I already had one interested publisher. She gave me the necessary information and said nothing about my status. Tomorrow we'd have the graduation rehearsal and awards assembly at Carnegie Hall.

That morning as usual Vickie woke me up on the phone, and we talked for a while. It was a beautiful, bright, and semi-windy day. I was wearing white jeans and a blue and white T-shirt and she a floor-length red dress. I met her at the subway —kissed her and teased her all the way to Seventh Avenue. When we got off the train, we saw some friends, and Vickie immediately went off with them. I went into a coffee shop, pissed as all hell. When I came out I saw Freya, a slender beauty; I took her bike and rode around in circles—free, I thought, free. From the sidewalk Freya asked:

"Don, aren't you glad to be getting out?"

"Well, I don't know if they're letting me out." Of course, I knew that they were.

"You'd think that after three years of you they'd have had enough!"

"Right on." And I was gone. I rode around the block until the rehearsal began.

We started to enter the hall. Official teachers were giving out report cards, and people were finding their seats. The chorus was practicing and practicing, occasionally going flat and getting yelled at by Mrs. Mandel, the music instructor. To the left of the stage stood Mr. Rogow with the Death Row List, those slated as non-grads.

"Mr. Rogow, am I in order?" He shuffled through the papers.

"I have you down as a non-grad," he huffed. I froze. I was in a state of shock.

"Who . . . failed me?"

"I don't know; that's not my job. All I have here is non-grad," he said sternly. I looked for Vickie—where was she— I ran outside—looked—inside—there she was on stage. I walked over, turned her around, and said, "Vickie, I'm not graduating."

"What!"

"Rogow has me down as a non-grad. Can you give me some money, I'll call Ken."

I saw Fran. She already knew about it.

"Listen, Don, you knew this was going to happen. You became the victim of everything you've been fighting against for other people. Now, because you're you and you have publicity, you can take this thing to court. You were failed on the basis of absence. There are many more students who were absent more times than you have been—well, maybe not as much, but you were doing something. You've *done* all the work. And when you weren't in school, you even mailed in the work."

Then Vickie spoke with a love and feeling I'll never forget.

"He's been concerned with everybody else, and that's what got him into this mess. You should be thinking about graduating; forget about going to court. It's about time you stopped helping people who don't even care."

Fran said, "Listen, so it will be an inconvenience. You go to summer school and get a 95 for the class because you've already passed the Regents'. But you have the opportunity to stop the shit from coming down. These people just can't be allowed to continue arbitrarily failing students."

I told Fran to speak to Ken when he got there. Meantime, I went to call the *Amsterdam News* to inform them about the shit. I thought to myself, Those motherfuckers, those motherfuckers . . . I wanted to string every one of them up. From the phone booth I could hear that awards were being read off. I knew that I was getting nothing, but I thought I heard my name read off, followed by a series of boos. When I finished calling, I came into the auditorium. Vickie, half laughing, said that she and I had won awards for "Cooperation in Government" (a slap in the face) and that she had been booed while receiving her award.

Those bastards were still jealous of my popularity outside the school and the love that Vickie and I had in the school that detached us from everything we had no desire to be part of. It was getting late—Warden Klein said that he wouldn't wait around for my lawyer because he had work to do back at school.

The rehearsal ended, and Ken made his appearance. He,

Fran, Vickie, and I went to the back where we discussed the situation. Ken, Vickie, and I left Carnegie Hall and went back to Ken's office where he called Klein. I wanted an all-out battle. I wanted to go to court. I knew that the cards were in my favor. I had saved every test and piece of work that I had done. I had even submitted essays on Malcolm X that Lambert hadn't even corrected.

But Ken, as usual, played it cool and bullshitted his way through the crisis by threatening to escalate the situation and distorting the ramifications that would follow if I wasn't set free. He and Klein made an agreement that the following morning I would be present in Klein's office with my speeches, English papers, and notes for my book. The crux of the problem lay with two tests I had failed, *Hamlet* and *Macbeth*. I had never read either from cover to cover and yet took the tests. I had fallen asleep while taking *Hamlet*. However, I had submitted two make-up papers, which were handed back to me, uncorrected, as being "intellectually insulting." Everyone else who read them said that they were good—or *at least* warranted correction for grammatical errors. Anyway, I appeared, with the presentation folder for my book: speeches, TV transcripts, writings, and the manuscript. The night before, Vickie and I had carefully taken out all the speeches and writing that had anything to do with Klein. Four times while reading through the manuscript Klein said, "I'll sue you if you print this." I asked why.

"Because I'm being misrepresented." I said nothing. He snickered.

I said, "Mr. Klein, I'm coming to you for justice; I've tried to be honest, and that's why I brought everything. Remember, I could have left certain pages home." He agreed and continued reading. In a thirty-page TV manuscript, he found one sentence referring to "a principal at Music and Art." He wanted to argue with me as to whether or not what I had said was true. The whole thing was like putting a lamb in a cage with a hungry wolf and expecting the wolf not to eat the lamb. When he opened the presentation folder and saw the numerous news clippings (many of which he admittedly had never seen before or I should say never entered on my confidential file), he called for Mrs. Forman, his secretary.

"Mrs. Forman, please get Mrs. Ackerman, Dean of Students, Mrs. Herman, Chairman of the English Department, and Miss Lambert." Only Mrs. Ackerman was present. He dictated the following memo:

TO WHOM IT MAY CONCERN: Donald Reeves has presented documentary evidence which indicates clearly that by his original writings, original speeches, participation in debates, discussions and conferences in this city as well as in various other cities throughout the State, he has in the past six months more than adequately satisfied the requirements for successfully completing the senior term of English at the high school level. I therefore declare him certified for graduation.

Richard A. Klein
PRINCIPAL

During the dictation I couldn't help grinning like a fool, almost laughing in Ackerman's face. I tried to stop. I bit my tongue and lips so hard they even started to bleed.

Klein then asked me to speak at a night class he was teaching over at City College. I had refused to do so prior to this, but I had to agree because the letter was still not in my hands. I rose, gathered my materials, shook his hand, and left. When I reached the door, Mrs. Herman, the devil's advocate, stepped in. As I looked back through the glass, I saw her slam her papers down on Klein's desk. She and Lambert had lost the battle and the war.

I went back to Ken's office and goofed off for a while, rehashing the whole scene. I told him that I wanted to sue. Vickie said, "SHUT UP!"

That night after I got back from City College, I explained the whole situation to my mother, who was always asking when my graduation was but never got an answer.

The following morning we had graduation ceremonies at Carnegie Hall. We had been told to dress "appropriately." I was wearing a brown, three-piece suit, Vickie a beautiful white pants suit and floor-length black coat. Many brothers and sisters wore clothing reflecting a pride in African culture. Some whites wore beautiful old-fashioned clothes or faded jeans. Our graduation was like a fashion show.

The ceremony started and continued as planned. Sandy, a friend of mine, turned to me and said, "Isn't anything going to happen?" We laughed.

After a couple of speeches harping on some idealistic egalitarian society, the action started.

Some brothers were in the corner with a Black Liberation flag. No one knew what they were going to do. Fineberg was over there trying to dissuade them from whatever it was they were up to. All eyes were on the brothers with the flag. I could hear an elderly Jewish woman behind me say, "That's what's spoiling everything; they're trying to take over." The brothers proceeded onto the stage, unfolded the flag, and stood behind the rostrum. They stretched the flag out behind Klein, who by this time was at the microphone pleading for someone to come up and help remove the brothers from the stage. No one moved. He kept pleading as another brother went to the other microphone and also started talking. The woman behind me thought Klein was "interpreting African." Both now were speaking simultaneously. I along with a lot of other students was laughing, not at the action, but at the parents screaming at each other—Black and white, as we "children" took it all in as just another incident. Some parents were even fighting, while others were shouting, "Get those black nigger bastards off the stage! It's terrible!" Klein backed down. The microphones were cut off. The brother was not alone on stage. He raised his right hand and delivered a Black Nationalist Pledge:

"One cause, one aim . . . POWER TO THE PEOPLE . . . POWER TO THE PEOPLE!"

Everyone was asked to stand for the pledge. Very few Black students rose. To the surprise of many, a white family stood for the pledge. No other family, Black or white, did the same. Then the elderly woman started clapping—she thought that the flag was a piece of artwork. Her relatives had to hold her hands and explain what was going on.

I did not identify with this kind of symbolic protest, but I identified with the cause. Finally, I rose from my seat, stood calmly. As soon as the pledge was over, the music and chorus started as if the incident was just another part of the ceremony. The diplomas were now being distributed. When it was Vickie's turn to receive her diploma, Terrie, who was always jealous of Vickie because of me, booed her. I was embarrassed and angry. At the same time I was expecting the same treatment, but in a much larger dose, maybe for a few minutes. But as I walked across the stage there was silence and a few claps. Klein gave me my diploma. I looked at him, shook his hand, and said softly:

"You've won, momentarily."

When I got off the stage I grabbed Fran, picked her up, kissed her, spun her around and around, and kissed her, and we laughed. I saw Vickie and kissed her—my mother and kissed her—my brother, I slapped five—Ken, I gave him the Black Power handshake . . . FREE AT LAST—FREE AT LAST!

Gone Away

So that any writer, looking back over even so short a span of time as I am here forced to assess, finds that the things which hurt him and the things which helped him cannot be divorced from each other; he could be helped in a certain way only because he was hurt in a certain way; and his help is simply to be enabled to move from one conundrum to the next—one is tempted to say that he moves from one disaster to the next. When one begins looking for influences one finds them by the score.

James Baldwin

I

HALLELUJAH. I was out. I remained for a while though after everyone else had gone. I sat there in Carnegie Hall staring at the empty stage, rows of empty seats, the few yellow and red flowers left in the vases by the red curtains. I felt hollow inside, uneasy. My mind recreated scenes of demonstrations, police, fires, friends, enemies, and affairs. I was already beginning to understand the feelings Darryl had tried to describe. I feared that I too would succumb to living solely in daydreams of misplaced memories. I had to get out of this hall immediately. I had to move on.

Later that night Ken, his main woman, Roberta, Vickie, and I had dinner at the glittering and colorful La Maganette Café. Ken had good news. He'd gotten me three jobs that would enable me to support myself through the first year of college. I would be working on Channel Five Metromedia TV, as an interviewer on "Black News," as a coach for the Harlem Sports Foundation, and as a consultant for the Board of Mediation for Community Disputes. I could see at the moment Ken told me of this news that Vickie appeared not to be happy, seemingly locked off in unappreciative, almost envious thoughts. I couldn't see why she felt this way, or why she gave me reason to believe she felt this way since all that was mine was also hers.

Within a few days two close friends of ours would be getting married at the Greater Emmanuel Baptist Church in Harlem. On the day of the wedding Vickie and I took the train up to Harlem and walked over to the church. It was a long walk. I can remember feeling self-conscious of being in Harlem with Vickie, as a *white* girl. On every block piercing eyes followed us. We got to the church. It was big, old, but very clean. It was the first wedding I'd ever been to. Red rugs lay on the floors in both aisles. Arthur, my friend who ran the elevators, was there, and so were many other students and teachers from school. After a long wait the ceremony began. Frank showed up looking real proud and handsome; Jackie was truly beautiful, more so than I'd realized before that moment when she entered the church doors. They were one couple in a thousand who had actually gone through the four-year nightmare and fulfilled their promises to each other when it was over. I knew Vickie was probably thinking about the same thing I was, about getting married. I squeezed her hand. She looked at me and smiled. Her eyes always seemed to glow when she was happy.

After showering Jackie and Frank with Uncle Ben's converted rice, we all went crosstown to a reception hall. Overlay's Jazz Band was playing. There was food and booze for everybody. People were dancing all over the place, taking pictures of each other and of Jackie and Frank. Vickie and I sat with Mr. Bacote, his date, and some other people from school.

Vickie talked about how different this whole atmosphere was from the "rich weddings" she frequently attended at country clubs. She just kept saying, "There's such a difference in wealth. So much more money is spent at Jewish weddings."

I said, "Yeah, but everybody's just as happy here, maybe even happier." She started biting on her bottom lip. "Such a difference."

"Well, do you want to leave?" I asked.

"Yeah." We split. The uneasy thought never left my mind that she probably dreaded marrying me under such similar "poor" conditions. The reality of no longer being Daddy's little girl, of being disowned by all her family if she married me, probably became frightfully clear to her that day.

II

Problems. Vickie was unable to get a job, and her father was threatening to send her away if she didn't get one soon. I started to panic. I just didn't know what I'd do without her. When people get to know each other really well, all the negative things they see standing between them somehow manage to be overlooked completely in the shadow of what they have in common that makes them one. By this time I would have done just about anything for Vickie. She was my entire world.

Ken got her a job in a post office which she couldn't accept because, in her words, "My father said I'd be working around too many black people." When I got both her and my brother jobs at the Commission on Resources for Youth, she made certain that I knew her father had said, "Things *are* changing," implying that I, a Black, could get her a job that she, a white person, couldn't get alone.

Just because Vickie and I were together, Jew and Black, didn't mean that either of us was any less racist toward the other's people. I thought that my prejudices were reactive (at that time they were). I had been with Vickie long enough to know when she was lying. Many times I had been on the other end of the phone with her while she told her parents she was out with friends, or had just gone for a ride. I knew now that she was *using* her father's name to say racist things that she herself believed in, but lacked the courage to say outright. She was capricious and did lack self-confidence. But even more than attitudes about race, our whole relationship had radically changed: the dependency role was changing, the tables had turned. *I* was now independent.

When we had first met and I was deaf, dumb, blind, she led me around to see the world, interpreted my feelings, set them down on paper for me, often had me stay clear of her racist friends and relatives, or had me hiding in back seats of cars or waiting *outside*. Now it was her turn to know how it felt. On all the jobs I had, most of the people I now associated with were Black and about Blackness. And the Black Identity of Manhood was now a necessary part of my well-being even if I knew that it (unfortunately) was visible and real in the eyes of those around me only as long as a white girl wasn't at my side. I knew Vickie found this unacceptable, but I was sure that her love for me would make it at least as tolerable as it had for me while I was waiting "outside" for her.

Day after day, things seemed to be going the wrong way. I had to start attending Jamaica Evening High School to take more math before Cornell would accept me. I enrolled in the wrong course and almost didn't get into Cornell. Vickie started running all over the city to various college placement agencies because she said that her parents didn't want her to be anywhere near where I was going to school. I told her I'd pay for her education. I'd work part-time during the year. I followed her all over asking, "Why? If you don't want to leave me, why are you willfully going to these places?"

She simply said, "I have to."

My brains were being scattered all over the place. I thought it would be good to take her out and bought two tickets for the Newport Jazz Festival at Madison Square Garden. We were sitting far up in the back in an empty section, listening to Herbie Mann, when some other people came in to sit behind us. I didn't look to see who they were. I started playing around with Vickie, teasing her about how this red floor-length thing she was wearing made her look like she just got out of a shower. (The material stuck to every curve on her body.) I started screaming and clapping when B. B. King came on. Vickie tried to calm me down, and I playfully moved away from her about four or five seats. Then I heard wild laughter and looked back to see what was going on. Some brothers and sisters were seated in back of us taking in all the action and were laughing and calling out, "Good white woman, lost your Black man." Vickie sat there motionless. I walked toward her slowly and saw that they had thrown paper cups at her. I picked the cups up from her lap, threw them down, and turned to the brothers and sisters, reaching for my knife as I did. I looked at them and they at me in silence. I suppose ignorance does make you brave. Now that I understood people's prejudices and hatreds, my actions became inhibited and functioned in reaction to those prejudices and hatreds. I was no longer my own man. I suppose I just didn't have the guts to cut them, so I sat down.

"Vickie, I'm sorry."

She looked at me, tears welling in her eyes, trying to break into a smile, "Well, at least they didn't throw stones this time."

I felt like shit when she said that. I felt totally worthless, like I shouldn't have permitted it to happen, I shouldn't have let anybody hurt her this way. I sat there with a feeling of emptiness inside me, almost nausea. I put my arms around her and held her tightly until the concert was over.

All during the night I was unable to sleep. I felt like I'd lost my balls, that I was a coward. I started banging on the wall in my room and screaming, "Why the fuck didn't I stab them, slash them, take their eyes out of their heads?" I was carrying on so much that I woke up Mom and Francis.

Mom asked, "Francis, what's going on?"

Francis turned on the light, saw me holding my head against the wall, and said, "Mom, I think he blew up."

"LORD JESUS, my son has blown up," Mom said half smiling. "What's wrong?" she asked gently. I told her nothing.

In the morning Vickie called, and she was steaming. She got right down to the point. She told me, "After all the places I've been to, I don't feel that I have to put up with that kind of shit . . ."

"Vickie, I'm sorry." That's all I could say.

III

Rrrring! The phone rang out in the heat of the night. I picked up the receiver and heard static. It was long distance, and an indistinguishable voice was at the other end repeating my name.

"Don, Don, is that you?"

"Could you speak louder? I can't hear you—who is this?"

I was startled. "Vickie, where are you?"

"I'm at White Woods."

"What?" I was panicking.

"It's a camp in Vermont."

I don't remember anything else she said although I did hear words, and the phone clicked at the other end. I held on to the receiver until I got a dial tone, and then a recording: THERE APPEARS TO BE A RECEIVER OFF THE HOOK, PLEASE HANG UP, PLEASE HANG UP, and then a loud Rrrrringing sound. I hung up empty.

I thought I was losing my mind. I couldn't think. I was unable to focus on any one thought in my head; everything was colliding and exploding. I ripped the phone from the wall. My heart was beating faster and faster. I was alone.

I had no friends except Ken, and he was busy most of the time catching up on the work he had missed by helping me during the past six months. I started drinking heavily, always managing to keep control of my mind in the outer limits. I

did things to ruin myself. I started failing the one course I had
in school, messing up my jobs, spending every penny that
came into my hands instead of saving for college. I just refused to accept that she had done this to me. I felt like a fool.

And yet another night, *Rrrring!* She was here in the city.

"Vickie."

"Why the hell have you been calling me?" she said angrily.

I sobered up quickly. "I haven't been calling you," I timidly replied, trying to hide my drunkenness.

"Dammit, I was brought home in the middle of the goddamn night because someone's been making calls at all hours
of the night at camp asking for me, and the person won't give
his name. And everyone that's picked up the phone says it
sounded like somebody black."

Why was she talking to me this way? "Wasn't me," I swore
earnestly. "Wasn't me, I tell you . . . Please, Vickie, I've
got to see you." A man should never beg a woman for her
body, but it got to a point where I was hungry, and I begged.

She'd be in the city for only a few nights. Her parents
would be home, but at 2:15 A.M. the candle in her window
would go out and five minutes after that she would meet me
on the lawn by the side of her house. I jumped off the lower
roof of our house to avoid waking Mom and Francis. (I
don't know how I managed not to break my legs.) I got on
my bike and rode the highway as fast as I could, zipping and
zagging between cars and trucks, to be there on time to see
the light go out. I must have looked like a madman—I only
had my pants on.

I left the bicycle down the block in some bushes and ran up
to her house, hiding behind parked cars and keeping in the
shadows as I did. The candle was flickering in the window.
At 2:15 it went out. I moved cautiously and quickly across
the street, like a black cat, and onto the lawn and hid in the
hedges by the side of the house, waiting and listening to
sounds of speeding cars on the highway nearby, feeling the
warmth of the summer's breeze cooling my sweat, anticipating what she would look like after all this time. And finally

she was there beside me naked and whispering in my ear not to make noise.

"Why are you doing this, Vickie?" I asked.

She didn't answer me, instead playfully pulled on my short and unkempt attempt at a beard. "It looks nice," she said.

"Vickie, please, tell me what's going on." But she just lay there silently on the grass, pulling me down onto her, pressing against me . . .

And we rolled over the grass like two maniacs romping in Eden. She understood my body and used it against me then, but I didn't care. I was fucking my brains away like some craven con set free for a fuck before death. Yet I knew there was more than sex involved, but right now what else could I feel about her except that she was probably the best fuck I ever had?

IV

I knew that sex was not the deepest reason I wanted her, but I kept myself half drunk each night so that my conscience wouldn't be fully pulverized with shame and disgust, loss of self-respect and manhood.

On the third night she returned to White Woods, leaving me with a scribbled map of its location. She told me her father had made her go, but I knew she was lying again. I received letters from her telling me of her asthma attacks and of all her wonderful friends at White Woods. By now, asthma was the only thing we had in common.

I called Ken up one night and told him I just had to see Vickie.

"Man," Ken said, "you're making a mistake. Let her go."

"Ken, I've got to go to her," I said.

"Don, can't you see it's all over?"

No, I couldn't see anything, and the next day I withdrew a considerable sum of money from the bank and bought Vickie an opal ring *bigger* than the one her parents had given her. Mine was even set in gold. I actually was trying to show her that I could give her as much monetarily as her parents. I was in the bidding to buy her off. And, of course, I got her an asthma inhaler.

I went to see Roberta before Ken and I left for the trip to White Woods. I think Ken arranged this meeting for me with Roberta. She spoke to me for a long while and told me that my thing with Vickie was no different from what was happening to thousands of other high school kids. I couldn't accept that even though I knew it was true; *my* thing just had to be deeper.

Roberta said, "How can you love her? You love what you had, and you feel sorry for what you might have had, but how could you love someone who's not what she was when you fell in love with her, who's doing what she's doing to you now? Make it easy on yourself, sugar—let her go."

"No." And I was gone.

Ken hardly spoke to me on the way up to White Woods. He just kept his eyes fixed on the road and fingers gripped on the wheel.

It was now very dark. There were no street lights, and we were in the middle of the woods running out of gas, barely able to see the ends of the winding roads beyond the range of the headlights. Ken, I could tell, was getting pissed off. I was following Vickie's directions as best I could, but we kept running into dead-ends. Ken blew up. "Shit man, where the hell *are* we?"

"Looks like they sent her far away . . . Ken, you're my main man. I really thank you for doing this for me."

He looked at me. "It's O.K., man. When I was a young cat, same thing happened to me with a redhead. Man, I was crazy about her. I drove all the way from New York City to Albany mad as hell one night because she'd left me. When I got there, she was with some cat . . ."

"A brother?"

"White guy. Man, we got into it. I was going to kill both of them, but fuck it. Mad as I was, I knew it wasn't worth it. Deal with it. If she loved me, she wouldn't have split." Then he shrugged his shoulders and said, "Just failing in style."

His saying that unnerved me, short-circuiting all kinds of impulses in my body and brain, leaving me uneasy inside.

Finally there was the sign: WELCOME TO WHITE WOODS, and Vickie came running out of the darkness toward the car's lights.

"What took you so long?" she asked, breathing heavily.

We drove back to a motel. All the way I listened to her tell stories of camp and her friends. She didn't look particularly overjoyed to see me.

Alone in the room I showed her the ring. She slipped it on and said, "I'll tell my father you gave it to me as a token of friendship." A punch in the mouth would have been easier to accept than hearing her say that.

"Vickie, just tell me straight: what's wrong?" She turned away as if I were pestering her and fired back, "I'm afraid of you. I just don't want to see you anymore. I want to live out my childhood. I'm a child, and I want to have fun. You're just too serious about things. People just don't care—all your speeches and traveling— You don't even *look* like a boy . . ."

I felt more let down by her than I was hurt. The more I listened, the more I realized how much of a child she really was, how much influence all those Jewish kids at the camp had on her. Her parents were smart to send her here. In this kind of surrounding with kids, all white, sharing her culture and background, Vickie, I realized (as painful as it was to swallow), had fulfilled her calling and was now truly Jewish and had made the decision her people applaud: to stay within the nation.

We fell asleep. In the morning she left. Yet before I called on Ken, I took the car and drove to the camp by myself. I had to see her one last time.

I knocked. A bushy-haired boy opened the door. Vickie was sitting on the bed in a red gown, sewing something, and was shocked to see me again. I entered the room eyeing the bushy-haired boy and sat on the bed.

"Vickie, I'd like to talk to you in private for a few minutes before I go."

"The two of you," she replied, "will have to settle that." I just couldn't believe she'd said that. I looked at the boy. I was at a loss for words, so I told him to come outside for a chat, thinking that I'd beat the shit out of him once he did. As we left the room, he turned and looked up at me, "You two can talk; I'll see her later tonight." And he walked off. I went back into the room closing the door behind me. "Who was that?" I asked.

She looked at me solemnly and replied, "He's my date, but actually there are two others. Would you like to meet them?"

"No, no." I said stunned.

"One's a grad student, going to be in med school. His mind isn't settled, but I'm keeping my fingers crossed until he's ready for me."

"Until *he's* ready for you?"

"Yes."

I thought it almost funny. Nice Jewish Doctor. Yet I found it unacceptable; all the stereotypes and printed trash on black/white relationships—what I had thought was trash was now the epitome of my relationship. I had felt so certain that this could never be true in my affair, never. She represented so much to me—hope, for one thing. She had given me confidence, in my view, to tell everyone our thing was different, clean, just two people. And maybe we were just two people going through an experience nobody else went through. But that's a lie.

I knew that now. Our thing was just *another* cheap cliché. My ego was crushed. I had thought so much of a person who thought so little of herself, who gained her self-confidence through destroying me when she *knew* I was at my weakest, when *she knew* how much she meant to me. That little Jewish boy had taken from me within a few days that which was part of me and, I had thought, my future. "How far have you gone?" I asked her, not wanting to know the answer. "Have you been sleeping with him?" Why had I even bothered to ask "How many times?"

"Three," she answered.

"Good-by, Vickie." And I walked out across the grass and to the car, before I realized that I'd forgotten my jacket and keys to the car. I went back only to find her with friends listening to her ridicule me in the hallway. "He's back againnnn," someone yelled. They were all laughing at me, and Vickie was fighting to control her own laughter.

I got my coat and left. I was a zombie and simply refused to think about any of it. I felt I'd been stripped of my manhood, lost my confidence and most of my mind. My nerves were shot. The only emotion left alive in me was hate.

V

On the way back to New York City I told Ken what had happened and asked him how everything looked to him now. He said, "You come off like four aces dealing with everybody else's problems but your own. As long as you have your people's best interests at heart, then you're a brother in my book. If I had thought you were insincere, I couldn't have dealt with you. But the thing I want to know, Reeves: Do you still have balls?"

I lied. I told him that I did.

It was night when we got into New York City, and we drove down to the Village.

"Let's see you score if you still have balls," Ken said smiling.

"Man, I'm finished with women."

"Bullshit! Let's see you score."

Reluctantly, I opened the door and got out of the car. I was trying, but I couldn't score. I almost got something going with a sister, but when she saw Ken waiting in the dark in his brown Thunderbird, she panicked and split. Ken roared with laughter.

"Well, you didn't score, but you've got guts," he laughed.

"I'll see you later." I got out of the car and took the subway up to 42nd Street. I went into a bar and swallowed as much whisky, vodka, and gin as my stomach could hold. I got thrown out of the bar, and my bag was stolen. I stumbled around carrying on in the street, bothering people until I caught sight of a sign: $5 LIVE SHOW—GIRLS, GIRLS, GIRLS.

I don't remember how many people were in the little, filthy, green, neon-lit room. The stripping music was on full blast playing on a broken needle, and everybody was hollering, "Ahhh, baby, more, more . . . pussy . . . pussy." There was a stage made of wood on which this ugly black woman was dancing, rubbing her butt with palm leaves, rolling on the ground, falling into a split-view of her pussy. I was cracking up watching those hungry bastards drool and pretend to catch those cunt hairs she threw them, licking their chops. I leaned over the knee-high black railing to touch her, to get one of those cunt hairs myself, and the man at the gate along with two other men carried me to a seat and screamed something in my face. I laughed. Things were spinning like a whirlpool.

A naked couple was on now: a white man, "a goddamn Forty-second Street Dick Sucker," dressed in a black star-spangled cowboy suit, holding a whip, which he snapped around the naked white woman's belly. "That's an abortion scar on your belly, baby," I screamed out, and everyone laughed. I looked around me at those hungry devils. "I've seen better pussy . . . ," I said. I looked at those starved dogs in the back of the room jerking off under newspapers. I realized that I was now a member of their ranks, a starved dog myself. Male chauvinist pig, castrated lamb. I laughed. The whole room was a whirlpool of vomit, and the nausea started to reach me. I was hurt, and I knew it, and I was trying to escape, running from myself. I walked out and down into the subway. It was either late night or early morning. Only two of us were in the car, me and a white boy who looked like a football player.

"I've got balls," I screamed out. I went over and challenged him to fight me. He got up and belted me in the mouth. I fell, just collapsed where I stood. I felt like I'd had an overdose of novocaine in my jaw. I thought he'd loosened

my teeth. My mouth quickly filled with bloody saliva. He
started to kick me, shooting for my balls, but that was the first
thing I covered. As soon as he stopped and started to walk
away, I went for him, catching him from behind the center
pole by his collar, wrapping my arm around his neck and
using the pole as leverage to choke him even harder. The
motherfucker squirmed like a worm. I let him go, and he
bolted for the door and into the next car, and the next. He
must have run to the last car. I took the bus home and stayed
there for a few days, recovering from a bad hangover.

One day Fran called. She'd returned from France and
wanted to see me. When she asked about Vickie and me, I
told her it was *all* over. We made plans to meet at a sidewalk
soul food café on West End Avenue. I was walking up to the
café, and I decided to call Lynn who lived nearby. First
thing she asked me was if it was true that I'd gotten Vickie
pregnant. "Everybody's heard about it." I just hung up the
phone as if I hadn't heard it. I hadn't put any pain in Vickie's
womb. So I was running from rumors now.

I had a long talk with Fran. She was quitting teaching because she couldn't be a "lesson-plan teacher simply giving out
assignments and tests." She was through with the system ("It
stinks"). And we talked about Vickie. I told her I thought it
was my fault that we'd broken up. She, in turn, gave me a
very bitter pill to swallow.

"I gave it a week before the two of you would break up.
David gave it a month. It was summertime. She didn't love
you as a person. It's what you were that she loved, never you.
She envied you more than you'll ever realize . . . You were
used, Don."

She must have had one hell of a time with me (and out of
me) without my ever knowing it. What an experience it must
have been for her; a beautiful Bloomingdale's baby who, for
all her life, had been penned in, denied the freedom girls her
age have the right to demand. Suddenly she found a tool to
bargain with, a black phallus, a Negro in her arms making
love to her, showing her the "thrills" of the other side. Her

parents (who never before gave her the love and attention she wanted), at the thought of a Negro with their daughter, got down on hands and knees pleading, "We'll give you anything dear, but please don't let that nigger get in your drawers." She had won, so I was now useless to her. *The chickens had come home to roost.* I had invited my own self-destruction through stubborn blindness and, I must admit, youthful idealism.

When the hate left, there was pain, then bitterness. Often it becomes necessary to revive the hate to ease the pain which comes at the thought that my judgment could be so poor. The affair was the culmination of broken trusts with the white race—the sequence of events that led to its end, the Iliad of an idiot.

VI

I severed my ties with the white world. I wasn't a racist. I just wasn't going out of my way again to have anything to do with white people. I went back to Brownsville to see Boss Reeves and tell him that he was right.

During the winter I had brought Vickie to Brownsville to see Boss Reeves and the people I loved most in America. Boss was shocked when I told him that Jewish parents had accepted me going out with their daughter, that what we knew of white people in Brownsville wasn't true anywhere else. He said, "You really mean they let *you* in the house? You eat off the sames plate with them? Them will let *you* marry their daughter?"

I had lied to him about those questions and told him, "Your days are finished. People are civilized now and respect each other as human beings. None of this tooth an' nail stuff you're always talking about."

I can remember how he sat there in his torn velvet robe, how his forehead became wrinkled as he leaned over the table and told me, "That's very strange, but I've been on this earth longer than you have, and I don't think things have changed from my days, but you think I'm old and foolish just because my life has come to this." He was alone, but he wasn't a fool. Maybe inconceivably cruel at times, but never foolish, except when he left my mother.

I was going back to tell him that I had lied about white people. I don't know why I felt it necessary for him to know that. I guess it was because I'd find it difficult to admit to him more than anybody else in the world that I had lied or made a fool of myself.

As I walked up New Lots Avenue, my mind was filled with a parade of scenes from 1965—murders, fires, rapes, glimpses of my brother, Derrick, Medrano, Pedro, and I roaming the streets together. In those days Brownsville was the entire world.

Our old house on Alabama Avenue was nearly falling apart, soon ready to crumble away to the rockpile remaining from the house next door where our Jewish neighbors used to live. (I've been told West Indians are the Black Jews of the world, *or at least America.*)

I rang the bell but heard no sound. I banged on the door. Peering through the window, I could see my father's shadow coming. I was wondering whether or not I could take him. He opened the door, startled to see me. He seemed to have shrunk.

"How tall are you?" he asked.

I went into the kitchen, which also seemed to have gotten smaller. The ceiling paint was peeling, walls cracking. He hadn't even bothered to take the dead mouse from the trap there beside the roach-sprayed bags of garbage next to the stove. Except for his room, the house was virtually empty. It was never really a *home* anyway. From the moment I entered the door, I felt sympathy for him instead of the hate I used to feel when I didn't understand why he did many cruel things. It seems inherently characteristic of West Indians, rich or poor, that they must have land to call their own, to build on or be buried in. I never knew what Boss Reeves did for a living except work for Greyhound all his life, for which he had a penny-sized twenty-years-of-service pin to show as proof. Yet he had sacrificed his offspring and wife to own land he could call his own and to boast that the fabulous ranch-type house near the Caribbean overlooking Montego Bay Airport was his. I don't think he himself will ever be able to afford to live in that house although it is his. So he has the land and the West Indian symbol of success.

Fanon was right. It is true, there is no native who does not dream of setting himself up in the settler's place. It is ironic that today the settlers still live in the house *owned* by the native; a native who cannot live in his own house, who is but another of ill fame and evil repute to all who do not understand him. Though wallowing in wretchedness, he is alive and well because he is strong. The bitterness has made him this way. Yet he has all he ever wanted, and he has paid the price for having it.

He was like his father, Más Obie. Boss will tell you that "Más Obie was a charitable man, a strong man, and a wise man," but no more. However, I have heard—not only from relatives—that Más Obie was a cruel man and died a wicked death "only Más Obie deserved." I was told, Más Obie never fed his children, yet he threw huge banquets for all the countryside. He wore the best clothes and shoes, but his children went naked. He walked tall while his family crawled. One day Más Obie was swept up by the river's swift and forceful currents, and his neck was thrust between two rocks where he was drowned and strangled by the vines he tried to use to pull himself free. Why Boss Reeves admires Más Obie I do not know.

Boss Reeves has taken from life the only meaning it has for him, and he is alone because of it, and he always lets me know that he *is* my father and I am *his* son. I am part of his *contribution* to the world. Yet he has always felt that the world was a conspiracy against him, to which I also was a party. This, I think, had tempered his hate and resentment through more than half a century of life in solitary confinement, not behind cement and bars of iron, but in the darkness of his closed mind. But he and I are alike in more ways than I care to admit.

I sat there eyeing him setting two eggs to boil, my inner ear hearing my mother tell me that I was just like my father, "just like him." And he sat down to ask me why I was here and asked, "Where is your white wife?"

I had come to talk about that, but just then it didn't seem to have any meaning.

"She's gone," I said. "But that's not why I'm here. I came to tell you that I was stubborn, and I didn't want to admit you were right. And I want you to know my view of the world was a lie. Not because I meant to tell you a lie. I just didn't have any sense. I shaped the world according to how *I* saw fit and refused to base my truths on what I see now, right in front of me . . ."

And I continued speaking, and then as if he hadn't heard a word he said sharply, "Why don't you shave your face? Look like a damn hippie." And he rose to get his two boiled eggs.

He turned and fixed his eyes on me. "Marry a nice brown-skin woman like your mother and stay with her. Don't follow me. Just leave them white people right where they are—don't go over there. The trick, my son, is to know where you stand and stay there."

Appendix A

CONTENTS: High School Rules and Regulations for Teachers and Students.

TO ALL NEW STUDENTS

The instructions that follow will help you review the regulations and practices of our school. Please read them with care and keep them in a notebook for future reference.

1. ATTENDANCE

You are to attend all classes and Study Halls indicated on your official Program Card. YOU ARE TO CARRY THIS PROGRAM WITH YOU AT ALL TIMES. Should a change of program be necessary, your Official Teacher will arrange for it and will note it on your copy of your Official Program Card.

You will receive additional instructions regarding attendance and punctuality.

In no case are you to leave the building before the end of the 8th period or before the end of your school day without an official early dismissal pass.

2.A. PUNCTUALITY

You are expected to arrive here in ample time for your first class. Plan your travel time so as to arrive at least ten minutes before the late bell rings. The late bell for the First Period rings at 8:40 A.M. If you have no First Period class, you are to arrive here in time for your Second Period assignment at 9:20 A.M. The late bell for the Second Period rings at 9:24 A.M. If you have neither a First nor a Second Period class, you are to arrive in ample time to get to the Locker Room and arrive in your Official Class on time for the Official Period. Should your late arrival occur after the Second Period and up to 11:00 A.M., you are to report to the Attendance Office (Room 113) where the proper Late Pass will be issued to you. After 11:00 A.M. report to the General Office for a pass and then at the end of Period 8 report to the Attendance Office in Room 113.

2.B. LATENESS TO SCHOOL, ABSENCE AND CUTTING

Please note the procedures with reference to Lateness to School, Absence and Cutting:

1. Students who are late to school report with their Program Card to the table in the Main Lobby for a Late Pass, proceed to deposit their outer clothing in the Locker Room, and then report to subject rooms.
2. Teachers will not admit students wearing or carrying outer clothing to any of their classes.
3. Each Student Must Carry A Program Card At All Times.
4. After the third unexcused lateness or absence, the parent may be summoned to school and interviewed by the Attendance Coordinator.
5. Cutting and Truancy:
   a. Where the student has incurred 2 or more truancies and/or cuts, his grade for the First Marking Period will be recorded as: "F".
   b. Where the student has incurred 4 or more in the first two marking periods, his grade will be recorded as: 55.
   c. Where the student has incurred 6 or more by the end of the semester, failure will be mandatory.
6. In addition, one or more of the following penalties may be imposed:
   a. Change of program
   b. Exclusion from graduation exercises
   c. Notation on Permanent Record Card
   d. Notation on college application and job reference form
   e. Exclusion from graduation exercises
   f. Withholding of graduation diploma.

3. Appropriate Dress

Our faculty and our Parents Association believe that the good taste and good sense of our boys and girls will induce them to wear *appropriate* dress in school and on the way to and from school. Appropriate standards of dress and grooming are observed in the world of business and social life.

The parents of students who offend against appropriate standards of dress and grooming will be consulted in regard to correcting the situation.

Outdoor Clothing: All outdoor clothing must be placed in the locker officially assigned for your use BEFORE YOU REPORT TO YOUR FIRST CLASS EACH DAY. You must allow time for this upon arrival at school each day in order to avoid lateness. Your outdoor clothing may not be removed from your locker until AFTER THE CLOSE OF YOUR LAST PERIOD CLASS.

4. Emergency Room

Illness must be reported to the school authorities without delay. Should you feel too ill to remain in class, your recitation teacher will give you a note that will admit you to the Emergency Room (Room 606). Upon receipt of such a note, you are to report to the Emergency Room at once. In case of serious illness, the teacher in charge of the Emergency Room will arrange with the Administrative Office for the issuance of an Early Dismissal Pass. NO VARIATION FROM THIS PROCEDURE IS PERMITTED.

5. Lunch Room

In accordance with your official Program Card, you are to report to the Students Cafeteria in the Basement for your regularly scheduled Lunch Period and occupy a definitely assigned seat. Unless special arrangement has been made by the Administrative Office, you are to remain in the Cafeteria for the full period, i.e., until dismissed by the teacher in charge.

All food, whether brought from home or purchased in the Cafeteria, is to be consumed in the Cafeteria. *No other room—no other part of the building is to be used as a Lunch Room.*

You will, of course, cooperate in keeping our Cafeteria orderly, clean and pleasant. The condition of the room and the care of table silver, chinaware and equipment are direct responsibilities of our students. Each table group is responsible for the condition of its table and the floor in the immediate vicinity.

About twenty-five minutes after the beginning of each Lunch Period, each table group will arrange for the clearing of its table and floor space. Dishes and tableware will be carried by students to the nearest receptacle. *At this time, each table group will make certain that neither paper nor food scraps remain on the floor in its area.*

6. LOCKER ROOM

You are not to use any locker which has not been officially assigned to you. You are not to loiter in the Locker Room. Except for the necessary interval for changing clothing for Health Education classes, no student may enter the Locker Room without a special pass obtainable *ONLY* in the Administrative Office.

7. PUBLIC TELEPHONE

You may use one of the public telephone booths located in Stairwell 9/10 opening off the Main Lobby just north of the elevators *Only In Cases Of Extreme Emergency* and if you have in your possession an official pass issued in your name by the School Secretary in the Administrative Office. *One of the telephone booths must be left available for faculty use at all times.*

8. LIBRARY

The Library is located on the Second Floor opposite the elevators. It is open to all students from 8:30 A.M. to 4:15 P.M. each school day without fee except for the usual fines imposed for keeping borrowed books overtime. After the first two weeks of a new term, you may spend any of your Study Periods in the Library if you will comply with these simple regulations:

   a. Report to the Library promptly at the beginning of the period.

   b. Sign the Library Register for that period so that you will not be marked absent from Study Hall.

If you have difficulty in finding the books you need, our Librarians will be glad to help you.

9. BOOKS

All books are city property. Since you enjoy their free use, you are expected to keep them covered and to return them in good condition. You will be required to pay for books lost or damaged.

10. LOST AND FOUND

If you have lost an article, you may be able to recover it by filing the properly completed form (REPORT OF LOST ARTICLE) in the box labeled for that purpose in the General Office. These forms are available through your Official Teacher. If your property has been turned into the Lost and Found Bureau, you will receive a notice.

11. FURNITURE

You are asked to be careful in handling furniture and equipment throughout the building. Aside from your general duty to preserve and care for public property, you will want to avoid any misuse of furniture, equipment or facilities that would inconvenience your teachers or fellow students.

12. OPENING AND CLOSING OF BUILDING

The building opens officially at 8:15 A.M. Please DO NOT ENTER BEFORE THIS TIME, unless you are assigned to help a teacher or wish to make a purchase in the Student Co-op. The Co-op is open from 8:00 to 8:35 A.M. each day.

Exit 9/10 is closed at 3:40 P.M. each day. Courtyard gates are closed and locked at this hour. *All students must leave when the warning gong sounds at 4:30* P.M. The building closes officially at 4:45 P.M.

13. GUIDANCE

If you have any personal problems that you would like to discuss, please see the Dean or the Assistant Dean in Room 113. If you have any program problems that need adjustment, your Grade Guide will be glad to help you.

14. Emergency Drills

a. *Fire Drill Instructions.* Three Gongs Repeated Four Times is the signal for a Fire Drill. You will instantly stop work, leave books and materials, except pocketbook, on your desk and follow your teacher in double file to the exit and stairway assigned for your room. Two competent Fire Drill monitors appointed by your teacher will assist in securing a rapid passing of all students from the room and will take their places last in the double lines.

Absolute silence must be maintained during the Fire Drill. Talking during a Fire Drill is a serious offense.

The usual signal for return is *one gong.* You will return to the classroom from which you started unless otherwise directed. *Absolute silence must be maintained until you return to your room.*

During a Fire Drill, *order, silence, speed* and *absolute obedience to commands* must be carried out to insure your safety in case of an emergency.

b. *Shelter Drill Instructions.* Five Gongs Sounded Three Times is the usual signal for a Shelter Drill. Upon recognition of the signal, your teacher will stop work and give directions in accordance with the situation. You will maintain silence, pay strict attention to the teacher in charge of the class or area of assignment and, upon being instructed by that teacher, report with your books to the Shelter Station assigned to your Official Class. You will receive detailed instructions from your Official Teacher concerning the several alternative signals for Shelter Drills and the procedures to be followed.

c. *"No Signal" Drill Instructions.* Each of your subject teachers for the room occupied and your Official Teacher will give you instructions for the "No Signal" Drill which is designed to afford maximum protection in case of a "sneak" air raid.

15. General Student Organization

The General Organization (G.O.), we hope, will include every student in our school as a regular member. It is your chief means for taking an active part in the affairs of our school. Loyalty to our school, therefore, should be the chief incentive for membership in the General Organization.

Besides, the General Organization is run by the students in our school in order to make possible many benefits which you would not otherwise be able to enjoy. By joining the G.O., you can get discounts at music and art supply stores, concerts, art exhibitions and sports events. In the school, you are entitled to admission to your term party and discounts on admission to almost all events which take place in the school. The chief reason for joining the G.O., however, is that you will want to take part in the life of the school and find satisfaction in friendly association with your fellow students.

16. ASSEMBLIES

The student body is divided into two groups for Assembly purposes. Assemblies take place on Fridays. When Group A is attending Assembly, Group B is having a long Official Period, each Official Class in its own room.

Assembly regulations are very simple:

a. Students should report *promptly* to the Auditorium and go *directly* to their assigned seats without pausing in aisles for conversation.
b. Each student should place books and other belongings on the floor under his seat. His desk should be drawn *up* and out of sight.
c. From the sounding of the initial fanfare until the dismissal of the Assembly, each student is expected to give his undivided attention to the Assembly program.

17. OFFICIAL CLASS PERIODS

Each school day, Monday to Thursday inclusive, there is a short Official Period. Attendance is checked and important notices are read to students at this time. On Fridays, when the class is not attending Assemblies, there is a long Official Period equal in duration to the Assembly period. This period provides a comfortable opportunity for students to discuss the affairs of the school community and to take part therein through the duly elected class representative, who is the link between the G.O. Council and the members of his Official Class.

18. WARNING: CITY COLLEGE GROUNDS AND BUILDINGS NOT OPEN TO PUBLIC

In order to protect its own students, the college authorities have restricted the buildings and facilities of the college—including the Lounge, the Snack Bar, the Bookshop, Library, etc.—to *their* students. In the effort to eliminate intruders, the college maintains at great expense private policemen whose duty it is to enforce the regulation. Intruders are normally turned over to the police. The students of our school are expressly warned against setting foot in any part of the College precincts. Aside from any police action to which they may make themselves liable, any of our students who violate this regulation may expect serious consequences.

Administrative Assistant

ALL TEACHERS FOR INFORMATION, GUIDANCE AND COMPLIANCE (NOT for publication to students)

1. CITYWIDE COORDINATOR OF SELECTIVE SERVICE FOR HIGH SCHOOL STUDENTS

The Board of Education has authorized the position of City-wide Coordinator of Selective Service counselling for high school students. If interested, please see Mr. Orfuss.

2. TEACHERS CAFETERIA ITEMS

  a. *Check Cashing and Large Bills*
     The Cafeteria is unable to cash personal checks or large bills for staff members.

  b. *Protocol in the Teachers Cafeteria*
     Our colleagues of the College are aware of the fact that the members of the High School of Music and Art faculty have precedence over the guest patrons of our Cafeteria; i.e., they are to be served first and should not hesitate to pass "visiting firemen" in order to make sure of getting lunch within the period.
        It is expected that all patrons of our Cafeteria—members of our faculty and guests from the College staff—will remove trays, paper bags, dishes, used ash trays and the like and place them on the side tables provided for the purpose in the North East corner of the dining room.

  c. *Building Security*
     The kitchen delivery door may not be used for entering the building. The only door for entrance or departure is the St. Nicholas Terrace door.

  d. *Dining Hours*
     In order to facilitate the preparation of food and the clean-

ing of the Cafeteria after one day's use and preparation for the following day, the faculty is reminded that the official hours of service are 8:30 A.M. to 2:00 P.M. No teacher may use the Cafeteria after 2:00 P.M. since their presence interferes with routine.

3. LEAVING THE ROOM

Members of the faculty are advised to restrict and limit the use of the authorized Hall Pass at all times. No other form or pass is to be used. They will keep a record of students leaving the room in a notebook, appointing a monitor to take care of this record. The date, name of student, time of leaving and returning will be noted. All students will be challenged for Hall Passes and only the regular Hall Pass will be accepted. Students who request the pass regularly and frequently should be reported *in writing* to Mrs. Ackerman, the Dean.

If a student walks out of a class without the express permission of the teacher, it is to be regarded as an act in open defiance of school authority and subject to whatever penalty the school deems appropriate. Will you, therefore, be good enough at such times to prepare an accurate list of the students who, without your permission, get up and walk out of your room while class is in session and submit this list, indicating the student's name and Official Class, to the Principal.

4. TEACHER RESPONSIBILITY IN CORRIDORS

Teachers are reminded that they must challenge all persons who are in the halls at times when classes are not changing. Students in halls must carry the official Hall Pass at all times. Notify the Administrative Office immediately, if questionable circumstances arise during such a challenge.

5. STUDY HALL REMINDERS

Study Hall supervisors and all other teachers should reinforce the following regulations concerning Study Hall procedures:
   a. The Study Hall is to be considered a regular class with assigned seats. Attendance must be taken promptly; lateness is to be challenged, recorded and—if excessive—reported. No floating from seat to seat is to be permitted.
   b. Excessive or regular departure from Study Hall is not to be

permitted. When departure is necessary, it may take place with the official Hall Pass ONLY. No handwritten passes may be issued.

c. Unenrolled students may not be permitted the use of the Study Hall. It must not become an assembly area for cutters or students from the Cafeteria.

d. There can be NO visitors, piano playing or eating. NO student may visit, frequent or use the area backstage without direct teacher supervision. Since the Study Hall supervisor's attention must be to the group in the Orchestra, nobody may be backstage unless an additional teacher is present.

6. Use Of Commercial Posters

Questions have arisen concerning the propriety of displaying in school halls travel posters and similar materials which show the names of private commercial firms and advertising slogans. While it is agreed that some outstanding designs can be found in commercial advertising, it is recommended that such materials not be used outside regular classrooms. In those cases where such materials are used, the names of the firms and their advertising slogans would have to be deleted or covered. On the other hand, the use of such materials in a classroom as part of regular instructional material for teaching design, lettering, techniques, etc., has definite value and would be fully justified.

7. Prohibition Against Requiring Pupil Purchase Of Workbooks, etc.

Purchase of all instructional materials by schools, including workbooks, textbooks, Regents review books, etc., which are proper and necessary in the implementation of the educational program are to be made from public funds. Materials of value in the educational program of a school should be ordered by the Principal from authorized lists or secured as non-list items by procedures previously announced. No teacher or supervisor may *require* individual pupils or their parents to purchase educational material in the form of workbooks, review books or "supplementary" textbooks. Unless such books are provided by the school, homework assignments or special projects dependent on the use of such books may not be assigned, nor may teachers use such material as a regular and continuous part of their classroom instruction.

Nothing is to be construed to prevent the purchase of workbooks, etc. by the Principal of the school from funds provided by the city. Such purchase is an educational judgment properly to be exercised by the head of the school. Where workbooks are so bought and the educational program enhanced, they should be used by pupils as *consumable* goods in the way they were designed.

8. JURY SERVICE FEES

The fees that staff members receive for service on jury duty are to be given to Mrs. Briggs for forwarding to the Bureau of Finance. However, in the event the payment to the juror includes an additional sum to cover carfare, such amount may be retained by the juror. Please note that the remittance should be made payable to the Administrator of Business Affairs and the back of the check or money order should indicate the juror's name, school, file number and the dates of jury service.

9. USE OF PERMANENT RECORD CARDS

All teachers are reminded that students or student aides may *NOT* check Permanent Record Cards.

Assistant Principal

Appendix B

BOARD OF EDUCATION'S
STUDENT BILL OF RIGHTS

Following is the text of the Board of Education's resolution on "Rights and Responsibilities for Senior High School Students."

1. In each high school there should be established an elective and truly representative student government with offices open to all students in good standing. All students should be allowed to vote. This government should be elected annually.

a. The student government shall have the power to allocate student activity funds, subject to established audit controls and the by-laws of the Board of Education. It shall also participate in making decisions in certain areas, including curriculum and disciplinary policies.

b. The representatives chosen by the student government shall meet at least monthly with the principal to exchange views, to share in the formulation of school student policies, to discuss faculty-student relations and any other matters of student concern.

2. A parent-student-faculty council, as established by previous Board of Education resolutions, shall meet monthly with the principal to discuss matters of common interest, make recommendations and to insure implementation of agreed upon innovations.

3. Official school publications shall reflect the policy and judgment of the student editors. This entails the obligation to be governed by the standards of responsible journalism, such as avoidance of libel, obscenity and defamation. Student publications shall provide as much opportunity as possible for the sincere expression of student opinion.

4. Students may exercise their constitutionally protected rights of free speech and assembly so long as they do not interfere with the operations of the regular school program.
　　a. Students have a right to wear political buttons, arm bands and other badges of symbolic expression.
　　b. Students may distribute political leaflets, newspapers, and other literature, without prior authorization at locations adjacent to the school.
　　c. Students shall be allowed to distribute leaflets, newspapers and other literature with prior authorization at specified locations and times designated within the school for that purpose. No commercial material, no obscene material and *nothing advocating racial or religious prejudice shall be permitted to be distributed within the school*. In noting these exceptions, it is clearly the intention of the Board of Education to promote the dissemination of diverse viewpoints and to foster discussion of all political and social issues. Decisions under this section restricting the distribution of literature within the school for the reasons stated above shall be made by the principal, or with his agreement by some other body which shall consist of students and faculty. Such decisions may be reviewed by the supervising assistant superintendent and later by the chancellor and the central board.
　　d. Students may form political and social organizations, including those that champion unpopular causes, providing they are open to all students and governed by the regulations pertaining to student government regarding extracurricular activities. These organizations shall have reasonable access to school facilities.

5. Students have the right to determine their own dress, except where such dress is clearly dangerous, or is so distractive as to clearly interfere with the learning and teaching process. This right may not be restricted, even by a dress code arrived at by a majority vote of students as Dr. Ewald Nyquist, Acting State Com-

missioner of Education, held this year in Decisions No. 8022 and 8023.

6. Students have the right to receive annually, upon the opening of school, a publication setting forth all the rules and regulations to which students are subject. This publication shall also include a statement of the rights granted to students. It shall be distributed to parents as well.

7. Students shall have the right to a fair hearing, as provided for in the State Education Law, which includes "representation by counsel, with the right to question witnesses against such pupils," prior to any disciplinary action which could result in suspension from classes for more than five days.

8. Any decision concerning student rights and responsibilities by school personnel is subject to discussion by the consultative council. Appeals from the decisions of the head of the school must first be lodged with the assistant superintendent in charge of the high schools, then the chancellor and finally the Central Board of Education. All such appeals shall be decided as quickly as possible.

EXPLANATION

This resolution is an attempt to state systematically the rights and responsibilities of senior high school students. In no way does it diminish the legal authority of the school and of the Board of Education to deal with disruptive students.

This resolution makes students responsible for their conduct and at the same time extends the range of their responsibility. It is meant to foster an atmosphere of trust so that students, parent, teachers and administrators can join in an active partnership in the educational process.

Appendix C

For High School Principals Association Use Only

COMMUNIQUE #3*

CONFRONTATION AND RESPONSE

The kind of student unrest now creating havoc in so many of our city high schools is a reflection of broader social unrest. Until recently spontaneous and without form, the more contemporary student movements are now rather precisely tooled, a battering ram to test and then destroy the "establishment."

The schools have been selected as the battleground; the method of attack is confrontation politics.

New York City's high school principals, individually and as an association, have long been spokesmen in the great libertarian tradition. We pride ourselves on our unequivocal endorsement of free speech, our confidence in free interchange in the marketplace of ideas, our support of the right of dissent.

Yet as educators and as citizens, we recognize that all the rights have limitations: laws of libel and slander, restriction in time of "clear and present danger," on freedoms that threaten the rights of others. Even the right to dissent has permissible limits.

Our problem is to reconcile opposites, to search for synthesis: to protect the historic right to challenge institutions without incur-

---

* As printed in the *High School Free Press.*

ring purposeless social disorientation. The problem is to define the limits of permissible dissent; and to respond with wisdom, courage, and conviction to dissent which exceeds these limits.

1. An Overview

We begin with affirmations. We affirm for our students the right—indeed the duty—of responsible dissent: of participation without turmoil, innovation without anarchy, and commitment without ideological orthodoxies. We affirm—indeed encourage— their right to test the non-violent limits of responsible freedom without allowing their corrupt fringe to seduce the innocent.

And, in our search for synthesis, we are guided by affirmations and convictions of our own: in reason, not sloganeering; in a responsive democracy which refutes charges of rigidity; and in effective channels of communication, not in the strong-arm tactics or in coercion.

We reject a policy of flabby drift. . . .

We define confrontation as we have learned to experience it: an attack on the viability of a school, using peripheral issues, non-negotiable demands, and calculated disorder to wrest control from the lawful authorities. The nature of the demands—not even the demands: rather, manifestos, political platforms, position papers —and the manner of their presentation—violent, sometimes wantonly destructive, using hostages as a political weapon—allow only one response: denial, simple, clear, and unequivocal.

Discussion perhaps. Negotiation, no.

A school's response to confrontation will be based on interplay of many factors: the nature of the school and its students, the maturity of its faculty, and the tone of the community, different tolerances, and finally, the personality, the posture, and the leadership of the principal.

2. The New Left: Composite Portrait

Our response must be based on an understanding of the conglomerate nature of the student left in these later years of the 1960's: part idealist, part nihilist, part shock troops of revolution; intellectually quite adult, often childish in the search for emotional joyrides, part deeply committed black nationalist, part alienated white liberal, and part elite corps of left fascism. Some have a sense of destiny; others, a greed for power. Together they wage deadly warfare—sometimes grimly, sometimes with gay and romantic abandon.

The new left is not monolithic. Quite the contrary, it is composed of many viewpoints and of many divergent groups. If it seems unified at the moment of confrontation, the unity is deceptive. With time, and under pressure, cracks will appear and caucuses surface.

3. THE CONFRONTATION SYNDROME

Unrest in New York City schools does not always follow precisely the same patterns. The following account describes the unfolding of a confrontation, from initial simmering to the moment of decision. It is composite reportage; not fantasy of fevered nightmare; the story of what happened, how it happened, and what we have learned. . . .

A. A PRE-CONFRONTATION MILIEU

Where student unrest is virulent, the period before the confrontation is characterized by vague dissatisfactions among the staff, the students, and the community, reflected in shifting and transient attacks: condemnation of the "insensitive principal," slanders against the "white, middle class" teachers, denunciation of censorship and repression.

Rumors inflame the staff, converting a silver comb into a switchblade knife, a stranger in the corridor into a rapist, a quarrel between two students into a race riot.

For every attack, there are a number of suggestions, a search for remedies. Each suggestion, each remedy has its partisans. The faculty begins to lose cohesiveness, to splinter.

B. THE CATALYST

A dramatic event serves to catalyze the discontent: riots at Columbia, demonstrations in Ocean Hill-Brownsville, the death of Martin Luther King. The activists, experiencing intolerable tension, sense the rendezvous with history. The school is brought to a fever pitch by sporadic surprise attacks: false alarms, cherry bombs, and threats to teachers keep everyone on edge.

The administrative machinery begins to erode: the intruders invade the school, cutting is uncontrolled, loiterers terrorize other students, disrupt classroom instruction. Teachers fear for their personal safety, react with increasing anxiety to fitful rumors, to arrogant and abusive flyers.

The administration temporizes, avoids decisive action, tries to compromise, to buy time, deceives itself with illusory peace.

C. The Confrontation Proper

Student activists present demands, a mix of the reasonable and the unreasonable, the negotiable and the non-negotiable. Disorders increase. Faculty demoralization—a sense of helplessness, of aloneness—reaches intolerable levels. New issues appear daily: irrelevant courses, the drop-out rate, the number of general diplomas.

For a school this is the moment of truth.

4. Guiding Principles

There are no neat formulas, only guidelines; no panaceas, merely options; and no miracles at all.

A. Recognize that there is no compromise with and no appeasing those who play confrontation politics.

B. Review your administrative machinery, the entire modus operandi, including procedures for selecting student leaders, for controlling discipline, and for coping with emergencies.

1. Insist that the activist use the established machinery (for requesting approval for posting notices, for amending the G.O. Constitution, etc.).

C. Review procedure for dealing with disorderly students, those who violate the instructional program or the academic atmosphere. To allow the number of disorderly students to multiply, uncontrolled, is disastrous.

D. Adopt a reasonable & liberal stance, but act decisively. The staff looks to the principal for leadership.

1. Administrative flexibility and reasonableness may not impress the extremists but the silent majority will be less ready for radicalization if negotiable requests receive serious consideration.

E. Be accessible and keep the lines of communication open. An administrator who is highly visible spreads assurance by his presence, reduces tension, senses the mood of his school, gives courage to the staff.

1. Hysteria feeds on rumour & ignorance. Keep the faculty informed.

2. Request the support of all groups—of parents, students, community leaders, and—above all others by far—of your staff.

3. Select for key positions staff members who are responsible and trustworthy.

F. In The Eye Of The Hurricane Remember:

1. Trained extremists will deliberately attack the values and personality structure of the administrators by a barrage of outrageous charges, obscene language, loud and strident voices, violent insults. Refuse to participate in such conferences.

2. Theirs is a struggle without quarter, fought with total commitment. It will demand and challenge our best efforts, as total a commitment, all our resources. It is a struggle without second chances.

a. Nail down rumors, identify slander, publicize the school's position.

b. Take the initiative. When subjected to politically inspired attacks (on vandalism, on rate of drop-outs) do not furnish a long litany of explanations and apologies, move over to the offensive.

3. Under attack we sometimes forget that time and struggle enervate the students, too, split them into caucuses, lead to defections.

a. It is as dangerous to exaggerate the numbers and powers of the militants as to minimize them.

b. It is perhaps as dangerous to overreact as to ignore danger signals.

4. Rely on your trusted and trained aides. Tackling every problem yourself is emotionally exhausting (and poor administration).

5. Unfolding of a Confrontation

For the purposes of this report confrontations are divided into 4 broad stages.

We may admit at the outset that there are a hundred gradations between them: that one can evolve into another in a twinkle of a furious exchange, that issues that threaten to radicalize large numbers in one school draw no response in another, and that our experience with confrontation is still too limited and the confrontations themselves are too varied to permit confident generalization.

Nevertheless, 4 broad stages are discernible, each with its own identifiable characteristics. For each, characteristic options are available.

A. THE MINI-CONFRONTATION

Confrontation and the mini-confrontation differ in the manner and the substance. In a confrontation the demands are non-negotiable, involving violations of laws and by-laws, injudicious capitulation to extremists, and distortions of sound educational practices (demands for control over finances, the right to hire and fire). In a mini-confrontation the demand is negotiable (for suggestion boxes, for the right to review cafeteria menus).

In some instances the demand (to use the school p.a. system improperly) is presented by a small handful—leaders without followers—with no potential for radicalizing the majority. In others both the demand and the manner are offensive (demand to use duplicating equipment for uncensored flyers) but the militants accept the administrative ruling.

1. Since not all confrontations are equally threatening, distinguish the mini-confrontation from the major, explosive threats to the school.

2. a. Again reasonable requests deserve a reasonable hearing.

   b. Requests to extend appropriate student participation should be welcomed with enthusiasm.

3. Wherever possible demands should be directed to aides who will reflect school policy or who will consult your more knowledgeable deputies. A request for duplicating equipment should be referred to the trained secretary, for the use of p.a. to the teacher in charge of announcements. Spare yourself the thousand demands on your time, the innumerable requests for your attention. Reserve for yourself only those decisions no one else can appropriately make.

4. The principal's response must be presented briefly, reasonably, and decisively.

B. THE SEARCH FOR A CAUSE

In the schools with well organized militants, the search for the issues which will radicalize the rest of the student body proceeds restlessly but persistently. The demands keep shifting, striking now at one issue, now at another. Now they claim censorship of the student newspaper, now bigotry by teachers; the food in the cafeteria is inedible and the choice restricted; assemblies are dull and irrelevant, the G.O. unrepresentative.

Some issues can be readily defused (e.g. a coke machine eliminates complaints about restricted offerings in the cafeteria) but others, despite your reasonableness and your best efforts, cannot. The restless search continues.

1. Where militants demand a hearing on a transient issue (complaints about an assembly program), they must submit the agenda and their recommendations in advance, allowing time for consideration and consultation. Transient issues may die stillborn.

2. Where the issues are more fundamental, adhere to standard, well-defined administrative procedures. Claims of censorship of the student newspaper should be referred to the faculty advisor and then to the Chairman of the English Department. Complaints about food may be reviewed by the dietician and a representative student committee—advisory groups to investigate, explore, and resolve the problem harmoniously; or to make recommendations for cabinet consideration.

3. Students' demands may have a cutting edge which, however threatening, must not lead us to reject their right to propose reforms; nor may we refuse them a machinery which without thoughtlessly and cavalierly violating established school policy, insures them proper consideration. A request for an SDS bulletin board, for example, may be referred to a broadly representative students' cabinet, the teacher in charge of publicity, the Fine Arts Department and the Administrative Assistant before reaching the principal for final approval. Deliberation at each level will prevent, by cumulative reinforcement—precipitate error without denying the request adequate attention.

C. Crisis: The Radicalization of Large Numbers

In more and more schools the search for a cause ultimately results in success. Masses of students are radicalized, accepting the militants' cause as their own. The school bubbles with a continual conspiratorial caucusing. Sometimes supported by dissident teachers and community extremists, they demand action—now. They insist on an immediate conference on the right to leave school during lunch or study periods, or unsupervised assemblies, on distributing libelous and obscene materials in the lobby. Their goal is to provoke the school authorities into error or action which win them more adherents.

Insist on a written statement of demands.

Insist on one to two days for study.

Refer demands to appropriate advisory groups for recommendation.

Where student participation in school government is widespread and meaningful and where broadly representative groups have a personal involvement in school activities (sing, athletic teams, clubs, a varsity show) the overwhelming majority will oppose disruption of these programs.

Reduce the potential for violence in a large, hostile mob. Milling in hallways, the cafeteria, the auditorium, the lobby outside your office; anonymous and emotionally variable; rendered immune to communication and reason by corrosive anger, by their intensity, and by their very numbers, the mob must be restored to sanity. Use trusted staff to subdivide the anonymous mass into smaller, identifiable, more rational groups and remove them to a calmer, less intense environment.

    a. Isolate the radical leadership from the followers.

    b. Take appropriate, forthright action.

Avoid provoking the students into escalating the ante. Avoid being similarly provoked yourself.

D. THE TIME FOR DECISION

All attempts to resolve the problem have failed, student clamor for an immediate hearing must be granted. The threat of violence to persons and property is real and imminent, the threat of anarchy within the building, of students rampaging through the hallways.

1. Meet with 3-5 student representatives, each identified by name and organization. Request their demands in writing.

    a. Teacher extremists, contained by peer counter-pressure, may not be admitted to the conference.

    b. Nor may community extremists. They may request a voice in the proceedings at a separate appointment.

2. To avoid psychological harassment and to insure the proper balance, the principal should be joined by 3-5 representative staff members. Your secretary or a tape recorder should record statements for future reference.

3. The principal's committee will display a reasonable and

responsive attitude and conspicuous good manners. Insist on similar good manners by the students.

4. Request time to consult and respond. Do not rush into concessions that may merely be preliminary to the next round of demands. Maintain the HSPA guidelines.

5. If the threat of violence is imminent, request standby police. Expel intruders. Arrest trespassers and lawbreakers.

6. If uncontrollable violence occurs, the closing of the school for a cooling-off period may be indicated. Request advice from the HSPA, your district office, and the Board in reopening.

7. Act firmly and with conviction. There is little to lose. The violence may assume the form of picketing and demonstrations outside the building.

a. Concentrate your energies on keeping the rest of the school functioning.

b. Request police barriers to prevent the demonstrators from interfering with normal operations.

c. Make emergency assignments to patrol corridors, doors, places of mass assemblage.

d. Request reasonable parents to keep their picketing children until they—and the situation— are stable.

1. Try to isolate leaders.

2. Take appropriate action against them.

e. Publicize your position broadly: the regulations, the rationale behind them, the nature and inevitability of punishment.

6. CONCLUSION

If a school staff has maintained the kind of decorum that is necessary for learning, has retained confidence in its professional ability, has developed a clear administrative machinery to cope with its problems, then the staff will act decisively in its moment of confrontation, refusing to be steamrolled into irreversible decisions.

If on the other hand, there has been an erosion of confidence in its professional ability, if the number of disorderly students is allowed to go unchecked, if the decision making process and responsibility for school discipline pass by silent sanction into riotous hands, if the administration reacts indecisively towards characteristic and insatiable demands, then student power will triumph. The staff will panic and search for a scapegoat. A school may die.

What is the survival rate of our beleaguered schools? Is a school's CQ—Confrontation Quotient—measurable, quantitative?

We only know that we cannot be sanguine. We are all vulnerable, none immune.

For those schools still not immediately beset by confrontation tactics, not yet daily embattled by disciplined extremists, review your preconfrontation status.

1. The new left leaders, trained in a hard and determined school, are masters of organized disruption.

2. A new sophistication is needed to understand and contain them.

3. Survival demands a constant state of readiness, total alertness, keen awareness—survival's price.

4. A flexible, reasonable and liberal posture creates a climate of opinion that tends to diffuse tension, prevents the radicalization of the moderates.

5. Anticipate the mood of your student body, the demands of the militants. Determine your posture in advance, not in the shrill atmosphere of charge and countercharge. The demands are predictable demands, and the predictable demands are subject to pre-planned responses.

Our future is uncertain, but we must not, dare not, temporize to avoid painful decisions. The problem will not disappear.

We place ourselves at a psychological disadvantage, ill equipped for conflict, unless we properly assess the ultimate objective of the new left. The school is the target, the symbol of the state, the epitome and embodiment of the society's corruptions. The leaders are programmed for total social disruption.

To confuse confrontation politics with traditional adolescent high-jinks, to identify the student protest movement as simply reformist, an expression of deeply felt aspirations and traditional youthful idealism is either naive or perverse.

We have sought, not always successfully, for synthesis—protecting the historic right to dissent without exceeding its permissible limits. We have tried to reconcile complex contradictions avoiding the frenzied escalation of violence, rejecting unprincipled capitulation.

THE RIGHTS AND RESPONSIBILITIES OF THE SENIOR HIGH SCHOOL STUDENT

as proposed by—

The High School Rights Committee of the N.Y.C. G.O. Council in consultation with the H. S. Student Mobilization Committee and the Third World Committee.

We, the students of the Senior High Schools of N.Y.C. do believe that in order to effectively pursue our reeducation, we must be guaranteed the following rights and responsibilities. The enumeration in this document of certain rights shall not be construed to deny or disparage others retained by students.

STUDENT GOVERNMENT

1. Each high school shall have an elected and truly representative Student Government in which all students may take part without faculty or administration limitation.

    a) Every student shall be allowed to vote; elections shall be held on a regular school day.

    b) The government shall be elected annually.

    c) Candidates for office shall be permitted to wage a "real" (unlimited) campaign with the use of all school facilities.

d) The student government shall have the right to act on all matters concerning students.

e) The student government shall be independent of the administration and the faculty adviser.

f) The student government shall have complete control over extra-curricular activities; student money shall be spent by students; all money raised by schools' extra-curricular activities shall go into a separate student bank account. Should any individual organization raise funds for itself, any such funds would be deposited in the student bank account in the name of that organization and shall be solely available for their own use.

g) The student government shall have free access to all school facilities without interference from the administration, or advisor.

h) No less than eight assembly programs per term shall be made available to the student government without interference from the administration.

2. There shall be established a School Liaison Board.

a) The School Liaison Board shall consist of 10 students, 4 teachers, the principal, and five representatives of the parent body. Each must have an official alternate.

b) The officers of the student government shall serve on the School Liaison Board; all remaining students shall be determined in a manner to be chosen by the students of each individual school.

c) The School Liaison Board shall meet at least once a week with dates and times to be determined by the Board.

d) Emergency meetings may be called by a majority vote of any one of the representative groups.

e) All recommendations and resolutions rendered by a majority vote of members at any official meeting of the School Liaison Board shall be considered final, absolute and binding on the faculty, administration and student body of each school.

f) The jurisdiction of the School Liaison Board will cover: any proposed changes concerning exams, programs, school year calendar, discipline, faculty, entrance requirements, curricular activities and general school policy.

g) With the use of continuing contracts, it would be beneficial to set up a system for evaluating each certified employee and make a decision as to the advisability of re-hiring or dismissing the individual at the end of each contract. The School Liaison Board shall be used for such a purpose.

h) The principal shall make available all information that concerns the School Liaison Board.

i) Every student has the right to an audience with the principal or School Liaison Board, as he chooses.

j) One third of the membership of each representative group shall constitute a quorum.

3. Faculty advisers shall be selected by the student groups and recommended to the administration for appointment. Each school shall specifically define the role and powers of these advisors.

4. There shall be a student member on the Board of Education with full voting privileges.

Freedom of Expression

1. Students shall have the right to distribute political leaflets, newspapers and other literature without prior authorization, without censorship and without fear that the ideas expressed will be recorded for future use against them, in or adjacent to the school, as long as the manner of distribution does not substantially block, obstruct or interfere with anyone else's rights.

2. School publications shall reflect the policy and judgment of the student editors, without censorship by the school administration, except cases concerning defamation and/or obscenities. All student groups shall be allowed access to the newspaper to advertise their activities and ideas.

3. Students shall have the right to wear buttons, armbands or other badges of symbolic expression.

4. All flag salutes, pledges of allegiance and other ceremonies of political loyalty are optional for both students and teachers.

5. Students shall have the right to choose their own dress, conduct and personal appearance.

6. Students have a right to meet on school property to discuss or express their opinions on any topic (e.g. a topic which is not a part of a prescribed school exercise). Students are entitled to freedom of expression, not only in the classroom, but everywhere in the school.

7. Students may form clubs, political and social organizations, including those which champion unpopular causes.

a) They shall have the power to govern themselves according to their own system.

b) These organizations shall have access to school facilities, with the ability to distribute its publications and publicize its point of view.

c) They shall have the right to invite outside speakers into the school regardless of their political beliefs.

d) These organizations may lobby for the purpose of changes in curriculum and school policy.

8. Students have the right to a lounge in which they may spend their free periods.

Freedom From Discrimination

1. Students shall be free from discrimination on the basis of ethnic background, sex, group membership, economic class, place of residence, or any other personal factor.

2. No law shall be made "respecting an establishment of religion, or prohibiting the free exercise thereof; or abridging the freedom of speech, or of the press; or the right of the people peaceably to assemble, and to petition" the administration "for a redress of grievances."

Due Process

1. The right to attend public school shall not be denied without due process of law.

a) Students shall receive annually, upon the opening of school, a publication giving adequate notice of all rules and regulations, this Student Bill of Rights, and the penalties which may be imposed for violations thereof. It shall be distributed to parents as well.

b) There shall be no suspension unless deemed necessary by the School Liaison Board.

c) Students shall have a fair hearing prior to suspension, expulsion, transfer, or any other serious sanction.

d) The right to counsel shall be upheld for all students, including those who cannot afford counsel.

e) Students shall have the right to counsel at all disciplinary proceedings which may have serious consequences.

f) Students shall have the right to confront the evidence against them, including the right of parents to see at any time, their children's records (i.e. permanent individual record card).

g) Students have the right to confront complaints, call friendly witnesses and cross examine hostile ones.

h) Students shall have the right to an impartial examiner, such as those afforded teachers facing dismissal.

i) The student shall have the right to an *effective* appeal from the decision at a disciplinary hearing, including the right to a transcript.

j) Students shall have the right to be free from forced self-incrimination.

k) Students shall have upon request, a hearing before the School Liaison Board.

2. Students and their parents shall have the right to file complaints against school officials before the School Liaison Board.

3. Students have the right to security in their persons, papers and effects against arbitrary search and seizures.

4. Students shall be free from the illegal use of police by school officials as an adjunct to their own authority, in the absence of crime or any threat of crime. Any use of police shall be subject to review by the School Liaison Board.

5. Students shall be free from the use of personal behavior files as a method of student evaluation.

6. Schools shall be open daily to parental observation.

7. The student body shall have the right to be free from the presence of any influence of federal, state or city agencies not directly involved in the educational process, unless sanctioned by the School Liaison Board, with the understanding that this right may be revoked by this same board.

8. Decisions concerning students' rights made by school personnel are subject to the jurisdiction of the School Liaison Board and may be appealed to the Assistant Superintendent, the Chancellor and then to the courts.

9. Students shall be free from the school's jurisdiction in all non-school activities, be it their conduct, their movements, their dress or their expression of their ideas. No disciplinary action may be taken by the school for out of school political activities provided that the student does not claim, without authorization, to speak or act as a representative of the school. When an out-of-school activity results in police action, it is an infringement on his liberty

for the school to punish that activity, or to enter it on the school records or report it to prospective employers or other agencies, unless authorized by the student. A student who violates any laws shall not be placed in jeopardy at school for an offense which is not concerned with the educational institution.

PERSONAL COUNSELING

1. All students shall have the right to receive information on abortion, and contraception. A personal counselor shall be provided with whom the student may consult without fear that it will be recorded on his record.

2. All students shall have the right to receive information on drugs. A personal counselor shall be provided with whom the student may consult without fear that it will be recorded on his record.

3. All students shall have the right to draft counseling at his school. A personal counselor shall be provided with whom the student may consult without fear that it will be recorded on his record.

CURRICULUM

1. There shall be a complete examination of all books and educational supplies upon request of the majority of the student body, and/or the School Liaison Board, and/or the majority of the minority groups.

2. There shall be no tracking system in the school, for example, to direct women into traditional "women's occupations," or to direct oppressed minorities into inferior occupations.

3. The school shall make available vocational training and work experience to all students.

4. All students shall have a pass-fail option for a grade in all minor subjects, since these grades are not considered when a student's grade-point average is computed for college entrance.

5. Students shall have the right to voluntarily choose electives.

6. Students shall have the right to take part in co-educational health education and hygiene classes.

7. No students shall be required to take Regents examinations.

8. There shall be instituted in each school library a minorities studies selection which shall include a section on women, and other minority groups.

9. Cultural exchange programs shall be permitted between schools with arrangements and programs to be decided upon by students.

FINANCIAL ASSISTANCE

1. All students shall be supplied with all school supplies, free transportation to and from school and other financial assistance which is needed by the student as a result of his attending school.

PROCESS OF AMENDMENT

1. This document may be amended by a two-thirds vote of the entire membership of New York City G.O. Council.

BOARD OF EDUCATION

OF THE CITY OF NEW YORK;

OFFICE OF THE SUPERINTENDENT OF SCHOOLS

Minutes of the City G.O. Council Meeting of February 18, 1970.

A vote was taken on the voting procedure. It was decided that the Council would vote on each section of the Bill with NO discussion; after the Bill was voted on, discussion was permitted and amendments would be made.

The results of the voting were:

Student Govt.
For: 54
Against: 10
Abstentions: 0

Freedom of Expression
For: 59
Against: 6
Abstentions: 3

Freedom from Discrimination
For: 59
Against: 0
Abstentions: 0

Due Process
For: 47
Against: 9
Abstentions: 3

Personal Counseling
For: 53
Against: 4
Abstentions: 2

Curriculum
For: 46
Against: 13
Abstentions: 0

Financial Assistance
For: 51
Against: 4
Abstentions: 3

Process of Amendment
For: 52
Against: 6
Abstentions: 1

The entire Bill was passed as presented to the Council.
No amendments were made.
The meeting was adjourned at 4:30 P.M.

Respectfully submitted
Bonni Schulman, *Secretary*